Handbook
of the
Irish Revival

The University of Notre Dame Press thanks the Keough-Naughton Institute

for Irish Studies and Notre Dame Ireland Council members

Tom and Judith A. Livingston Moore

for making this publication possible.

HANDBOOK OF THE IRISH REVIVAL

Edited by Declan Kiberd and P.J. Mathews

An Anthology of Irish Cultural
and Political Writings
1891—1922

UNIVERSITY OF NOTRE DAME PRESS
NOTRE DAME, INDIANA

First published in 2015 by Abbey Theatre Press
Dublin, Ireland
www.abbeytheatre.ie

Published in the United States in 2016 by
University of Notre Dame Press
Notre Dame, Indiana 46556
undpress.nd.edu

Library of Congress-in-Publication Data

Names: Kiberd, Declan, editor. | Mathews, P. J. (Patrick J.), 1969- editor.
Title: Handbook of the Irish Revival : an anthology of Irish cultural and
    political writings 1891-1922 / edited by Declan Kiberd and P. J. Mathews.
Description: Notre Dame, Indiana : University of Notre Dame Press, 2016.
    Includes bibliographical references.
Identifiers: LCCN 2016024810 | ISBN 9780268101305 (hardback) |
    ISBN 0268101302
    (hardcover) | ISBN 9780268101312 (paper)
Subjects: LCSH: Ireland—Intellectual life—20th century. |
    Ireland—Intellectual life—19th century. | Ireland—Social life and
    customs—20th century. | Ireland—Social life and customs—20th century.
    Ireland—Social conditions—20th century. | Ireland—Social
    conditions—19th century. | English literature—Irish authors. | BISAC:
    HISTORY / Europe / Ireland. | HISTORY / Modern / 20th Century.
Classification: LCC DA959.1 .H36 2016 | DDC 941.5082—dc23
LC record available at https://lccn.loc.gov/2016024810

∞ *This paper meets the requirements of ANSI/NISO Z39.48-1992
(Permanence of Paper).*

NOTE ON THE EDITORS

Declan Kiberd is the author of a number of books on the Revival, among them *Inventing Ireland, Synge and the Irish Language, Idir Dhá Chultúr* and *Ulysses and Us*. He is Keough Professor of Irish Studies at University of Notre Dame and was Visiting Professor at Université de Paris, Sorbonne 3 and Magdalene College, Cambridge. He served on the board of directors of the Abbey Theatre and has been a director of the Yeats International Summer School. He taught Anglo-Irish Literature and Drama for thirty-two years at University College Dublin.

P. J. Mathews is a Senior Lecturer in the School of English, Drama and Film at University College Dublin, and has written widely on Irish literature and theatre. He is the author of *Revival: the Abbey Theatre, Sinn Féin, the Gaelic League and the Co-operative Movement* (Field Day, 2003) and editor of *The Cambridge Companion to John Millington Synge* (CUP, 2009). A Member of the governing board of RTÉ, he is also Director of Academic Podcasting for UCDscholarcast (www.ucd.ie/scholarcast), and an Associate Member of the Irish Studies Colloquium, Université Sorbonne Nouvelle-Paris 3. He was appointed Naughton Fellow and Visiting Associate Professor of English at the University of Notre Dame for 2007-08, and was Director of the Parnell Summer School, 2002-05.

CONTENTS

CHRONOLOGY

1900 John Redmond elected chair of Irish Parliamentary Party
First publication of poems of Seathrún Céitinn
Maud Gonne founds Inghinidhe na hÉireann (Daughters of Erin)
Visit by Queen Victoria countered by Gonne's Patriotic Children's
Treats
1902 Augusta Gregory, *Cuchulain of Muirthemne*
Frank Fay's essays on national theatre in the *United Irishman*
Gregory and Yeats, *Cathleen Ní Houlihan*
1903 Wyndham's Land Purchase Act
Augusta Gregory, *Poets and Dreamers*
Yeats visits United States
1904 George Bernard Shaw, *John Bull's Other Island*
Launch of *Dana* journal
Horace Plunkett, *Ireland in the New Century*
Michael Davitt, *The Fall of Feudalism in Ireland*
Arthur Griffith, *The Resurrection of Hungary*
Abbey Theatre opens
J. M. Synge, *Riders to the Sea*
1904 Glenarm Feis, Antrim
1905 Sinn Féin founded by Arthur Griffith
George Bernard Shaw's *John Bull's Other Island* turned
down by the Abbey Theatre
D.P. Moran, *The Philosophy of Irish Ireland*
Patrick Pearse studies bilingualism in Belgium
1907 J.M. Synge, *The Playboy of the Western World* and
The Aran Islands
Riots and dockers strike in Belfast
1908 Irish Women's Franchise League founded
Inception of Irish Transport and General Workers' Union
Universities Act passed
Old Age Pension introduced
1910 Foundation of Irish Countrywomen's Association
1911 Kuno Meyer, *Ancient Irish Poetry*
George Moore's first volume of *Hail and Farewell*

1912   Signing of Ulster Covenant
Third Home Rule Bill
Anti-Catholic riots in Belfast

1913   Foundation of Ulster Volunteer Force, of Irish Citizen Army
and of Irish Volunteers
Dublin Lock-Out
Tagore's *The Post Office* at Abbey Theatre

1914   Gun-running by UVF and Irish Volunteers
Outbreak of World War One
Home Rule introduced and suspended until end of war
Split in Volunteers
Redmond's speech at Woodenbridge supports recruiting
for British army
W.B. Yeats, *Responsibilities*
James Joyce, *Dubliners*

1915   Irish Republican Brotherhood reorganised
Funeral of O'Donovan Rossa

1916   Easter Rising—executions and imprisonments
Battle of Somme
Execution of Roger Casement
James Joyce, *A Portrait of the Artist as a Young Man*
Thomas MacDonagh, *Literature in Ireland*

1917   Irish Convention
W.B. Yeats, *The Wild Swans at Coole*

1918   Threat of conscription
Influenza epidemic kills millions worldwide
Success of Sinn Féin at polls
Address by Cumann na mBan to US President and Congress

1919   Democratic Programme of First Dáil Éireann
Éamon De Valera attends Peace Conference and visits USA
War of Independence

1920   Government of Ireland Act introduces partition
War of Independence continues

1921	Anglo-Irish Treaty follows truce
	W.B. Yeats, *Michael Robartes and the Dancer*
1922	Treaty approved in Dáil Éireann
	Michael Collins forms government
	Foundation of Irish Senate
	Civil War begins
	Assassination of Collins
	State executes seventy-seven republicans
	James Joyce, *Ulysses*
1923	De Valera calls an end to hostilities
	Cosgrave founds Cumann na nGaedheal
	Free State enters League of Nations
	Yeats receives Nobel Prize for Literature
	Launch of *Irish Statesman*
1924	Reorganisation of national army
	Daniel Corkery, *The Hidden Ireland*
1925	Collapse of Boundary Commission
	Liam O'Flaherty, *The Informer*
1926	Foundation of Fianna Fáil
	Sean O'Casey, *The Plough and the Stars*
1927	Assassination of Kevin O'Higgins
	Fianna Fáil enters Dáil Éireann

ACKNOWLEDGEMENTS

WE ARE GRATEFUL to Senator Fiach Mac Conghail,
Director, for the invitation to compile this collection and
for his willingness to publish it under the imprint of the
Abbey Theatre, many of whose playwrights appear in the
volume. That invitation arose towards the end of *The
Theatre of Memory* three-day seminar conducted at the
Abbey Theatre in January 2014. Both Fiach and Aideen
Howard, Literary Director, gave invaluable advice and
support at all stages of the production, which was directed
with immense kindness and efficiency by Myra McAuliffe,
Head of Communications. Thanks also to Heather Maher,
Marketing Assistant, for her enthusiasm and attention to
detail on this project.

In our early work in sourcing texts we had the assistance
of two fine scholars: Emma Venter and Bebhinn Whelan.
Thanks are due also to Lisa Caulfield and the Keough-
Naughton Institute of Irish Studies, University of Notre
Dame, whose Dublin director, Kevin Whelan, gave us many
fruitful suggestions.

We are also very grateful to the following for help with
various themes: Dr. Giulia Bruna, Robert Ballagh, Professor
Gregory Castle, Dr. David Clare, Dr. Brian Crowley, John
Dillon, Professor John Hobbs, Dr. Aoife Lynch, Professor
David McConnell, David McKinney, Professor Lucy
McDiarmid, Dr. Angus Mitchell, Dr. Deirdre Mulrooney,
Dr. Ríona Nic Congáil, Seán Ó Mórdha, Dr. Elaine Sisson,
Dr. Feargal Whelan, Catherine Wilsden. The Irish Revival
Network organised a seminar in the course of which its
members, some just named, alerted us to many issues and
themes. We are grateful as always to the excellent staff at the
National Library of Ireland for much assistance.

Beth Kiberd and Audrey Murtagh made a number of very valuable suggestions, as always, and we are grateful for their perspectives.

We are indebted also to Ciarán Ó Gaora, Jura Afanasjevs and David Cairnduff for their work in designing this book in a way that does honour to the Revival writers who feature in it; thanks also to Bríd Ní Chuilinn of Repforce Ireland, and to Cormac Kinsella for his mix of literary insight and marketing skill.

Thank you to Trocadero and the Keough Naughton Notre Dame Centre, Dublin, for their generous financial support.

Not for the first time, the editors of the volume and Directors of the Abbey Theatre are indebted to President Michael D. Higgins, Uachtarán na hÉireann.

We offer our deep gratitude to Professor Owen Dudley Edwards for his great generosity and wise advice, and to Bonnie Dudley Edwards for her kind help too.

Above all, our thanks go to Dr. Máire Doyle for her indispensable care in processing all aspects of the volume. In her work, creative audacity was chastened only by sound scholarly scruple.

Declan Kiberd
P. J. Mathews
Dublin—January 2015

PERMISSIONS

WE WISH TO thank the following for their kind permission
to reproduce material: Macnaughton Lord Representation
and the Estate of Sean O'Casey for passages from *The Plough
and the Stars*, *Drums Under the Windows* and *The Story
of Thomas Ashe*; the Society of Authors and the Estate of
Bernard Shaw for passages from 'A Visit to Skellig Michael',
'Safe Holidays in Ireland', and from the *Irish Statesman*; the
extract from *My Own Story* by Peadar Ó Laoghaire, trans.
Sheila O'Sullivan, is reproduced with kind permission of Gill
& Macmillan and the Estate of Sheila O'Sullivan; Random
House Group for the extract from *Inglorious Soldier* by Monk
Gibbon, published by Hutchinson; the Bureau of Military
History for the rights to quote passages from the depositions
of Helena Molony, Sean Keegan, and Louise Gavan Duffy;
the extract from *The Splendid Years* is reproduced with the
kind permission of Dave Kenny, Dave@davekenny.com; the
Capuchin Provincial Archives for permission to use passages
from Fr. Aloysius Travers' Diary in the *Capuchin Annual
1941(42)*; the Estate of Maud Gonne for extracts from *A
Servant of the Queen* and the letter to W.B. Yeats in 1916;
C.S. Lewis Company Ltd. and Houghton Mifflin Harcourt
Publishing Company for the excerpt from *Surprised by
Joy* © 1956 by C.S. Lewis and renewed 1984 by Arthur
Owen Barfield, all rights reserved; United Agents and the
National Library of Ireland for four sentences that form the
predictions by Mary Battle, recorded in notebook NLI 30481
by W.B. Yeats; Cormac K. H. O'Malley and Mercier Press for
passages from *On Another Man's Wound* by Ernie O'Malley;
the Estate of Thomas Bodkin for extracts from 'Modern Irish
Art'; to Ríona Nic Congáil for extracts from her translation
of Úna Ní Fhaircheallaigh's *Smaointe Ar Árainn* and to

the Estate of Úna Ní Fhaircheallaigh; Peadar Ó Gaora and
An Gúm for the extract from *Mise* by Colm Ó Gaora, trans.
Delcan Kiberd; and the Estate of Padraic Colum.

Every effort has been made to trace all current holders of
copyright: should any have been overlooked, please contact
the Abbey Theatre and due acknowledgement will be made
in future printings.

In compiling a book that seeks to offer a comprehensive
range of material from the period in question, it has been
necessary to include only extracts from many of the works
included herein. Omissions from texts are signalled by
means of ellipsis within paragraphs and additional line
spacing between paragraphs. In presenting the selection
to readers, we have sought at all times to remain true to
each author's central argument or idea. Texts were chosen
to illustrate artistic, cultural and political debate in the
years between 1891 and 1922: most of these were published
in the period but a number appeared only afterward and
we have cited the date of publication (or of depositions
lodged) under each heading. Given the richness of material
available and the constraints on space, many texts which
we would like to have included are not in this volume. Our
hope is that we have encouraged readers to make their own
further explorations.

PUBLISHER'S INTRODUCTION

Handbook of the Irish Revival edited by Declan Kiberd and
P.J. Mathews is the first publication from Abbey Theatre
Press. Following *The Theatre of Memory Symposium* in 2014,
it became apparent that the Abbey Theatre could play a
role in broadening the discourse around theatre and society
by bringing together artists, scholars and members of the
general public.

The Theatre of Memory Symposium paid particular
attention to the artistic challenges of social and historical
commemoration. During the concluding symposium session
Declan Kiberd observed the relative difficulty of accessing
some of the seminal texts of the Irish Revival and so
Handbook of the Irish Revival was born.

Of course, publishing is nothing new for the Abbey
Theatre. Even before its opening in 1904 its forerunner, The
Irish Literary Theatre, published *Beltaine* edited by
W.B. Yeats. Subsequently, *Beltaine* was replaced by the more
ambitious *Samhain*, an occasional review. Both magazines
included articles relating to theatre and occasional play
texts. In addition, in 1905, the new theatre itself undertook
the publication of certain plays produced by the company.
This is a tradition that we have revived in recent years by
collaborating with publishing houses to publish programme-
playscripts of all new plays on the Abbey and Peacock stages.

We acknowledge this tradition and we hope that
Handbook of the Irish Revival will be a resource to our
artists and audiences alike.

Fiach Mac Conghail
Director of the Abbey Theatre

INTRODUCTION

T HE IRISH REVIVAL, which took place between
1891 and 1922, was an extraordinary era of literary
achievement and political ferment. This period
generated not only a remarkable crop of artists of world
significance, but also a range of innovative political thinkers
and activists, among the most influential that Ireland has
produced. In contrast to the darker nineteenth century,
the Revival stands out as an intense phase of intellectual
rejuvenation that fashioned a new civic culture outside
the scope of institutional religion, the colonial state
and conventional politics. It created multiple forums in
which intellectual exchange and artistic excellence were
encouraged, and where freedom of expression was upheld.
Yet many of the achievements, complexities and nuances of
this largely progressive and intellectually inquiring moment
remain hidden. The aim of this publication is to provide a
set of readings and keynote statements to reflect the range
and intensity of cultural exchanges.

Most of the significant figures of the time made ample
use of the newspapers and literary journals to promote their
views and various causes, and to take part in contemporary
cultural debates. Even high literary figures like W.B. Yeats
and James Joyce embraced popular journalism as a means of
engaging with the political ideas of the time and influencing
opinion. Meanwhile, anti-establishment figures such as
Alice Milligan and James Connolly, who did not have access
to the mainstream press, set up their own newspapers. Yet
despite the wealth and importance of this material to the
shaping of modern Irish culture, many of these formative
essays remain out-of-print, uncollected and unavailable
to all but a select readership. At a time of national

introspection during the Decade of Commemorations, and in response to a welcome trend of greater public familiarity with recently-available archival sources—such as the 1911 census and Bureau of Military History files—this volume, it is hoped, will facilitate a deeper engagement with the many and varied voices of the period.

The intention here is to return to the moment that produced these texts and to see the contributors as they saw themselves: to recognise the sense in which each contribution to the developing debate was at the mercy of its moment of enunciation. It seems appropriate, as we reflect on the various significant centenaries being marked over the coming years, that the writings of those who shaped the country should be available. As key eyewitness accounts of the period (some taken as far back as the late 1940s) become available, an opportunity to engage in-depth with hitherto unknown sources presents itself. The hope is that the perspectives and insights of unjustly neglected writers and texts can be made current again, to citizens, to commentators and to all who partake in, or care about, national debates. Many of the important contributors to the national conversation a century ago were characterised by a marked idealism but also by a conviction that ideas could become a basis for practical action: a deep investment in the future was born out of an intense engagement with the past. Nearly all of them lived intensely in the present moment; took ideas more seriously than their own careers; and contributed brilliantly to debate. Few of them made much money but most of them were as intellectually enriched by the critiques of their opponents as by the thinking of their allies. They savoured the value of dissent, and openly challenged the established ideas and practices of the day.

Many of their contemporaries were so engaged in action that they left no memorable texts: but they should not be forgotten. Nevertheless, this was a supremely articulate generation, whose members, writing in the heat of the moment, had some sense that they were also addressing their successors. Readers of these pages will quickly recognise that many of the ideas and challenges that the Revival generation faced have their own iterations in the present moment. In this regard, their debates about citizenship, dissent, personal liberty, education, political accountability, and sovereignty have the potential to vivify national deliberations in post-Celtic-Tiger Ireland. As the Irish Revival demonstrated, moments of stasis can also give birth to moments of profound creativity and social change. These essays and articles illustrate the extraordinary reawakening of intellectual life and the rebirth of civic action in Ireland, decades after a devastating famine, and in the wake of the political implosion which followed the Parnell era. They demonstrate admirably the ability of a society to diagnose the political and cultural ills that beset it for over a century, and show how ideas and civic participation could change reality. The best of them impel us to imagine our futures as audaciously as they imagined theirs.

If anything characterises the era it is the belief that the gap could be closed between ideas and actions, between the aims of artists and the ideas of the wider community. This extraordinary generation of dynamic people thought about and agitated for a range of political ideas including: political sovereignty, female suffrage, the rights of the working classes, agricultural co-operation, unionism, republicanism, and pacifism, among others. As people variously questioned the coercive forces of empire, Christianity, capitalism, patriarchy, militarism, industrialism and nationalism, they discovered new modes of thinking and living in the alternative forms of socialism, theosophy, feminism, pacifism, and Celtic spirituality. Some even chose to reinvent themselves by adopting a 'new' ancient language. Yet we should not be seduced into thinking that the Revival was a great communal moment of liberal and harmonious revelation. There were serious ideological differences between many who considered themselves to be 'Revivalists'. Undoubtedly much of the cultural activity was of a progressive nature and was enabling in its definition of alternative pathways for the Irish to follow on the challenging journey into the modern world. But there were also Revivalist figures who saw in the project of reconnection with the ancient past an opportunity to advance more conservative agendas. Further, there were prominent thinkers who felt that the entire Revivalist project was bogus and fraudulent. Within these pages the wide spectrum of debate is given a hearing. While the aim is to reveal something of a Revival *zeitgeist*, we have been keen to explore points of contention and divergence, and to present the vigour of fractious debate as it unfolded over the period.

Different versions of the Revival have been produced at different historical moments. Some of the best critiques of the era were produced by people who were directly involved or who were in close proximity. Figures as diverse as J.M. Synge, Eva Gore-Booth, James Joyce and Sean O'Casey were central players but were not slow about highlighting some of the absurdities and exclusions of the movement. In the early years of independence, however, attempts were made to appropriate the Revival to suit the agendas of the time. Those who commemorated often sought to control the discourse in ways which made them seem the logical successors. In that process, much was forgotten—Connolly's socialism; the dead in World War One; the role of radical women; the part played by the 1913 Lock-Out. Exclusive focus on the *literary* revival had the effect of cutting off the artistic energies of the period from the political forces that informed them, thereby transmogrifying the movement into an elitist one of high cultural exchange between a privileged few. In a parallel manoeuvre, certain revolutionary figures, notably Pearse, were singled out in hagiographical treatments as the saviours of the spiritual nation and the embodiments of Catholic martyrdom. By contrast, in more recent decades, the tendency has been to dismiss and demonise the Revival as the source of many Irish ills and a repository of many backward tendencies. Some critics, indeed, have been determined to remove one of the most innovative and progressive writers, James Joyce, from the Revival context that informs all of his work, on the basis that that movement could only ever produce insular, nativist art. Much, too, has been made of the apparent division between the 'elite' directors of the Abbey Theatre and the nationalist 'rioters' at Synge's *Playboy of the Western World*. The fact is that the conflicting groups were close enough to have the argument in a shared language, as part of the robust exchange of the times. It is ironic that Synge, whose play polarised so much opinion, can now be seen as the subtlest cultural commentator of all—he was, in the words of Jack B. Yeats, 'a keen observer of political conditions', as well as the author of the Abbey's first global masterpiece. His words illuminate almost every theme explored in this volume.

It may well be the case that the challenge of extreme idealism so apparent in the Revival seems impossible to answer without feeling an adverse judgement by the past on the present. The resort to military action by some members of the Revival generation in one theatre of action or another—in Ireland or mainland Europe or even further afield—has also called forth adverse judgements by present thinkers on the people of the past. Whether as extreme idealists or as determined militarists, that generation may induce in many a sense of shame—based on a feeling that we in our bureaucratic risk-averse lives can never measure up to that extraordinary range of exaltation and ruination. Yet it is possible that many actions of the Revival generation surprised even their agents—it was probably as hard for them to believe in the reality of what they were doing as it would be for most of us to think of emulating them now— whether putting lives on the line in battle or writing global masterpieces. The 1916 Rising may seem almost inevitable to a reader of some of these writings but it took not just most of the authorities, but even some of its progenitors, by surprise. W.B. Yeats was unhinged by the moment, yet had in the past been a member of the IRB and went to his grave convinced that a play he co-wrote helped to bring about the event. In an earlier decade, he might have been a more active participant; in a later one, an arch-critic.

During the Revival, artistic creation and intellectual debate happened at breakneck speed. The catching-up with the American and French revolutions (and with the United Irishmen) was accompanied by moments of ideological surplus in which the protagonists far exceeded the norms and potentials of their own age. They often accused one another of being 'belated' yet they were also futuristic—to such a degree that more than a century later we are still learning how to be the contemporaries of radical thinkers like James Joyce and Hanna Sheehy Skeffington. The Revival generation, even as it moved to a future that was exciting to the extent that it was unknowable, felt a need to establish a lineage with the past—with Celtic saga, bardic poetry, authors and orators, Grattan, Emmet—but this may have been because it was aware of the immense break with that past that its innovations represented. Not only did it temporarily divest some nineteenth-century leaders and writers (for example, O'Connell and Carleton) of much of their 'afterglow', but it may also have deprived the generations that followed of the sense of being able to make a significant contribution—the 'mediocrity' complained of by returned soldiers in Britain of the 1920s had its equivalent feeling in Ireland, perhaps creating the beginning of an unconscious resentment against a charismatic generation that had sucked up so much air from the future as well as the past.

Now may be the moment to reclaim the intellectual inheritance of the Irish Revival in all of its diversity and contradiction as an empowering, robust and creative republic of letters. The writings collected here belong finally to nobody—not to the various state elites who have claimed them, nor to other elites who ignore them, nor to the rebels who feel that they are theirs by default. But they are always available to those who want to attend to what their voices actually said. The less familiar texts make the over-familiar ones seem somewhat strange—almost as strange as they must have seemed to their original readers. And anyone who finds them strange is beginning to read them aright. We do not know them still—but they may yet help us to know ourselves. ∎

A Country in Paralysis?

THE DEFEAT OF the second Home Rule Bill in 1893 marked a
catastrophic turn of events for Irish nationalist advance in the
Westminster Parliament. In an instant the great Home Rule
aspiration of the Parnell years was lost with the overwhelming
rejection of Gladstone's bill in the House of Lords. In truth, the
Lords' veto killed any chance of achieving Home Rule until the
power of the upper house to block new legislation indefinitely
was removed in 1911. With the Irish Parliamentary Party deeply
riven by the Parnell split and demoralised by the failure of
Home Rule, the next two decades would be characterised by
a decline in faith in constitutional politics and the emergence
of a new approach to Irish problems. The idea, which rapidly
gained traction, was to mobilise and apply the latent national
intelligence of the country to the practical and cultural needs
of Ireland. Central to this 'self-help' strategy was the belief
that Ireland had accepted London as the centre of culture
and civilisation for too long, and that the time had come for
the Irish people to regenerate their own intellectual terms of
reference and narratives of cultural meaning.

Much of the impetus for this new movement for revival
came from a heightened resolve to transcend the forces of

decline and degeneration that had taken hold in Ireland throughout the nineteenth century, notwithstanding gains made by tenant farmers following the Land War. The spectre of the Great Famine haunted a country that had lost millions of people to starvation and emigration. Also in decline were the Anglo-Irish landowning class who had dominated the political and cultural life of Ireland in the eighteenth century. In that stagnant interval between the fall of Parnell and the emergence of a new revolutionary generation, much of the literature and thought of the period would focus on the causes of the deep paralysis and provincialism in Irish life, and on ways of overcoming these. Central to this endeavour was a radical re-evaluation of the Irish language, a renewed belief in Irish innovation, and a deep commitment to the development of a robust civic culture to serve the needs of the putative citizens of Ireland. At a political level, growing disillusionment with Westminster would lead to a developing realisation that Ireland's interests would be best served as a sovereign nation outside the empire.

J.M. SYNGE

'A LANDLORD'S GARDEN IN COUNTY WICKLOW'

(1907)

A STONE'S THROW FROM an old house where I spent several summers in County Wicklow, there was a garden that had been left to itself for fifteen or twenty years. Just inside the gate, as one entered, two paths led up through a couple of strawberry beds, half-choked with leaves, where a few white and narrow strawberries were still hidden away. Further on was nearly half an acre of tall raspberry canes and thistles five feet high, growing together in a dense mass, where one could still pick raspberries enough to last a household for a season. Then, in a waste of hemlock, there were some half-dozen apple trees covered with lichen and moss, and against the northern walls a few dying plum trees hanging from their nails. Beyond them there was a dead pear tree, and just inside the gate, as one came back to it, a large fuschia filled with empty nests. A few lines of box here and there showed where the flowerbeds had been laid out, and when anyone who had the knowledge looked carefully among them many remnants could be found of beautiful and rare plants.

All round this garden there was a wall seven or eight feet high, in which one could see three or four tracks with well-worn holes, like the paths down a cliff in Kerry, where boys and tramps came over to steal and take away any apples or other fruits that were in season. Above the wall on the three windy sides there were rows of finely-grown lime trees, the place of meeting in the summer for ten thousand bees. Under the east wall there was the roof of a greenhouse, where one could sit, when it was wet or dry, and watch the birds and butterflies, many of which were not common. The seasons were always late in this place—it was high above the sea—and redpolls often used to nest not far off late in the summer; siskins did the same once or twice, and green-

J.M. Synge, born in 1871, came of age during the heyday of the Home Rule movement and registered the cultural and political aftershock of the fall of Parnell in nearly everything he wrote. In the decade before his early death in 1909 he brilliantly captured, in stark gothic terms, the prolonged state of exhaustion and paralysis that characterised Irish life in the interregnum between Parnell's death and the emergence of a new revolutionary generation. The botanical stalemate in the landlord's garden described here represents the wider deadlock in Irish political life after the defeat of the Second Home Rule Bill in 1893. In an unguarded meditation on his own Ascendancy roots, Synge is keen to mark the decline of the landlord class without forgiving its sins. This is a highly nuanced essay in which he portrays a degenerate →

→ and discredited class
on the verge of extinction
but also acknowledges its
past cultural achievements
in the age of Swift and
Grattan. The attempt by
the boy-narrator to make
contact with the local lad
who invades the garden
is revealing. In this robust
encounter the boys
re-enact in microcosm
the familiar roles of
landlord and agitator. Of
particular significance is
the attempt by the narrator
to forge a new code of
honour outside the official
sanctions of British law
and adult authority.

finches, till the beginning of August, used to cackle endlessly in the lime trees.

Everyone is used in Ireland to the tragedy that is bound up with the lives of farmers and fishing people, but in this garden one seemed to feel the tragedy of the landlord class also, and of the innumerable old families that are quickly dwindling away. These owners of the land are not much pitied at the present day, or much deserving of pity, and yet one cannot quite forget that they are the descendants of what was at one time, in the eighteenth century, a high-spirited and highly cultivated aristocracy. The broken greenhouses and mouse-eaten libraries, that were designed and collected by men who voted with Grattan, are perhaps as mournful in the end as the four mud walls that are so often left in Wicklow as the only remnants of a farmhouse. The desolation of this life is often of a peculiarly local kind, and if a playwright chose to go through the Irish country-houses he would find material, it is likely, for many gloomy plays that would turn on the dying away of these old families, and on the lives of the one or two delicate girls that are left so often to represent a dozen hearty men who were alive a generation or two ago. Many of the descendants of these people have, of course, drifted into professional life in Dublin or have gone abroad, yet, wherever they are, they do not equal their forefathers, and where men used to collect fine editions of *Don Quixote* and Molière, in Spanish and French, and luxuriantly bound copies of Juvenal and Persius and Cicero, nothing is read now but Longfellow and Hall Caine and Miss Corelli. Where good and roomy houses were built a hundred years ago, poor and tawdry houses are built now, and bad bookbinding, bad pictures, and bad decorations are thought well of, where rich bindings, beautiful miniatures and finely carved chimney pieces were once prized by old Irish landlords.

To return to our garden. One year the apple crop was unusually plentiful, and every Sunday inroads were made upon it by some unknown persons. At last I decided to lie in wait at the dangerous hour—about twelve o'clock—when the boys of the neighbourhood were on their way home from Mass, and we were supposed to be busy with our devotions three miles away. A little before eleven I slipped out, accordingly, with a book, locked the door behind me, put the key in my pocket, and lay down under a bush. When I had been reading for some time, and had quite forgotten the thieves, I looked up at some little stir and saw a young man, in his Sunday clothes, walking up the path towards me. He stopped when he saw me, and for a moment we gazed at each other with astonishment. At last, to make a move, I said it was a fine day. 'It is indeed sir,' he answered with a smile, and then he turned round and ran for his life. I realised that he was a thief, and jumped up and ran after him, seeing, as I did so, a flock of small boys swarming up the walls of the garden. Meanwhile the young man ran round and round through the raspberry canes, over the strawberry beds and in and out among the apple trees. He knew that if he tried to get over the wall I should catch him, and that there was no other way out, as I had locked the gate. It was heavy running and we both began to get weary. Then I caught my foot in a briar and fell. Immediately the young man rushed to the wall and began scrambling up it, but just as he was drawing his leg over the top I caught him by the heel. For a moment he struggled and kicked, then by sheer weight I brought him down at my feet, and an armful of masonry along with him. I caught him by the neck and tried to ask his name, but found we were too breathless to speak.

For I do not know how long we sat glaring at each other, and gasping painfully. Then by degrees I began to upbraid him in a whisper for coming over a person's wall to steal his apples, when he was such a fine well-dressed, grown-up young man. I could see that he was in mortal dread that I might have him up in the police courts, which I had no intention of doing, and when I finally asked him his name and address he invented a long story of how he lived six miles away, and had come over to this neighbourhood for Mass and to see a friend, and then how he had got a drought upon him, and thought an apple would put him in spirits for his walk home. Then he swore he would never come over the wall again if I would let him off, and that he would pray God to have mercy on me when my last hour was come. I felt sure his whole story was a tissue of lies, and I did not want him to have the crow of having taken me in. 'There was a woman belonging to the place,' I said, 'inside in the house helping the girl to cook the dinner. Walk in now with me, and we'll see if you're such a stranger as you'd have me think.' He looked infinitely troubled, but I took him by the neck and wrist and we set off for the gate. When we had gone a pace or two he stopped. 'I beg pardon,' he said, 'my cap's after falling down on the over side of the wall. May I cross over and get it?' That was too much for me. 'Well, go on,' I said, 'and if I ever catch you again woe betide you.' I let him go then, and he rushed madly over the wall and disappeared. A few days later I discovered, not at all to my surprise, that he lived half-a-mile away, and was intimately related to a small boy who came to the house every morning to run messages and clean the boots. Yet it must not be thought that this young man was dishonest; I would have been quite ready the next day to trust him with a ten-pound note. ■

EMILY LAWLESS—*from*:

'FAMINE ROADS AND FAMINE MEMORIES'

(1898)

IT HAS SOMETIMES seemed to me as if every great event, especially if it be of the more tragic order, ought to have some distinctive cairn or monument of its own; some spot at which one could stand, as before a shrine, there to meditate upon it, and upon it alone. Such a shrine—though only in my own eminently private mental chapel—the great Irish Famine of 1846-47 possesses, and has possessed for more years than I can now readily reckon. Whenever I think of it there rises before me one particular spot, in one particular corner of Connemara; one particular cluster of cabins, or rather wrecks of cabins, for roofs there have been none since I knew it first. There they stand, those poor perishing memorials, and yearly the nettles spread a little further across their hearthstones, and yearly the slope on which they rest crumbles a little nearer to the sea, and yearly the rain batters them a little more down, and the green things cluster more closely around them, and so it will be till one day the walls too will roll over, and the bog from above will overtake them, and the last trace of what was once a populous village will have disappeared, without so much as a *Hic Jacet* to say where it stood.

Certain words and certain combinations of words seem to need an eminently local education in order adequately to appreciate them. These two words, 'Famine road,' are amongst the number. To other, larger minds than ours they are probably without any particular meaning or inwardness. To the home-staying Irishman or Irishwoman they mean only too much. To hear them casually uttered is to be penetrated by a sense of something at once familiar and terrible. The entire history of two of the most appalling years that any country has ever been called upon to pass through seems to be summed up, and compendiously packed into them.

Emily Lawless was born in 1845 as the devastating impact of the Great Famine was being felt across Ireland. She grew up in a wealthy landowning family in Lyons House, County Kildare, but spent many childhood summers with her mother's family in Tuam, County Galway. She is best remembered as the author of novels such as *Hurrish* (1886), which explored social conditions in rural Ireland in the run up to the First Home Rule Bill, and *Grania* (1892), a romance set on the Aran Islands. Another novel, *With Essex in Ireland* (1890), was widely acclaimed and admired by Gladstone for its fidelity to historical detail. Lawless was a pioneering figure of the Irish Revival who combined a deep interest in history and natural science with a literary sensibility. Her style is distinguished by a forensic attention to →

Other mementoes of the Famine, besides its roads, exist of course in Ireland. As his train lounges through its flat central counties the intelligent stranger must have more than once observed some erratic looking obelisk, or other odd development of the art of the builder. If he bestirs himself to inquire what it is, he will be pretty certain to be told that it is a 'Famine work', as though bad architecture and empty stomachs had a natural connection! There are plenty of such abortive 'Famine works' scattered over the country, but the Famine roads were the official ones—the ones longest persisted in, and in the vast majority of cases, alas! they were the most absolutely futile and abortive of all.

If the Famine road has disappeared, however, other traces of the Famine, or rather of the pre-Famine condition of things, are still to be seen. Only if you have eyes to see them though and if the indications—worn almost to invisibility by this time—are sufficiently familiar to make themselves felt as you look around you. Turning towards the higher ground you can count a succession of small humps or projections along the top of the ridge. There is one with a gable end still visible to help the reckoning. Fifty years back those projections were all villages, or groups, at any rate, of from three to ten cabins. In those pre-Famine days the rural population throughout Ireland was all but incredibly dense. The fact that nearly four hundred thousand one-roomed cabins are stated by the Registrar General to have disappeared between the census before and after the Famine, is alone sufficiently indicative of the change. Of such one-roomed cabins these villages probably all consisted. They were apparently unconnected with one another, even by a 'bohereen', yet this now utterly vacant hillside must have hummed in those days with life,

and been as busy with its comings and goings as any
village green.

The mere bald enumeration of the number of lives
extinguished in this one county of Galway during those two
years of famine is enough to make one ask oneself how any
man or woman living there at the time retained his or her
sanity. Many did not. The list of those, well above the reach of
actual hunger, who broke down, mind and body alike, from
mere pressure upon their vital forces; from pity, from a sense
of unutterable horror, is greater than would be believed, or
than has ever been set down in print. And can anybody
reasonably wonder? Take the mere official reports; the report,
for instance, of one county inspector in this very district, and
you will find him speaking of a hundred and fifty bodies picked
up by himself and his assistants along a single stretch of road.
Multiply this fifty-fold, and ask yourself what that means?

   And if upon the roadsides, what of the less easily attainable
places? Think of the thousands of solitary cabins and sheilings
high on the hillsides? Think of the little congeries of similar
cabins, such as these whose wrecks lie around us here; of the
groups collected round their hearths, so large at first, growing
smaller and smaller day by day, until none were left to carry
out the dead. Think of the eyes lifted to heaven here upon these
very slopes on which we are today indolently strolling. Think
of the separate hell gone through by each individual father
and mother of all that starving multitude. And when all hope
was over, when the bitter draught was almost drunk, the end
had almost come, that end which must have been so welcome,
because there were none left to live for, think of the lying down
to watch the vanishing away of this familiar green landscape in
the last grey mists of death. ■

PEIG SAYERS—*from*:

PEIG

A Battle That Never Happened
(1936)

(TRANSLATED FROM IRISH BY DECLAN KIBERD)

Peig Sayers was born in
Dún Chaoin in 1873. Her
early memories were of
charismatic local leaders
of the Land League, some
of whom fled to the United
States on the run from
crown forces. She was a
gifted storyteller, whose
memories were eventually
written down by her son.
Without a dowry, she
married a farmer from the
Blasket Islands, whose
austere life of 'thuas seal,
thíos seal' (good times,
bad times) she chronicled
with a vivid wit tempered
only by the conviction
that 'the old life will soon
be gone.' She was right.
By the time she died in
Dingle in 1958, the Blasket
was quite empty. But her
book *Peig*, a set text for
schoolchildren, gave her a
strange kind of immortality.

A RUMOUR WENT OUT across the community at that time that Maurice Ferriter in the upper townland was to be evicted from his piece of farm on the following week. That was the time when the people of Corca Dhuibhne stood up for their rights. Thomas Martin of the Black Fields was Captain of the Land League and whatever he decreed was done by all the boys. For that reason, they were well advised by him as to what they should do on the evil day.

Never had there been such hue and cry, nor such commotion, in the parish of Ballyferriter as there was on the date ordained by the bailiffs for the dispossession of Maurice. Every man, young or old, who could grip any kind of weapon, was proceeding to the spot decided upon by Captain Martin.

I well remember how, around mid-day, the Master closed the school door, and any among us who burned with ardour went eastward on foot to the Red Hill, from which we had a good view of the crowds.

Even though we were not beside them and didn't know quite what they were up to, we saw a terrifying sight—hundreds of men, young and old, each with a weapon on his shoulder. Those without pikes had hoes or poles or many other implements that looked quite destructive.

After that, I heard people say that were it not for the parish priest, who brokered a truce, nobody could have known what might have happened, for when the foreign army arrived—police, sheriff and bailiff—somebody fired a missile at them. No sooner had that happened than the foreign captain gave his men the order to do mischief.

If he did, Captain Martin gave an order to his own men: 'Fix bayonets!' said the foreign captain, 'Fix pikes, boys!' said the Gaelic captain. No sooner was that said than hundreds of

pikes and poles were in the air, but the parish priest arrived
and immediately made a peace.

My strong opinion is that the foreign army would never
have got safely away, because some of Martin's men had
dug deep trenches in the roadway. But my sadness and my
ruin! The takers of bribes are always in our midst and will be
forever. A lump of money had gone to some man who spied
for the foreign army and who warned it not to return by
the road on which it had come, but to take a different route
because the way before them was mined with trenches.

The police affected unconcern and went back by this
different way. It's well for them that they did, for the Gaels
had worked out a strategy that, once they trapped the foreign
army, they would fall upon it from the rear. It's likely there
would have been a horrific battle. It was better that things
turned out as told. At any rate, nobody lay dead or injured
afterwards. ■

'...we saw a terrifying sight—hundreds of
men, young and old, each with a weapon
on his shoulder. Those without pikes had
hoes or poles or many other implements
that looked quite destructive.'

DOUGLAS HYDE—*from*:

'THE NECESSITY FOR DE-ANGLICISING IRELAND'

(1892)

Douglas Hyde, a pioneering language activist, scholar, and writer was born in Castlerea, County Roscommon, in 1860. The son of a Church of Ireland rector, he identified at an early age with the Irish language which he heard spoken by the country people of Roscommon. As an activist, Hyde's approach to Irish was radical and refreshing. He promoted the idea that the spoken language of ordinary people was as worthy of attention and encouragement as the scholarship of antiquarians and philologists. This groundbreaking essay was originally delivered as a lecture to the Irish National Literary Society, Dublin, in 1892. It marks a sea-change in attitudes towards the language and played an important role in the founding of the Gaelic League the following year, led by Hyde himself. The essay had profound repercussions beyond ↗

WHEN WE SPEAK of 'The Necessity for De-Anglicising the Irish Nation', we mean it, not as a protest against imitating what is best in the English people, for that would be absurd, but rather to show the folly of neglecting what is Irish, and hastening to adopt, pell-mell, and indiscriminately, everything that is English, simply because it is English.

This is a question which most Irishmen will naturally look at from a national point of view, but it is one which ought also to claim the sympathies of every intelligent unionist, and which, as I know, does claim the sympathy of many.

If we take a bird's-eye view of our island today, and compare it with what it used to be, we must be struck by the extraordinary fact that the nation which was once, as everyone admits, one of the most classically learned and cultured nations in Europe, is now one of the least so; how one of the most reading and literary peoples has become one of the *least*-studious and most *un*-literary, and how the present art products of one of the quickest, most sensitive, and most artistic races on earth are now only distinguished for their hideousness.

I shall endeavour to show that this failure of the Irish people in recent times has been largely brought about by the race diverging during this century from the right path, and ceasing to be Irish without becoming English.

I shall attempt to show that with the bulk of the people this change took place quite recently—much more recently than most people imagine—and is, in fact, still going on. I should also like to call attention to the illogical position of men who drop their own language to speak English, of men who translate their euphonious Irish names into English

monosyllables, of men who read English books, and know
nothing about Gaelic literature, nevertheless protesting as a
matter of sentiment that they hate the country which at every
hand's turn they rush to imitate. imposed . Not by choice!!

I wish to show you that in Anglicising ourselves
wholesale we have thrown away with a light heart the best
claim which we have upon the world's recognition of us as a
separate nationality. What did Mazzini say? What is Goldwin
Smith never tired of declaiming? What do *The Spectator* and
Saturday Review harp on? That we ought to be content as an
integral part of the United Kingdom because we have lost the
notes of nationality, our language, and customs.

It has always been very curious to me how Irish
sentiment sticks in this half-way house; how it continues to
apparently hate the English, and at the same time continues
to imitate them; how it continues to clamour for recognition
as a distinct nationality, and at the same time throws away
with both hands what would make it so. If Irishmen only
went a little farther they would become good Englishmen
in sentiment also. But, illogical as it appears, there seems
not the slightest sign or probability of their taking that step.
It is the curious certainty that come what may, Irishmen
will continue to resist English rule, even though it should
be for their good, which prevents many of our nation from
becoming unionists upon the spot. It is a fact, and we must
face it as a fact, that although they adopt English habits and
copy England in every way, the great bulk of Irishmen and
Irishwomen over the whole world are known to be filled
with a dull, ever-abiding animosity against her and, right
or wrong, to grieve when she prospers, and joy when she is
hurt. Such movements as Young Irelandism, Fenianism, Land

→ Irish language circles
andsounded many of the
key ideas of the period. The
focus on self-sufficiency
and cultural sovereignty
provided a blueprint
for many subsequent
Revival movements to
follow. Importantly, Hyde
recognised a profound
paralysis and cultural
split-mindedness in the
tendency of Irish people to
imitate the very thing that
they constantly professed
to detest—English
culture. Notwithstanding
his detachment from the
political arena, Hyde's
reappraisal of the Irish
language as a positive
force can be regarded as
a significant de-colonising
gesture. Yet he was
careful not to insist on
a re-imposition of Irish,
preferring instead to
encourage it where it
was still spoken. Hyde, like
many leading Revivalists,
exhibited a paranoia about
the negative influence
of English popular →

→ culture in Ireland
which was to become a
major obsession of the
guardians of the new Irish
State post-1922. However,
his central point that
Ireland, after centuries of
degeneration, could once
again distinguish itself
as a centre of cultural
innovation, was hugely
enabling. In 1937 Hyde
became the first President
of Ireland under the new
constitution of that year.

Leagueism, and Parliamentary obstruction seem always to gain their sympathy and support. It is just because there appears no earthly chance of their becoming good members of the empire that I urge that they should not remain in the anomalous position they are in, but since they absolutely refuse to become the one thing, that they become the other; cultivate what they have rejected, and build up an Irish nation on Irish lines.... *Ireland is not simply what England is, not though*

In order to de-Anglicise ourselves we must at once arrest the decay of the language. We must bring pressure upon our politicians not to snuff it out by their tacit discouragement merely because they do not happen themselves to understand it. We must arouse some spark of patriotic inspiration among the peasantry who still use the language, and put an end to the shameful state of feeling—a thousand-tongued reproach to our leaders and statesmen—which makes young men and women blush and hang their heads when overheard speaking their own language. Maynooth has at last come splendidly to the front, and it is now incumbent upon every clerical student to attend lectures in the Irish language and history during the first three years of his course. But in order to keep the Irish language alive where it is still spoken—which is the utmost we can at present aspire to—nothing less than a house-to-house visitation and exhortation of the people themselves will do; something, though with a very different purpose, analogous to the procedure that James Stephens adopted throughout Ireland when he found her like a corpse on the dissecting table. This, and some system of giving medals or badges of honour, to every family who will guarantee that they have always spoken Irish amongst themselves during the year. But unfortunately, distracted as we are and torn by contending

factions, it is impossible to find either men or money to carry
out this simple remedy, although to a dispassionate foreigner—
to a Zeuss, Jubainville, Zimmer, Kuno Meyer, Windisch,
or Ascoli, and the rest—this is of greater importance than
whether Mr. Redmond or Mr. MacCarthy lead the largest wing
of the Irish Party for the moment, or Mr. So-and-So succeed
with his election petition. To a person taking a bird's-eye-view
of the situation a hundred or five hundred years hence, believe
me, it will also appear of greater importance than any mere
temporary wrangle, but, unhappily, our countrymen cannot be
brought to see this.

On racial lines, then, we shall best develop, following the
bent of our own natures; and, in order to do this, we must
create a strong feeling against West-Britonism, for it—if we
give it the least chance, or show it the smallest quarter—will
overwhelm us like a flood, and we shall find ourselves toiling
painfully behind the English at each step following the same
fashions, only six months behind the English ones; reading
the same books, only months behind them; taking up the
same fads, after they have become stale there, following
them in our dress, literature, music, games, and ideas, only a
long time after them and a vast way behind. We will become,
what, I fear, we are largely at present, a nation of imitators,
the Japanese of Western Europe, lost to the power of native
initiative and alive only to second-hand assimilation. I do
not think I am overrating this danger. We are probably at
once the most assimilative and the most sensitive nation in
Europe. A lady in Boston said to me that the Irish immigrants
had become Americanised on the journey out before ever
they landed at Castle Gardens. And when I ventured to

regret it, she said, shrewdly, 'If they did not at once become Americanised they would not be Irish.' I knew fifteen Irish workmen who were working in a haggard in England give up talking Irish amongst themselves because the English farmer laughed at them. And yet O'Connell used to call us the 'finest peasantry in Europe.' Unfortunately, he took little care that we should remain so. We must teach ourselves to be less sensitive; we must teach ourselves not to be ashamed of ourselves, because the Gaelic people can never produce its best before the world as long as it remains tied to the apron strings of another race and another island, waiting for it to move before it will venture to take any step itself.

In conclusion, I would earnestly appeal to everyone, whether unionist or nationalist, who wishes to see the Irish nation produce its best—surely whatever our politics are we all wish that—to set his face against this constant running to England for our books, literature, music, games, fashions, and ideas. I appeal to everyone whatever his politics—for this is no political matter—to do his best to help the Irish race to develop in future upon Irish lines, even at the risk of encouraging national aspirations, because upon Irish lines alone can the Irish race once more become what it was of yore: one of the most original, artistic, literary, and charming peoples of Europe. ∎

D.P. MORAN—*from*:

'THE FUTURE OF THE IRISH NATION'

(1899)

TAKE ALL SUCH literature as *Speeches from the Dock* from the hands of Irish youth. The little squint-eyed bit of nationality, the spirit of impotent hate and surly growl, which we get from such sources, do no good under present conditions. On the contrary, the sentimental and ineffective sulks which these books put most of us into do us a great deal of material harm. Even abroad, the '98 spirit, the spirit which causes us to sit down and put our hats on when 'God Save the Queen' is struck up, shuts us out from a great many avenues that would lead to our better material well-being: and it creates an anti-Irish prejudice in England which falls hardly on the Irish working classes in the British towns and cities. Why not make a decent job of it while we are about it, and fire the whole national bag of tricks into oblivion—send *Speeches from the Dock* and the likes of it after our language, customs, literature, and self-respect? Let us be Irish as the lowland Scotch are Scotch. Let us shout that God may save the Queen or anyone else whom it may serve our policy to toady to at the moment. Let us work up an ambition in the hearts of Irish youth to become empire-makers and civilisers of the heathen. If the rebel sentiment against serving the empire were removed I do not think it would be too much to say that hundreds of Irish boys out of the National and Christian Brothers' schools, would rise to the front ranks of empire-makers and load their pockets with riches. As it is they stop at home and stultify themselves, or go abroad organising insurrections which never come off. If Ireland became politically 'loyal' as the logical extension of her other back-slidings she would, in no way, I submit, hasten the passing of the nation. And think of what we should gain: we should get cartloads of the English praise that we thirst after . . .

David Patrick Moran, one of the leading polemicists and cultural commentators of the Revival period, was born in Manor, County Waterford in 1869 and educated at Castleknock College, Dublin. He championed the interests of an upwardly mobile Catholic middle class and was hostile to Protestant influence in Ireland. These ideas were expressed in *The Leader* newspaper which he founded in 1900 and in a book, *The Philosophy of Irish Ireland* (1905), in which this earlier essay of 1899 is collected. Here Moran registered his deep disillusionment with the stasis of nationalist politics in the post-Parnell period. The Irish tendency to loudly profess nationalist ideals, he believed, was never followed up with committed action. →

→ In Moran's view,
energies should be
invested in making
Ireland culturally rather
than politically distinct.
In this way an aspiring
Catholic bourgeoisie
could make significant
advances within the empire
rather than following a
republican dead-end.
Moran's commitment to
ethnic nationalism led
him to champion the Irish
language as a barrier to
foreign influence.

…The state of Wales, where political union is not questioned, contrasted with the state of Ireland, where we have been working all the century to hoist the harp without the crown, bears its own eloquent witness: the language wars on the Continent proclaim them, and we have the echo of the voice of the Irish-hating Spenser ringing out from three hundred years ago: 'for it hath ever bene the use of the conquerors to dispise the language of the conquered, and to force him by all meanes to learne his.' There is one great advantage which a language movement has over a political agitation, and advantage which must appeal to a people sick to despair with disappointed hopes—it cannot be betrayed by any leaders. The death of one man, or the stupidity and cowardice of a section in an hour of crisis, cannot render years of labour worse than useless: every move is a step forward and a step that cannot be blotted out. A movement of this kind stands like a cone upon its base, not like so many of our disastrous agitations, a cone upon its apex with one man holding it in place. ■

JAMES JOYCE—*from*:

'IVY DAY IN THE COMMITTEE ROOM'
(1914)

WHAT'S THE DIFFERENCE between a good honest bricklayer and a publican – eh? Hasn't the working man as good a right to be in the Corporation as anyone else – ay, and a better right than those shoneens that are always hat in hand before any fellow with a handle to his name? Isn't that so, Mat? said Mr. Hynes, addressing Mr. O'Connor.

—I think you're right, said Mr. O'Connor.

—One man is a plain honest man with no hunker-sliding about him. He goes in to represent the labour classes. This fellow you're working for only wants to get some job or other.

—Of course, the working classes should be represented, said the old man.

—The working man, said Mr. Hynes, gets all the kicks and no halfpence. But it's labour produces everything. The working man is not looking for fat jobs for his sons and nephews and cousins. The working man is not going to drag the honour of Dublin in the mud to please a German monarch.

—How's that? said the old man.

—Don't you know they want to present an address of welcome to Edward Rex if he comes here next year? What do we want kowtowing to a foreign king?

—Our man won't vote for the address, said Mr. O'Connor. He goes in on the Nationalist ticket.

—Won't he? said Mr. Hynes. Wait till you see whether he will or not. I know him. Is it Tricky Dicky Tierney?

—By God! perhaps you're right, Joe, said Mr. O'Connor. Anyway, I wish he'd turn up with the spondulics.

James Joyce, born in 1882, was educated at University College Dublin where he rubbed shoulders with a talented generation of significant Revival figures. His early short stories were published in the *Irish Homestead*, the journal of the Irish Agricultural Organisation Society edited by George Russell. Joyce was rightly critical of many Revivalist tendencies and fads, especially the pronounced bias towards rural experience. Nonetheless, *Dubliners* (1914) repeatedly draws attention to a deep paralysis and provincialism in Irish life not unlike that diagnosed by Douglas Hyde two decades earlier in his 'de-Anglicising' essay. In Joyce's view, Ireland was dominated by the twin forces of an authoritarian Catholic Church that was removed from the realities of the people, and a physical force nationalist tradition that was intellectually →

→ underdeveloped. In
'Ivy Day in the Committee
Room' Joyce offers a
scathing critique of a
mindset characterised by
a boozy nostalgia for the
Parnell era and by a chronic
inability to imagine a better
future. In this extract, Mr.
Hynes, who wears an ivy
leaf to mark the anniversary
of Parnell's death, draws
attention to the neglect of
the working class in Irish
politics. He also criticises
the greasy expediency of
the nationalist politician,
Tierney.

The three men fell silent. The old man began to rake more cinders together. Mr. Hynes took off his hat, shook it and then turned down the collar of his coat, displaying as he did so, an ivy leaf in the lapel.

—If this man was alive, he said, pointing to the leaf, we'd have no talk of an address of welcome.

—That's true, said Mr. O'Connor.

—Musha, God be with them times! said the old man. There was some life in it then. ■

AUGUSTA GREGORY—*from*:

'IRELAND REAL, AND IDEAL'

(1898)

A LITTLE TIME AGO, when staying among fishermen and peasants on one of the isles of Aran, I took up an old volume of *Don Quixote* that had strayed there from some Galway saleroom. And as I read in it the story of his stay at the castle of the Duke and Duchess, the idea grew upon me that as he and his squire appeared in the eyes of the their hosts, so do we Irish appear in English eyes, looking at us with half-tolerant, half-impatient patronage from the other side of the Channel. They see in us one part boastful quarrelsome adventurer, one part vulgar rollicking buffoon.

But we begin to think after all that truth is best, that we have worn the mask thrust upon us too long, and that we are more likely to win at least respect when we appear in our own form. There is a great deal of Sancho and a great deal of Don Quixote in the nature of my countrymen, but what I, living among them, see, is the ready, adaptable, sagacious nature of the one, interwoven with the dignified spiritual nature of the other, the champion of lost causes and of shadowy ideals.

It is not the fault of the English public of today that they see him otherwise. There is a stage tradition and a literary tradition against him. The tourist who comes to Ireland finds in the country, like all other tourists, 'what he brings with him', and a car-driver or a professional beggar is called upon to supply the food he desires. And the Englishman who stays at home looks to Westminster for representatives of our race. He sees there a confused crowd of politicians crying out to their opponents and to each other, saying in their exaggerated way more than they mean—fighting men, not representing their people at home any more than the old fighting men, Finn and his companions, represented the

Lady Gregory, one of the towering figures of the Irish Revival, was born Augusta Persse at Roxborough House, County Galway in 1852. Her interest in Irish folklore, language and literature intensified after the death of her husband, Sir William Gregory, in 1892. Her residence at Coole Park became a spiritual home of the Irish Revival where she hosted many of the influential writers of the period, notably W.B. Yeats. Gregory was one of the innovators behind the Irish Literary Theatre (1899) and a founding director of the Abbey Theatre (1904). She was a pioneering playwright whose work is distinguished by her use of folklore and her inventive deployment of Hiberno-English based on the dialect of her locality, Kiltartan, County Galway. This essay, published in the influential journal *Nineteenth Century* in November 1898, highlights the extent to which a new →

→ Revival ethos was beginning to manifest itself at a grassroots level across Ireland. Gregory identified the progress made by emerging movements such as the Gaelic League and the co-operative movement in improving the material conditions and the cultural life of the Irish people. She also drew a sharp distinction between the 'confused crowd of politicians' in Westminster pursuing failed strategies, and the new alliance of energetic organisers like Douglas Hyde and Horace Plunkett committed to innovative ideas of renewal and 'self-help'.

dwellers in the valleys when they shouted defiance from one mountain top to another, and when 'every step they made was heard through the firmament.' We in our grey valleys are rather pleased with the echo of the shouting. It gives us a sociable sense of connection with the outer world. If we are moved now and then to a sigh, it is over the quarrels of our heroes amongst themselves, and we murmur, like our countryman who found his fighting cocks had pecked each other to death on the way to a match, 'Wouldn't you think they'd have known they were on the one side?'

The bacillus of politics has exhausted its feeding ground for the present. It is only when it finds us susceptible to infection again that a new fever will run through our blood. And there is no conspicuous leader to excite the imagination. 'We don't hear much of Parliament now,' and old man said to me the other day, 'since Parnell died.' Parnell had filled the foreground. There are some who still refuse to believe he can be dead. 'He was not the prophet of our spiritual future,' one of our writers says, 'he was not the hero of our highest ideals, but he was the only hero we knew.' Since the hewing down of that great overshadowing tree other growths have had a chance of stretching towards the sunlight, and new forces are coming into play. It is through one or two of these new forces, the Society of Agricultural Co-operation and the Gaelic League that I will try, in this quiet moment, to show the character of our Sancho-Quixote of today. ■

MICHAEL DAVITT—*from*:

THE FALL OF FEUDALISM IN IRELAND

(1904)

WHY SHOULD NOT the Irish people make a persistent demand, inside and out of Parliament, for the fullest measure of freedom to which, as a separate nationality among civilised peoples, we are in every sense, and on every rational ground, entitled? Why should Ireland not be a state in the freest and fullest sense in which Holland, Denmark, Belgium, Switzerland, Bulgaria, Servia, and Greece are nations? On the grounds of abstract justice, of historic claim, or racial right—or on that of England's failure in Ireland—our demands could not, in reason, be disputed. England has not alone failed to win our assent to her selfish dominion over us; she has shown her incapacity to rule Ireland either for its contentment or prosperity, or for her own advantage and peace. The present condition and prospects of a depopulated country, after centuries of English lordship, and a hundred years of direct rule over us, is alone a full commendation of the system of government which has reduced it to the level of the poorest country in Europe, and made it the only civilised land on earth in which a hardy and prolific race is persistently diminishing in numbers.

Nationhood is not a decaying but a growing force, and is gaining new vitality in Europe. It will be found that the principle of nationality, rooted as it is in the very foundations of human society, will grow stronger and more virile as education and enlightenment spread among the people, while imperialism, with its tendency to military rule, crushing taxation, and constant provocation to wars, will breed the diseases of its own decay and downfall. In Great Britain, parliamentarism or imperialism must die. They cannot live together. The growth of military power,

Michael Davitt, founder of the Land League, was born in Straide, County Mayo in 1846. Childhood memories of his family's eviction for non-payment of rent had a huge bearing on his political formation. Throughout his life he supported the causes of tenant farmers, the labour movement, prison reform, and anti-imperialism. Davitt was a pioneer in the deployment of organised passive resistance as a political tactic. He endured as a key figure, linking the era of the Land War with the emergence of Sinn Féin. This account of the overthrow of the landlord class in Ireland was written shortly after Davitt lost faith in the Westminster parliament and resigned his seat in protest over the conduct of the Boer War. In this extract, Davitt advances the claim for a sovereign Irish nation as an inalienable right →

→ commensurate with that
of other small European
nations. He also delivers
a caustic critique of
rampant British imperialism
based on his recent
travels in South Africa.
Although Davitt frames his
narrative in racial terms
as a struggle between the
Anglo-Saxons and the
Celtic Irish, he is always
aware of the role of class
in political domination.
The advancement of
political rights for the
Irish, he argues, would
undoubtedly have positive
repercussions for 'the
toiling millions of Great
Britain' suffering under the
burdens of landlordism,
capitalism and imperialism.

increasing armaments, aggressive politics which provoke international disputes, expeditions for the subjugation of so-called savage races, all mean a constant danger to social peace and to true progress, with increasing taxation upon those who look to parliamentary government as the best protection for their trading interests and liberties. Imperialism is necessarily impatient of constitutional control, and will not always submit to its restraining influence. Since 1895 an imperialist policy has added over twenty-five millions a year to the expenditure of British and Irish taxes. What good has accrued to the people of Great Britain in exchange for this astounding extravagance? Two hundred millions of taxes have been wasted in the war engineered by jingoism, in South Africa. Is there a human being alive today who will ever live to point to a single shilling's worth of benefit resulting from that waste of money to the taxpayers who must foot the bills?

I contend that an Ireland independent of all English control and interference would be of far greater advantage to the working classes of Great Britain than an Ireland ruled and ruined under Dublin Castle on the principles of imperialism—that is, for landlords, aristocrats, and moneylenders. A free Ireland would mean a House of Commons free for the British, a Protestant Parliament left to a Protestant people, and Catholic members relegated to their own country. It would mean a saving of three millions a year in British taxes, according to Giffen, while trade and commerce would go on, under the new conditions, just as smoothly and at least as flourishing as today.

The rational solution of the whole Irish question lies in the complete severance of the parliamentary connection between Great Britain and Ireland. I have shown, I hope, clearly and convincingly, how the complete autonomy of Ireland would be no injury, wrong, or menace to the people of Great Britain. On the other hand, we have either to continue to see our country slowly dying from the poison of imperialism, and have it identified with or incorporated in a system which is the very negation of Celtic nationality, or we must resolutely demand and strenuously labour to obtain the full freedom of Irish rule which will alone avert the complete ruin of the fatherland of the race.

It is to progress in this direction that the Irish movement tends. It seeks no reforms in the betterment of the economic and social conditions of our population, or in the democratic government of Ireland by its own people, that are not in harmonious line and in sympathetic co-operation with the industrial and political enfranchisement of the working classes in Great Britain from the burden of landlordism in field, workshop, coalmine, factory, city office, and domestic hearthstone—and in the making of laws in the Imperial Parliament. ■

A Thought Revival

BY THE TIME that Douglas Hyde issued his warning against becoming a pale imitation of the neighbouring island, major English artists such as George Eliot had exposed the degree to which, at a time of apparent imperial glory, her own country had become largely derivative in medicine, scholarship or banking theory, when compared with Germany or France. The challenge for the Irish was clearer than ever: there was no point in being the province of a province.

For some thinkers, interesting options presented themselves: either to turn to Paris with its radical republican politics and experimental art, or to reconnect with the buried energies of a traditional Irish culture exemplified in the Irish language. But there were problems with either choice. The cosmopolitanism of Parisian culture seemed at times to shade into a shallow consumerist internationalism, itself verging on decadence and quite unconnected with the experience of ordinary Irish people. And the attempt to speak Irish again would entail a laborious reversal of the process by which the people had painfully mastered English as a language fitted to the modern world. Some argued for an internationalism which, though socialist, was often rooted in the rare privilege of overseas travel. Others spoke up for a Gaelic culture which might entail a return to the culture of the common people *or* to the aristocratic codes of ancient Ireland. The debate was honest and invigorating, but some of the more astute analysts recognised a familiar old falseness in the very choices being posed: J.M. Synge, for instance, found on the Aran Islands many elements of the culture of Left Bank Paris, and Patrick Pearse argued that you could Europeanise writing in Irish without de-Gaelicising it.

All agreed on the need for new forms of art and thought in which an unfettered Irish mind could become metropolitan to itself. Ultimately, not even Paris or Aran could serve as models to a generation determined on self-invention, on deriving only from itself. The intensity with which its artists explored ancient myths—whether Cuchulain or Odysseus—was rooted in a modern desire to unlock the psyche of every person.

Ireland would itself provide a test-case of modernity to the outside world; hence the intense interest taken by overseas scholars and commentators not only in the Celtic past but also in the Irish present.

STANDISH O'GRADY—*from*:

'A WET DAY'

(1899)

A T SCHOOL AND in TCD I was an industrious lad and worked through the curriculums with abundant energy and some success, yet in the curriculums never read one word about Irish history and legend, nor ever heard one word about those things from any of my pastors and masters. When I was twenty-three years of age, had anyone told me—as later on a professor of the Dublin University actually did—that Brian Boroma was a mythical character, I would have believed him. I knew absolutely nothing about our past; not through my own fault, for I was willing enough to learn anything set before me, but owing to the stupid educational system of this country. I knew Sir Samuel Ferguson and was often his guest, but I knew him only as a kind, courteous, and hospitable gentleman; no one ever told me that he was a great Irish poet.

I think I was in my twenty-fourth year when something happened which has since then governed the general trend of my life and through me that of others. In a country-house in the west of Ireland, near the sea, I had to stay indoors one rainy day, and though my appetite for literature was slender enough then, in default of other amusements I spent the time in looking over the books in the library. So I chanced upon O'Halloran's *History of Ireland* in three volumes—the first history of Ireland into which I had ever looked.... I was greatly interested, perhaps excited: 'How,' I thought, 'was all this interesting history of my own country never brought before my notice by anyone?' None of the pastors or masters had ever uttered a hint.

Returning to Dublin, and with a determination to learn more of this fascinating subject, I found my way—how I don't know—to the Royal Irish Academy where Mr. Mac

Standish James O'Grady was born in Berehaven, County Cork, in 1846. After graduation from Trinity College, Dublin, he practised law but ultimately turned to full-time writing. A chance encounter at the age of twenty-three with a volume of Irish history changed his life. In his books he resuscitated the ancient Celtic hero, Cuchulain, as a model of proud self-reliance for the declining Anglo-Irish aristocracy, whose weaknesses he flayed in commentaries (one example of which follows here). A unionist in politics, he was deeply national in his cultural interests, finding in ancient legends the energies of a renovated Irish consciousness →

→ (most notably in *History of Ireland: Heroic Period 1878-80*). Between 1900 and 1906 he edited the influential *All-Ireland Review*. He left his native land in 1918, by which time the country was in the throes of a cultural revival which his writings had inspired, but which sealed the ultimate doom of the Anglo-Irish elite: the social class to which alone he felt allegiance. O'Grady died on the Isle of Wight in 1928.

Sweeney, the librarian, was very kindly and helpful to me in my Irish studies. . . . Then, and how I again forget— probably through the advice of Mr. Mac Sweeney, I lighted on O'Curry's *Manners and Customs of the Ancient Irish* and his MSS, 'Materials of Irish History'. Here, owing to the numerous and often lengthened quotations in which he indulged, I was introduced for the first time, to the wonder-world of Irish heroic and romantic literature. That, indeed, was a revelation. Theories concerning ancient Irish history: Nemedian, Firbolgic, etc., I then dropped absolutely and went into the literature itself, whenever I could find it in the *New Atlantis*; in the *Revue Celtique*; in the publications of the Ossianic Society; in Crowe's manuscript translations, or wherever else I could arrive at it. I had not gone far before I discovered that the Tuatha Dé Danan, whom I had heretofore regarded as a race of conquerors as historical as the Normans, were in fact the gods of the pagan Irish, and that of course the races preceding them, Partholonians and so forth, were of the same nature, and represented more primitive divine dynasties.

'For the honour of the Ireland' I beg to state that this discovery was made and printed here in Ireland before it was announced to the students of Europe by M. de Jubainville, the eminent French-Breton scholar. It was really no great discovery at all, for the fact is quite patent in the heroic and romantic literature; yet, be the cause what it may, no one ever announced it before. Everyone had rationalised or euphemerised *The Book of Invasions*. Of course, like everyone else who has ever dipped into this antique Irish literature, I could not fail to be deeply affected by the great story of Cuchulain's heroic defence of Ulster

against the banded host of the rest of Ireland. This story
kept simmering in my imagination and finally eventuated
in my writing the *History of Ireland: Heroic Period, Vols.
I. and II.* Naturally I was a good deal laughed at. I did
not mind that, but certainly was disappointed that so few
people bought the book. Nevertheless, time worked in my
favour, and after a few years the whole impression—a score
or so each year—was quite bought off. I have not had a copy
myself for a great many years, and this is the more singular
seeing that the price was almost prohibitive, viz., 15s. So
my juvenile enthusiasm concerning the 'heroic period' was
justified by results. I need hardly add that I could not get
a publisher for that work: I had to print and publish at my
own expense.

Now, though the whole impression was sold off, this
did not take place till after the lapse of many years and, in
the meantime, though I still continued my studies in Irish
history, I had come to think that writing was not my forte.
However, though the professors and educated classes in
general laughed at or ignored me, a good many young men
and young women quite unknown to me did not, such as:
Miss Tynan, Miss Eleanor Hull, Mr. Yeats, Mr. Rolleston
and others. These young people, growing up and going to
London, were good enough to talk about *The Heroic Period.*
So London publishers wrote to me and asked me to send
them something for publication, and this is the origin of
my other works: *Finn and his Companions*, the *Flight
of the Eagle*, and others. The fact reminds me of a noble
utterance of Finn, who otherwise was a little inclined to the
strong assertion of his own incontestable merits: 'Small, in
sooth, was my considerations in Erin till my sons and my

grandsons, and my gallant nephews and grandnephews grew up around me.'

Frankly, I do not like writing about myself, but on consideration, and in thinking over the matter from different points of view, I believe that this account of the accident of the wet day and an old library at hand, which started me as a writing man, will not be unwelcome to those who take an interest in the history of Anglo-Irish literature. It looks like an accident, a mere chance, and yet I don't think it was quite such. If the fall of a sparrow is provided for, possibly so was that wet day in the west of Ireland. ∎

'I think I was in my twenty-fourth year when something happened which has since then governed the general trend of my life and through me that of others.'

STANDISH O'GRADY—*from*:

'THE GREAT ENCHANTMENT'

(1900)

ARISTOCRACIES COME AND go like the waves of the sea, and some fall nobly and others ignobly. As I write, this Protestant Anglo-Irish aristocracy, which once owned all Ireland to the sea, is rotting from the land in the most dismal farce-tragedy of all time, without one brave deed, without one brave word. Our last Irish aristocracy was Catholic, intensely and fanatically Royalist and Cavalier, and compounded of elements which were Norman-Irish and Milesian-Irish. They worshipped the crown when the crown had become a phantom or a ghost, and the god whom they worshipped was not able to save them, or himself. They were defeated and exterminated. They lost everything, but they never lost honour, and because they did not lose that, their overthrow was bewailed in songs and music which will not cease to sound for centuries yet:

> Shaun O'Dwyer a Glanna,
> We're worsted in the game.

Worsted they were, for they made a fatal mistake, and they had to go; but they brought their honour with them, and they founded noble or princely families all over the Continent.

Who laments the destruction of our present Anglo-Irish aristocracy? Perhaps in broad Ireland not one. They fall from the land while innumerable eyes are dry, and their fall will not be bewailed in one piteous dirge or one mournful melody.

They might have been so much to this afflicted nation; half-ruined as they are, they might be so much tomorrow. But the curse that has fallen on the whole land seems to have fallen on them with double power—the understanding paralysed, the will gone all to water, and for consequence a sure destruction. None of them noticed it, but I did . . . when

they seemed to be giving the country a lead not one of the
anti-landlord newspapers of Dublin touched the land question,
or uttered an unfriendly word concerning them. The war
of classes stopped—stopped utterly. As a class our landed
gentry were becoming popular—nay, very popular. The people
thought they were about to lead them, and upon a matter
concerning which all Ireland was in virtual unanimity; a great
question—great, essentially, and involving gigantic issues.
This marvellous opportunity, thrust into their hands by kind
Destiny, they flung away, and for what? ■

'They worshipped the crown when the
crown had become a phantom or a ghost,
and the god whom they worshipped was
not able to save them, or himself. They
were defeated and exterminated.'

W.B. YEATS

O'GRADY AS ELEGIST FOR ANGLO-IRELAND

(1922)

STANDISH O'GRADY, UPON the other hand, was at once all passion and all judgement. And yet those who knew him better than I assured me he could find quarrel in a straw.... Indeed, I wanted him among my writers because of his quarrels, for, having much passion and little rancour, the more he quarrelled, the nobler, the more patched with metaphor, the more musical his style became, and if he were in his turn attacked, he knew a trick of speech that made us murmur, 'We do it wrong, being so majestical, to offer it the show of violence.' Sometimes he quarrelled most where he loved most. A unionist in politics, a leader-writer on the *Daily Express*, the most conservative paper in Ireland, hater of every form of democracy, he had given all his heart to the smaller Irish landowners, to whom he belonged, and with whom his childhood had been spent, and for them he wrote his books, and would soon rage over their failings in certain famous passages that many men would repeat to themselves like poets' rhymes. All round us people talked or wrote for victory's sake, and were hated for their victories—but here was a man whose rage was a swan-song over all that he had held most dear, and to whom for that very reason every Irish imaginative writer owed a portion of his soul. ■

W.B. Yeats was born in Dublin in 1865, but spent most of his childhood in Sligo and then at school in London. He won early fame for poems and prose on Celtic themes and legends. Inspired by O'Grady's re-telling of Irish hero-tales, he became a founder of the Irish Literary Theatre in 1899 and of the Abbey Theatre in 1904. He fell in love with Maud Gonne in 1889 and she served as both his muse and as his initiator into advanced nationalism. He secured a global audience for Irish literature, wining the Nobel Prize in 1923, but he never forgot his generation's debt to Standish O'Grady, recalled in a passage from *The Trembling of the Veil.*

ALICE MILLIGAN

'WHEN I WAS A LITTLE GIRL'

(n.d)

As a boy in Sligo Yeats was taught by his family to fear Fenian rebels but, like many young people of unionist background, he felt the insurgent counter-appeal of nationalist voices. So it was for Alice Milligan, born in Omagh, County Tyrone, in 1866. Many Protestants identified more with the geography of Ireland than with its history, and in her early twenties Milligan co-wrote a travel book with her father: *Glimpses of Erin*. While serving as a young teacher in Derry she began to study Irish and soon became a nationalist. On the night of Parnell's death she wrote: 'I am in the enemy's camp; if I had but the means, I would go to Dublin to be with the people who feel as I feel.' The following poem was much anthologised. To the end of her life (1953) Milligan remained loyal to her family, nursing a brother through a terminal illness in a Northern Ireland in which she felt nonetheless 'interned'.

When I was a little girl,
In a garden playing,
A thing was often said
To chide us, delaying:

When after sunny hours,
At twilight's falling,
Down through the garden walks
Came our old nurse calling–

'Come in! for it's growing late,
And the grass will wet ye!
Come in! or when it's dark
The Fenians will get ye'.

Then, at this dreadful news,
All helter-skelter,
The panic-struck little flock
Ran home for shelter.

And round the nursery fire
Sat still to listen,
Fifty bare toes on the hearth,
Ten eyes a'glisten –

To hear of a night in March,
And loyal folk waiting
To see a great army of men
Come devastating –

An army of Papists grim,
With a green flag o'er them,
Red-coats and black police
Flying before them.

But God (Who our nurse declared
Guards British dominions)
Sent down a fall of snow
And scattered the Fenians.

'But somewhere they're lurking yet,
Maybe they're near us',
Four little hearts pit-a-pat
Thought, 'Can they hear us?'

Then the wind-shaken pane
Sounded like drumming;
'Oh!' they cried, 'tuck us in,
The Fenians are coming!'

Four little pairs of hands,
In the cots where she led those,
Over their frightened heads
Pulled up the bedclothes.

But one little rebel there,
Watching all with laughter,
Thought, 'When the Fenians come
I'll rise and go after'.

Wished she had been a boy
And a good deal older –
Able to walk for miles
With a gun on her shoulder.

Able to lift aloft
The Green Flag o'er them
(Red-coats and black police
Flying before them);

And, as she dropped asleep,
Was wondering whether
God, if they prayed to Him,
Would give fine weather.

J.M. SYNGE

'THE IRISH INTELLECTUAL MOVEMENT'

'Le Mouvement Intellectuel Irlandais' in *L'Européen*,
31 May 1902
(TRANSLATED BY MICHAEL EGAN)

After graduation from
Trinity College, Dublin,
in 1893 John Millington
Synge engaged in private
studies of language and
music in Germany and
France. In Paris he lived
in the Latin Quarter,
attending lectures on
Celtic mythology by Henri
D'Arbois de Jubainville, as
well as studying Breton.
Paris was not only the
intellectual capital of
the nineteenth century
but also the crucible in
which new forms of Irish
consciousness were being
forged. While there, Synge
met the young James
Joyce and the militant
nationalist Maud Gonne,
briefly enlisting in her ↗

THE RELATIVE PEACE which has reigned in Ireland over recent years seems to be coming to an end.... [W]e are on the threshold of a new period of political agitation. Now if one wishes to analyse the progress made since the death of Parnell, before looking at this new period, what would one find? Apart from the admittedly useful Local Government Act and some other measures, years have passed without any really significant legislative events. The skill of Redmond, Dillon, and other Irish politicians is undeniable, but no real popular leader has arisen, and in Ireland nothing gets done without the influence of such a dominant personality. However, in a certain sense this period has been fertile, perhaps the most fertile of the last century, since it has seen the birth or at least the blossoming of three movements of the utmost significance: the Gaelic League (an association for the preservation of the Irish language); a movement for the development of agriculture and animal husbandry, and finally, a new intellectual activity which is even now creating a new literature for us.

These three movements are intimately linked; it is rare to find someone who is interested or active in one of the three movements who is not also concerned with the others. However, here I am going to talk of the third of them, which is the one that is generally more interesting.

When, towards the end of the seventeenth century, the Irish language ceased to be used as a literary tongue, all of the intellectual traditions of the country were lost. From this moment on, it was the descendants of English immigrants who made the literature instead of the descendants of the prior Celtic races. Since these writers possessed neither a tradition nor a language of their own, the more gifted of them almost always went to England, with the result that their works do not belong to us. Among them, reference can be made to those three writers who are so remarkable in English literature: Burke, Goldsmith, and Sterne.

This state of affairs lasted a long time, but little by little a growing knowledge of the English language among the populace, and a more complete assimilation of people of English extraction, endowed the country with a new literary terrain. In 1794 William Carleton was born in Tyrone and thirty years later he published his *Traits and Stories of the Irish Peasantry*, a book which became famous and marked the definitive debut of modern Irish literature. From this moment on, Irish writers have been both numerous and prolific. Especially around the year 1848 there were novelists; young people who were half-political, half-literary; there were also poets and savants whose main concern was the treasure of national antiquity.

Nevertheless, it cannot be denied that all of the literature that was produced during the first three quarters of the last century contained little of any real literary value. The national feeling was too fervent, too conscious, as it were, in most of these writers with the result that their prose degenerated easily into an overcharged rhetoric whereas with their poetry they believed that they had accomplished enough merely if they sang of the ancient glories of Ireland. Moreover, the literary men of this era were writing in a language which had not yet been perfectly assimilated by the people around them. It follows that their vision of the English language remained devoid of that special intimacy which alone can give rise to great works of literature.

→ Irlande Libre movement. A more lasting influence was W.B. Yeats, who advised Synge to abandon literary criticism and go for creative inspiration to the Aran Islands. By the time Synge wrote this essay for a French readership in 1902, he was proficient in the Irish of Aran but not yet known for the plays which would become even more famous than those which he praises here.

Looking at the present generation, one notes that these shortcomings have lessened if they have not disappeared completely. With a broader cultural outlook, the national feeling is no longer a dominant obsession and, little by little, the English language has become a virtual maternal tongue in the greater part of Ireland. It is especially in the work of W.B. Yeats, the writer of genius who leads the new school of Irish poetry, that the true extent of this advance can be seen. Yeats's national feeling, although it remains as profound as that of his predecessors, does no more than give a distinctive character to the atmosphere in which blossom the delicate creations of his imagination.

Furthermore, his rhythms, composed with a curiously intelligent simplicity, offer evidence of a deep knowledge of the English language. No one could criticise in a few lines the whole work of W.B. Yeats who is, of course, not unknown in Paris. He has published in *L'Ermitage* where M. Davray spoke of him a long time ago and his name has been seen more than once already in the *Mercure de France*. I will remark merely on the strange beauty of his lyric poems without, however, being able to omit reference to the names of two of his books. *The Secret Rose* is a prose work and *The Shadowy Waters* a little verse drama possessed of a rare beauty of language and feeling.

Apart from Mr. Yeats we have a poet, George Russell, whose extraordinary imagination does not always express itself in a fully satisfactory form. In the two volumes which he has published to date, one may find some small pieces which are almost perfect side by side with a lot of works of no value.

Two or three minor poets have produced collections of some interest recently but I will make no comment on them here in order to concentrate on the Literary Theatre. This theatre is the centre of the intellectual movement. The first production took place in May 1899. *The Countess Cathleen* of W.B. Yeats was presented first of all. In that play, Cathleen, a sort of lady of the manor at a time of famine in Ireland, sells her soul to devils in order to help the people who are starving to death around her castle. That seems innocent enough, but there are still people in Dublin who are of so orthodox a persuasion as to find themselves outraged by the presentation of such a scenario. A certain disapproval was expressed by the clergy, and at every presentation of the play there were drunkards who, apparently scandalised, poured forth vituperations for the benefit of Mr. Yeats and his colleagues.

That piece was followed by a play entitled *The Heather Field* by Edward Martyn, a disciple of Ibsen, at least in his manner of writing. The plot was of the simplest. An Irish landowner living on his demesne in the midst of his tenants finds himself embarrassed by his lack of funds. Being a dreamer and an idealist, instead of looking for a practical way out, he imagines that he can convert his heather field into fertile land and thus recoup great profit. The field in question is a huge heath close to his house. Work is soon begun. The heather is burnt and the land is sown at considerable expense. The wife of the landlord, a woman of a hard-headed materialistic nature, is horrified, foreseeing very clearly that all of this will bring ruin and not salvation. Finally, losing patience, she sends for two doctors to certify the insanity of her husband so that she herself can take control of his affairs. However, the doctors dare not give a definitive diagnosis and this means that the situation continues unresolved until the spring. One day the young son of the landlord goes off to take a horse ride in the heather field. He comes back at noon jubilant and overjoyed. Father, he cries, the field is beautiful. Heather is growing everywhere there! At his father's feet he throws a huge bouquet that he has just picked. The father, seeing the collapse of all his dreams, becomes mad in earnest.

This brief account unveils nothing of the drama. This dreamer who places his faith in his grand chimerical hopes has been transformed by the skill of the author into a truly attractive character. In contrast to his brutally realistic wife, he wins all the sympathy. At least that is what happened when the play was put on in Dublin. Encouraged by their success there, the piece was staged in London. There, with the exception of a few literary savants, however, nobody understood the intimate meaning of the action. Audiences were unmoved. According to the reviews, the wife was in the right, and the husband was but 'a dangerous and impractical person.'

In the second year of the Literary Theatre, plays by Edward Martyn and George Moore were given with considerable success and it was in October last year that a play was staged most recently. *Diarmuid and Grania*, a play written in collaboration by W.B. Yeats and George Moore was staged, and it was followed by a lovely play written for the occasion in Irish by Douglas Hyde. It was the first time a play in Irish had been played on a big stage and the cheap seats in the theatre were snapped up by the enthusiastic members of the Gaelic League. Despite the importance of this organisation (and as it happens so often in the movements which are of their nature popular), there is an element of the ridiculous apparent in its public events, side by side with which are feelings of infinite depth. Thus, at the beginning of the play's first night, it was hard to keep a straight face at the sight of the beautiful Irish ladies of the Gaelic League all around the theatre talking non-stop in the most woeful Irish with their young clerks and working men who were quite pale with enthusiasm. But, it happened that during an interval in *Diarmuid and Grania*, according to local custom, the people in the galleries started to sing. They sang old, well-known songs. Until that moment those melodies had never been sung in unison by so many voices with the ancient Irish words. A shiver went through the auditorium. In the lingering notes there was an incomparable melancholy, like the cry of a nation. One after another, faces could be seen leaning into their programmes. We wept.

Then the curtain lifted and the play resumed amid an atmosphere of deep emotion. We had just sensed the soul of a people floating in the auditorium. ▪

JOHN EGLINTON—*from*:

DANA

A Thought Revival
(1904)

CERTAINLY NOTHING IS more alien to the spirit of *Dana* than to hold up, as some recent publicists have done, the ignorance and obscurantism of the Catholic people of Ireland to the derision of the Orange Party, which is, all things considered, probably on a lower moral plane itself.

At the same time, as Catholicism is the religion of the vast majority of the Irish people, it is, perhaps, natural that those who seriously criticise religious affairs should be mostly concerned with Catholicism. After all, Irish Protestantism is so largely a mere phase of political ascendancy.

Another interesting question is raised by Mr. Gibson in his contention that a man should confine his criticism to 'the thoughts and doings of those with whom he is most closely in touch, with whom his judgement may be of some weight.' Presumably Mr. Gibson refers to public, not private, criticism. In any case the advice is sound, but it is often difficult to act on. Should an Irish nationalist, say, never criticise unionism, but always follow nationalists? Are we always to play the part of 'candid friend' to our own side? The *rôle* is never a pleasant one at the best, but even the 'candid friend' is criticising people with whom he does not agree. Criticism, in the very nature of the case, must always come from a more or less 'external standpoint'. The essential thing to demand is that it be honest, competent and fair. In the interests of 'mental efficiency' a man may properly criticise a belief or a policy which he regards as wholly false or vicious: the conditions are that he shall be courteous; that he shall never substitute abuse for argument; and that he shall fairly listen and give publicity to the opinions he criticises. That certainly is the ideal of *Dana*. ■

John Eglinton was the pen name of W.K. Magee, born in Dublin in 1868. He worked at the National Library from 1898 until 1922. He co-edited (with Frederick Ryan) *Dana*, a journal which called for a movement in critical thought to match that of the language revival. Casting himself in the role of counter-revivalist, Eglinton argued that much writing of the period sentimentalised the more 'backward' elements of Irish life and that the main interests of ordinary people lay in extirpating the very conditions which had made the Gaelic cult possible. A champion of cosmopolitanism in art, Eglinton was a major antagonist of the Revival, yet his vibrant contributions to intellectual debate made him somehow an intrinsic part of it. He left Ireland in 1923 and died in 1961.

GEORGE RUSSELL (AE)—*from*:

'VILLAGE LIBRARIES'

(1906)

George Russell was born in Lurgan in 1867 but grew up in Dublin, where he was a fellow student at art school with W.B. Yeats. He himself won a measure of fame not only as a painter and mystic poet but also as a great enabler of the young writers of the Revival. A lifelong theosophist, he was also a pragmatic and energetic activist. He worked for many years for the rural co-operative movement under the direction of Horace Plunkett in The Irish Agricultural Co-operative Society. This was one of those 'self-help' movements which, along with the Gaelic League, Abbey Theatre, and Sinn Féin, added vibrancy to community life in the first decade of the twentieth century. From 1905 to 1923 Russell edited *The Irish Homestead*, in which the following appeared at the close of March, 1906.

W E BELIEVE IF village libraries are to be extended in Ireland we must encourage individual effort, and not rely too greatly on the ratepayers.... A library of two or three hundred books can be obtained for ten or fifteen pounds.... We think libraries of general literature will supply the lack in the present system of national education, and by awakening a general all-round intelligence, make people far more receptive of the ideas on special subjects inculcated by lecturers and instructors under the county schemes.

Even apart from this it is of the greatest importance that the farmers in Ireland should have a culture suited to their class. Culture of some kind we must have in a country or it becomes barbarous, and the standard of life, morals, and civilisation sinks lower and lower. When land purchase has been completed, and the great families, who, however inadequately, kept up the tradition of a cultured class in Ireland, are gone, as they will go for the most part—for families with wealth untied by local possessions will inevitably gravitate to other countries—what kind of a country will it be from the intellectual point of view?

There are no bookshops in Ireland outside Dublin, Belfast, Cork, Derry, Limerick, and perhaps one or two other towns. In other countries the peasant has his library. We in Ireland must try not to lose all interest in the higher thought or culture of the world. In the democracy of the future every man must be his own duke. It is all very well burning the *Harmsworth Magazines*, but are the people who burn providing themselves with good literature? Is the burning merely a spiteful act, or is it the outcome of a genuine national culture spreading in Ireland? We hope it

is, for the present indifference to books, to ideas, makes the
country a barbarous desert to the educated man.

The Gaelic League boasts of selling half-a-million
publications yearly, but most of these are textbooks, and
it has not yet touched the fringe of providing a national
literature. People won't continue learning a language when
the literature in that language is not easily accessible, is
expensive, is not modern, and does not reflect their own life.
The Gaelic movement may produce such a literature, but
while we wait we must advocate good libraries of Anglo-
Irish literature, and of the best books of the world. There
are many districts in Ireland as uninfluenced by books as if
they were in the centre of the Sahara. ∎

CONSTANCE MARKIEWICZ—*from*:

'WOMEN, IDEALS AND THE NATION'

(1909)

Constance Gore-Booth was born in 1868 into an Anglo-Irish family which owned the estate of Lissadell, near Sligo, where she and her sister Eva were childhood friends of W.B. Yeats. She became a suffragist while studying art at the Slade School in London. In 1900 she married the wealthy Polish aristocrat and artist, Count Casimir Markiewicz. Settling in Dublin in 1903, the couple became active in those societies where advanced nationalism overlapped with experimental painting and theatre. In 1908, under the inspiration of Maud Gonne, she joined Inghinidhe na hÉireann (Daughters of Erin) as well as Sinn Féin. She delivered a trenchant lecture to university students at a meeting of Inghinidhe in 1909.

ALL THIS POINTS to the one way in which the women of Ireland can help their country and, indeed, many of them are already doing so. And it is a movement too that all creeds, all classes, and all politics can join in. We have the Irish Industrial Development Associations, and the Sinn Féin organisations, both working very hard for this object, but there is still much to be done.

It is not enough just vaguely to buy Irish goods where you can do so without trouble, just in a sort of sentimental way. No, you must make Irish goods as necessary to your daily life as your bath or your breakfast. Say to yourselves, 'We must establish here a voluntary protection against foreign goods.' By this I mean that we must not resent sometimes having to pay an extra penny for an Irish-made article—which is practically protection—as the result of protection is that native manufacturers are enabled to charge the extra penny that will enable their infant factory to live and grow strong, and finally to compete on absolute equal terms with the foreign-made article.

Every Irish industry that we manage even to keep in existence is an added wealth to our nation, and therefore indirectly to ourselves. It employs labour which serves to keep down the poor rates, and to check emigration. The large sums of money it turns over benefits every other trade in the country. So you also will benefit, for the richer the country, the better price you will be able to command for your services in the professions and trades, and the more positions will be created to which you may aspire.

If the women of Ireland would organise the movement for buying Irish goods more, they might do a great deal to help their country. If they would make it the fashion to dress in Irish clothes, feed on Irish food—in fact, in this as in everything, *live really Irish lives,* they would be doing something great. And don't let our clever Irish colleens rest content with doing this individually, but let them go out and speak publicly about it, form leagues, of which 'No English Goods' is the war-cry. Let them talk and talk, publicly and privately, never minding how they bore people—till not one even of the peasants in the wilds of Galway but has heard and approved of the movement.

I daresay you will think this all very obvious and very dull, but patriotism and nationalism and all great things are made up of much that is obvious and dull, and much that in the beginning is small, but that will be found to lead out into fields that are broader and full of interest. You will go out into the world and get elected on to as many public bodies as possible, and by degrees through your exertions no public institution—whether hospital, workhouse, asylum, or any other—and no private house—but will be supporting the industries of your country.

Ireland wants her girls to help her to build up her national life. Their fresh, clean views of life, their young energies, have been long too hidden away and kept separate in their different homes. Bring them out and organise them, and lo! you will find a great new army ready to help the national cause. The old idea that a woman can only serve her nation through her home is gone, so now is the time: on you the responsibility rests. No one can help you but yourselves alone, you must make the world look upon you as citizens first, as women after. For each one of you there is a niche waiting—your place in the nation. Try and find it. It may be as a leader, it may be as a humble follower—perhaps in a political party, perhaps in a party of your own—but it is there, and if you cannot find it for yourself, no one can find it for you.

If you are fitted for public work take up any that is within your reach, so long as you feel that you can do it. Ireland wants reforming, sweeping clean from ocean to ocean, and it is only the young people can do it.

Since the Union we have been steadily deteriorating: all our ideals have been gradually slipping from us. Let us look all these facts bravely in the face, and make up our minds to change them.

We know that the government of England is responsible for all this. First, for the famine, with its deaths and desolations, by which our people were taught to beg and to appeal and look to England and our fine national spirit was taught to be submissive.

Emigration—another policy sent to us from England— has helped to build up another great nation at Ireland's expense. The men and women whom she could least afford to lose were the ones who so often had to go, leaving the weak and the feeble to continue their own race.

But what has done us most harm of all is a system of government calculated to foster all that was low or mean in our nature—treachery, place-hunting—besides all the petty, mean vices that follow on the idea that commercial prosperity and nothing else is the highest ideal of life. These ideas and many more, we have been allowing a subtle foe to graft on our national character at her will. ■

MARY COLUM —*from*:

LIFE AND THE DREAM

(1947)

T HE VIGOROUS INTELLECTUAL life of the city was open to the students who wanted it, and even those who didn't could not have missed taking some of it in through the pores. If we learned about the past of literature in the classrooms, we learned about the present of literature, what literature was, outside from the men who were making it. Dublin was a small city, the suburbs stretched out to a distance, but the centre, the old part of the city, was circumscribed and bristled with movements of various kinds—dramatic, artistic, educational; there were movements for the restoration of the Irish language, for reviving native arts and crafts, for preserving ancient ruins, for resurrecting native costume, an array of political movements: here, too, were the theatres and the tearooms and pubs which corresponded to the café life of the continental city. In the centre, too, were the headquarters of the clubs and societies, some at war with each other, but all exciting and, somehow, focused towards one end—a renaissance. Between Abbey Street and College Green, a five minutes' walk, one could meet every person of importance in the life of the city at a certain time in the afternoon.

The city was then drama-mad, and every actor with an ambition to play any drama, ancient or modern, tried it out in Dublin; if it passed the test of a Dublin audience, it could pass anywhere, it was the fashion to say, and Dublin believed the dictum. Certainly we saw the most diverse kinds of dramatic entertainment, all the way from *Oedipus Rex*, played by Martin Harvey and staged by Reinhardt, to Mrs. Patrick Campbell in *Hedda Gabler* and Sarah Bernhardt and Mrs. Patrick Campbell in Maeterlinck's *Pelléas and Mélisande*....

Born in 1887 at Collooney, County Sligo, Mary (Molly) Maguire studied at University College Dublin, being a frequent attendee at the Abbey Theatre and Theatre of Ireland (set up in 1906). She was a schoolteacher and with Thomas MacDonagh a co-founder of the *Irish Review* in 1911. She married poet and playwright Padraic Colum in 1912 and two years later the couple migrated to New York. In the 1920s and '30s she was regarded as one of the foremost literary critics in the United States—her essays on Virginia Woolf and Rebecca West being very influential. She and her husband's collected essays on her most famous college classmate appeared after her death under the title, *Our Friend James Joyce* (1958). Her literary masterpiece *Life and the Dream* (1947) vividly evokes what it was like to be a young woman in Revival Dublin.

The Comédie Française, as it always did in its provincial tours, took in the needs of the students, and the French seventeenth-century classical drama was played, including the pieces on our course. The acting of the Comédie Française was strikingly different from that of the English companies and was supposed to be the type that native Irish players could take for a model; indeed it was passed around that the real name of the great French actor Coquelin was Coghlan, and that his family had originated in Limerick. But at this period the Irish were claiming almost everybody of distinction as Celtic or Gaelic if not Irish. ■

'The city was then drama-mad...'

Movements and Manifestos

IN JAMES JOYCE'S novel, *A Portrait of the Artist as a Young Man* (1916), the protagonist, Stephen Dedalus, brings the narrative to a close with his declared intention to 'forge in the smithy of my soul the uncreated conscience of my race.' In this famous declaration Joyce's hero vents his frustrations on an authoritarian Catholic Church and an oppressive colonial regime that have combined to stifle the development of independent thinking in Ireland. Joyce was critical, too, of the inadequacies of Irish nationalist traditions that were physically brave but intellectually under-developed. What he lamented above all was the absence of secular traditions of thought in Ireland—a republic of letters that could forge its own conscience and connect to the best of the world's thought. Ironically, a distinctly Irish republic of letters was coming into being at the very moment that Joyce lamented its absence.

Not only did the Revival produce a cadre of exceptional writers who would make their contribution to world literature but it also witnessed a huge upsurge in the level of civic participation and activism across Irish life. People in their thousands gathered in meeting rooms all over the country to debate the issues in secular and democratically-run societies

and organisations. Many were energised and empowered
by the idea that connecting with forgotten traditions might
enable progress and modernisation on Irish terms. The wider
availability of print technology and the rise of niche newspapers
and journals greatly facilitated intellectual exchange and
activism of all sorts. At this time it was possible for Irish men
and women to join a whole range of clubs, leagues, and societies
dedicated to sport, the Irish language, agricultural co-operation,
music and theatre. As the new century unfolded a fresh set of
more radical, anti-establishment ideas—socialism, women's
suffrage, trade unionism, pacifism, anti-conscriptionism—
presented themselves as the basis for organisation and
activism. In this period of ideals, manifestos and action, people
embraced the opportunity to organise in new forms beyond
those sanctioned by the British state, the Churches and the
established politicians.

What is most striking, however, is the speed with which
cultural and intellectual energies and activities across these
networks of activism transformed into military organisation in
response to the Home Rule crisis of 1912, and in the context of
a militarist *zeitgeist* sweeping Europe. Growing disenchantment

with the efficacy of the Westminster Parliament in the north
and south of Ireland undoubtedly helped the causes of
those committed to the use of arms to bring about change.
This period of movements and manifestos culminates in
the declaration of Irish sovereign independence in the 1916
Proclamation. The right of the insurgents to bear arms in the
name of the Irish people continues to generate vigorous debate.
However, it is significant that the manifesto of the nation is
recognisably informed by the democratic, non-sectarian ideas
of citizenship that underwrote civic activities in parish halls and
meeting rooms all over Ireland in the decades leading up to the
1916 Rising.

MICHAEL CUSACK

'A WORD ABOUT IRISH ATHLETICS'

(1884)

N O MOVEMENT HAVING for its object the social and political advancement of a nation from the tyranny of imported and enforced customs and manners can be regarded as perfect if it has not made adequate provision for the preservation and cultivation of the national pastimes of the people. Voluntary neglect of such pastimes is a sure sign of national decay and of approaching dissolution.

The strength and energy of a race are largely dependent on the national pastimes for the development of a spirit of courage and endurance. The corrupting influences which, for several years, have been devastating the sporting grounds of our cities and towns are fast spreading to the rural population. Foreign and hostile laws and the pernicious influence of a hitherto dominant race drove the Irish people from the trysting places at the crossroads and the hurling fields, back to their cabin where, but a few short years before, famine and fever had reigned supreme. In these wretched homes . . . the Irish peasant too often wasted his evenings and his holidays, in smoking and card-playing.

A few years later a so-called revival of athletics was inaugurated in Ireland. The new movement did not originate with those who have ever had any sympathy with Ireland or the Irish people. Accordingly labourers, tradesmen, artists, and even policemen and soldiers were excluded from the few competitions which constituted the lame and halting programme of the promoters. Two years ago every man who did not make his living either wholly or partly by athletics was allowed to compete. But with this concession came a law which is as intolerable as its existence in Ireland is degrading. The law is that all athletic meetings shall be under the rules of the Amateur Athletic Association of England, and that any

Michael Cusack was born in Carron, County Clare in 1847. He was an accomplished hurler, footballer and cricketer, and an early advocate of Irish sports. A committed nationalist, he was known for his outspoken views and was caricatured as the xenophobic 'Citizen' in James Joyce's *Ulysses*. On 11 October 1884 Cusack published a letter in the *United Ireland* newspaper. Arising from this, a meeting was arranged in Hayes's Commercial Hotel, Thurles, County Tipperary on 1 November 1884. At this inaugural gathering, the 'Gaelic Athletic Association for the Preservation and Cultivation of National Pastimes' was founded. Maurice Davin was elected president, Michael Cusack, John Wyse Power and John McKay elected secretaries, and Archbishop Thomas William Croke, Charles Stewart Parnell and →

→ Michael Davitt were
invited to become patrons.
The GAA rapidly became
a hugely successful
grassroots movement. Its
organisational structure—
from parish to all-Ireland
levels—became a model
for subsequent Revival
movements such as
the Gaelic League
and, later, Comhaltas
Ceoltóirí Éireann.

person competing at any meeting not held under these rules should be ineligible to compete elsewhere. The management of nearly all the meetings held in Ireland since has been entrusted to persons hostile to all the dearest aspirations of the Irish people. Every effort has been made to make the meetings look as English as possible—foot-races, betting, and flagrant cheating being their most prominent features. Swarms of pot-hunting mashers sprang into existence. They formed Harrier Clubs, for the purpose of training through the winter, after the fashion of English professional athletes that they might be able to win and pawn the prizes offered for competition in the summer.

We tell the Irish people to take the management of their games into their own hands, to encourage and promote in every way every form of athletics which is peculiarly Irish, and to remove with one sweep everything foreign and iniquitous is the present system. The vast majority of the best athletes in Ireland are nationalists. These gentlemen should take the matter in hand at once, and draft laws for the guidance of the promoters of meetings in Ireland next year. The people pay the expenses of the meetings, and the representatives of the people should have the controlling power. It is only by such an arrangement that pure Irish athletics will be revived, and that the incomparable strength and physique of our race will be preserved. ∎

OBJECTS OF THE IRISH NATIONAL LITERARY SOCIETY

(1892)

THE OBJECTS OF the Irish National Literary Society are as follows:

1. The Circulation of Irish Literature
2. Lectures and Discussions
3. Concerts of Irish Music
4. The Establishment of Lending Libraries

The Society has now taken rooms in 4, College Green, Dublin, where the members hold social and musical meetings, with fortnightly debates or lectures on Irish subjects.

The following monthly public lectures have also been or are to be delivered under the auspices of the Society:

Aug 22 1892, 'Irish Literature: Its Origin, Environment, and Influence' (Inaugural Address), by George Sigerson, M.D., F.R.U.I.

Nov 25, 'The Necessity of De-Anglicising the Irish Nation' by the President, Douglas Hyde, LL.D.

Dec 15, 'The Antiquities of Tara' (illustrated) by George Colley, B.L.

Jan 20, 1893 'Owen Roe O'Neill' by Rev. T. Finlay, S.J.

Feb 17, 'Battle of the Curlew Mountains' by Standish O'Grady

March 24, 'The Celtic Leaven in English Literature,' by Richard Aske King, M.A.

April 2, 'James Barry, R.A.' by Count Plunkett, B.L.

May 19, 'Nationality and Literature' by W.B. Yeats

June 23, 'Irish Orators' by J.F. Taylor, B.L. ∎

This society was established by W.B. Yeats with the support of John O'Leary in 1892. Its primary aim was to combat the indifference of Anglo-Irish intellectuals towards Irish cultural matters by fostering literary debate. It also addressed the dearth of critical scrutiny of Irish literature due to the lack of a vigorous periodical press. The intention was to create as much impact as possible on national opinion and taste by encouraging Irish readers to look on Ireland as a centre of literary excellence. The society played an important role in raising standards of criticism and introducing new thinking. Many of the key ideas of the Revival were first aired before the members of the Irish National Literary Society. Douglas Hyde delivered his famous 'De-Anglicising' lecture at this forum in 1892.

⊛ ⊛

from:

THE GAELIC LEAGUE ANNUAL REPORT

(1894)

The Gaelic League was
founded on 31 July 1893
at a meeting in 9 Lower
O'Connell Street, Dublin.
Douglas Hyde presided
with Charles Percy
Bushe, James Michael
Cogan, William Hayden
S.J., Patrick J. Hogan,
Martin Kelly, Eoin MacNeill,
Patrick O'Brien and
Thomas O'Neill Russell
in attendance. The aim of
the society was to keep
the Irish language spoken
in Ireland. Very quickly it
became a popular mass
movement that promoted
classes in the Irish
language and encouraged
the development of Gaelic
cultural life through music
and drama. The League
created a new civic space
outside the influence of the
Churches, political parties
and the British state, where
people from a range of ↗

RULES OF THE GAELIC LEAGUE

I.

The object of this Society is to keep the Irish language spoken in Ireland.

II.

No matter of religious or political difference of opinion shall be admitted into the proceedings of this Society.

The foregoing are fundamental rules, and cannot be altered or abolished.

MEETINGS OF THE CENTRAL BRANCH

Meetings were held weekly on Tuesday evenings at 4, College Green. With the exception of the first few weeks, when the number of members was small, the meetings were well attended throughout the year. A number of ladies were generally among the audience. At first the proceedings were carried on half in Irish, half in English, or possibly more in English than in Irish. Later on, Irish became more and more generally used, and in the meetings towards the close of the session, Irish was used almost exclusively. The proceedings consisted of discussions of various points relative to the movement, original papers in Irish, readings of Irish prose and poetry, Irish recitations and Irish songs....

CLASSES

In September two classes were formed; one for beginners, under Mr. R. MacS. Gordon; another for more advanced pupils under Mr. T. O. Russell. Later on, a conversation class was formed, and was attended by all the learners. As the principle on which this class was conducted may form a good model for other classes throughout the country, it may be well to state it in detail.

The phrases to be translated into Irish were taken from a phrasebook. The book most used in this class was De Fiva's *Guide to French Conversation*. An English phrase was read aloud, and any idiomatic speaker of Irish present was invited to give a translation in Irish. The conductor of the class then wrote the Irish on a blackboard. If several correct and distinct translations were forthcoming, they were all usually taken down, especially when they exemplified the different usages of different localities. The learners were expected to copy the Irish phrases with the English equivalents into their notebooks. ∎

→ social, religious and political backgrounds could meet on the basis of their shared interest in the Irish language. This may explain why so many of the revolutionary generation were members. After independence, the Gaelic League found itself in obvious alignment with the interests of the new Irish state and seems to have lost its popular appeal for that very reason.

HORACE PLUNKETT

THE AIMS OF THE CO-OPERATIVE MOVEMENT

(1894)

The Irish Agricultural Organisation Society was set up on 18 April 1894 to encourage co-operation among a new class of small farmers who had secured land as a result of recent land acts. This movement was led by Horace Plunkett, R.A. Anderson, Fr. Tom Finlay and George Russell, and spread rapidly across the country. It undertook to educate farmers in modern agricultural practices and to encourage the formation of co-operative societies and credit unions. The co-ops played an important role in breaking the economic stranglehold of the gombeen class of publican-shopkeepers. Like the GAA and the Gaelic League, the co-op societies were organised locally and affiliated nationally. They were run democratically and promoted a non-sectarian and non-political ethos. The IAOS had a transformative influence on the cultural life and civic infrastructure of rural Ireland.

T HE CHIEF INDUSTRY of Ireland is agriculture. The welfare of the country can be seen to depend almost entirely on the welfare of the agricultural industry . . . Among all the remedies suggested to deal with the depression of agriculture, none seemed to offer any real aid to the farmer except protection and that was unattainable. No one had suggested combination on the lines of co-operative enterprise in all other trades and in the agriculture of various foreign countries. The idea prevailed that farmers were uncombinable atoms—more especially Irish farmers. This proposition I have been combating for some few years. The creamery movement had demonstrated its falsity. I now proposed to extend the movement to apply combination to every branch of the farmers' business. This I held to be a mere question of propaganda, and propaganda a question of money and influential backing. I propounded a scheme for the formation of a society (the IAOS) to send paid organisers to organise co-op societies throughout Ireland and generally to instruct the farming community upon what can be done by co-operation. ■

OPENING STATEMENT OF THE IRISH LITERARY THEATRE
(1899)

The origins of the Abbey Theatre lie in the foundation of an experimental theatre company, the Irish Literary Theatre, in 1899. Led by Augusta Gregory, W.B.Yeats, George Moore, and Edward Martyn, the group was funded by nationalist and unionist supporters. This initiative was a self-conscious attempt to provide an alternative to Dublin's commercial theatres, which were heavily reliant on British touring companies. The idea was to encourage Irish playwrights to inaugurate an Irish theatre for Irish audiences. Over a three-year span the company experimented with Irish myth, folklore and dialect, and also mounted the first professional production of a play in Irish—Douglas Hyde's, *Casadh an tSúgáin*. A major concern was to uphold high literary standards and to offer a more edifying idea of Irish character than the stereotypes of the London stage.

WE PROPOSE TO have performed in Dublin, in the spring of every year certain Celtic and Irish plays, which whatever be their degree of excellence will be written with a high ambition, and so to build up a Celtic and Irish school of dramatic literature. We hope to find in Ireland an uncorrupted and imaginative audience trained to listen by its passion for oratory, and believe that our desire to bring upon the stage the deeper thoughts and emotions of Ireland will ensure for us a tolerant welcome, and that freedom to experiment which is not found in theatres of England, and without which no new movement in art or literature can succeed. We will show that Ireland is not the home of buffoonery and of easy sentiment, as it has been represented, but the home of an ancient idealism. We are confident of the support of all Irish people, who are weary of misrepresentation, in carrying out a work that is outside all the political questions that divide us. ▪

OBJECTS OF INGHINIDHE NA HÉIREANN

(Daughters of Ireland)

(1900)

Maud Gonne (1865–1953) founded Inghinidhe na hEireann out of the frustration of being excluded, as a woman, from advanced nationalist clubs like the Celtic Literary Society. The aim of the group was to contribute to the revival of Irish culture, and to promote separatist and republican thinking. Gonne and her colleagues actively opposed royal visits to Ireland and openly campaigned against British army recruitment drives that targeted Irishmen. ↗

1. The re-establishment of the complete independence of Ireland.

2. To encourage the study of Gaelic, of Irish Literature, History, Music and Art, especially amongst the young, by the organising and teaching of classes for the above subjects.

3. To support and popularise Irish manufacture.

4. To discourage the reading and circulation of low English literature, the singing of English songs, the attending of vulgar English entertainments at the theatres and music halls, and to combat in every way English influence, which is doing so much injury to the artistic taste and refinement of the Irish people.

5. To form a fund called the National Purposes Fund, for the furtherance of the above projects.

RULES

1. The Inghinidhe na hÉireann, remembering that they are all workers in the same holy cause, pledge themselves to mutual help and support, and to stand loyally by one another.

2. Each member must adopt a Gaelic name by which she shall be known in the association.

3. Each member shall pledge herself to aid in extending and popularising Gaelic as a spoken tongue, and to advance the Irish Language movement by every means in her power.

4. Each member shall pledge herself to support Irish manufactures, by using as far as possible Irish made goods in her household and dress.

5. Each member shall adopt the badge of the association. The price of the badge shall be 2s. 6d.

6. Members wishing to resign from the association shall give one week's notice, and return her badge, when the price shall be refunded, provided her subscription be paid up to date.

7. Each member shall pledge herself not to lend her badge to anyone outside the association, without special permission from the Committee.

8. Each member must be three months in the association before she receives the badge. ■

→ The organisation also played a crucial role in the emergence of the Irish theatre, with Maud Gonne taking the lead role in the iconic first production of *Cathleen Ní Houlihan* in 1902. Prominent members of the organisation included Jennie Wyse-Power, Anna Johnston (Ethna Carbery), Annie Egan, Alice Furlong and Maire T. Quinn. Many Inghinidhe na hEireann members would become Cumann na mBan activists in advance of the 1916 Rising.

from:

MANIFESTO OF THE ULSTER LITERARY THEATRE

(1904)

One of the notable features of the Irish theatre movement was the important contribution of Ulster playwrights such as Alice Milligan, George Russell and James Cousins. Influenced by developments in Dublin, Bulmer Hobson and Lewis Purcell (David Parkhill) set about founding an adjacent, yet separate, theatre company in Belfast with the help of playwrights Rutherford Mayne, Samuel Weddell, Gerald McNamara and Harold Morrow. Their manifesto, published in the literary journal *Uladh* in 1904, aimed to connect with a national consciousness and also pledged to articulate Ulster's regional distinctiveness. In the three decades of its existence, the ULT specialised in the production of political satires and rural comedies and often parodied the fondness for mythology and poetic drama so evident among their counterparts in Dublin.

W E RECOGNISE AT the outset that our art of the drama will be different from that other Irish drama which speaks from the stage of the Irish National Theatre in Dublin, where two men, W.B. Yeats and Douglas Hyde, have set a model in Anglo-Irish and Gaelic plays with a success that is surprising and exhilarating. Dreamer, mystic, symbolist, Gaelic poet, and propagandist have all spoken on the Dublin stage, and a fairly defined local school has been inaugurated. We in Belfast and Ulster also wish to set up a school, but there will be a difference.

At present we can only say that our talent is more satiric than poetic. That will probably remain the broad difference between the Ulster and the Leinster schools. But when our genius arrives, as he must sooner or later, there is no accounting for what extraordinary tendency he may display. Our business is, however, to plod along gathering matter for his use, practising methods, perfecting technique and training actors.

We hope to publish a short play with each number. These plays will all be by Ulster writers. A page or more will be devoted to Gaelic, and the rest of the magazine to essays,

short poems, and illustrations . . . we do not aim at being
sixpence-worth; we aim at being priceless, for honesty
and good purpose are priceless. If we do not attain to all
this, we shall at least attain to something unique in Ulster,
smacking of the soil, the winds on the uplands, the north
coast, the sun and the rain, and the long winter evenings.

Uladh will be non-sectarian and non-political; each
article will be signed by the writer as an expression of his
own views; other views may be put forward in another
number. In any case, our pages will be kept free from
the party-cries of mob and clique and marketplace. Our
contributors are mostly young men, of all sects and all
grades of political opinion. ■

'At present we can only say that
our talent is more satiric than
poetic. That will probably remain
the broad difference between the
Ulster and the Leinster schools.
But when our genius arrives, as he
must sooner or later, there is no
accounting for what extraordinary
tendency he may display.'

from:

REPORT ON THE INAUGURAL FEIS NA nGLEANN
(1904)

Feis na nGleann
(the Glens Feis) was an
initiative of a number of
influential Ulster Revivalists
to celebrate the Gaelic
heritage of the Glens
of Antrim. Until the
mid-nineteenth century
the Irish language was
widely spoken in this
region. The first feis was
held in Glenariff in July
1904 and featured a busy
programme of language,
music and dance
competitions. The event
was supported by an array
of important Revival figures
such as F.J. Bigger, Eoin
MacNeill, Roger Casement,
Ada McNeill, John
Campbell and Barbara
McDonnell. Horace
Plunkett was invited to
award the prizes at this
event, demonstrating
the close collaboration
between the co-operative
movement and the Gaelic
League. This report of
the inaugural feis was
published in the *Ballymena
Weekly Telegraph* on 9
July 1904.

WATERFOOT NEVER IN its history before had such a crowd of people along its streets and shore as on that memorable 30 June 1904, when the 'Feis na nGleann' was held. All the schools in the Glens were closed to enable the children to attend, cars brought in visitors and competitors from every part of the Glens, while motor cars and steam yachts conveyed the more wealthy observers to the place. The Raghery (Rathlin) folk were well represented. And Holden's Hall, a most fortunate erection, was crowded from 10.00 a.m. till the small hours of the next morning by excited, curious, homely, and fashionable crowds.

Athletic games, such as an caman, running, jumping, etc., were contested on the shore, dancing on the greens around the hall on specially erected platforms; while inside singing, fiddling (that's the pan-Gaelic way of it), whistling, story-telling, and reciting went on all day until six o'clock, when the competitions were concluded and the building cleared for the evening concert, at which quite a number of celebrities were present, including Sir Horace Plunkett, who distributed the prizes and made a hopeful speech on the industrial revival and the good work done by the Gaelic League.

It was stated that about 4,000 people came and went about the Feis during the day. The syllabus certainly afforded something for everyone's interest. This syllabus was like everything else, characteristically Irish in design, with good black and white work by Joseph Campbell, illustrating local places of interest[.] ■

SINN FÉIN RESOLUTIONS

(1905)

RESOLUTIONS PASSED ON the 28 November 1905, at the public meeting which followed the first annual convention of the National Council of Sinn Féin, 1905.

1. That the people of Ireland are a free people, and that no law made without their authority or consent is or can ever be binding on their conscience. That the general council of county councils presents the nucleus of a national authority, and we urge upon it to extend the scope of its deliberation and action; to take within its purview every question of national interest and to formulate lines of procedure for the nation.

2. That national self-development through the recognition of the duties and rights of citizenship on the part of the individual, and by the aid and support of all movements originating from within Ireland, instinct with national tradition, and not looking outside Ireland for the accomplishment of their aims, is vital to Ireland.

The United Irishman
9 December 1905

The outbreak of the Boer War in 1899 had a seismic effect on the Irish political landscape. Prior to this moment, advocates for a sovereign, independent Irish nation tended to meet in secret organisations such as the Irish Republican Brotherhood. The Boer conflict, however, greatly assisted the emergence of a new non-clandestine separatist politics outside the domain of the Irish politicians attending Westminster. Widespread demonstrations against the war signalled a growing critique of the foreign policies being pursued by the British empire in the name of the Irish people. Arthur Griffith (1872–1922), editor of the newly founded *United Irishman* newspaper (1899), was a prominent opponent of the war and an advocate for the withdrawal of Irish politicians from Westminster. He was a key figure in the founding of a new separatist political organisation, Sinn Féin, in 1905.

from:

PATRICK PEARSE'S LETTER TO EOIN MACNEILL ON THE FOUNDING OF ST. ENDA'S SCHOOL

(1908)

St. Enda's secondary school for boys was founded by Patrick Pearse (1879–1916) in 1908. The radical and experimental ethos of the school was informed by revivalist ideas about the importance of the Irish language to the formation of national character. Pearse studied bilingual teaching in Belgium and was greatly inspired by that model. He was keen to replace colonial modes of education that promoted rote learning and fetishised examination success. Instead he encouraged more liberal ideas, placing value on individuality and imagination. Pearse's interest in early-Christian Ireland and in the heroic deeds of Cuchulain was reflected in the curriculum. The increasing involvement of staff members in military organisation was also mirrored in the distinctive form of patriotic masculinity encouraged at St. Enda's.

I WONDER WHETHER I can interest you in a project which, as I think you know, I have had at the back of my head for the past two or three years and which, if I can see my way clear, I am now more than ever anxious to proceed with? It is the project of a high school for boys in Dublin on purely Irish Ireland lines. The arguments in favour of the establishment of such a school are irresistible. There is no *Irish* high school in Ireland. There is no high school for Catholic boys conducted by laymen in Ireland. My idea is, if possible, to fill this twofold need.

There are a number of Gaelic Leaguers in Dublin and throughout the country who have brought up their children more or less Irish-speaking and who are now anxiously looking round for a school which would provide these children with a genuine *Irish* education, while at the same time of a high standard generally.... Among the features of my scheme would be:

1. An *Irish* standpoint and 'atmosphere'.
2. *Bilingual teaching* as far as possible.
3. All language teaching on the *Direct Method*.
4. Special attention to science and 'modern' subjects generally, while not neglecting the classical side.
5. Association of the pupils with the shaping of the curriculum, cultivation of observation and reasoning, 'nature study', and several other points to which I have devoted a good deal of thought.
6. Physical culture, Irish games etc.
7. Above all, formation of character. ∎

ELLICE PILKINGTON—*from*:

'THE UNITED IRISHWOMEN: THEIR WORK'

(1911)

W E ARE TIRED of seeing our sons die in foreign countries because they are too poor to live in Ireland. We are maddened by the sad look in the eyes of the returned Irish-American girl who hates the discomfort of her Irish home. We are prematurely aged by too much hard lonely work. We are sorry for our old people to whom we cannot give the care that old age deserves. We are frightened by disease. We dread the horrors of the lunatic asylums. We are now awake to the fact that relief from all these troubles will only come to us from within ourselves. We must band together, join hands and hearts and work not half-heartedly and in sorrow but joyfully, at times merrily, ever looking to where the sun is breaking through the cloud. We have a great inheritance of youth and hope, and we have only to put out our hands to take it and to pass it on to our children when our day's work is done. ∎

The society of the United Irishwomen—a forerunner of the Irish Countrywomen's Association—was founded in May 1910 by a small group of largely Protestant women in Bree, County Wexford. Affiliated to the IAOS, the aim was to improve living standards in rural Ireland through education and co-operation. The ethos was non-sectarian and non-political. One of the early pioneers of the movement was Ellice Pilkington (1869–1936) who outlined the objectives of the movement in this essay. By drawing attention to the drudgery and oppressions of rural life, she critiqued the idealising tendencies of some urban-based revivalists. Many of the aspirations articulated here are remarkably close to some of the aims outlined in the 'Democratic Programme of the First Dáil'.

'ULSTER'S SOLEMN LEAGUE AND COVENANT'

(1912)

The introduction of the Third Home Rule Bill to the British Parliament in April 1912 provoked a huge reaction from Ulster unionists. Mass protests against the proposed legislation proved the strength of unionist resistance to constitutional change. Central to this campaign, led by Edward Carson (1854–1935) and James Craig (1871–1940), was a document known as 'Ulster's Solemn League and Covenant'. On 28 September 1912 the Ulster Unionist Council organised rallies in support of the covenant. In total 218,206 men signed the document while 234,046 signatures were gathered by the Ulster Women's Unionist Council. The Ulster Covenant pledged loyalty to the king and empire but registered a loss of faith in the parliamentary process in Westminster. The implicit threat of armed resistance to Home Rule was soon backed up by the formation of the Ulster Volunteer Force in January 1913.

BEING CONVINCED IN our consciences that Home Rule would be disastrous to the material well-being of Ulster as well as of the whole of Ireland, subversive of our civil and religious freedom, destructive of our citizenship and perilous to the unity of the Empire, we, whose names are underwritten, men of Ulster, loyal subjects of his Gracious Majesty King George V, humbly relying on the God whom our fathers in days of stress and trial confidently trusted, do hereby pledge ourselves in solemn covenant throughout this our time of threatened calamity to stand by one another in defending for ourselves and our children our cherished position of equal citizenship in the United Kingdom and in using all means which may be found necessary to defeat the present conspiracy to set up a Home Rule Parliament in Ireland. And in the event of such a parliament being forced upon us we further solemnly and mutually pledge ourselves to refuse to recognise its authority. In sure confidence that God will defend the right we hereto subscribe our names. And further, we individually declare that we have not already signed this Covenant.

The above was signed by me at _____
Ulster Day, Saturday 28th September 1912.

God Save the King

THE CONSTITUTION OF THE IRISH CITIZEN ARMY

(1913–1914)

1. That the first and last principle of the Irish Citizen Army is the avowal that the ownership of Ireland, moral and material, is vested of right in the people of Ireland.
2. That its principal objects shall be:
   a. To arm and train all Irishmen capable of bearing arms to enforce and defend its first principle.
   b. To sink all differences of birth, privilege and creed under the common name of the Irish people.
3. That the Citizen Army shall stand for the absolute unity of Irish nationhood and recognition of the rights and liberties of the world's democracies.
4. That the Citizen Army shall be open to all who are prepared to accept the principles of equal rights and opportunities for the people of Ireland and to work in harmony with organised labour toward that end.
5. Every enrolled member must be, if possible, a member of a Trades Union recognised by the Irish Trades Union Congress.

GOD SAVE THE PEOPLE

Reasons why the workers should join the Irish Citizen Army

1. Because it is controlled by leaders of your own class.
2. Because it stands for Labour and the principles of Wolfe Tone, John Mitchel and Fintan Lalor.
3. Because it has the sympathy and support of the Dublin Trades Council.
4. Because it refuses to allow in its ranks those who have proved untrue to Labour.

WORKERS, don't be misled; trust only those ye know and have suffered for your class.

JOIN THE CITIZEN ARMY NOW!

The Irish Citizen Army was founded on 23 November 1913 by Jack White (1879–1946), with the encouragement of James Larkin. Sean O'Casey served as the secretary and Constance Markiewicz as treasurer. This initiative was partly inspired by the brutal treatment of striking workers by the Dublin Metropolitan Police during a demonstration in O'Connell Street during the 1913 Lock-Out. The aim was to protect workers in clashes with the police during strikes and demonstrations. It was also a means of instilling discipline within a labour movement that was often characterised as listless and badly organised. Under the leadership of James Connolly the ICA joined forces with the Irish Volunteers and the IRB to take part in the 1916 Rising. ICA volunteers were drawn largely from Dublin's unskilled working class and fought to defend the rights of labour in a sovereign Irish nation.

CONSTITUTION OF THE IRISH VOLUNTEERS

The Irish Volunteers (Óglaigh na hÉireann) were founded on 25 November 1913, eight months before the outbreak of World War One, as a response to the earlier formation of the Ulster Volunteer Force. Eoin MacNeill, a leading figure in the movement, made unrequited overtures to Ulster unionists at the outset, appealing to the fact that the Ulstermen were kinsmen of the Irish Volunteers of 1782 and of the 'Antrim and Down insurgents of 1798'. He also stressed the 'defensive and protective' function of the movement in an early manifesto. The organisation was armed during the Howth gun-running operation on 26 July 1914 and rapidly drew support from all sections of nationalism, from moderate Home Rulers to advanced republicans. The movement split in September 1914 when John Redmond urged volunteers to enlist in the British army for service during World War One.

ADOPTED AT THE FIRST IRISH VOLUNTEER CONVENTION
(ABBEY THEATRE, DUBLIN, SUNDAY, 25 OCTOBER 1914)

I.—OBJECTS

1. To secure and maintain the rights and liberties common to all the people of Ireland.
2. To train, discipline, and equip for this purpose an Irish Volunteer Force.
3. To unite in the service of Ireland, Irishmen of every creed and of every party and class.

II.—ENROLMENT FORM TO BE SIGNED BY ALL IRISH VOLUNTEERS

I, the undersigned, desire to be enrolled for service in Ireland as a member of the Irish Volunteer Force. I subscribe to the constitution of the Irish Volunteers and pledge my willing obedience to every article of it. I declare that in joining the Irish Volunteer Force I set before myself the stated objects of the Irish Volunteers, and no others. ■

CUMANN NA mBAN

Irish Women's Council

(1914)

Cumann na mBan was founded on 2 April 1914 in Wynn's Hotel, Dublin in support of the cause of the Irish Volunteers. From the outset this movement retained its independence, drafting its own constitution and appointing its own executive. Members regarded themselves as allies rather than subordinates of the Volunteers. In 1915 the organisation split over the issue of whether volunteers should join the British war effort. Cumann na mBan played a crucial role in the 1916 Rising and the War of Independence in relation to intelligence gathering, communications, propaganda, commandeering supplies and provision of first aid. The movement campaigned against proposed conscription of Irishmen and supported Sinn Fein in the 1918 election. A key figure, Constance Markiewicz, was appointed Minister for Labour in the First Dáil in 1919.

I. — OBJECTS

1. To advance the cause of Irish liberty.
2. To organise Irishwomen in furtherance of this object.
3. To assist in arming and equipping a body of Irishmen for the defence of Ireland.
4. To form a fund for these purposes to be called 'The Defence of Ireland Fund'.

Miss L. Nic Shambraidhin proposed the adoption of the Constitution of the organisation.

Mrs. M. Kettle seconded. Miss Agnes O'Farrelly presided. Resolution passed unanimously.

II. — CONSTITUTION

1. For the time being the direction of the branches will be carried on by the provisional committee.
2. Branches will be formed throughout the country, pledged to the Constitution, and directed in a general way by the provisional committee.
3. Members will be expected in addition to their local subscription to support the Defence of Ireland Fund by subscription or otherwise.
4. The affiliation fee for branches shall be 5/- per annum. ■

POBLACHT NA hÉIREANN

(THE PROVISIONAL GOVERNMENT OF THE IRISH REPUBLIC
TO THE PEOPLE OF IRELAND, 1916)

The Proclamation is the
fundamental document
of the 1916 Rising, which
explained the actions of
the rebels and outlined a
vision for an Irish Republic
to be founded by the
insurgents. It was read by
Patrick Pearse, president
of the newly formed
provisional government, on
the steps of the General
Post Office on Easter
Monday. The document
declared Irish sovereign
independence by rejecting
the British claim over
Ireland. Furthermore, it
proposed a radical new
form of government for
Ireland by changing the
status of the Irish people
from that of subjects of a
monarch, to equal citizens
before the law. Reference
to 'the dead generations'
invoked the memory of
injustice under British
rule, and recalled the
repeated attempts by Irish
revolutionaries to assert
their freedom over the
previous centuries. The
Proclamation addressed ↗

Irishmen and Irishwomen:

In the name of God and of the dead generations from which she receives her old tradition of nationhood, Ireland, through us, summons her children to her flag and strikes for her freedom.

Having organised and trained her manhood through her secret revolutionary organisation, the Irish Republican Brotherhood, and through her open military organisations, the Irish Volunteers and the Irish Citizen Army, having patiently perfected her discipline, having resolutely waited for the right moment to reveal itself, she now seizes that moment, and, supported by her exiled children in America and by gallant allies in Europe, but relying in the first on her own strength, she strikes in full confidence of victory.

We declare the right of the people of Ireland to the ownership of Ireland, and to the unfettered control of Irish destinies, to be sovereign and indefeasible. The long usurpation of that right by a foreign people and government has not extinguished the right, nor can it ever be extinguished except by the destruction of the Irish people. In every generation the Irish people have asserted their right to national freedom and sovereignty; six times during the past three hundred years they have asserted it in arms. Standing on that fundamental right and again asserting it in arms in the face of the world, we hereby proclaim the Irish Republic as a sovereign independent state. And we pledge our lives and the lives of our comrades-in-arms to the cause of its freedom, of its welfare, and of its exaltation among the nations.

The Irish Republic is entitled to, and hereby claims, the allegiance of every Irishman and Irishwoman. The Republic guarantees religious and civil liberty, equal rights and equal opportunities of all its citizens, and declares its resolve to pursue the happiness and prosperity of the whole nation and of all its parts, cherishing all the children of the nation equally, and oblivious of the differences carefully fostered by an alien government, which have divided a minority in the past.

Until our arms have brought the opportune moment for the establishment of a permanent National Government, representative of the whole people of Ireland and elected by the suffrages of all her men and women, the Provisional Government, hereby constituted, will administer the civil and military affairs of the Republic in trust for the people.

We place the cause of the Irish Republic under the protection of the Most High God, Whose blessing we invoke upon our arms, and we pray that no one who serves that cause will dishonour it by cowardice, inhumanity, or rapine. In this supreme hour the Irish nation must, by its valour and discipline and by the readiness of its children to sacrifice themselves for the common good, prove itself worthy of the august destiny to which it is called.

Signed on behalf of the Provisional Government:

Thomas J. Clarke
Seán MacDiarmada
Thomas MacDonagh
P.H. Pearse
Eamonn Ceannt
James Connolly
Joseph Plunkett

→ 'Irishmen and Irishwomen' as equals and accepted the right of women to vote. It guaranteed religious and civil liberties, and undertook to extend equal opportunities to all citizens. The seven signatories of the Proclamation undertook to act in trust as the provisional government of the Irish Republic pending the election of a national government by the sovereign Irish people.

THE DEMOCRATIC PROGRAMME OF THE FIRST DÁIL ÉIREANN

(1919)

The First Dáil came into being when the seventy-three Sinn Féin members elected in the 1918 Westminster election declined to take their seats in the London Parliament and set up an independent Irish assembly in Dublin. The remaining twenty-six Unionist and six Irish Party MPs were invited to attend but declined. The first Dáil met for its inaugural session in the Mansion House on 21 January 1919. On this occasion the Democratic Programme was proposed by Richard Mulcahy (1886–1971) and agreed unanimously without a debate. The document marks a clear and unequivocal endorsement of the principles of government outlined in the Proclamation of 1916. However, it also reflected the priorities of the Labour Party, which opted not to ↗

W E DECLARE IN the words of the Irish Republican Proclamation the right of the people of Ireland to the ownership of Ireland, and to the unfettered control of Irish destinies to be indefeasible, and in the language of our first President, Pádraíg Mac Piarais, we declare that the Nation's sovereignty extends not only to all men and women of the Nation, but to all its material possessions, the Nation's soil and all its resources, all the wealth and all the wealth-producing processes within the Nation, and with him we reaffirm that all right to private property must be subordinated to the public right and welfare.

We declare that we desire our country to be ruled in accordance with the principles of Liberty, Equality, and Justice for all, which alone can secure permanence of Government in the willing adhesion of the people.

We affirm the duty of every man and woman to give allegiance and service to the Commonwealth, and declare it is the duty of the Nation to assure that every citizen shall have opportunity to spend his or her strength and faculties in the service of the people. In return for willing service, we, in the name of the Republic, declare the right of every citizen to an adequate share of the produce of the Nation's labour.

It shall be the first duty of the Government of the Republic to make provision for the physical, mental and spiritual well-being of the children, to secure that no child shall suffer hunger or cold from lack of food, clothing, or shelter, but that all shall be provided with the means and facilities requisite for their proper education and training as Citizens of a Free and Gaelic Ireland.

The Irish Republic fully realises the necessity of abolishing the present odious, degrading and foreign Poor

Law System, substituting therefore a sympathetic native scheme for the care of the Nation's aged and infirm, who shall not be regarded as a burden, but rather entitled to the Nation's gratitude and consideration. Likewise it shall be the duty of the Republic to take such measures as will safeguard the health of the people and ensure the physical as well as the moral well-being of the Nation.

It shall be our duty to promote the development of the Nation's resources, to increase the productivity of its soil, to exploit its mineral deposits, peat bogs, and fisheries, its waterways and harbours, in the interests and for the benefit of the Irish people.

It shall be the duty of the Republic to adopt all measures necessary for the recreation and invigoration of our Industries, and to ensure their being developed on the most beneficial and progressive co-operative and industrial lines. With the adoption of an extensive Irish Consular Service, trade with foreign Nations shall be revived on terms of mutual advantage and goodwill, and while undertaking the organisation of the Nation's trade, import and export, it shall be the duty of the Republic to prevent the shipment from Ireland of food and other necessaries until the wants of the Irish people are fully satisfied and the future provided for.

It shall also devolve upon the National Government to seek co-operation of the governments of other countries in determining a standard of social and industrial legislation with a view to a general and lasting improvement in the conditions under which the working classes live and labour. ■

→ contest the 1918 election to avoid splitting the Sinn Féin vote. Drafted by the Labour leader, Thomas Johnson, it augmented the socialist aspirations of the new republic. Notable aims include the provision for 'the physical, mental, and spiritual well-being' of the nation's children; the abolition of the British Poor Law System; and the improvement of the conditions of workers.

from:

THE ANGLO-IRISH TREATY

(1921)

The Anglo-Irish conflict lasted until a truce was called on 11 July 1921. On 11 October formal negotiations began between the Irish and the British at 10 Downing Street, concluding in the signing of the Anglo-Irish Treaty on 6 December 1921. The Treaty granted the right to an Irish Parliament and executive. However, it fell short of recognising Irish sovereign independence. Instead, it proposed for Ireland the same constitutional status as Canada: a Dominion of the Empire to be known as the Irish Free State. The Treaty also underwrote the right of the newly established Northern Ireland Parliament to opt out of the new constitutional arrangements, thus paving the way for the partition of the island. It further insisted on an oath of allegiance to the British monarch. The leading opponent of the agreement, Éamon de Valera (1882–1975), led a walk-out of anti-Treaty deputies from the Second Dáil in January 1922, beginning a sequence of events that would lead to civil war.

1. Ireland shall have the same constitutional status in the community of Nations known as the British Empire as the Dominion of Canada, the Commonwealth of Australia, the Dominion of New Zealand, and the Union of South Africa, with the Parliament having powers to make laws for the peace, order and good government of Ireland and an Executive responsible to that Parliament, and shall be styled and known as the Irish Free State.

2. Subject to the provisions hereinafter set out, the position of the Irish Free State in relation to the Imperial Parliament and government and otherwise shall be that of the Dominion of Canada, and the law, practice and constitutional usage governing the relationship of the Crown or the representative of the Crown and of the Imperial Parliament to the Dominion of Canada shall govern their relationship to the Irish Free State.

3. The representative of the Crown in Ireland shall be appointed in like manner as the Governor-General of Canada, and in accordance with the practice observed in the making of such appointments.

4. The oath to be taken by members of the Parliament of the Irish Free State shall be in the following form:

   I ... do solemnly swear true faith and allegiance to the Constitution of the Irish Free State as by law established and that I will be faithful to H.M. King George V, his heirs and successors by law, in virtue of the common citizenship of Ireland with Great Britain and her adherence to and membership of the group of nations forming the British Commonwealth of Nations. ∎

Language Revival

WHEN DOUGLAS HYDE and his companions founded the Gaelic League in 1893, there were only six books in print in Irish. The language had long ceased to be a medium of intellectual exchange, being spoken mainly by small farmers and fisher-folk in the poorer districts of the west of Ireland. It had become, in the words of Matthew Arnold, 'the badge of a beaten race', associated in the popular mind with backwardness and deprivation. Some were so ashamed of speaking it that they refused to have their cases in court tried in Irish, even when an occasional liberal judge was willing to do this.

For centuries the colonial authorities had discouraged and even penalised the use of Irish, yet it had been allowed to survive in most places until the early nineteenth century as a sort of 'colour bar', marking off native from planter. In that context, the decision by hundreds of thousands suddenly to master English must be understood as, at least in part, an attempt to frustrate the binary, Manichean nature of a divided colonial society.

All of these elements stacked the dice against the gamble by Hyde and his companions. Yet the story of the language revival would be like that of previous near-death experiences in Gaelic culture. Back in 1601, the defeat of Gaelic chieftains at Kinsale might have signalised the death of a Gaelic culture but instead gave rise to a literary revival in the language, as ruined bards turned to the common people as to a new audience. Likewise, after the tragedy of Parnell's fall in 1891 and the frustration of the Home Rule Bill in 1893, young people in particular turned from politics to culture in the attempt to explore and update a threatened identity.

As the social power of the Anglo-Irish waned after various land reforms, their leaders were faced with a choice—either to identify with the culture of their previous underlings or to make one final attempt to disable it. Some, like Yeats and Synge, took the former view, perhaps even seeing in the doomed princes of the Gaelic past an image of their own class, and in the response of the bards an example of how to cope with the present crisis. Others, notably a group of professors at Trinity College Dublin, tried to block all attempts to ratify Irish as a valid subject of study in state schools. They denounced the leaders of the League as nostalgists, bent on returning Ireland to a medieval mindset just when it seemed about to become modern.

The Gaelic League was, like many national movements, Janus-faced. Some of its members probably did dream of a return to the past, but many more were 'critical traditionalists', keen to modernise in a non-imperial way. They stressed the links between language revival and the cultural self-belief that produced a more vibrant industry, agriculture, and sense of community, as well as a radically innovative kind of modern literature.

EUGENE O'GROWNEY—*from:*

PREFACE TO *SIMPLE LESSONS IN IRISH*

(1894)

Born in Athboy, County
Meath, Eugene O'Growney
(1863–1899) developed
his interest in the study of
Irish while training for the
priesthood at the national
seminary, Maynooth
College. He was appointed
to the Chair of Irish there in
1891 and was made editor
of the *Gaelic Journal* in
1894. Like many priests,
he saw the language as a
bulwark against unbelief.
The *Simple Lessons*
first appeared in the
Weekly Freeman, before
being published in five
pamphlets. They sold in
hundreds of thousands. ↗

THE FOLLOWING COURSE of *Simple Lessons* in Irish has been drawn up chiefly for the use of those who wish to learn the old language of Ireland, but who are discouraged by what they have heard of its difficulties. A language whose written literature extends back for over a thousand years, and which has been spoken in Ireland for we know not how many centuries, must naturally differ in many ways from the modern language now generally studied. But the difficulties of Irish pronunciation and construction have always been exaggerated.

As I myself was obliged to study Irish as a foreign language, and as I have been placed in circumstances which have made me rather familiar with the language as now spoken, I have at least a knowledge of the difficulties of those who, like myself, have no teacher. I have tried to explain everything as simply as possible and I have the satisfaction of knowing that these lessons during their appearance in the *Weekly Freeman*, and afterwards in the *Gaelic Journal*, have made some thousands of Irish people acquainted with what is really our national language.

I am convinced that a person who speaks Irish, can learn to read and write the exercises of their lessons in a month, and I believe that one totally unacquainted with the language can master the pronunciation of every word in the lessons (Parts I and II) in six months.

The following plan of working out the exercises of the lessons appears to be the best.

1. First, let the student go over the lesson, translating the Irish lessons into English, and writing out the translation.
2. Let him then re-translate into Irish, comparing with the original.
3. Lastly he may translate the English exercises into Irish.

To those who, in many ways, have assisted in the construction of these lessons, I offer my hearty thanks. The Archbishop of Dublin first suggested the bringing out of a series of lessons, in which the pronunciation of each word should be indicated in accordance with some simple phonetic system, and His Grace afterwards took a large share in developing and applying that system. I am also indebted to Mr. C. P. Bushe, Mr. John MacNeill, Mr. J. H. Lloyd, Father Hickey, Mr. MacC-Dix, and many others, for valuable suggestions. ■

→ The Fenian John O'Leary had once suggested that learning Irish was beyond the power of the human brain, but the *Lessons* offered a reassuringly simple method by which the language could be self-taught. Their popularity was well in excess of their effectiveness. O'Growney, fighting poor health, migrated to the United States and died in California.

LOUIS PAUL-DUBOIS—*from*:

CONTEMPORARY IRELAND

(1908)

Louis Paul-Dubois was a
French sociologist whose
sympathetic study *l'Irlande
Contemporaine* was
published in English in 1908,
becoming a sort of bible
among some intellectual
leaders of the Revival. It was
critical of British policy and
it offered a sophisticated
panoptic analysis of the
various strata of society,
notable especially for its
study of poor people. It
was sceptical of attempts
by British educational
policymakers to keep
religion out of school
classrooms, rather
gleefully documenting the
subterfuges adopted by
teachers and students to
get around this. He attacked
the national schools for their
policy of anglicisation and
wrote with sympathy of the
language revival movement.
The following passage
captures the enthusiasm
of early learners at Irish
classes, which functioned a
little like the adult education
movement favoured by
socialist activists in other
countries.

B UT THE STRANGER is most forcibly struck when he attends some Irish class in a poor quarter in Dublin, or even London, and perceives how serious, deep, and infectious is the enthusiasm of the crowd—young and old, clerks and artisans for the most part, with an 'intellectual' here and there—who are gathered together in the ill-lit hall. To these there is no doubt the thought of learning anything, and above all of learning a language other than English, would never have occurred at any other time, but now after their day's work, they sit here with an O'Growney in their hands, with shining eyes, and strained looks, greedily listening to the lesson, following with their lips, *con amore*, the soft speech of their teacher.

Evidently here are people who have been transformed to the core of their being by this somewhat severe study, and by the importance of the social role which they wish to play, and which in fact they do play. Here, as elsewhere, the Gaelic movement has given an object, a goal, an ideal, to lives which, from their conditions, are often empty in these respects. Those who are in a position to know say indeed that few people of national feeling have taken up the study of Irish without being quickly aware of its strengthening and stimulating influence, without being fascinated by it as by a revelation. This shows that the language is for the children of Erin neither a dead language nor a strange one, but an integral part of their nature, a second self, an element of themselves that they had forgotten.

The English which they speak with a remarkable native accent is, as has often been remarked, an English learnt from books, and full of absurd Irishisms which have remained locked up within their brains, a heritage of which they were not aware; it is an English built artificially upon a Gaelic substructure. ■

ROBERT ATKINSON—*from*:

DR. ATKINSON'S EVIDENCE TO THE ROYAL COMMISSION

The Irish Language and Irish Intermediate Education

GAELIC LEAGUE PAMPHLETS—NO. 14

(1899)

I DO NOT REGARD this language as in a settled state. There are numerous *patois*, but there is no standard of speech absolutely accepted by everybody.... Not only is the language, as I say, so unsettled that it is impossible for the child to get real educational training out of it, such as he can get from almost any other language I know, but there is extremely little literature that he can get to read. If a boy learns his French, or learns his Latin, he has the whole world before him in choice of what to read. But I have been surprised in seeing even now, after so many years during which the beauties of Irish literature have been talked of, how little has been done that really could be usefully or properly brought before children. Those stories, my lord, are not all fit for children. There is a story mentioned here—*Toruigheacht Dhiarmuda agus Ghráinne*—it is put in there, and they are examined in portions of it. Well, passages are selected, but I assure you the book itself is not fit for children, and I can only say I would allow no daughter of mine of any age to see it.

You mentioned Dr. Hyde. Well, he published some stories—of course there was nothing ethically wrong about them, but so low! I do not want to know about the vulgar exploits of a dirty wretch who never washed his feet, and who put that forward ostentatiously . . .

There was a book published not very long ago—a large book in two volumes—in which there is an immense quantity of stories given, and there is a translation of them, too. Now, all I can say is that no human being could read through that book, containing an immense quantity of Irish matter, without feeling that he had been absolutely degraded by contact with it—filth that I will not demean myself even to mention. ∎

Robert Atkinson was born in 1839 and became professor of Celtic, Sanskrit and Romance Languages at Trinity College Dublin. With his Trinity colleague, the classicist J.P. Mahaffy (1839–1919), he took fright at the success of the Gaelic League, which he saw as a front for 'separatism'. In 1899, at a government commission set up to explore the ratification of the study of Irish on the secondary school curriculum, he denigrated the modern dialects as a degeneration from the classical language and said that the older literature was often 'low in tone'. Some of its texts he would ban from his home. Stung by these strictures, Hyde presented statements from British and continental scholars on the value of Irish literature. Irish was ratified and Atkinson died in 1908.

W.B. YEATS—*from*:

'THE ACADEMIC CLASS AND THE AGRARIAN REVOLUTION'
(1900)

W.B. Yeats played a part in bringing public opinion behind the Gaelic League's crusade for the ratification of Irish in the school syllabus. In February 1900 he called upon Members of Parliament to use the old Parnellite methods of obstruction to insert the teaching of Irish into an Education Bill. His father, John Butler Yeats (a graduate), had joked that Trinity College Dublin did not as a rule produce distinguished minds, but the son went farther, accusing it of being provincial, 'which the Literary Society is not, and the Gaelic League ↗

'A LL FOLKLORE IS essentially abominable.' If a professor at an English university were to say these things in any conspicuous place, above all before a Commission which he hoped would give his opinion an expression in action, he would not be reasoned with, but his opinion would be repeated with a not ill-humoured raillery and his name remembered at times with a little laughter. Dr. Hyde has understood, however, and perhaps rightly understood, that the conditions of Ireland are so peculiar that it is necessary to answer Dr. Atkinson, lest, as I should imagine, some imperfectly educated priest in some country parish might believe that Irish literature was 'abominable', or 'indecent'—to use another favourite word of Dr. Atkinson— and raise a cry against the movement for the preservation of the Irish language....

The true explanation is that Dr. Atkinson, like most people on both sides in politics of the generation which had to endure the bitterness of the agrarian revolution, is still in a fume of political excitement, and cannot consider any Irish matter without this excitement. If I remember my Bible correctly, the children of Israel had to wander forty years in the wilderness that all who had sinned a particular sin might die there, and Ireland will have no dispassionate opinion on any literary or political matter till that generation has died or fallen into discredit. One watches with an irritation, that sometimes changes to pity, members of Parliament, professors, eminent legal persons, officials of all kinds, men often of great natural power, who cannot talk, whether in public or private, of any Irish matter in which any living affection or enthusiasm has a part without becoming bitter with the passion of old controversies in which nobody is any longer interested.

Trinity College Dublin makes excellent scholars, but it does not make men with any real love for ideal things or with any fine taste in the arts. One does not meet really cultivated Trinity College men as one meets really cultivated Oxford and Cambridge men. The atmosphere of what is called educated Dublin is an atmosphere of cynicism—a cynicism without ideas which expresses itself at the best in a wit without charm.... [O]ur academic class understands in some dim way that its influence is passing into the hands of men who are seeking to create a criticism of life which will weigh all Irish interests, and bind rich and poor into one brotherhood. ■

→ is not.' Hyde's warning against producing a shabby, imitation-England was having its effect. By 1906 the League secured the use of Irish as the language of instruction in Gaeltacht schools. By 1909 Irish was ratified as a compulsory subject for matriculation at the National University, at which Hyde (another TCD graduate) was made a professor.

GEORGE MOORE—*from*:

'LITERATURE AND THE IRISH LANGUAGE'

(1900)

George Moore was born in County Mayo to a landed Catholic family in 1852. His novel *A Drama in Muslin* (1886) mocked the imitation of English ways at the coming-out of the daughters of Anglo-Ireland at the Dublin Castle Ball. Fifteen years later, Moore returned to Ireland and became a keen supporter of the Irish Literary Theatre (for which with W.B. Yeats he co-wrote *Diarmuid and Grania* in 1901). He was an enthusiast also for the language movement, but whenever his Irish tutor called for a class at his home in Ely Place, Moore invariably had his butler say that he was 'out'. He published *The Untilled Field* (1903), a book of stories which in its Irish-language version *An tÚrGhort* was published as a parallel text for learners in the Gaelic League. In 1911 he abandoned Dublin and he went on to satirise the Revival in his three-volume account *Hail and Farewell* (1914 and after). He died in London in 1933.

FELLOW COUNTRYMEN, THE language is slipping into the grave, and if a great national effort be not made at once to save the language it will be dead in another generation. We must return to the language. It came we know not whence or how; it is a mysterious inheritance, in which resides the soul of the Irish people. It is through language that a tradition of thought is preserved, and so it may be said that the language is the soul of race. It is through language that the spirit is communicated, and it is through language that a nation becomes aware of itself.

We want our language; we desire it with our whole heart and soul. Our desire may be foolish, unpractical, unwise, according to the lights of the English nation at the present moment, but our desire is our desire, our folly is our own, and if we wish to start ill-equipped in the business race of the world, knowing no language which is understood outside of Ireland, shall we be gainsaid like children? But this is not our desire; our desire is to make Ireland a bilingual country—to use English as a universal language, and to save our own as a medium for some future literature. ■

AN tATHAIR PEADAR Ó LAOGHAIRE—*from*:

MY OWN STORY

(TRANSLATED FROM IRISH BY SHEILA O'SULLIVAN)

(1915)

Peadar Ó Laoghaire (Peter O'Leary) was born in 1839 in County Cork and grew up in the Gaeltacht of Muskerry. One of many Catholic priests who supported the revival of Irish, he published *Séadna* in serial form in 1894 and as a book in 1904. It concerns the life of a cobbler who made a bargain with the devil. He published an autobiography *Mo Sgéal Féin\My Own Story*, in which he recalled his crusade for 'caint na ndaoine', the speech of ordinary people rather than classical Irish, as the basis for a modern literature. This was in accord with the naturalist aesthetic which argued that literature was merely a form of recorded speech. The popularity of *Séadna* helped to advance Ó Laoghaire's belief that the Munster dialect should provide the standard form of modern Irish, despite the rival claims of Connacht and Ulster. He died in Cork at the age of eighty.

IMAGINE THAT Daniel O'Connell thought that if Irish were seven miles under the sea and English the language of Irishmen, their English would be as good as his own. But if not, why not? Because under that veneer of broken English their minds were still stocked with the beautiful, noble, expansive riches of the Irish language. Now that wealth has been lost by those of the Irish language who have lost the Irish tongue. Some of them, conscious of the devastation, are trying to salvage that wealth, but it is easier to squander riches than to retrieve them.

If the two languages had been fostered together from the time that the Irish people began to converse among themselves in English to any extent, the two tongues would have helped each other, and given each other a strength and exactitude impossible to one language only. That was not done and the result was evident. When the two languages were mixed without any effort to cultivate either of them, many people were adrift in both of them. That was what caused Diarmuid Moynihan to say:

> The biggest fools in the land of Erin
> Are the fools without Béarla and without Gaeluinn.

But I heard reports of a society that was to be founded for
the purpose of fostering the Irish language, and keeping
it alive orally among the people. I was very pleased when
I heard the news, and heard also that a young priest in
Maynooth was the originator of the effort.

The years went by. It is not necessary for me to give
here any account of the labours and the events of those
years. Perhaps, however, it is not out of place for me to say a
very little about the movement. Pondering on this, I realised
that we had nothing whatever, in the shape of a book, to
put in the hands of any child for the purpose of teaching it
Irish. As a result of my reflections, I decided to write a book
especially for our young people, a book that would be free
from the faults present in most of the language of the poets:
a book that would have language suitable to the young, and
pleasing to the young. That was the consideration which
impelled me to write *Séadna*. The book pleased all, both
old and young. It was read to the aged and it pleased them.
They heard something coming to them from the pages
of a book. It pleased the young because there was a great
resemblance between the Irish of that book and the English
which they themselves spoke. ▪

FREDERICK RYAN—*from*:

'IS THE GAELIC LEAGUE A PROGRESSIVE FORCE?'

(1904)

THAT THE GAELIC League is popular goes without saying. It may or may not be popular with the governing classes—though from them it has met with a benevolent neutrality, if not an encouragement, which no previous national movement ever received—but it is certainly popular with the people, the Church, and the press. In fact, the Gaelic League has got to the stage when its 'popularity' might well be embarrassing to its best friends.

On what scientific grounds, then, is the revival of Irish urged? It is pressed on the ground that it was once the national language of Ireland and that in adopting it again, Ireland will be differentiating herself from all other nations and proving her own individuality. Moreover it is contended that English literature and habits of thought are debased and debasing, whilst the Irish language and literature is superior and elevating.

These arguments have always appeared to me rather faulty. In the first place, individuality in man or nation is not a thing to be directly sought; it is a by-product of the whole nature. When a man has to deliberately emphasise his individuality by artificially doing something out of the common, real individuality is at a minimum. What really gives a noble distinction to a man or nation is not the language they speak or the kind of dress they wear: it is their culture, their science, their art. When we meet a man whose conversation and bearing exhibit independence of character and freshness of outlook we say we have met a man of 'individuality'. But 'individuality' is probably the last thing of which such a one is consciously thinking. And I confess when I see the young men and women rushing to acquire the rudiments of Irish (and it seldom gets beyond that) in

Frederick Ryan was born in 1873 in Dublin. He combined a lifelong crusade for socialist values with a commitment to the Irish Literary Revival. He became secretary to the Irish National Theatre Society in 1902, to which he contributed a seminal 'social problem' play, *The Laying of the Foundations*. With John Eglinton he co-edited *Dana*, a major if short-lived journal of secular ideas, to which he contributed this essay, which was critical of conservative elements within Gaelic revivalism. He worked for the Irish Socialist Party, collaborating with James Connolly. In the later part of his career he edited *Egypt* (1911–1912), a journal in which the English aristocrat Wilfrid Scawen Blunt promoted national independence. He died at Blunt's home in England in 1913.

order to show they are not as other nations, the phenomenon seems to me to have something of pathos in it. Let me, however, not be misunderstood. The desire for political independence is admirable; that counts for real manhood. Only a nation of slaves would contentedly resign themselves to be governed by another nation.

But the mere desire to speak another language does not of necessity at all correlate with the active desire for political freedom. On the contrary, the Gaelic League leaders do not seem to be at all keen lovers of liberty as plenty of the mere English-speaking Irishmen before them. To make Irish, or even the desire to acquire it, the test of nationalism would shut out some of the best men who have served the cause of Irish liberty in the past. Parnell, for instance, assuredly wrought for Ireland at least as well, according to his lights, as any man who ever lived, but Parnell did not know Irish or endeavour to learn it. In fact it has often seemed to me that the language movement has acted as a soothing rather than a stimulating influence on the political movement. If the Irish people could be lulled to rest with a new toy in the shape of a new tongue, their English governors need not grieve. And it is to a realisation of this fact that I attribute, in some degree, the participation in Gaelic League work of men who would not connect themselves with any other national work whatever. One of the historic methods of political reactionaries is to turn any really progressive movement into harmless channels; a foreign war is a favourite device for accomplishing such an end; it provides a distraction and produces a crop of military problems in place of the political ones which previously occupied the stage. May not a language movement, then, unconsciously serve a similar end? And if the people are content to let the substance of liberty go for the gewgaw of a new grammar, so much the better—for the reactionaries.

Because there is undoubtedly a good deal of extravagance, to use a mild word, in the claim that medieval Irish literature can supply the place for a modern mind of modern literature. And in saying this I do not in the least disparage the beauty of the old literature in its place and as a light on the age that produced it. But as each age has to live in itself and face its own problems, so we have to live by present lights and not by those of, say, Brian, who himself had to do the same.

The truth is, however, that most of the leaders of the Gaelic League appear to desire a return to medievalism in thought, in literature, in pastimes, in music and even in dress. And the fact that this desire is impossible of realisation does not affect those who proclaim it, and does not lessen its practical injuriousness.

The truth is that modern knowledge and the positivist spirit are correlative and to keep out the one it would be necessary to keep out the other also. And to keep out both is, I think, the aim, explicit or implicit, of many Gaelic Leaguers, whose ideal is a purely folk-ideal—a folk literature, a folk drama, and a folk art. All the while to correct the shortcomings of English sciences (whatever they may be) by advocating the study of Gaelic which has no modern scientific literature whatever, good or bad, positivist or otherwise, is like trying to save yourself from the heat of the frying pan by jumping into the fire.

Let me, however, not be thought to be making a partisan case. All public movements and especially such subtle movements as that under discussion have mixed and diverse results, and their total effect cannot be expressed in any single formula. Thus there is to be set on the other side of the account the fact that the League has brought a spirit of study into the country, has evoked a great amount of self-sacrificing work that in itself compels admiration, whatever its ultimate result, and in addition has stimulated a feeling of indifference for England that is a needed variation on the traditional Irish attitude towards England of appeal, apology and abuse.

A nation is not morally raised by dwelling on its own past glories or its neighbour's present sins; it is raised by increasing its ability to deal with its present problems— political, economic, and social—in a spirit of equity and a spirit of knowledge. But these beneficent spirits can be evoked and nourished quite efficiently, it seems to me, without putting on Ireland the enormous burden of adopting what is now virtually a new language. For no better reason than the sentimental one that she once spoke it. The truth is that, given the solution of our political problems, the solution of the others will merely depend on all the modern light we can get, whilst the stress laid on the teaching of Gaelic tends to obscure even some of these. Thus, for instance, the degradation of taste deplored by Father Dinneen and others is not the result of speaking English—it is a result of the industrial system, of long hours and fatiguing work in towns, with scanty leisure, and is more or less characteristic of all modern industrial communities. So far, however, from evading that industrialism most Gaelic Leaguers stand for its extension, without, at the same time bothering themselves much or sympathising much with the attempts to control and mitigate its evils by socialist reformers in other countries. No medieval literature can possibly supply any guidance on these complicated but inevitable issues[.] ∎

STEPHEN GWYNN—*from*:

'IN PRAISE OF THE GAELIC LEAGUE'

(1904)

T O HIS QUESTION, therefore, 'Is the Gaelic League a progressive force?' I answer with another, 'What would you put in place of it?' That the League has done much—that it has brought a spirit of study into the country, has evoked a great amount of self-sacrificing work, and has stimulated a much-needed feeling of indifference for England—he admits. We may fairly ask, what other lever would have heaved Ireland so far out of its stagnant apathy? It is hard to understand how an organisation which has admittedly accomplished these things could be other than a progressive force.

Mr. Ryan assails the Gaelic League with an *a priori* argument. *A priori*, it is wasteful when you have a language convenient for all uses, which is also the key to a great literature, to acquire with labour a new language which has a literature insignificant by comparison. I answer, *a priori*, that a national education ought be founded on a national literature, that the literature of England cannot be accepted as the national literature of Ireland, and that the great bulk of the national literature of Ireland, of the record of Irish thought and imagination, is written in Irish.

A posteriori, on practical grounds, I argue that it is not regarded as waste of time for English or Irish boys to learn Latin and other languages, merely as educational gymnastics, and that Gaelic for Irish people affords a means of such gymnastics, along with the advantage of maintaining the spirit of nationality. Further, that the revival of Gaelic has quickened intellectual life in outlying country places, and has given a recognised value to knowledge and scholarship, too often only valued before by their owners, and not always even

Born in Rathfarnham, Dublin, in 1864, Stephen Gwynn grew up in Donegal, before attending Oxford University. He served as secretary to the Irish Literary Society, while working as a journalist in London; and was elected Member of Parliament for the Irish Parliamentary Party in 1906. The following article was written for *Dana* shortly after his return to Ireland in 1904. He was a supporter of the Gaelic League and a founder with George Roberts of the Revivalist publishing house, Maunsel and Company. He enlisted in the British forces in World War One. A moderate nationalist, he formed a Centre Party in 1919 in a futile attempt to counteract the polarisation of politics. Thereafter, he was better known for his literary works and he died in 1950.

by them. As for the view that there is any natural opposition
between the study of Gaelic and the study of English
literature, my own experience is wherever one finds a young
man in a Gaelic-speaking district interested in good English
books, he is always heart and soul with the Gaelic League. I
have also found many applying themselves zealously to study
in Gaelic who never read anything in their lives before but a
local newspaper or a cheap novelette. These people were no
'slaves of the industrial system': they were peasants living as
peasants have always lived, but they showed *in English* very
little sign of taste or discrimination. You may get the truly
Irish mind thinking in English and nourished in English,
but in a thousand cases you will lose it. I have known a man
who in Irish was a lover and a critic of fine literature, but
in English was an uneducated peasant, yet his English was
better than that of most English labourers. Taken young,
on top of his Irish training, he could have assimilated what
he wanted in English literature; he could have been given
through Irish that love of reading which through English had
never tempted him. ∎

J.M. SYNGE

'CAN WE GO BACK INTO OUR MOTHER'S WOMB?'

(A LETTER TO THE GAELIC LEAGUE BY A HEDGE SCHOOLMASTER)

(1907)

MUCH OF THE writing that has appeared recently in the papers takes it for granted that Irish is gaining the day in Ireland and that this country will soon speak Gaelic. No supposition is more false. The Gaelic League was founded on a doctrine that is made up of ignorance, fraud, and hypocrisy. Irish as a living language is dying out year by year: the day the last old man or woman who can speak Irish only dies in Connacht or Munster—a day that is coming near—will mark a station in the Irish decline which will be final a few years later. As long as these old people who speak Irish only are in the cabins the children speak Irish to them—a child will learn as many languages as it has need of in its daily life—but when they die the supreme good sense of childhood will not cumber itself with two languages when one is enough. It will play, quarrel, say its prayers and make jokes of good and evil, make love when it's old enough, write if it has wit enough, in this language which is its mother tongue. The result is what could be expected beforehand and it is what is taking place in Ireland in every Irish-speaking district.

I believe in Ireland. I believe the nation that has made a place in history by seventeen centuries of manhood, a nation that has begotten Grattan and Emmet and Parnell will not be brought to complete insanity in these last days by what is senile and slobbering in the doctrine of the Gaelic League. There was never till this time a movement in Ireland that was gushing, cowardly, and maudlin, and yet now we are passing England in the hysteria of old women's talk. A hundred years ago Irishmen could face a dark existence in Kilmainham Jail, or lurch on the halter before a grinning mob, but now they fear any gleam of truth. How are the mighty fallen! Was there ever a sight so piteous as an old and respectable people setting

Written in fury after members of the League had participated in the agitation against *The Playboy of the Western World*, Synge's open letter was not published until long after he was dead. He did not share in the League's optimism that Irish could ever again become the spoken language throughout Ireland—and he feared that a difficult transition back to Irish might leave many people inarticulate in either language. He was also critical of the forms of Irish spoken by many learners outside the Gaeltacht, who tended to pronounce words with an English intonation. Consistent as ever, he felt that just as Irish should not be imposed in English-speaking areas; neither →

→ should English be imposed on Gaeltacht schoolchildren. He derided the implication by some Leaguers that a knowledge of Irish would permit them to read the ancient sagas and legends in the original language. Yet he also recognised that the League was doing more than any other organisation to combat demoralisation in Irish-speaking districts.

up the ideals of Fiji because, with their eyes glued on John Bull's navel, they dare not be Europeans for fear the huckster across the street might call them English.

This delirium will not last always. It will not be long—we will make it our first hope—till some young man with blood in his veins, logic in his wits and courage in his heart, will sweep over the backside of the world to the uttermost limbo, this credo of mouthing gibberish. (I speak here not of the old and magnificent language of our manuscripts, or of the two or three dialects still spoken, though with many barbarisms, in the west and south, but of the incoherent twaddle that is passed off as Irish by the Gaelic League.) This young man will teach Ireland again that she is part of Europe, and teach Irishmen that they have wits to think, imaginations to work miracles, and souls to possess with sanity. He will teach them that there is more in heaven and earth than the weekly bellow of the brazen bull-calf and all his sweaty gobs, or the snivelling booklets that are going through Ireland like the scab on sheep, and yet he'll give the pity that is due to the poor stammerers who mean so well though they are stripping the nakedness of Ireland in the face of her own sons. ■

PATRICK PEARSE

A GAELIC MODERNISM?

(1904 and after)

H OSTS OF OUR writers can give us admirable
photographic reproductions of Irish dialogue. That
is good, but it is not the best thing. It is literature
only in the limited sense in which a verbatim report of
a Parliamentary debate is literature.... Style and form
are essential. The true literary artist is like a painter as
compared with a photographer. The one gives back what he
sees transformed into something radiant and gracious by
the impression of his own personality, the other produces
a mere mechanical copy. Style after all is another name for
personality. One cannot always stick the folk formula and
genealogies are out of fashion.

['Reviews', *An Claidheamh Soluis*, 14 March 1903: 3.]

The lesson that *Séadna* has taught us was that in writing
your prime care must be, not to imitate this or that dead
or living writer, but first and foremost to utter *yourself.*
While style in the ordinary acception is essentially personal
and peculiar to an author, there is such a thing as the
'style' of a period, or the style of a national literature.... If
Séadna may be taken as a foretaste then we may say that
the Irish prose of tomorrow, whilst retaining much of the
lyric swing and love of melody of later Irish prose, will
be characterised by the terseness, the crispness, the plain
straightforwardness of what is best in medieval Irish
literature. It will be found in the speech of the people, but it
will not be the speech of the people, for the ordinary speech
of the people is never literature, though it is the stuff of
which literature is made.

['*Séadna* and the Future of Irish Prose', *An Claidheamh Soluis*,
24 September 1904: 8.]

Patrick Pearse was born in Dublin in 1879 and was called to the bar in 1901. He had joined the Gaelic League while still in his teens, becoming editor of its journal *An Claidheamh Soluis* in 1902. His father was a monumental sculptor with allegiance to the English arts-and-crafts movement, while his mother came from Irish speakers in County Meath. These influences shaped his love of Gaelic tradition, as did repeated visits to Connemara, where he had a cottage in Ros Muc. He supported those in the League who believed that a modern literature must found itself on current idiom; but he also believed that writers should incorporate the lessons and even forms of classic authors into their work. His aim was the creation of a modernist literature in Irish, connected equally to its own past and to 'the mind of contemporary Europe'. Here are extracts from four separate essays outlining his thoughts.

We hold the folk tale to be a beautiful and gracious thing
only in its own time and place . . . and its time and place are
the winter fireside, or the spring sowing time, or the country
road at any season. Thus, we lay down the proposition that a
living literature *cannot* (and if it could), should not be built
upon the folk tale. The folk tale is an echo of old mythologies:
literature is a deliberate criticism of actual life. . . . Why
impose the folk attitude of mind, the folk conventions of
form on the makers of literature? Why set up as a standard of
today a standard at which Aonghus Ó Dálaigh and Seathrún
Céitinn would have laughed? . . . Two influences go into the
making of every artist, apart from his own personality, if
indeed personality is not in the main only the sum of these
influences: the influences of his ancestors and that of his
contemporaries. Irish literature if it [is] to live and grow,
must get into contact on the one hand with its own past and
on the other with the mind of contemporary Europe. . . .
This is the twentieth century and no literature can take rook
in the twentieth century which is not of the twentieth century.
We want no Gothic revival.

> ['About Literature', *An Claidheamh Soluis*, 26 May 1906: 6.]

[Some] have seen in the traditional style the *debris* of
an antique native culture. We see in it simply a peasant
convention, which in its essentials, is accepted by the folk
everywhere. . . .

'Traditionalism' is not essentially Irish. . . . The traditional
style is not the *Irish* way of singing or declaiming, but the
peasant way; it is not, and never has been, the possession of
the nation at large, but only of a class in the nation. . . .
Our artists (we refer in particular to singers and reciters)
must imbibe their Irishism from the peasant since the
peasants alone possess Irishism, but they need not and must
not adopt any of the peasant conventions. . . . They need not be
afraid of modern culture.

> ['Traditionalism', *An Claidheamh Soluis*, 9 June 1906: 6-7.] ∎

An Irish Literature in English?

EVEN BEFORE THE Great Famine of the 1840s, Irish people had begun to abandon Irish and speak English. They recognised that it would be the language of international modernity, essential for those who wished to engage in commerce or to emigrate to Britain, North America or Australia. It was necessary even for those insurgents who fought British rule: whether to defend themselves in court, or to issue statements which might prick the conscience of liberal well-wishers in the English-speaking world. While the Irish language offered one secure basis for the separatist claim to recognition as a distinct nation, English became the language in which the nationalist case could most effectively be made.

Such a usage—in speeches from the dock, in letters threatening landlords, or in appeals to English radicals—helped also to liberate the English language in Ireland from some of its more negative historic meanings. Previously, most sentences uttered in English would have been an order, a condescension or an insult, but suddenly the language seemed capable of many other inflections.

The skill with which the people mastered English has never been fully recognised for the intellectual achievement it was—least of all by those authorities in independent Ireland of the twentieth century who tried without much success to reverse the process. The speed of the changeover was so great that many people continued to think in Irish while using English words, developing in the process a kind of bilingual weave in an English as Irish as it was possible for that language to be.

J.M. Synge, hearing the islanders of Aran speak English in this new way, found in that idiom a challenge to him as an artist. 'Has any bilingual writer ever been great in style, *crois pas?*' he asked himself in a notebook. By such means was created the 'Celtic note' in literature, sounded in the language that would eventually be called Hiberno-English. Some Gaelic purists denounced it as a faked-up, hybrid lingo, neither good Irish nor good English but an artificial artistic invention: but it was rooted in the ordinary people's sudden discovery of the expressive potentials of English, which had all the excitement and surprise made possible when any group learns how to project its thoughts and feelings through a new medium. The process was little different from that by which African-Americans took up such instruments as the violin and clarinet, teasing from these an altogether new sound called jazz.

By the end of the nineteenth century, a generation of artists
and scholars was making the discovery that to translate Ireland
into English was in fact to invent the country (or invent it all
over again). Just as every translation presupposes an 'original',
so was the case here—many wished to know the sources for
the beautiful works rendered. But some of the translators
themselves noticed that phrases which had begun to sound
clichéd in Irish, acquired in English a new beauty in their very
deviation from the norms of an English itself becoming rapidly
jaded by journalese. Synge was just the most famous of an entire
school of authors who found that if you translated Irish word-
for-word into English, the results often sounded rather like
poetry. Whether such translations were enough in themselves,
or products of a transitional moment on the journey back to an
Irish-speaking nation, remained an open question. However, the
expressive achievement in English provided inspiration right
across the world, from artists of a decolonising India or Africa to
the writers of the Harlem Renaissance.

STOPFORD A. BROOKE—*from*:

'THE NEED AND USE OF GETTING IRISH LITERATURE INTO THE ENGLISH TONGUE'

(1893)

IRISH LITERATURE IS not to Ireland what English literature is to England. The mass of the Irish people know nothing of it, and care little about it. That they should know, and should care will do more for the cause of a true nationalism than all our political angers. Moreover, with the perishing of the Irish language as the tongue of the people—and it is perishing with accelerating speed—the popular interest that once gathered round her past literature is vanishing away. A few scholars still love and honour it, and know the tongue in which it is written, but the politicians on both sides and most of the peasantry have lost their lingual tie to the past: they have no literary nationality. It is a great pity, and the Welsh were wiser than the Irish. A people who are only politically national are weaker in national sentiment than a people who love their ancient literature and language, and Ireland is day by day suffering a greater national loss than she imagines. She will bitterly regret it unless she repent and work meet for repentance. She knows less of her literature than the French and Germans know of it.

Translation, then, is our business. We wish to get the ancient Irish literature well and statelily afloat on the worldwide ocean of the English language, so that it may be known and loved wherever the English language goes.

. . . Irishmen of formative genius should take, one by one, the various cycles of Irish tales, and grouping each of them round one central figure, such as Manannán or Cuchulain or Finn, supply to each a dominant human interest to which every event in the whole should converge. It would then be possible to add to each of these cycles either a religious centre such

Born in Donegal in 1832, Stopford Brooke was educated at Trinity College Dublin, before becoming a chaplain in Berlin and London. He broke with the Church of England, opting instead for the Unitarian creed. He was a spiritual adviser to monarchs as well as a fashionable and popular public lecturer. In 1893 he was chosen by a committee of disparate personalities to give the inaugural address of the Irish Literary Society in London, from which the following extracts are taken. He wrote many influential books on English poets from Shakespeare to Tennyson. His lectures, along with the early poetry of Yeats, helped to raise the profile of Irish literature in England. He died in 1916.

as the Holy Grail was to the Arthurian tales, or a passionate centre such as the love of Lancelot and Guinevere, and this would knit together the reworking of each cycle into an imaginative unity....

Hidden away in these tales there is lying unused a mass of poetic material, and of such historic interest as belongs to the science of folklore which is rapidly perishing. The young men and women who speak Irish have fled from Ireland; the old who speak their own language, or who have kept their tales in memory are dying out. In twenty years it will be too late to do this work. And it will be a great pity if it is not done. ■

'Translation, then, is our business. We wish to get the ancient Irish literature well and statelily afloat on the worldwide ocean of the English language, so that it may be known and loved wherever the English language goes.'

DOUGLAS HYDE—*from*:

'THE NECESSITY FOR DE-ANGLICISING IRELAND'

(1892)

Douglas Hyde was caught in a strange dilemma. He was at once the foremost propagandist for the revival of the Irish language and at the same time scholar-in-waiting to the Irish literary renaissance in English. Although convinced that the national mind expressed itself most easily in Irish, he was too cultured to deny the immense achievements of those earlier Irish authors who had written in English, especially figures of the nineteenth century such as Thomas Moore and Thomas Davis in whose lyrics a national spark burned. So the famous lecture on 'de-Anglicisation', which began by regretting the way in which Irish separatists love to denounce that England which at every moment they rush to imitate, moved towards its conclusion by recommending, entirely without irony, some classic works by Irish writers of English.

I HAVE NOW MENTIONED a few of the principal points on which it would be desirable for us to move, with a view to de-Anglicising ourselves, but perhaps the principal point of all I have taken for granted. That is the necessity for encouraging the use of Anglo-Irish literature instead of English books, especially instead of English periodicals. We must set our face sternly against penny-dreadfuls, shilling-shockers, and still more, the garbage of vulgar English weeklies like *Bow Bells* and the *Police Intelligence*. Every house should have a copy of Moore and Davis. In a word, we must strive to cultivate everything that is most racial, most smacking of the soil, most Gaelic, most Irish, because in spite of the little admixture of Saxon blood in the north-east corner, this island *is* and *will* ever remain Celtic at the core [.] ■

DOUGLAS HYDE—*from*:

LOVE SONGS OF CONNACHT

'A Ógánaigh an Chúil Cheangailte / Ringleted Youth of My Love'

Love Songs of Connacht, a collection edited and published as a book by Douglas Hyde in 1893, was a best-seller. It offered to learners a text in Irish on one side of the opened pages and Hyde's own translation into an Anglo-Irish 'poetic' version on the other. At the bottom of the second page, Hyde generated a looser, more literal translation in Hiberno-English prose. These passages were much admired and quoted, providing later writers such as J.M. Synge and Augusta Gregory with a viable medium. W.B. Yeats wrote in a Preface to a later, limited edition in 1904 that Hyde's prose versions were 'even better than his verse ones.' The very success of Hyde's collection caused the defeat of its primary purpose. Instead of popularising Irish-language literature, it made the creation of a national ⁊

Tá píora binn eile ann a bpáṡmaoro an páö ceuöna, "peult an eólair" aṡur ir aoiöinn an páö é. Ir aṡ cur i ṡ·céill atá ré ṡo mbíonn eólar öúbalta aṡur ṡéir-inntinn meuöaiṡte ṡo món, aṡ an té atá i nṡpáö. Tá an ṡpáö mar peult, aṡur tá ré mar peult-eólair mar ṡeall ar an ṡ-caoi ann a n-orṡlann ré ár ṡ-ceuö-ṗaċa, ṡo mbiömío öúbalta níor euötroime níor beóöa aṡur áilleaċt an traoṡail i ṁoċt nár ċuiṡeaman amaṁ ṡo ötí rin é. Aṡ ró an píora air ar Laörar, aöṗán naċ ṗéiöir a ṗáṗuṡaö i öte-anṡa ar biċ ar a ṁillreaċt aṡur ar a ṗíor-ċaoine.

A Óṡánaiṡ an Ċúil Ċeanṡailte.

A óṡánaiṡ an ċúil ċeanṡailte
  Le a raiö mé real i n-éinṗeaċt
Ċuaiö tu 'péir, an bealaċ ro
  'S ni ċáiniṡ tu öo m'ṗeuċaint.
Ṡaoil mé naċ nöeunṗaiöe öoċar öuit
  Öá ötiucṗá, a'r mé ö'iarraiö,
'S ṡur b'í öo ṗóiṡín ċabairṗeaö rólár
  Öá mbeiöinn i Lár an ṗiaöṗair.

Öá mbeiöeaö maom aṡam-ra
  Aṡur airṡeaö ann mo póca
Öeunṗainn bóiċrín aiċ-ṡiorṗaċ
  Ṡo öorar tiṡe mo reóirn,
Mar ṗúil le Öai ṡo ṡ-eluinnṗinn-re
  Torann binn a bṗóiṡe,
'S ir ṗaö an Lá ann ar ċooail mé
  Aċt aṡ rúil le blar öo póiṡe.

Δ'r ŕaoil me a rτóirín
    ᵹo mbuḋ ᵹealaċ aᵹur ᵹrian ċu,
Δ'r ŕaoil mé 'nna ḋiaiᵹ rin
    ᵹo mbuḋ rneaċτa ar an τrliaḃ ċu,
Δ'r ŕaoil mé 'nna ḋiaiᵹ rin
    ᵹo mbuḋ lóċrann o Ḋia ċu,
No ᵹur ab τu an reulτ-eólair
    Δᵹ ḋul rómam a'r mo ḋiaiᵹ ċu.

Ġeall τu ríoḋa 'raiτin ḋam
    Callaiḋe* 'rḃróᵹa árḋa,
Δ'r ġeall τu τar éir rin
    ᵹo leanrá τríḋ an τrnáṁ mé.
Ní mar rin aτá mé
    Δċτ mo rᵹeaċ i mbeul bearna,
ᵹaċ nóin a'r ᵹaċ maiḋin
    Δᵹ reuċainτ τiᵹe m' aċar.

Δᵹ ro aḃrán fír-ṁilir eile τá corṁúil le ríora ar Ċúiᵹe Muṁan τá ré ċoṁ binn rin, aċτ creiḋim ᵹur aḃrán Connaċτaċ é. Τá an ráḋ rin "reulτ an eólair" ann ran bríora ro mar an ᵹ-ceuḋna. Ir follaraċ ᵹo ḃfuil ré ḃrirτe ruar ᵹo mór aᵹur naċ ḃfuil an τ-iomlán ann.

___

* rórτ rᵹáile no cáir, creiḋim.

→ literature in English seem all the more possible. A leader of the movement to save Irish, Hyde became inadvertently one of the first exponents of the Anglo-Irish literary revival. Unluckily for him, his twenty-year campaign to save the language coincided with the emergence of a group of Irish authors destined to write masterworks of global reach in English.

There is another melodious piece in which we find the same
expression, "star of knowledge," and a lovely expression it
is. It is making us understand it is, that there be's double
knowledge and greatly increased sharp-sightedness to
him who is in love. The love is like a star, and it is like a
star of knowledge on account of the way in which it opens
our senses, so that we be double more light, more lively
and more sharp that we were before. We understand then
the glory and the beauty of the world in a way we never
understood it until that. Here is the piece of which I spoke,
a song which cannot be surpassed in any language for its
sweetness and true gentleness.

RINGLETED YOUTH OF MY LOVE.

Ringleted youth of my love,
    With thy locks bound loosely behind thee,
You passed by the road above,
    But you never came in to find me;
Where were the harm for you
    If you came for a little to see me,
Your kiss is a wakening dew
    Were I ever so ill or so dreamy.

If I had golden store
    I would make a nice little boreen
To lead straight up to his door,
    The door of the house of my storeen;
Hoping to God not to miss
    The sound of his footfall in it,
I have waited so long for his kiss
    That for days I have slept not a minute.

I thought, O my love! you were so—
    As the moon is, or sun on a fountain,
And I thought after that you were snow,
    The cold snow on top of the mountain;

And I thought after that, you were more
Like God's lamp shining to find me,
Or the bright star of knowledge before,
And the star of knowledge behind me.

You promised me high-heeled shoes,
And satin and silk, my storeen,
And to follow me, never to lose,
Though the ocean were round us roaring;
Like a bush in a gap in a wall
I am now left lonely without thee,
And this house I grow dead of, is all
That I see around or about me.*

---

* Literally. O youth of the bound back hair, With whom I was once together. You went by this way last night, And you did not come to see me. I thought no harm would be done you If you were to come and ask for me, And sure it is your little kiss would give comfort. If I were in the midst of a fever.

If I had wealth And silver in my pocket, I would make a handy boreen To the door of the house of my storeen; Hoping to God that I might hear The melodious sound of his shoe, And long (since) is the day on which I slept, But (ever), hoping for the taste of his kiss.

And I thought, my storeen, That you were the sun and the moon, And I thought after that, That you were snow on the mountain, And I thought after that you were a lamp from God, Or that you were the star of knowledge Going before me and after me. ▪

MARY COLUM—*from*:

LIFE AND
THE DREAM

(1947)

By far the most popular of all the *Love Songs of Connacht* were those in which frustrated young women had given utterance to a repressed sexuality—often voiced by rural women compelled to marry a local farmer in a match made for economic rather than romantic reasons. In the decade of the 1890s, when professors of Trinity College Dublin could accuse Irish-language literature of sexual indecency, and when many marriages in both upper and lower classes were forced on ↗

HEN, DR. DOUGLAS Hyde's translations of *The Love Songs of Connacht* threw us all into the same sort of excitement that Herder's translations of folk poetry or Percy's *Reliques of Ancient English Poetry* had thrown people into in the eighteenth century. These anonymous west of Ireland songs were mostly women's love songs, and they were unlike any love poetry we read in other languages. They had a directness of communication, an intensity of emotion which, I think, is the special Celtic gift to literature. It was odd that in a country where romantic love was not part of the social organisation, where it was even mocked at, where marriages were arranged and were even a sort of deliberate alliance between families, there should have been love poetry of such a high kind. We read these songs in the original and in the striking translations so often that we knew them by heart. The occasional carelessness of Douglas Hyde's language seemed to be all right in these versions of folk poetry. A stylist could easily find fault with some of the words . . . but we knew it was grand love poetry.

It was the poetry of youth, yearning, and unsophistication. And not only this, but it was the special expression of the women of the race we belong to, women who were married to men whom they barely knew, who took it for granted that marriage was a destiny they had to accept, but love was an aspiration of the heart and spirit to be expressed in beautiful words by people who had never handled a book except a prayer book.

The Love Songs of Connacht and the new translations of the old sagas set everybody on fire with a desire to have a national literature and to revive a national life. A spirit that had been long asleep awoke. It was surprising that the English government, which proclaimed Land League meetings and threw the Irish Members of Parliament into jail for some little political offence, took no notice, or only favourable notice, of this new ardour for native culture. One would think that even a child of ten would have realised that all this was bound to develop towards another and more determined fight to throw off the English yoke. ■

→ reluctant young brides, these piercing lyrics rang out with a defiant appeal to the heart. They permitted young women like Mary Colum, educated by the nuns of her secondary school on strict standards of Victorian gentility, to reconnect with the vibrant sexuality of pre-Famine Ireland. Hyde's collection was equally challenging to sexual puritanism and to repressive class codes. As young men and women mingled freely at Gaelic League weekend events in country houses (often under the baleful eye of some local parish priest), a whole new sexual order seemed possible.

PATRICK PEARSE

TO THE EDITOR, AN *CLAIDHEAMH SOLUIS*

Patrick Pearse, in his
earlier and more dogmatic
years as a Gaelic League
crusader, may have shared
Hyde's admiration for the
poems of Thomas Davis
and Samuel Ferguson, but
he was adamant that the
Irish mind could express
itself in an unfettered way
only in the native language.
Unintentionally, he drove
the young James Joyce
away from his own classes
in Irish by his propensity
to accompany praise for
the expressive beauty of
the Irish language with
denunciations of the inferior
intellectual and emotional
possibilities of English.
The growing national and
international success of ↗

May 13th, 1899   27 Gt. Brunswick St.,
Dublin.

Dear Sir,

Ireland is notoriously a land of contradictions and of shams, and of Irish contradictions and shams. Dublin is assuredly the hot bed. We have in the capital of Ireland 'Irish' national newspapers whose only claim to nationality is that they run down—whilst they imitate—everything in English; we have 'Irish' nationalist politicians who in heart and soul are as un-Irish as Professor Mahaffy; we have a 'national' literary society which is anti-national without being so outspoken as Trinity College. Apparently the only thing necessary to make a man or an institution Irish is a little dab of green displayed now and again to relieve the monotony, a little eloquent twaddle about the 'children of the Gael' or a little meaningless vapouring about some unknown quantity termed 'Celtic Glamour'. Take away the dab of green, strip off the leafy luxury of words and what have you? The man or the institution is as English as Lord Salisbury. Newspapers, politicians, literary societies are all but forms of one gigantic heresy that like a poison has eaten its way into the vitals of Irish nationality, that has paralysed the nation's energy and intellect. That heresy is the idea that there can be an Ireland, that there can be an Irish literature, an Irish social life, whilst the language of Ireland is English.

And lo! Just as the country is beginning to see through the newspapers and the literary societies, here we have the Anglo-Irish heresy springing up in new form, the 'Irish' Literary Theatre. Save the mark! Much ink has been spilled in our newspaper offices over this same 'Irish' Literary Theatre, but I note that not a single 'national' daily impeaches it on the only ground, on which details apart, it is impeachable; namely, that literature written in English cannot be Irish. Why waste time in criticising stray expressions when the whole thing is an imposture, a fraud, a heresy? Had Mr. Yeats and his friends called their venture, the 'English Literary Theatre', or simply 'The Literary Theatre', I would have been the last in the world to object to it. But in the name of common sense, why dub it 'Irish'? Why not select Hindu, Chinese, Hottentot or Eskimo? None of these would be true, for a play in English, if it is a play at all, must be English literature, but any one of them would be quite as appropriate as 'Irish'. What claim have these two English plays to be called 'Irish' literature? None in the world, save that the scene in each is laid in Ireland. Is then, *Timon of Athens* Greek literature? Is *Romeo and Juliet* Italian literature? Is *Quentin Durward* French literature? Is the *Vision of Don Roderick* Spanish literature? When Greece, Italy, France and Spain claim these works as their respective properties, then may Ireland claim *The Countess Cathleen* and *The Heather Field* as her own.

The 'Irish Literary Theatre' is, in my opinion, more dangerous—because [less] glaringly anti-national—than Trinity College. If we once admit the Irish literature in English idea, then the language movement is a mistake. Mr. Yeats's precious 'Irish' Literary Theatre may, if it develops, give the Gaelic League more trouble than the Atkinson-Mahaffy combination. Let us strangle it at its birth. Against Mr. Yeats personally we have nothing to object. He is a mere English poet of the third or fourth rank, and as such he is harmless. But when he attempts to run an 'Irish Literary Theatre', it is time for him to be crushed.

Very sincerely yours,
P.H. Pearse

→ Irish writing in English led him to argue, while still in his teens, that a national literature could be created only in the Irish language. Ironically, he would himself in the fullness of time win fame for his writings in English as well as in Irish, and for his advanced views on bilingualism in the educational process.

D.P. MORAN—*from*:

'THE BATTLE OF TWO CIVILISATIONS'

(1900)

Moran was a member of the Irish Literary Society in London where he earned his living as a journalist. Having returned to Ireland, he edited *The Leader*, a journal in which he promoted the ideal of an 'Irish Ireland'. This would be a purist nation devoted to Catholicism, Gaelic sports, and the Irish language. In this spirit, he showed a special genius for coining abusive terms to describe anyone he suspected of promoting English values: 'West Briton', 'shoneen' (little John), 'sourface'. He never mastered the Irish language himself but even after independence continued to crusade against 'foreign' culture, such as jazz music and modern dancing. He died in 1936.

THEN YET ANOTHER Irish make-believe was born, and it was christened 'The Celtic Note', Mr. W. B. Yeats standing sponsor for it. The 'Celtic Renaissance' was another name invented about this time, and we were asked to pride ourselves on the influence we had exerted, and would continue to exert on English literature. The birth of the 'Celtic Note' and the discovery of what Irish literature was really made of, caused a little stir amongst minor literary circles in London, but much less stir in Ireland itself, where the 'Irish National' demand for the *Mirror of Life*, the *Police Gazette*, and publications of a like kind, showed no signs of weakening. The people, when they showed any evidence of interest whatever, asked what these gentlemen were driving at. Their backers thereupon put them up proudly on a pedestal and said, 'Hats off, gentlemen; these are mystics.' Never, indeed, was truer sentence uttered. Mystics they were and are, for a mystic is assuredly a man who deals in mysteries, and mysteries are things which the limited human mind cannot understand. The whole situation was really charged with the comic element. A muddled land which mistook politics for nationality and English literature for Irish, which confused black with white, was offered the services of a few mystics: 'But, man, it's too many mysteries we have already,' no one had the courage to say, 'and what Ireland wants is not men to muddle her with more mysteries, but men who can solve some of the too many already in stock.'

However, it must be admitted that the mystics served a useful purpose, though it was by no means the one they intended. By making a serious and earnest effort to create a distinct Irish literature in English they pushed forward the question, 'What is Irish literature?' The Gaelic League took up a logical and uncompromising position, fought a sharp and, as it proved, a decisive campaign, and last summer Mr. W.B. Yeats, though he has since wobbled, formally surrendered his sword, and Irish literature henceforward was not to be thought of outside the Irish language. ■

'A muddled land which mistook politics for nationality and English literature for Irish, which confused black with white, was offered the services of a few mystics...'

W.B. YEATS—*from*:

'THE LITERARY MOVEMENT IN IRELAND'

(1899)

W.B. Yeats contributed to a collection of essays in which he defined a programme for Irish writing, marking it off clearly from English literature, which (he held) celebrated only victories. The 'triumph of failure' mode of writing would prove potent later in the hands of writers as different as Patrick Pearse and Samuel Beckett; but here Yeats also seeks to show just how ancient were the works now passing from Irish to English among country people. In this way, he wrote also to answer critics such as D.P. Moran who attacked the 'Celtic note' as a mere halfway house between two authentic cultures. Moran argued that, 'the Gael must be the element that absorbs', but even he accepted Thomas Davis's ideal of the Irish people as a composite race. The real debate among revivalists was about whether the literature produced either in Irish or in English should be national or cosmopolitan in tone.

WE ARE PREPARING, as we hope, for a day when Ireland will speak in Gaelic, as much as Wales speaks in Welsh, within her borders, but speak, it may be, in English to other nations . . . Already, as I think, a new kind of romance, a new element in thought, is being moulded out of Irish life and traditions, and this element may have an importance for criticism, even should criticism forget the writers who are trying to embody it in their work, while looking each one through his own colour in the dome of many-coloured glass.

Contemporary English literature takes delight in praising England and her empire, the master-work and dream of the middle class, and though it may escape from this delight, it must long continue to utter the ideals of the strong and wealthy. Irish intellect has always been preoccupied with the weak and with the poor, and now it has begun to collect and describe their music and stories, and to utter anew the beliefs and hopes which they alone remember. It may never make a literature preoccupied with the circumstance of their lives, like the 'peasant poetry', whose half-deliberate triviality, passionless virtue, and passionless vice has helped so many orderly lives; for a writer who wishes to write with his whole mind must knead the beliefs and hopes which he has made his own, with the circumstance of his own life. Burns had this preoccupation, and nobody will deny that he was a great poet, but even he had the poverty of emotions and ideas of a peasantry that had lost, like the middle class into which it would have its children absorbed, the imagination that is in tradition without finding the imagination that is in books. Irish literature may prolong its first inspiration without renouncing the complexity of ideas and emotions which is the inheritance of cultivated men, for it will have learned from the discoveries of modern learning that the common people, wherever civilisation has not driven its plough too deep, keep a watch over the roots of all religion and romance. ■

W.B. YEATS

HIBERNO-ENGLISH

(1902)

H E [DOUGLAS HYDE] has begun to get a little careless lately. Above all I would have him keep to that English idiom of the Irish-thinking people of the West which he has begun to use less often. It is the only good English spoken by any large number of Irish people today, and we must found good literature on a living speech. English men of letters found themselves upon the English Bible, where religious thought gets its living speech. Blake, if I remember rightly, copied it out twice, and I remember once finding a few illuminated pages of a new decorated copy that he began in his old age. Byron read it for the sake of style, though I think it did him little good, and Ruskin founded himself in great part upon it. Indeed, we find everywhere signs of a book which is the chief influence in the lives of English children. The translation used in Ireland has not the same literary beauty, and if we are to find anything to take its place we must find it in that idiom of the poor, which mingles so much of the same vocabulary with turns of phrase that have come out of Gaelic. Even Irish writers of considerable powers of thought seem to have no better standard of English than a schoolmaster's ideal of correctness. If their grammar is correct they will write in all the lightness of their hearts about 'keeping in touch', and 'object-lessons', and 'shining examples', and 'running in grooves', and 'flagrant violations' of various things. Yet, as Sainte-Beuve has said, there is nothing immortal except style. One can write well in that country idiom without much thought about one's words; the emotion will bring the right word itself, for there everything is old and everything alive and nothing common or threadbare. I recommend to the Intermediate Board—a body that seems to benefit

Now that Irish had been recognised as a language worthy of study by the Intermediate Board of Education, W.B. Yeats began to agitate for a similar recognition of Hiberno-English as the language which most people actually spoke. His tongue may have been only partly in his cheek. He admitted that his attempt to create a national literature and theatre in English was somewhat paradoxical, 'for English is the language in which the Irish cause has been debated and we have to struggle against traditional points of view'. Nevertheless, a subtle use of English would help to liberate the 'language of occupation' from many of its more negative historic meanings.

by advice—a better plan than any they know for teaching children to write good English. Let every child in Ireland be set to turn a leading article or a piece of what is called excellent English, written perhaps by some distinguished member of the Board, into the idiom of his own countryside. He will find at once the difference between dead and living words, between words that meant something years ago and words that have the only thing that gives literary quality—personality, the breath of men's mouths. Zola, who is sometimes an admirable critic, has said that some of the greatest pages in French literature are not even right in their grammar: 'They are great because they have personality.' ■

'Let every child in Ireland be set to turn a leading article or a piece of what is called excellent English, written perhaps by some distinguished member of the Board, into the idiom of his own countryside.'

WILLIAM ROONEY

'IS THERE AN ANGLO-IRISH LITERATURE?'

(1899)

I T IS DIFFICULT to understand the position of these guardians of the national taste. We have, in spite of ourselves, an English-reading public in Ireland, supplied with an illimitable periodical literature wholly British in tone. The National School kept us wholly ignorant of ourselves and our history throughout childhood; this vendetta of the hyper-Gaelic element would deprive us of all the writings likely to hold for us the ghost of a national tradition, hope, or sentiment. Surely no one is insane enough to imagine that we can de-Anglicise Ireland by teaching the people to regard as non-Irish the writings of Davis, Mitchel, Mangan, and their *confrères* and followers? Father O'Hickey, one of the leaders of the present Gaelic movement, has admitted that an essay of Davis first directed his attention to Irish. Are we to shut off all possibility of stirring others in the same fashion? Are we to ask the young men and women who are so unfortunate as never to have heard Irish spoken to give up reading until they are able to satisfy themselves with the literature of Gaelic Ireland? Are we further to force those of our kith and kin who can write to go over to the service of the enemy because they are unable to give their thoughts to us in a tongue which, through no fault of theirs, they do not know? I am not by any means to be taken as an *ad misericordiam* appeal for the creators of an Irish literature in English. They have a *raison d'être*, and the popularity that their works have won, and still find, amongst the most Irish of Irishmen, is a proof of their truth to Ireland, and their service to her cause.

The Gaelic cause will be far better advanced by encouraging the reading of this literature than by reviling it. It is primarily and principally intended to keep Ireland Irish; being so it is the most potent weapon for those parts of Ireland where Gaelic has been lost. ∎

William Rooney was born in Dublin in 1873 and joined the Gaelic League at the age of twenty. As a cultural nationalist, he helped to formulate the policy that only after political freedom could the native culture be fully protected and developed. This thinking had a major influence on Pearse's notion of 'an Ireland not merely free but Gaelic, not merely Gaelic but free.' It led Rooney to make probing criticisms of the parliamentary nationalists for failing to be more assertive in promoting Irish. With Arthur Griffith he founded the *United Irishman* paper. He was also known as a poet. He died in 1901 at the age of twenty seven. In the following extract he questions those purists of the Gaelic League who denied that the English language writings of Young Ireland in the 1840s were an element of the national literature.

ETHNA CARBERY

'MO BHUACHAILL CAEL-DUBH\MY BLACK SLENDER BOY'

(1902)

Ethna Carbery, born
Anna Johnston in County
Antrim in 1866, was a close
associate of Maud Gonne,
with whom she founded
Inghinidhe na hÉireann
in 1900. By then she had
become known, along with
Alice Milligan, as publisher
of The Northern Patriot and
The Shan Van Vocht, in
whose columns writers like
Katharine Tynan and James
Connolly began to appear.
On marrying the folklorist
Seumas MacManus in
1901, she adopted the
pen-name Ethna Carbery
(many Revivalists adopted
a pseudonym in order to
assert a Gaelic identity
or to conceal an English
one). She died in 1902.
Her husband published
her poetry and songs to
remarkable success. Here
is a translation from one
of the most famous Gaelic
love songs from The Four
Winds of Eirinn.

My Black Slender Boy, as you step on your way
To the dewy-wet fields at the dawning of the day;
My heart in my dreams hears the ring of your shoe,
And roams in the dawn through the clover with you.

My Black Slender Boy!—on my father's grass browse
Of sheep a full hundred, and twenty fine cows,
And my mother has webs of blue woollen go leor,
And linen and gold for my fortune, *a stór*.

My Black Slender Boy, you have nothing but health—
Yet your diamonds of eyes are far rarer than wealth:
Your mouth of white pearls, and your locks of the jet,
Would buy all my fortune and leave me in debt.

My Black Slender Boy, though my father may frown,
And my proud mother pass you with scorn in the town,
While they bargain at making a match for me there,
With Red Ulic Keown in the heat of the fair—

I love you the more, Love, because of their hate,
If you whispered me, 'Come,' I would fly to you straight—
Ay, over the bog to you, jewel of mine—
And leave them their pride and their gold and their kine.

But what can a poor *cailín* do till you speak?
With your hand in my hand, and your kiss on my cheek,
I would wander the world with you, singing for joy,
My store-house of treasure, my Black Slender Boy.

THOMAS MACDONAGH—*from*:

LITERATURE IN IRELAND
'The Irish Note'
(1916)

O NE FEARS TO draw conclusions too general from particular points of difference between Irish and English, in vocabulary and in grammar. The one thing worth knowing in the matter, as far as we are concerned here, is that there are wide differences, which prove different mental habits, different social conditions, different literary traditions. English writing is full of metaphor that cannot be understood without knowledge of historic events which have not affected Ireland: Shakespeare's plays are indeed, as has been said, nothing but strings of popular sayings. Irish has a different set of historic memories and of popular sayings. These have come into Anglo-Irish, but not in full force, and Anglo-Irish is the simpler for it. New images have to be supplied from current life in Ireland; the dialect at its best is more vigorous, fresh and simple than either of the two languages between which it stands. It is indeed by its colloquial directness that you will know the true Anglo-Irish work. Some of our best poems indeed have no word or phrase which alone could be labelled Irish. On the other hand there appear at present quantities of so-called Celtic poems, plays, stories, which, for all their Irish phrases, and indeed because of them, are obvious shams. A writer of these could turn almost any sentence into his 'Celtic'. Where I have said 'Which are obvious shams' just now, he would say something like this: 'And, Johnny, I give you my hand on it this night, 'tis out and out humbugs they are surely.' One of the most powerful writers of recent years, the late J.M. Synge, was very often merely 'Celtic' in his phraseology, though far more often rich and right. His fault in the matter was that he crammed his language too full of rich phrases. He said that he used no form of words that he had not actually heard. But this probably means that he took note only of the striking things, neglecting the common stuff of speech. ■

Thomas MacDonagh was born in Cloughjordan, County Tipperary in 1878. He became a teacher at St. Enda's School while studying at University College Dublin, where he was appointed lecturer in English in 1911. He was an editor of *The Irish Review* and took a leading role in organising the Irish Volunteers (whose rules appeared in the *Review* in 1914). Poet and playwright, he was also a critic. In *Literature in Ireland: Studies Irish and Anglo-Irish*, published after his execution as a leader of the 1916 Rising, he supported Yeats's and Synge's view of the vitality of dialect. Like many intellectuals, he feared that official Irish and official English were being destroyed by vulgar journalism. His precepts had a softening effect on the theories of Pearse, leaving him more open to the achievements of Irish writers in English.

Theatre Matters

DOUGLAS HYDE'S APPEAL to Irish people to stop looking to London and to make Ireland a centre of cultural innovation once again had reverberations beyond the Gaelic League. As the nineteenth century drew to a close, a vibrant generation of playwrights, actors, directors and theatre-goers emerged across the country with the express purpose of working towards the inauguration of distinctively Irish forms of theatre. Many were motivated by a growing dissatisfaction with the predictable offerings of the established commercial theatres, generally imported from the London stage. Most committed themselves to the novel aim of producing plays by Irish playwrights for Irish audiences. This ideal inspired the founding of the Irish Literary Theatre by W.B. Yeats, Augusta Gregory and Edward Martyn (1859–1923). It also motivated the endeavours of talented actors such as Willie Fay and Máire Nic Shiubhlaigh who divided their time between theatre commitments and paid employment elsewhere. When these two constituencies came together to perform *Cathleen Ní Houlihan* in 1902, a new national theatre movement was born that would eventually find a home in the Abbey Theatre.

The form that a new Irish theatre might take was hotly debated in the newspapers and the periodical press, demonstrating the importance of the theatre in an era before the emergence of radio and cinema. If writers like W.B. Yeats and Alice Milligan favoured a drama founded on a rediscovery of Irish myth and legend, the critic John Eglinton worried that such an approach would not express the realities of ordinary people. James Joyce was, likewise, concerned that an inward turn would cut the Irish movement off from important developments in European theatre. However, he didn't anticipate the emergence within a few short years of the great genius of twentieth century Irish theatre—J.M. Synge. The author of *The Playboy of the Western World* had soaked up many of the radical ideas of *fin de siècle* Europe (as Joyce had) but was also deeply engaged with the folk imagination of his compatriots. He regarded his drama as a great collaboration between himself and the fiercely imaginative people he met in his travels all over Ireland. Significantly, the controversy over the *Playboy* demonstrated not only the centrality of theatre to national debate but also the important role that the Abbey Theatre could play in promoting freedom of expression in Irish society.

Despite innumerable challenges, controversies and rivalries, the
development and progress of the theatre movement during
the Irish Revival attests to the innovation, determination, and
ultimate success of a disparate band of people committed to
the development of the dramatic arts in Ireland. From humble
beginnings in various impromptu and amateur associations, they
succeeded in the establishment of an Irish National Theatre with
a permanent home in Abbey Street. Within two decades, a body
of drama of international significance had been created, a Nobel
Prize had been conferred on the movement's leading figure,
and a state endowment had been secured by the theatre.

AUGUSTA GREGORY—*from*:

OUR IRISH THEATRE

(1913)

The setting up of the Irish Literary Theatre in 1899 marks the beginning of an extraordinary period of innovation in Irish drama that would culminate in the founding of the Abbey Theatre in 1904. As Augusta Gregory recalls in this account, the initiative was set up by W. B. Yeats and herself to produce the work of Irish playwrights at a time when opportunities open to new dramatists were few. Together with Edward Martyn and George Moore, they raised the money to have a number of plays performed once a year in a Dublin venue. They aspired to create an Irish national theatre and encouraged artistic experiment. Although, controversially, the company engaged English actors in its early productions, it quickly established a collaborative relationship with the Fay brothers who created an Abbey Theatre style of acting. The Abbey Theatre was successful in producing a number of playwrights of international significance including W. B. Yeats, Augusta Gregory, J. M. Synge, and Sean O'Casey.

O N ONE OF those days at Duras in 1898, Mr. Edward Martyn, my neighbour, came to see the Count [de Basterot], bringing with him Mr. Yeats, whom I did not then know very well, though I cared for his work very much and had already, through his directions, been gathering folklore. They had lunch with us, but it was a wet day, and we could not go out. After a while I thought the Count wanted to talk to Mr. Martyn alone, so I took Mr. Yeats to the office where the steward used to come to talk—less about business I think than of the Land War or the state of the country, or the last year's deaths and marriages from Kinvara to the headland of Aughanish. We sat there through that wet afternoon, and though I had never been at all interested in theatres, our talk turned on plays. Mr. Martyn had written two, *The Heather Field* and *Maeve*. They had been offered to London managers, and now he thought of trying to have them produced in Germany where there seemed to be more room for new drama than in England. I said it was a pity we had no Irish theatre where such plays could be given. Mr. Yeats said that had always been a dream of his, but he had of late thought it an impossible one, for it could not at first pay its way, and there was no money to be found for such a thing in Ireland.

We went on talking about it, and things seemed to grow possible as we talked, and before the end of the afternoon we had made our plan. ■

HARRY PHIBBS

'IRISH NATIONAL CLUBS 1900-1907'

(1953)

N THE CELTIC Literary Society there was evidently a focus point for protest meetings, such as protesting the Dublin Corporation giving an address to visiting British royalty.

The beginnings of the Abbey Theatre took place in meetings of this club. The members got together at the suggestion of Arthur Griffith to celebrate Samhain. For this, Alice Milligan wrote a play called *The Deliverance of Red Hugh*, and the members got up some tableaux. This affair was held in the Antient Concert Rooms, and it was after this meeting that William Butler Yeats declared that these Dublin boys and girls provided him with the acting talent he desired for his Irish Theatre. Members of the cast were: Dudley Digges as Red Hugh; W.G. Fay, Frank Fay, and Thomas Cuffe.

While this club was supposed to be a literary and dramatic club, it was generally known that there was some inner organisation devoted to the cause of freedom and providing the spark for activities. I was not a member of this inner organisation, which undoubtedly was the IRB. ■

Harry Phibbs was born in 1885 and joined the Celtic Literary Society in 1900. He was a talented artist and sketched many of the prominent nationalist figures of the period. He was a frequent caller at Cathal McGarvey's tobacco shop, An Stad, on North Frederick Street, a noted meeting place for cultural nationalists and political activists. Here he regularly met a variety of literary and political figures including Michael Cusack, James Joyce, Oliver St.John Gogarty, Sean T. O'Kelly, and Patrick Pearse. This account of the origins of the Abbey Theatre is taken from his deposition to the Bureau of Military History.

ALICE MILLIGAN—*from*:

'STAGING AND COSTUME IN IRISH DRAMA'

(1904)

Alice Milligan was an influential figure in the early phase of the Irish theatre movement. She was particularly interested in the ancient Irish past and was among the first of the Irish playwrights to dramatise the heroic deeds of the Fianna. She contributed a play, *The Last Feast of the Fianna*, to the Irish Literary Theatre but was keen to ensure that Irish drama would not become the preserve of the literati. The *tableaux vivants* or 'living pictures' form was used to great effect by her. Milligan handled this theatrical mode with striking effect to breathe life into mythical and historical personages from the ancient past. She worked hard to encourage productions in local halls all over the country and was happy to share her experience and expertise with amateur societies and theatre groups. This essay, published in the popular magazine *Ireland's Own* on 30 March 1904, offers practical hints on costume-making including tips on male and female costume, head dress, gold ornaments and weaponry.

A T THE PRESENT time, when we hear in every part of the countryside of more or less successful attempts to produce national dramas, it has occurred to me that it would be profitable to many amateur stage managers to have the benefit of my long and varied practical experience.

Anticipated difficulty and doubt with regard to costume and mounting have often deterred societies from attempting pieces of an ancient, historical and legendary character, whilst they will quite readily undertake the production of long and difficult dramas such as the *Colleen Bawn* and *Robert Emmet*.

The ninety-eight period of history is that with which popular dramas of the present day have made them most familiar, but as far as costume goes it is much more difficult to put upon the stage. To mount a play of this period entails the hiring of military costumes and wigs from London or Liverpool and even the civilian dress, especially that of men, cannot be accurately provided without considerable expense.

When we go back to more remote times the same difficulties do not present themselves, for we find ourselves in the fortunate era, when all garments, including those of royalty, were home made, and when neither dressmakers nor tailors were required to cut out and stitch up close-fitting garments. In our reproductions we can also dispense with the aid of skilled cutters or machine stitching. Good taste in blending colours, skill in manipulating drapery, and some knowledge of the fashions in olden days will serve us instead. Simplicity of make will be found to be quite compatible with artistic beauty, and stage magnificence can be attained without extravagance.

Without further preface I will proceed to tell how to clothe, deck, and arm for battle a whole company of Irish warriors, chiefs, and kings; how to represent ladies of high or low degree as well as bards, clerics and druids. It will be well also to give some hints as to the costume of foreigners or the Danish medieval and Elizabethan eras, who would be expected to put in an appearance in dramas of action. . . . ■

'Simplicity of make will be found to be quite compatible with artistic beauty, and stage magnificence can be attained without extravagance.'

JOHN EGLINTON

'WHAT SHOULD BE THE SUBJECTS OF A NATIONAL DRAMA?'

(1898)

John Eglinton (W.K. Magee)
was one of the most
talented literary critics of
the Revival period who kept
abreast of the new literary
and theatrical developments
of the day. He worked as
a librarian in the National
Library of Ireland and had
access to many of the
important literary figures
of the Irish Revival in that
capacity. In this essay
Eglinton challenged W.B.
Yeats's view that a new Irish
drama should be based
on a recovery of Irish myth
and legend—especially at
a time when the deeds of
Cuchulain and the Fianna
had not yet been translated
into English. In Eglinton's
opinion, the problems of
the modern world could
not be expressed in terms
of ancient stories and
characters beloved of the
cognoscenti but unknown
to the majority of Irish
people. His preference
was for a literature more
obviously connected
to 'the world of modern
sympathies' rather than
one invested in an ancient
idealism.

SUPPOSING A WRITER of dramatic genius were to appear in Ireland, where would he look for the subject of a national drama? This question might serve as a test of what nationality really amounts to in Ireland—a somewhat trying one, perhaps, yet it is scarcely unfair to put the question to those who speak of our national literature with hardly less satisfaction in the present than confidence in the future. Would he look for it in the Irish legends, or in the life of the peasantry and folklore, or in Irish history and patriotism, or in life at large as reflected in his own consciousness? There are several reasons for thinking that the growing hopes of something in store for national life in this country are likely to come to something...

The ancient legends of Ireland undoubtedly contain situations and characters as well suited for drama as most of those used in the Greek tragedies which have come down to us. It is, nevertheless, a question whether the mere fact of Ireland having been the scene of these stories is enough to give an Irish writer much advantage over anyone else who is attracted by them, or whether anything but *belles lettres*, as distinguished from a national literature, is likely to spring from a determined preoccupation with them. *Belles lettres* seek a subject outside experience, while a national literature, or any literature of a genuine kind, is simply the outcome and expression of a strong interest in life itself. The truth is, these subjects, much as we may admire them and regret that we have nothing equivalent to them in the modern world, obstinately refuse to be taken up out of their old environment and be transplanted into the world of modern sympathies. The proper mode of treating them is a secret lost with the subjects themselves. It is clear that if Celtic traditions are to be an active influence in future Irish literature they must seem to us worthy of the same compliment as that paid by Europe to the Greeks; we must go to them rather than expect them to come to us, studying them as closely as possible, and allowing them to influence us as they may....

In short, we need to realise in Ireland that a national drama or literature must spring from a native interest in life and its problems and a strong capacity for life among the people. If these do not, or cannot exist, there cannot exist a national drama or literature. ▪

'There are several reasons for thinking that the growing hopes of something in store for national life in this country are likely to come to something...'

JAMES JOYCE—*from*:

'THE DAY OF THE RABBLEMENT'

(1901)

Although James Joyce is best known as a leading novelist of the twentieth century, he was also deeply interested in theatre. As a student at University College Dublin, he attended the opening production of the Irish Literary Theatre and applauded enthusiastically, unlike his fellow students who objected to Yeats's *Countess Cathleen*. Joyce was a devoted follower of Ibsen and had high hopes that the new theatre movement in Dublin would stage the best of contemporary European drama, as well as home-grown plays. He was bitterly disappointed, however, when he read that the programme planned for the 1901 season would feature only a play in the Irish language and one based on Irish legend. Deeply annoyed by the lack of commitment ↗

N O MAN, SAID the Nolan, can be a lover of the true or the good unless he abhors the multitude, and the artist, though he may employ the crowd, is very careful to isolate himself. This radical principle of artistic economy applies specially to a time of crisis, and today when the highest form of art has been just preserved by desperate sacrifices, it is strange to see the artist making terms with the rabblement. The Irish Literary Theatre is the latest movement of protest against the sterility and falsehood of the modern stage. Half a century ago the note of protest was uttered in Norway, and since then in several countries long and disheartening battles have been fought against the hosts of prejudice and misinterpretation and ridicule. What triumph there has been here and there is due to stubborn conviction, and every movement that has set out heroically has achieved a little. The Irish Literary Theatre gave out that it was the champion of progress, and proclaimed war against commercialism and vulgarity. It had partly made good its word and was expelling the old devil, when after the first encounter it surrendered to the popular will. Now, your popular devil is more dangerous than your vulgar devil. Bulk and lungs count for something, and he can gild his speech aptly. He has prevailed once more, and the Irish Literary Theatre must now be considered the property of the rabblement of the most belated race in Europe.

Meanwhile, what of the artists? It is equally unsafe at present to say of Mr. Yeats that he has or has not genius. In aim and form *The Wind Among the Reeds* is poetry of the highest order, and *The Adoration of the Magi* (a story which one of the great Russians might have written) shows what Mr. Yeats can do when he breaks with the half-gods. But an aesthete

has a floating will, and Mr. Yeats's treacherous instinct of adaptability must be blamed for his recent association with a platform from which even self-respect should have urged him to refrain. Mr. Martyn and Mr. Moore are not writers of much originality. Mr. Martyn, disabled as he is by an incorrigible style, has none of the fierce, hysterical power of Strindberg, whom he suggests at times, and with him one is conscious of a lack of breadth and distinction which outweighs the nobility of certain passages. Mr. Moore, however, has wonderful mimetic ability, and some years ago his books might have entitled him to the place of honour among English novelists.

In such circumstances it has become imperative to define the position. If an artist courts the favour of the multitude he cannot escape the contagion of its fetishism and deliberate self-deception, and if he joins in a popular movement he does so at his own risk. Therefore, the Irish Literary Theatre by its surrender to the trolls has cut itself adrift from the line of advancement. Until he has freed himself from the mean influences about him—sodden enthusiasm and clever insinuation and every flattering influence of vanity and low ambition—no man is an artist at all. But his true servitude is that he inherits a will broken by doubt and a soul that yields up all its hate to a caress, and the most seeming-independent are those who are the first to reassume their bonds. But truth deals largely with us. Elsewhere there are men who are worthy to carry on the tradition of the old master who is dying in Christiania. He has already found his successor in the writer of *Michael Kramer,* and the third minister will not be wanting when his hour comes. Even now that hour may be standing by the door. ■

→ to European drama, he vented his anger in this essay written for the college magazine, *St. Stephen's.* When the college refused permission for it to be published, Joyce put it out as a pamphlet with the help of Francis Skeffington (1878–1916). In the essay Joyce disparages the under-developed state of Irish drama, and criticises the leaders of the Irish theatre movement for bowing down to popular taste rather than following their own artistic convictions.

FRANK J. FAY—*from*:

'THE IRISH LITERARY THEATRE'

(1901)

Frank Fay was born in Dublin in 1870 and educated in Belvedere College. He developed a deep interest in theatre from an early age and, along with his brother Willie, was to have a profound influence on the development of Irish acting. He was recruited by Arthur Griffith as drama critic for the *United Irishman* and demonstrated a wide knowledge of contemporary theatre practices. In early newspaper articles Fay strongly advocated the idea of an Irish language theatre, but he became a crucial figure in the development of the Abbey Theatre, and in the elaboration of a distinctive Abbey style of acting. This was characterised by careful attention to the spoken word and by an economy of movement on stage. His memorable roles on the Abbey Theatre stage include Cuchulain in Yeats's *On Baile's Strand* and Shawn Keogh in the first production of Synge's *The Playboy of the Western World*. In this essay he answers Joyce's criticisms of the Irish Literary Theatre but also defends his right to make them.

SHOULD LIKE TO refer, before concluding, to an article which I have just read, entitled 'The Day of the Rabblement', and which I consider makes some grossly unjust assertions about the Irish Literary Theatre. The writer, James A. Joyce, adopts a rather superior attitude. He accuses the Irish Literary Theatre of having 'surrendered to popular will', although it 'gave out that it was the champion of progress and proclaimed war against commercialism and vulgarity.' One would be glad to know in what way the Irish Literary Theatre has pandered to popularity. Is it by producing a play in Irish? I ask this because Mr. Joyce speaks of 'sodden enthusiasm and clever insinuation and every flattering influence of vanity and low ambition.' But I have yet to learn that either the Irish Literary Theatre or the Irish language movement is popular. Surely they both represent the fight of the minority against the 'damned compact majority.' Mr. Joyce sneers at Mr. Yeats, Mr. George Moore and Mr. Martyn, but sneering at these gentlemen has become so common that one wonders why Mr. Joyce should fall so low. Lastly, Mr. Joyce accuses the Irish Literary Theatre of not keeping its promise to produce European masterpieces. If he will read *Samhain* he will see that the Irish Literary Theatre still hopes to do that. That it has not done so, is mainly a matter of money. Those who write and talk so glibly about what the Irish Literary Theatre ought to do and ought not to do are people who have no idea of the difficulties such an institution has to contend with. Patience, good Mr. Joyce, and your desires for the masterpieces may have fulfilment. This article of Mr. Joyce's with another, are published in pamphlet form because they have, it seems, been suppressed by Father Delany, who would not let them appear in *St. Stephen's*, and therefore, I hope, they will be widely read. ∎

AUGUSTA GREGORY AND W.B. YEATS—*from*:

CATHLEEN NÍ HOULIHAN

(1902)

BRIDGET (*to the* OLD WOMAN): Will you have a drink of milk, ma'am?

OLD WOMAN: It is not food or drink that I want.

PETER (*offering the shilling*): Here is something for you.

OLD WOMAN: That is not what I want. It is not silver I want.

PETER: What is it you would be asking for?

OLD WOMAN: If anyone would give me help he must give me himself, he must give me all.

PETER *goes over to the table staring at the shilling in his hand in a bewildered way, and stands whispering to* BRIDGET.

MICHAEL: Have you no one to care for you in your age, ma'am?

OLD WOMAN: I have not. With all the lovers that brought me their love I never set out the bed for any.

MICHAEL: Are you lonely going the roads, ma'am?

OLD WOMAN: I have my thoughts and I have my hopes.

MICHAEL: What hopes have you to hold to?

OLD WOMAN: The hope of getting my beautiful fields back again; the hope of putting the strangers out of my house.

MICHAEL: What way will you do that ma'am?

One of the most influential plays of the early theatre movement was *Cathleen Ní Houlihan* produced in St. Teresa's Hall, Clarendon Street, Dublin on 2 April 1902. This play marked the beginning of a ground-breaking collaboration between a talented band of actors under the direction of Frank and Willie Fay, and the playwrights of the Irish Literary Theatre. Starring Maud Gonne in the title role, it was a huge popular success and was revived many times. Set near Killala, County Mayo, it recalls the United Irishmen rebellion of 1798, and blends ideas of Fenian revolution with Celtic other-worldliness. The play draws heavily on the Gaelic →

→ *aisling* tradition in which Ireland is personified as a woman who inspires male heroic action. Yeats had this play in mind when he later wrote the lines 'Did that play of mine send out / Certain men the English shot?' It was much parodied by post-independence writers such as Sean O'Casey and Denis Johnston who regarded it as the apotheosis of a dangerous, unthinking nationalism.

OLD WOMAN: I have good friends that will help me. They are gathering to help me now. I am not afraid. If they are put down today they will get the upper hand tomorrow. (*She gets up.*) I must be going to meet my friends. They are coming to help me and I must be there to welcome them. I must call the neighbours together to welcome them.

MICHAEL: I will go with you.

BRIDGET: It is not her friends you have to go and welcome, Michael; it is the girl coming into the house you have to welcome. You have plenty to do; it is food and drink you have to bring to the house. The woman that is coming home is not coming with empty hands; you would not have an empty house before her. (*To the* OLD WOMAN) Maybe you don't know, ma'am, that my son is going to be married tomorrow.

OLD WOMAN: It is not a man going to his marriage that I look to for help.

PETER (*to* BRIDGET): Who is she, do you think, at all?

BRIDGET: You did not tell us your name yet, ma'am.

OLD WOMAN: Some call me the Poor Old Woman, and there are some that call me Cathleen, the daughter of Houlihan. ■

THOMAS KEOHLER—*from*:

'THE IRISH NATIONAL THEATRE'

(1905)

A LARGE AND DISTINGUISHED audience assembled on Tuesday evening, December 27th last, to witness the opening performances of the Irish National Theatre Society at the new theatre in Abbey Street, provided for them through the munificence of Miss Horniman. During the course of the week in which the Society held the boards the attendance thinned a little, but towards the end it recovered itself considerably, so that the closing night was probably the best from the point of numbers after the first.

To one who had watched not only the career of the Society since its beginning with sympathy and interest, but the much larger and older movement of which it forms a part—namely, that slow awakening of the latent imaginative faculties of the country which is gradually feeling its way towards self-expression in the arts—the occasion was one of great interest and importance. Indeed it was much more. One felt keenly aware that it was a critical moment big with opportunity, and that, for a generation at any rate, the fate of national drama was trembling in the balance.

One felt inclined to forget, in the enthusiasm of the opening performance, the real work of the Society is but beginning, that it has yet to make itself felt as a compelling and gripping force in the country, and through years of stern and unremitting labour to justify by solid achievement its existence and—shall I say it—the hanging of its trophies in the vestibule. To be nicely housed, to have willing authors, pleasant plays, good actors and approving audiences is much, but it is not enough. Unless the Society is merely trifling with drama as a dilettante, no one of its members should ever feel that it has accomplished its purpose until the theatre in Abbey Street has become a distributing house of ideas, and the centre of a great intellectual movement in the country. For I trust that Ireland will never forget that art is the companion of thought and life, and not the plaything of effeminacy and degeneration. ∎

Thomas Keohler was born in Belfast in 1873 and moved in Dublin literary circles where he befriended influential figures such as George Russell and James Joyce. He worked as company secretary at Hely's stationers. Keohler published a collection of poems, *Songs of a Devotee* in 1908 and contributed essays to journals including *Shanachie* and *Dana*. He was keenly interested in drama and was involved in a number of Dublin theatre societies. This review published in *Dana* marks a hugely significant moment in the development of Irish drama—the opening of the Abbey Theatre, then known officially as the Irish National Theatre Society, on 27 December 1904. The plays performed on this occasion were *On Baile's Strand* by W.B. Yeats and *Spreading the News* by Augusta Gregory. The move to Abbey Street was funded by a wealthy English patron, Annie Horniman (1860–1937).

W.B. YEATS—*from*:

OPENING SPEECH AT THE ABBEY THEATRE *PLAYBOY* DEBATE
(1907)

The first performance of J.M. Synge's *Playboy of the Western World* in January 1907 immersed the Abbey Theatre in a heated controversy and placed it at the very heart of national debate. Some audience members, outraged by Synge's colourful language and 'unflattering' portrayal of a west of Ireland community, attempted to disrupt the performances during the opening week. Throughout the disturbances, the Abbey Theatre directors defended the right to have the play performed without interruption, and called in the police to maintain order. During a public debate on the controversy, Yeats, as a director of the *de facto* national theatre, valiantly defended civil liberties against conservative elements within Irish nationalism. In time, Synge's play was recognised as a work of genius. The right to free expression would be assailed again by regressive censorship measures later introduced by the new Irish state.

IT HAS BEEN said in today's *Freeman* that the forty dissentients in the pit were doing their duty because there is no government censor in Ireland. The public, it is said, is the censor where there is no other appointed to the task. But were these forty—we had them counted upon Monday night and they were not more—alone the public and the censor? What right had they to prevent the far greater number who wished to hear from hearing and judging? They themselves were keeping the plays from the eyes and ears of its natural censor. We called to our aid the means which every community possesses to limit the activities of small minorities who set their interests against those of the community—we called in the police. There is no stalwart member of the Sinn Féin party who would not do the same if he were to find a representative of that active minority—the burglars—fumbling with the lid of his strong box. We think it is folly to say that we cannot use the laws common to all civilised communities to protect ourselves and our audience against the tyranny of cliques. At no time would we have ever hesitated to do what we have done. When the *Countess Cathleen* was denounced with an equal violence we called in the police. That was in '99, when I was still President of the '98 Association of Great Britain. ■

they tried to silence him, but he retaliated by silencing them.

EUGENE O'NEILL—*interview*:

'ON THE IRISH PLAYERS'

(1923)

THE LATEST O'NEILL drama, *Anna Christie,* is now being played in London, and *The Hairy Ape* will go there in the Fall. At the same time Kathe Deutsch, 'Germany's Sarah Bernhardt', will be playing a leading role in *The Hairy Ape* at Berlin. Paris will see the French version of *The Emperor Jones* at the Odeon, the Government-endowed theatre, in September, and about the same time *The Emperor Jones* and *The Hairy Ape* will be billed in Stockholm.

But it is doubtful if all these European productions will mean as much to Eugene O'Neill as the experience of having Lennox Robinson produce his Yankee play *Diff'rent,* conceived and written in Provincetown, on the boards of the little Abbey Theatre in Dublin. *Diff'rent* is a Cape Cod play.

Mr. O'Neill chuckles when he thinks about it. 'You know,' he said, 'everybody in it is a hard-bitten New Englander. Think of putting that piece on in Ireland.'

Eugene O'Neill is proud of his Irish ancestry. No wonder. His daddy, who thrilled thousands of American theatre audiences, hailed from Kilkenny.

The second American in this branch of the O'Neill family wants to cross the sea to bask in the atmosphere of the Gaelic Renaissance, to sit at the fireside of 'AE', the Irish philosopher, and to taste the flavour of the Literary Revival which went back for its inspiration to Ireland's cultural beginnings and produced such interpreters as Yeats and Synge, Lady Gregory and James Joyce. Indirectly, Eugene O'Neill drank from the same fountain.

'I'm all Irish,' he said in his interview for the *Globe.* 'I have always wanted to go to Ireland. My father, of course, knew the old Irish legends and folklore. I started to study Gaelic, but it was too difficult and I had to give it up.'

In September 1911 the Abbey Theatre was invited by Liebler & Co. to tour America for seven months. This marked a significant milestone for the company and signalled its growing influence beyond Irish shores. The tour was marred by organised protests against the *Playboy of the Western World,* which generated much publicity. The American playwright, Eugene O'Neill (1888–1953), attended the productions in New York and later recalled this moment as an important one in the development of his own dramatic writing. He was struck by the simplicity of the Abbey Theatre method, in comparison to the melodramas of the →

→ commercial theatres.
Indeed, critics have pointed
to the influence of Synge
in O'Neill's fondness for
braggarts and dreamers.
He, in turn, influenced Irish
theatre when a number of
his plays were staged by
the Dublin Drama League
in the 1920s. The following
interview was published
in the *Boston Globe*,
8 July 1923.

'You will understand why I want to go to Ireland if I tell you that I first saw the possibilities for dramatic realism when I witnessed a performance of the Irish players in New York.'

'My early experience with the theatre through my father really made me revolt against it. As a boy I saw so much of the old, ranting, artificial, romantic stage stuff that I always had a sort of contempt for the theatre.'

'It was seeing the Irish players for the first time that gave me a glimpse of my opportunity. The first year that they came over here I went to see everything they did. I thought then and I still think that they demonstrated the possibilities of naturalistic acting better than any other company.'

'In my opinion the Moscow Art Players could not hold a candle to the original Abbey Theatre Company, which toured America.' ■

'You will understand why I want to go to Ireland if I tell you that I first saw the possibilities for dramatic realism when I witnessed a performance of the Irish players in New York.'

MÁIRE NIC SHIUBHLAIGH —*from*:

THE SPLENDID YEARS

(1955)

O F COURSE, IN a city where the greater part of the
public turned to the stage for entertainment, where
the Irish National Theatre Society and its various
offshoots worked for the creation of a national drama and
a new school of acting, it was hardly surprising that most
of the younger folk were dabbling in the amateur theatre.
Almost all the national clubs, literary, political or otherwise,
were associated with theatrical groups in the young years of
the dramatic movement. Many young nationalists appeared
as players with amateur companies, and a lot of the political
clubs, led by Arthur Griffith's Cumann-na-nGaedheal, had
dramatic societies attached, either as a means of gathering
funds or of disseminating propaganda. All over the city, in
small halls and concert rooms, and, when they were available
for hire, in the Abbey or Rotunda, or the Queen's, little
amateur stage groups of the most varied kinds were always
appearing, and although not all of them were important,
either because of the plays they produced or of the standards
they achieved in presentation, they were at least interesting
to watch, if only because of the people whom they managed
to enlist as members, as players or writers or producers. At
that time the most unexpected people in Dublin: poets,
writers, artists, revolutionists, were interested in the theatre;
everyone was ready to discuss a new play or the work of a
player. The arrival of a new Irish dramatist—and most of the
young writers at this period wrote for the stage at some time
or other—would create a notable stir, and a controversial
play was always certain to evoke widespread discussion—
sometimes, as was the case with Synge, a lot of bitter
argument and ill-feeling. ■

Máire Nic Shiubhlaigh (1883–1958), was one of the most talented actors of the Irish theatre movement. Early stage roles include Delia Cahel in *Cathleen Ní Houlihan* and Nora Burke in Synge's *Shadow of the Glen*. She played an important part in the founding of the Abbey Theatre but objected to the involvement of the theatre's patron, Annie Horniman. In 1906 she and a number of disgruntled Abbey Theatre colleagues founded the Theatre of Ireland—a more overtly nationalist company that resisted moves to professionalise their theatre practices along the lines of the Abbey. Nic Shiubhlaigh was an active republican who took part in the 1916 Rising as a leading Cumann na mBan figure. She also supported the work of the Irish Women's Franchise League. Her memoir, *The Splendid Years*, endures as one of the most vivid accounts of theatrical life and political activism of the period. In this passage she describes the variety and intensity of theatrical activity in Dublin and its centrality to cultural and political debate.

W.B. YEATS—*from*:

'THE IRISH DRAMATIC MOVEMENT'

(LECTURE TO THE ROYAL ACADEMY OF SWEDEN)

(1923)

The award of the Nobel Prize for Literature in 1923 conferred international distinction on W.B. Yeats and on the wider Irish Literary Revival that he led. Significantly, he used the occasion of his Nobel lecture to reflect on the struggles and achievements of the Irish theatre movement. In his speech Yeats recalled the early battles and remembered the contributions of Edward Martyn and Annie Horniman. He praised, too, the input of talented actors and the importance of the language and stories of the Irish people. Above all, he recognised Augusta Gregory and J.M. Synge as his great collaborators, and felt their presence beside him as he received the prestigious award. ↗

I HAVE CHOSEN AS my theme the Irish Dramatic Movement because when I remember the great honour that you have conferred upon me, I cannot forget many known and unknown persons.... The modern literature of Ireland, and indeed all that stir of thought which prepared for the Anglo-Irish War, began when Parnell fell from power in 1891. A disillusioned and embittered Ireland turned away from parliamentary politics; an event was conceived and the race began, as I think, to be troubled by that event's long gestation. Dr. Hyde founded the Gaelic League, which was for many years to substitute for political argument a Gaelic grammar, and for political meetings village gatherings, where songs were sung and stories told in the Gaelic language. Meanwhile I had begun a movement in English, in the language in which modern Ireland thinks and does its business; founded certain societies where clerks, working men, men of all classes, could study those Irish poets, novelists, and historians who had written in English, and as much of Gaelic literature as had been translated into English. But the great mass of our people, accustomed to interminable political speeches, read little, and so from the very start we felt that we must have a theatre of our own. The theatres of Dublin had nothing about them that we could call our own. They were empty buildings hired by the English travelling companies and we wanted Irish plays and Irish players. When we thought of these plays we thought of everything that was romantic and poetical, for the nationalism we had called up—like that every generation had called up in moments of discouragement—was romantic and poetical. It was not, however, until I met in 1896 Lady Gregory, a member of an old Galway family, who had spent

her life between two Galway houses, the house where she was
born and the house into which she was married, that such a
theatre became possible. All about her lived a peasantry who
told stories in a form of English which has much of its syntax
from Gaelic, much of its vocabulary from Tudor English,
but it was very slowly that we discovered in that speech of
theirs our most powerful dramatic instrument, not indeed
until she began to write.... It is too soon yet to say what will
come to us from the melodrama and tragedy of the last four
years, but if we can pay our players and keep our theatre
open, something will come. We are burdened with debt, for
we have come through war and civil war and audiences grow
thin when there is firing in the streets. We have, however,
survived so much that I believe in our luck, and think that
I have a right to say I end my lecture in the middle or even
perhaps at the beginning of the story. But certainly I have
said enough to make you understand why, when I received
from the hands of your King the great honour your Academy
has conferred upon me, I felt that a young man's ghost
should have stood upon one side of me and at the other a
living woman in her vigorous old age. ∎

→ This was a generous
speech from a man with
a fondness for locating
himself at the centre
of the action. Here
he demonstrated an
understanding of an idea,
much cherished by Synge,
that theatre is, above all
else, the most collaborative
of all the arts.

W.B. YEATS—*interview*:

'STATE ENDOWMENT FOR ABBEY THEATRE'

(1925)

Although the Abbey
Theatre managed to
survive World War One,
the War of Independence
and its curfew, and the
Civil War, it found itself
in deep financial trouble
by 1923. Arguably the
rise of cinema had a
more devastating effect
on the box office than
wartime disruption. In June
1923 Yeats and Gregory
wrote to President
W.T. Cosgrave offering the
theatre to the Irish people
in return for an annual
state subsidy. Their wish,
above all, was to have the
Abbey Theatre officially
recognised as the National
Theatre of Ireland and, in
that regard, free from the
arbitrary pressures of the
commercial world. Despite
the fact that Cosgrave
took little interest in the
Abbey Theatre and was
known to boast that he
had never attended a
performance there in his
life, his minister for finance,
Ernest Blythe, managed ↗

SENATOR YEATS, IN the Abbey Theatre on Saturday night, thanked the government for an endowment of £850 to the Theatre and expressed the hope that it would be continued. It was, he said, an act of intelligent generosity.

They had become the first state-endowed theatre in any English-speaking country, but the example of their country would probably be followed. All nations except the English-speaking nations and, he believed, Venezuela, had considered that their theatres were a most important part of national education and had endowed those theatres that they might not have to lower their quality through the struggle for existence.

There were probably some people there that night who gave them their sympathy during their first struggles, some who would remember evenings when they had hardly more than a dozen people in the house. It had been a long and anxious labour and especially in recent years, for when they had established their popularity and gathered together a company of great talent, war and civil war scattered their audience once more and the impossibility of paying adequate salaries compelled players, long irreplaceable, to join English or American companies.

BRILLIANT COMPANY

Now they could assure them that this government subsidy and their continued support would enable them to keep a brilliant company, and to offer in the future, as in the past, a means of expression in Irish dramatic intellect.

'Neither Lady Gregory nor John Synge nor I ever thought of this theatre as an educational theatre in the ordinary sense of the word: we had nothing to teach but clarity of expression, and that for the most part was taught not by us but by the opportunity of the stage, and the opportunity that you gave by your critical enthusiasm. The credit belongs to dramatists, actors and audiences—they have been worthy of one another.'

The Irish oratory, he said, of the period of the old Irish Parliament was among the greatest of modern times. Their own Oireachtas was far more representative of the people but the day of oratory was past, and not only here, but everywhere in the modern world.

THEIR OWN PROBLEMS

They had, however, created in that little theatre an assembly where they could discuss their own problems and life, and he thought they had the right to claim that they had founded an art of drama and an art of acting which were of the first rank. The fame of the theatre had gone everywhere. ▪

→ to convince him to support the request. On Saturday 8 August 1925, Yeats announced the news that the Abbey Theatre would be accepting a subsidy from the Free State government to the value of £850, making it the first state-endowed theatre in the English-speaking world. His speech was reported in the *Irish Independent* on 10 August 1925.

SEAN O'CASEY—*from*:

THE PLOUGH AND THE STARS
Act 1
(1926)

Sean O'Casey was born on 30 March 1880 into a lower middle class Protestant family in Dublin's north inner city. Despite a debilitating eye condition and a disrupted education, he became the leading Abbey Theatre playwright of the first decade of Irish independence. O'Casey was an influential activist with the Gaelic League, the trade union movement, and the Irish Citizen Army. He was deeply committed to labour politics and a vocal critic of the middle-class biases of Irish nationalism. ↗

THE COVEY (*with contempt*): Th' job's stopped. They've been mobilised to march in th' demonstration to-night undher th' Plough an' th' Stars. Didn't you hear them cheering th' mugs. They have to renew their political baptismal vows to be faithful in seculo seculorum.

FLUTHER (*forgetting his fear in his indignation*): There's no reason to bring religion into it. I think we ought to have as great a regard for religion as we can, so as to keep it out of as many things as possible.

THE COVEY (*pausing in the taking off of his dungarees*): Oh, you're one o' the boys that climb into religion as high as a short Mass on Sunday mornin's? I suppose you'll be singin' songs o' Sion an' songs o' Tara at th' meetin', too.

FLUTHER: We're all Irishmen, anyhow, aren't we?

THE COVEY (*with hand outstretched, and in a professional tone*): Look here, comrade, there's no such thing as an

Irishman, or an Englishman, or a German or a Turk; we're all only human bein's. Scientifically speakin', it's all a question of the accidental gatherin' together of mollycewels an' atoms.

PETER (*comes in with a collar in his hand, he goes over to mirror, Left, and proceeds to try to put it on*).

FLUTHER: Mollycewels an' atoms! D'ye think I'm goin' to listen to you thryin' to juggle Fluther's mind with complicated cunundhrums of mollycewels an' atoms?

THE COVEY (*rather loudly*): There's nothin' complicated in it. There's no fear o' th' Church tellin' you that mollycewels is a stickin' together of millions of atoms o' sodium, carbon, potassium o' iodide, et cetera, that, accordin' to th' way they're mixed, make a flower, a fish, a star that you see shinin' in th' sky, or a man with a big brain like me, or a man with a little brain like you!

FLUTHER (*more loudly still*): There's no necessity to be raisin' your voice; shoutin's no manifestin' forth of a growin' mind. ■

→ His Dublin plays were intentionally iconoclastic and revisionist, expressing a new post-war mentality that questioned the solidifying orthodoxies of the new state. *The Plough and the Stars* caused heated controversy in 1926 when it interrogated the heroic narrative of the 1916 Rising. This episode tested the resolve of the Abbey Theatre to retain its independence in a new era of government subsidy.

The Natural World

THE IRISH FAMINE had shown that the natural world could, at a whim, turn from being a great provider, to a nurturer of disease and death. In this catastrophic disaster, the vengeance visited by nature was widely understood by the ruling classes as a stroke of divine providence to punish a degenerate people. This may explain why so many Revivalists, some of whom had lost faith in Christianity, were keen to renegotiate the Irish relationship with nature and the environment, and to rediscover in the natural world a storehouse of inspiration and sustenance, rather than a repository of gothic horror. Yeats's, 'The Lake Isle of Innisfree', is exemplary in this regard. The poem subtly addresses cultural memories of a vengeful nature and proposes, instead, a sustainable, harmonious human relationship with the natural world. It also praises the virtue of modest self-reliance—the very quality that Malthusian economists regarded as lacking in the Irish.

The renewed interest in the natural world also owed a great deal to the pronounced hostility to the modern, urban, industrial culture of empire that informed much Revivalist thinking. It is not surprising, therefore, that the Revival would promote the idea of the spontaneous, rural Irish Celt as an

antidote to the conventional, urban Anglo-Saxon. Within the
hidden recesses of Celtic tradition could be found energising
and heroic attitudes to nature that were forged in opposition
to the measured austerity and sedentary contemplations of
the Christian world. Thanks to modern innovations such
as the bicycle, it was possible, too, for a wider section of the
population to visit sites of ancient significance and natural
beauty. Likewise, the rediscovery of the Gaelic tradition
of dinnseanchas (lore of places) revealed much about the
intimate relationship between culture and landscape in Irish
tradition, and challenged attempts to codify the landscape
according to imperial standards and schemas.

 Not all Revivalists, however, regarded the discoveries of
modern science as alien to the Irish temperament. Central
figures like Emily Lawless and J.M. Synge were deeply
interested in natural science and were as inspired by the
ideas of Charles Darwin and Herbert Spencer as they were
by Standish O'Grady's Celticism. Yet they were aware,
too, that scientific models and methodologies developed
elsewhere did not always explain Irish conditions accurately.
Both Lawless and Synge were alert to the limits of imperial

cosmopolitanism and promoted, instead, the development
of scientific thinking along local lines. Throughout his work,
Synge's own commitment to the nuanced portrayal of locality
is an interesting combination of new ideas of regionalism
promoted by the French school of geographers and older
dinnseanchas traditions.

Much of the literature of the period is heavily invested
in representing Ireland as a place of unsurpassed beauty and
vitality—especially those regions on the western seaboard
that were most affected by the Famine. This was a significant
development at a time when Irish schoolchildren were taught
more about the railway systems of the United Kingdom than
about the physical features of their homeland.

W.B. YEATS

'THE LAKE ISLE OF INNISFREE'

(1893)

Arguably Yeats's best-known poem, 'The Lake Isle of Innisfree' was published in an early collection, *The Rose* in 1893. It registers the deep nostalgia for Sligo that Yeats felt while living among 'the pavements grey' of London. The poem can be easily critiqued as an example of twee Revivalism in its promotion of rural pastoral values over the challenges of modern urban life. However, it can also be interpreted as a rallying call for the Irish Revival. The passionate vow to return to Innisfree at a time when people were leaving Ireland in their thousands is a bold statement of confidence in Irish possibility. In its celebration of viable self-sufficiency, the poem strikes the keynote of the period and can be read as a rousing self-help manifesto.

I will arise and go now, and go to Innisfree,
And a small cabin build there, of clay and
    wattles made:
Nine bean-rows will I have there, a hive for
    the honey-bee,
And live alone in the bee-loud glade.

And I shall have some peace there, for peace
    comes dropping slow,
Dropping from the veils of the morning to
    where the cricket sings;
There midnight's all a-glimmer, and noon
    a purple glow,
And evening full of the linnet's wings.

I will arise and go now, for always night
    and day
I hear lake water lapping with low sounds
    by the shore;
While I stand on the roadway, or on the
    pavements grey,
I hear it in the deep heart's core.

J.M. SYNGE—*from*:

'AUTOBIOGRAPHY'

(1896–1907)

O NE EVENING WHEN I was collecting on the brow of a long valley in County Wicklow, wreaths of white mist began to rise from the narrow bogs beside the river. Before it was quite dark I looked round the edge of the field and saw two immense luminous eyes looking at me from the base of the valley. I dropped my net and caught hold of a gate in front of me. Behind the eyes there rose a black sinister forehead. I was fascinated. For a moment the eyes seemed to consume my personality, then the whole valley became filled with a pageant of movement and colour, and the opposite hillside covered itself with ancient doorways and spires and high turrets. I did not know where or when I was existing. At last someone spoke in the lane behind me—it was a man going home—and I came back to myself. The night had become quite dark and the eyes were no longer visible, yet I recognised in a moment that they called the apparition—two clearings in a wood lined with white mist divided again by a few trees which formed the eye-balls. For many days afterwards I could not look on these fields even in daylight without terror. It would not be easy to find a better instance of the origin of local superstitions, which have their origin not in some trivial accident of colour but in the fearful and genuine hypnotic influence such things possess upon the prepared personality.

Before I abandoned science it rendered me an important service. When I was about fourteen I obtained a book of Darwin's. It opened in my hands at a passage where he asks how can we explain the similarity between a man's hand and bird's or bat's wings except by evolution. I flung the book aside and rushed out into the open air—it was summer and we were in the country—the sky seemed to have lost its blue

Unlike some Revivalists who embraced mythic and otherworldly modes of thought, Synge was always curious about scientific and rationalist explanations of nature. He joined the Dublin Naturalists Field Club in his teens and learned much from the talks and field trips given by some of the leading botanists, anthropologists and ornithologists in Ireland. The young Synge, influenced by Wordsworth, was greatly inspired by his solitary encounters with the natural world. He was also conscious of the influence of the protean Irish landscape on the imagination.

and the grass its green. I lay down and writhed in an agony of
doubt. My studies showed me the force of what I read, [and]
the more I put it from me the more it rushed back with new
instances and power. Till then I had never doubted and
never conceived that a sane and wise man or boy could doubt.
I had of course heard of atheists but as vague monsters
that I was unable to realise. It seemed that I was become
in a moment the playfellow of Judas. Incest and parricide
were but a consequence of the idea that possessed me. My
memory does not record how I returned home nor how long
my misery lasted. I know only that I got the book out of the
house as soon as possible and kept it out of sight, saying
to myself logically enough that I was not yet sufficiently
advanced in science to weigh his arguments, so I would do
better to reserve his work for future study. In a few weeks or
days I regained my composure, but this was the beginning.
Soon afterwards I turned my attention to works of Christian
evidence, reading them at first with pleasure, soon with
doubt, and at last in some cases with derision. ■

EMILY LAWLESS—*from*:

'NORTH CLARE: LEAVES FROM A DIARY'

(1899)

OUR WHOLE AUTHORISED flora is indeed to my mind an exasperating piece of business, and I can never help wishing that if it was going to be so inadequate, its inadequacy had at least taken less provoking and unlooked-for lines. With regard to two of its departments I feel a positive sense of personal grievance. Our own mountains, and our own sea! To be told that we lag behind England—flat, prosaic England—in the number of our 'mountain' or 'highland' plants is already sufficiently trying, but when it comes to being gravely assured by Mr. Watson that out of what he calls his 'Atlantic type' we have but a miserable thirty-four plants, to Wales and England's sixty-two. Well, I can only say that I consider such a statement to be an outrage! Are we going to put up with such an invasion of our few prerogatives? Can any patriotic, any commonly self-respecting Irish botanist accept for a moment so palpably prejudiced and hostile a judgment? Let us, I say for my part, not accept it. Arise, botanic Celts, and glut your ire! Let us have an entirely new botany, based upon an entirely new system and classification, and let not the name of the hostile and anti-Irish botanist be so much as named in it! ◼

As well as being a leading novelist, Emily Lawless was also an accomplished botanist at a time when female participation in the sciences was discouraged. A theory she formulated in relation to plant fertilisation in the Burren drew the attention of Charles Darwin, who wrote to her requesting further information. One of the recurring motifs in her nature writing is the idea that Ireland has been misrepresented by modes of scientific description that have been derived elsewhere and do not take into account the specificities of indigenous flora and local ecosystems. Although written in a light-hearted style, this essay, published in the influential London journal *Nineteenth Century*, questions the appropriateness of imperial classifications in an Irish context, and argues instead for native scientific models and approaches.

WILLIAM ROONEY—*from*:

'IRISH TOPOGRAPHY'

(C. 1900)

William Rooney was a leading member of the Celtic Literary Society and a political activist who contributed articles on a variety of cultural topics to Arthur Griffith's *United Irishman*. In this essay he criticises the geography syllabus in Irish schools for its concentration on the features and characteristics of the British empire. Such a view of the world, argued Rooney, had the effect of alienating schoolchildren from their own localities, about which little was taught. Rooney advocated the reinstatement of Gaelic place names and pointed out their value as rich repositories of local knowledge and cultural memory. After the 1916 Rising the original Gaelic ↗

A MONG THE MANY other subjects which the national schools, and in fact most other educational institutions in Ireland, have tabooed is Irish topography. 'Of the geography of the British isles,' says the Intermediate programme, a 'minute knowledge will be required.' 'A general knowledge of the geography of the British Empire, with special knowledge of the geography of the railway systems of the United Kingdom,' say the civil service programmes. And the unfortunate scholar is primed with the height of Mount Everest, the length of the Ganges, the density of the Dead Sea, and the junctions of the London and North-Western, but of Ireland he is told next to nothing, since a knowledge of anything Irish is not a factor in competitive examinations. Hence, we grow up with the haziest ideas about Irish places, except for such towns as Belfast or Cork or Derry, have only the dimmest acquaintance with the lakes, mountains, plains and rivers that go to make Ireland, know somewhat more about Timbuctoo than Tullamore, and are more certain of the source of the Nile than the Shannon. It is hoped that one of the earliest school texts the Gaelic League produces will be an Irish geography in Irish, which will do something towards dissipating the ignorance and apathy that surround the subject in our day schools, and indeed in every department of our daily life.

An effort should be made to get our boards to set up on all their public notices the Gaelic names of villages and parishes, to have their electoral divisions known by their Gaelic titles, and in every other way possible to disseminate knowledge of the local history of our people. This history lies locked up in our topography: the natural features of our land, its hills and hollows, its woods and morasses, its riverheads and estuaries; all these are plain to the man who can read our topography. Though he has never seen a certain place, its name will disclose to him, as certainly as if he were native to it, what manner of place it is. The value of such knowledge cannot be over-estimated. It is a priceless heirloom, for the loss of which no amount of commercial success can compensate. It is a book that is always to our hand, a well-spring of inspiration that can never run dry; a treasure for the humblest as for the highest; a spell that charms equally the poet and toiler; a message that whispers of yesterday, and fits us for tomorrow. ■

→ titles of a number of Anglicised place names were reinstated, such as Cobh (Queenstown) and Dún Laoghaire (Kingstown). In 1946 a branch of the Ordnance Survey (An Coimisiún Logainmneacha) was established with the purpose of researching the place names of Ireland in order to provide authoritative Irish language forms of those names.

AGNES O'FARRELLY—*from*:

SMAOINTE AR ÁRAINN

(1902)

(TRANSLATED FROM IRISH BY RÍONA NIC CONGÁIL)

Agnes O'Farrelly (Úna
Ní Fhaircheallaigh) was
born in Virginia, County
Cavan in 1874. She was
educated at University
College Dublin and was
a founder member of
the Irish Association of
Women Graduates and
Candidate Graduates
in 1902. O'Farrelly was a
leading member of the
Gaelic League executive
committee and a founding
member of Cumann na
mBan. She was appointed
lecturer in Modern Irish
at UCD in 1909 and
succeeded Douglas Hyde
as professor in 1932. From
1898 she spent a number
of summers visiting the
Aran Islands to improve
her spoken Irish and to
advance the work of the
Gaelic League there. Her
accounts of Aran life
were published in *An
Claidheamh Soluis* and
republished as *Smaointe
ar Árainn* in 1902. ⌐

I DID NOT KNOW the true Gaels until the first time that I went west of the Shannon, almost three years ago. That's the truth, indeed even though I had always thought that I was an Irish person, just like many generations of my family before me.

In the English-speaking regions, we do our best to be Irish people, but somehow, we do not properly understand how to be so. I don't claim that the people do not feel a great love for their country in the areas all over Ireland in which Irish was not alive during our lifetime. They undoubtedly do, and often maybe more so than the Irish speakers themselves. But the fact of the matter is that the thoughts and customs of the English are ruining us without our knowledge in such places. Those bad habits and more besides came to us with the foreign language, and for that reason, the blame does not rest on us exactly, but on the people who came before us.

I spent the greater part of the day in that way, going around the Galway neighbourhood, but the next day, I left the old city behind me and I was out on the ocean, heading for Aran of the Saints—moving and moving steadily until we left Black Head to the south behind us, and we could see the islands of Connemara ahead of us. At last I saw what appeared to be a whale raising his back out of the waves— you would say it was a grey whale—and it was not long before another raised itself in the same way, and after a little while, a third one.

But then all changed shape, so that each one of them looked like they were becoming a big stone. They were getting bigger by the minute: they were the Aran Islands! Drawing towards them, it was hard for anyone to imagine that there are people, and a lot of people too, living on them. It was hard to imagine that there is a livelihood for a man or a beast in such a rough, stony place. It was not long, however, until five curraghs came out from one of the islands. The little steamship I was on stopped until they reached us, the crews in them competing with each other to see who would be the first to be able to put their goods on board.

Looking around me, I thought I had landed in a different world—flannel or blue woollen clothes worn by the men and red flannel on the women who were sitting at the end of the curraghs; they wore shoes of cowhide from which the fur had not been removed, wearing them on their feet just as it grew on the animals, and stranger still, a new language was being spoken on every side of me—and to say that that was the language of my ancestors and here was I a foreigner without knowledge of it or the customs of my own country. Who is to blame? Me or the people who came before me? Everything that happened here, happened in almost the same manner close to the second island, and, finally, we reached the harbour and landing-place in Inis Mór, the largest and richest of the Aran Islands, but, of course, that is not to say that the richness of this life is available in any of the islands. It is not indeed but, instead of that, what should be said is that there is not as much distress and poverty weighing on and afflicting the people of this island as their relatives on the other islands. ∎

→ Here O'Farrelly expresses a view, gaining currency at this time, that the truest expression of Irishness was to be found among the Irish-speaking people of the west of Ireland. Such essentialist thinking was later parodied by writers like Flann O'Brien in his novel *An Béal Bocht* (1941).

EVA GORE-BOOTH

'WOMEN'S RIGHTS'

(1906)

Eva Gore-Booth was born at Lissadell House, County Sligo in 1870 into the privilege of an Anglo-Irish land-owning family. She renounced aristocratic values at an early age and dedicated her life to political activism to further her feminist and socialist ideals. She published poetry in journals such as the *Irish Homestead*, *Temple Bar*, and the *Yellow Book*, and also wrote a number of plays. Her poems were collected and edited by Esther Roper in 1927. Informed by her deeply-held political convictions, much of her poetry reveals an interest in the natural world, spiritualism and the occult. In this poem she questions the patriarchal idea that biology is destiny and portrays male dominance as a contravention of the natural order. In contrast, radical feminist ideas are aligned with the unfettered rhythms of nature.

Down by Glencar Waterfall
There's no winter left at all.

Every little flower that blows
Cold and darkness overthrows.

Every little thrush that sings
Quells the wild air with brave wings.

Every little stream that runs
Holds the light of brighter suns.

But where men in office sit
Winter holds the human wit.

In the dark and dreary town
Summer's green is trampled down.

Frozen, frozen everywhere
Are the springs of thought and prayer.

Rise with us and let us go
To where the living waters flow.

Oh, whatever men may say
Ours is the wide and open way.

Oh, whatever men may dream
We have the blue air and the stream.

Men have got their towers and walls,
We have cliffs and waterfalls.

Oh, whatever men may do
Ours is the gold air and the blue.

Men have got their pomp and pride—
All the green world is on our side.

WILLIAM BULFIN—*from*:

RAMBLES IN ÉIRINN

(1907)

THERE WERE THREE canal boats at the station or dock, all laden with fine trunks of ash or oak or beech from the woods of the district. I believe timber cut from Irish woods, and destined for English sawmills, is at present one of the most important items in the traffic of the Irish canal. Here you have a twofold object lesson in the crying need that exists in Ireland for an Irish government to govern Ireland in the interests of the Irish nation. The weed-grown and half-idle canal recalled the problem of cheap transit which meets you everywhere in the country, and the boatloads of timber going seaward recalled the problem of deforestation....

The problem of deforestation is tragically eloquent of the evils of foreign rule in Ireland. A wise native Government, drawing inspiration from national needs and national interests, would derive from Irish forests a permanent and considerable revenue. Under foreign rule Ireland is being denuded of her beautiful woods. The axe and cross-cut are at work in all directions. A mania for tree slaughter seems to have afflicted the landlords. Hundreds of acres of pine and ash and oak are felled every year, and in very few instances are any trees planted to replace the ones that have been cut down. Twenty years ago one of the landlords of the West was asked why he did not plant trees on his waste lands, and he replied:

'What! Plant trees to give cover to my damned tenantry to fire slugs at me? Not much.'

A few days ago I asked a farmer in southern Offaly why he did not plant, and he said:

'Plant, indeed! Why should I? Is it to give more cover to the landlord's pheasants and hares? Besides he

William Bulfin was born in Birr, County Offaly in 1863 and was educated at Galway Grammar School. He emigrated to Argentina in 1884 and succeeded in becoming the owner and editor of the *Southern Cross* newspaper in Buenos Aires. Bulfin supported the Gaelic League and Sinn Féin and promoted their activities in Argentina. Between June 1902 and January 1903 he travelled by bicycle around Ireland and published his observations on Irish life, landscape, and economy as *Rambles in Éirinn*. Bulfin's son, Éamonn, →

would come down on me some day and claim all my trees as he is doing now.'

Down by the skirts of the bog, where the wild wind and the threshing rain have washed away the grass and mould, you may see the stumps of giant pines that gave sylvan beauty to the landscape two hundred years ago. If meteorological data reached back so far we should find that the rainfall in Ireland has increased since the seventeenth century. Even today the rainfall is greater in the western than in the eastern districts.

The effect of forests on climate is common knowledge in other countries. It is Greek to the average man in rural Ireland. The reason is plain. The people have had no sympathetic and scientific State guidance as the people who till the soil have had in other countries, and the infamous legislation which deprived the tenant of compensation for his improvements placed a premium on slip-shod methods. But now there is a change. The land laws are far from being perfect yet, but they give the tenants a right in their farm. They can improve their land now with a reasonable assurance that their improvements will not be confiscated. Consequently, they can plant; and everyone who has the ear of the agrarian and pastoral communities should make a propaganda in favour of tree planting. The Press should teem with articles dealing with afforestation. At present Sinn Féin alone is in this department of journalism, as indeed it is, sad to say, in too many other works of a constructive nature. Every journal in Ireland that honestly wishes to serve the country should deal earnestly and luminously with re-afforestation. ∎

GEORGE BERNARD SHAW—*from*:

'A VISIT TO SKELLIG MICHAEL'

(1910)

YESTERDAY I LEFT the Kerry coast in an open boat, 33 feet long, propelled by ten men on five oars. These men started on 49 strokes a minute, a rate which I did not believe they could keep up for five minutes. They kept it without slackening half a second for two hours, at the end of which they landed me on the most fantastic and impossible rock in the world: Skellig Michael, or the Great Skellig, where in south west gales the spray knocks stones out of the lighthouse keeper's house, 160 feet above calm sea level. There is a little Skellig covered with gannets—white with them (and their guano)—covered with screaming crowds of them. The Bass Rock is a mere lump in comparison: both the Skelligs are pinnacled, crocketed, spired, arched, caverned, minaretted; and these gothic extravagances are not curiosities of the islands: they are the islands: there is nothing else.

The rest of the cathedral may be under the sea for all I know: there are 90 fathoms by the chart, out of which the Great Skellig rushes up 700 feet so suddenly that you have to go straight up stairs to the top—over 600 steps. And at the top amazing beehives of flat rubble stones, each overlapping the one below until the circle meets in a dome—cells, oratories, churches, and outside them cemeteries, wells, crosses, all clustering like shells on a prodigious rock pinnacle, with precipices sheer down on every hand, and lodged on the projecting stones overhanging the deep huge stone coffins made apparently by giants, and dropped there God knows how.

…I tell you the thing does not belong to any world that you and I have lived and worked in: it is part of our dream world. And you talk of your Hindhead! Skellig Michael, sir, is the Forehead. ∎

George Bernard Shaw, born in Dublin in 1856, was one of the most significant literary figures of the English-speaking world during his lifetime. He was, however, only peripherally involved with the Irish Revival. Yeats commissioned him to write *John Bull's Other Island* for the Abbey in 1904 but declined to produce it due to its elaborate staging demands. The Abbey did produce another play of his, *The Shewing Up of Blanco Posnet*, in 1909 at a time when it was prohibited in London. Shaw visited Ireland often and wrote effusively about the natural beauty of his homeland. In a letter written on 18 September 1910 he described a visit to the Skellig Islands off the coast of Kerry, and showed that he could be as inspired and moved by the beauty of the Irish landscape as the most enthusiastic Revivalist.

GEORGE MOORE—*from*:

SALVE

Hail and Farewell

(1912)

Born in 1852 George
Moore left his home at
Moore Hall, County Mayo
in 1852 to pursue his
artistic ambitions in Paris.
There he discovered the
work of Zola and was
greatly influenced by
developments in French
naturalism. His volume
of essays, *Parnell and
His Island* (1887), caused
controversy in Ireland due
to his scathing critique of
Irish life. Moore became
involved with the Revival
through the Irish Literary
Theatre, which produced
his *Bending of the Bough*
in 1900. He made Dublin
his home from 1901 to
1910. His memoir, *Hail
and Farewell* (1911-14) is
a humorous account of
his involvement in the
Irish Revival which often
focuses on the petty
rivalries between the
leading figures.

AE CALLED FOR me as he had promised, and we went away together on bicycles—myself on a new machine bought for the occasion, AE on an old one that he had ridden all over Ireland, from village to village, establishing co-operative creameries and banks. And side by side we rode together through the early streets to Amiens Street Station, where we took second-class tickets to Drogheda—an hour's journey from Dublin. At Drogheda we jumped on our bicycles again; two tramps we were that day, enjoying the wide world, and so intoxicating was the sunlight that it was with difficulty I kept myself from calling to AE that I felt certain the Gods would answer us. I would have done this if a river had not been passing by, and such a pretty river—a brook rather than a river.

As we rode to Newgrange along smooth roads, between tall hedges, the green undulating country flowing on either side melting into grey distances, AE told me that we should see at Newgrange the greater temples of the Druids, and through his discourse the hope glimmered that perhaps we might be more fortunate at Newgrange than we had been at Dowth. It was only reasonable that the Gods should show themselves to us if they deemed us worthy, and if we were not worthy— who were worthy among living men? The Presbyterian ministers would be absent from Newgrange, and we rode on, AE thinking of Angus and his singing birds, myself of Midir at the feast among the spears and the wine cups, his arm around Etain, the two passing through the window in the roof, and how all that the host assembled below saw was two white swans circling in the air above the palace.

The same landscape that had astonished me at Dowth lay before me, the same green wilderness, with trees emerging like vapour, just as in AE's pastels. My eyes closed, and through the lids I began to see strange forms moving toward the altar headed by Druids. Ireland was wonderful then, said my dreams, and on opening my eyes Ireland seemed as wonderful in the blue morning, the sky hanging about her, unfolding like a great convolvulus. My eyes closed; kind and beneficent Gods drew near and I was awakened by a God surely, for when I opened my eyes a giant outline showed through the sun-haze miles away.

Has Angus risen to greet us, or Mac Lir come up from the sea? I asked, and, shading his eyes with his hand, AE studied the giant outline for a long time.

'It's Tara', he said, 'that you're looking at. On a clear evening Tara can be seen from Newgrange.'

Tara! Tara appearing in person to him who is relating the story of her lovers! And certain that there was more in this apparition than accidental weather, I started to my feet. At that moment sounds of voices called me back again to 1901—the voices of clergymen coming through the gate, and askance we watched them cross the field and go down on their hands and knees.

'Let us go, AE. Yes, let us go to Tara and escape from these Christian belly-gods.' ∎

ROBERT LLOYD PRAEGER—*from*:

SAORSTÁT ÉIREANN
'The Fauna and Flora of Ireland"
(1932)

Robert Praeger was born in 1865 in Holywood, County Down and was educated at Queen's University Belfast. He worked as a civil engineer with Belfast City Water Commission and held a post at the National Library of Ireland from 1893 to 1924. He is most distinguished as one of Ireland's leading naturalists and nature writers. His works include *The Botanist in Ireland* (1934), *The Way that I Went* (1947), *Some Irish Naturalists* (1949) and *Natural History of Ireland* (1950). He was awarded the gold medal of the Royal Horticultural Society on two occasions and later became its President. He was also elected President of the Royal Irish Academy, and of the British Ecological Society. Praeger believed that the protection of Ireland's heritage was a ↗

THE MAIN PART of the story of our animals and plants, then, is that since the Ice Age they have migrated into Ireland from the great land mass lying to the eastward, chiefly across land surfaces which have long since disappeared under the sea. Migration from Europe undoubtedly still goes on, but much more slowly owing to the presence of the intervening channels, which offer formidable obstacles. The fauna and flora have not yet recovered from the catastrophe of the Ice Age, and even in the absence of any climatic or other change, they will probably continue to alter slowly—chiefly by additions—for a long time to come.

Were that the whole of the story—were the Irish fauna and flora merely reduced English ones—comparatively little interest might attach to them. But when we find among our native plants and animals—particularly among the former—a number which do *not* occur in Great Britain, or which are absent from continental Europe, our curiosity is aroused. Where did they come from? Are they special forms which originated in Ireland, and have not spread as yet beyond our country? Or are they European species which have died out elsewhere and now remain in Ireland alone? Or have they come from more distant places arriving in Ireland by longer and less direct routes than that *via* England and France, or Scotland and Scandanavia? There can be no doubt as to this: for although they occur in Ireland, all have their main development, their headquarters, elsewhere. They divide into two main groups—one of southern and European origins, found mainly about the Pyrenees or Mediterranean, and the other northern and American, being spread widely across the northern part of that continent. To the former belong the London Pride, found wild chiefly along the west coast of Ireland; the strawberry-tree, much more local, and confined to the Killarney region; the beautiful large-flowered butterwort, so abundant in Kerry and Cork, and three kinds of heath, all confined to the bogs of Galway and Mayo. ■

→ responsibility shared by all citizens and, as the first President of An Taisce, enshrined this as a key objective.

Mind, Emotion, Spirit

AS CELTIC ARCHAEOLOGISTS dug down into the bogs, exhuming ancient treasures and everyday artefacts, people came to realise that the land was an image of the human mind. Every level that was stripped back revealed layers of past existence, long forgotten but still recoverable as a history of the Irish consciousness. The land, indeed, often functioned in the same way as the unconscious being explored by the new science of psychoanalysis. It was filled with lost objects and despised potentials, once neglected or rejected but now brought to the light of serious care and analysis. As W.B. Yeats put into print many of the fairytales of the west of Ireland, he showed a sharp awareness of the links between such lore and the developing psychological sciences. He conjectured a link between 'moods' and 'fairies', arguing in the *Irish Theosophist* of 1892 that 'the fairies are the lesser spiritual moods of a universal mind.' In a late poem, Yeats likened the process of digging up graves and ancient objects to the way in which analysis reconnects people with repressed impulses, brought back into conscious recognition:

> They but thrust their buried men
> Back in the human mind again.

The landscape seemed to project an infinite store of communal memories but also a vast range of human emotions. Rapid changes in weather and cloud formation could make the same townland appear under many different guises (sunlit; dreary; sullen; melancholic) at various times of the day. Hence the recurrence of shape-changing characters in Celtic legend, for the world which they and the storytellers inhabited seemed protean, ductile and even transient. The suffering of the people through years of famine had created in some a certain scepticism about nature, for they had trusted it absolutely only to be disappointed by the crop failure. The constant flux of lives and setting reinforced in many people a melancholy fatalism about this material world, along with a strong conviction that there must be a better world elsewhere, beyond this place of mortality and limitation. Yet nature also continued to offer a way into these deeper spiritual zones, and the landscape was often read as a sort of sacred text, created by divinity, whose mind could be decoded by close attention to small detail. Again and again, writers of the Revival noted the ability of rural people to integrate pagan codes into the belief-system of Christianity, so that each seemed complementary rather than opposed.

W.B. YEATS

'IRISH FAIRIES'

(1890)

WHEN I TELL people that the Irish peasantry still believe in fairies, I am often doubted. They think that I am merely trying to weave a forlorn piece of gilt thread into the dull grey worsted of this century. They do not imagine it possible that our highly thought of philosophies so soon grow silent outside the walls of the lecture room, or that any kind of ghost or goblin can live within the range of our daily papers. If the papers and the lectures have not done it, they think, surely at any rate the steam-whistle has scared the whole tribe out of the world. They are quite wrong. The ghosts and goblins do still live and rule in the imaginations of the innumerable Irish men and women, and not merely in remote places, but close even to big cities. . . .

At Howth, for instance, ten miles from Dublin, there is a 'fairies path', whereon a great colony of otherworld creatures travel nightly from the hill to the sea and home again. There is also a field that ever since a cholera shed stood there for a few months, has broken out in fairies and evil spirits.

Sligo is, indeed, a great place for fairy pillaging of this kind. In the side of Ben Bulben is a white square in the limestone. It is said to be the door of fairyland. There is no more inaccessible place in existence than this white square door; no human foot has ever gone near it, not even the mountain goats can browse the saxifrage beside its mysterious whiteness. Tradition says that it swings open at nightfall and lets pour through an unearthly troop of hurrying spirits. To those gifted to hear their voices the air will be full at such a moment with a sound like whistling. Many have been carried away out of the neighbouring villages by this troop of riders. I have quite a number of records beside me, picked up at odd times from

A good deal of W.B. Yeats's work was informed by his idea that the richness of the Irish folk imagination owed much to the enduring rhythms of Irish life. He was consoled by the fact that Ireland had not been transformed by the homogenising forces of industrial capitalism as Britain had over the course of the nineteenth century. Yeats liked to challenge the ideas of utilitarian thinkers like Jeremy Bentham who regarded the rise of the newspapers and the spread of industrialisation as a victory of reason →

→ and progress over the forces of myth, superstition and folk beliefs. From Yeats's perspective, however, such modernising forces were to blame for emptying the world of mystery and imagination. This essay, published in the London magazine *The Leisure Hour* in October 1890, is an attempt to offer a positive reappraisal of the Irish folk imagination at a time when secular and rationalist thinking is in the ascendant.

the faithful memories of old peasants. Brides and new-born children are especially in danger. Peasant mothers, too, are sometimes carried off to nurse the children of the fairies. At the end of seven years they have a chance of returning, and if they do not escape then are always prisoners. A woman, said still to be living, was taken from near a village called Ballisodare, and when she came home after seven years she had no toes—she had danced them off. It is not possible to find out whether the stolen people are happy among 'the gentry', as the fairies are called for politeness. Accounts differ. Some say they are happy enough, but lose their souls, because, perhaps, the soul cannot live without sorrow. Others will have it that they are always wretched, longing for their friends, and that the splendour of the fairy kingdom is merely a magical delusion, woven to deceive the minds of men by poor little withered apparitions who live in caves and barn laces. But this is, I suspect, a theological opinion, invented because all goblins are pagans. Many things about fairies, indeed, are most uncertain. We do not even know whether they die. An old Gaelic poem says, 'Death is even among the fairies', but then many stories represent them as hundreds of years old.

The world is, I believe, more full of significance to the Irish peasant than to the English. The fairy populace of hill and lake and woodland have helped to keep it so. It gives a fanciful life to the dead hillsides, and surrounds the peasant, as he ploughs and digs, with tender shadows of poetry. No wonder that he is gay, and can take man and his destiny without gloom and make up proverbs like this from the old Gaelic—'The lake is not burdened by its swan, the steed by its bridle, or a man by the soul that is in him.' ∎

GEORGE SIGERSON—*from*:

'FAND AND CUCHULAIN'

(1905)

George Sigerson was born in County Tyrone in 1836 and studied medicine in Galway, Cork and Paris, where he worked under Charcot, an early diagnostician of schizophrenia. Sigerson returned to Ireland, working as a neurologist in Dublin. He was fascinated by the way in which the cycles of Irish history moved from periods of torpor to times of hyper-activity (even insurrection). He thus became one of the subtler analysts of the psychological underpinnings of the Revival. In *Bards of the Gael and Gall* (1907), he noted how the progress of the hero Cuchulain was marked by phases of 'long inexplicable debility' (during which the warrior sometimes had to send substitutes to fight his battles) followed by periods of sudden arousal (as in the famous 'riastra' or 'battle rage')—an analysis similar to this theory of Celtic psychology.

APPENDED TO THIS legend, there is a concluding statement, seemingly added by some Christian copyist. It explains that 'the demoniac power was great before the Faith, and such was its greatness, that the demons used to corporeally tempt the people, and show them delights and secrets, as of how they would be in immortality.'

There are passages here, as in other ancient Gaelic legends, of interest to the physiological psychologist. Unwittingly, the writers have enumerated many signs of extreme nervous excitability in Cuchulain, such as the distortion of his face in battle, his convulsive leaps, his long inexplicable debility, into which he was thrown by strokes of wands, and from which he rouses suddenly. Symptoms similar, in many respects, are found in cases of 'induced lethargy', or hypnotic trance. It is remarkable, also, that when aroused, Cuchulain seeks a certain place (as if 'suggested') and there beholds a vision of Fand. The Druids, by their incantations, seemed to possess the power of inducing hypnosis.

Descriptions such as those given, though exaggerated, were founded on observed facts, and are quite in harmony with our knowledge of neurotic exaltation in Celtic races. ∎

MARY BATTLE

PROPHECIES

(1898)

1. Mary Battle knows when it is going to rain because she sees green in the sky she says 'Isn't it as natural to see green in the sky as purple in the fire!' Purple in the fire is another of her signs of rain.

2. Mary Battle says that sickness travels like a ring. You see a ring of all kinds of colours and the more yellow the worse the sickness travels in the air. It looks like 'a ring made by a man exercising horses.' It is like this and that size. Wherever it lights the sickness is. Sometimes a woman in a white dress goes in front of it.

3. She sees the clouds get all red like blood before a violent death. One day last week she told me she had seen it over towards Knocknarea—we were at Rosses—and that somebody would be killed or there would be war. She has seen it before a man was killed the year before. Two days after she told me a child was burned to death in Sligo. She thinks that was a fulfilment. ■

W.B. YEATS

'THE VALLEY OF THE BLACK PIG'

(1896)

Mary Battle foretold a great war, which might occur when a black pig (or boar) came out of Ben Bulben mountain in Sligo. This kind of prophecy was widespread among rural communities in the west of Ireland, who often cast the coming battle as one of liberation from the British empire. But to Yeats—and perhaps also to Battle—the prediction signalised not the end of the English occupation but rather Armageddon, the conflict which would mark the end of the world and the moment of apocalypse. Yeats's poem suggests that a peasantry, exhausted by imperial abuse and living in melancholy darkness, can expect deliverance not from earthly powers but from God, who will be the bringer of light. The black pig was once a god in mythology, whose flesh was to be worshipped, but in more recent times it has been stigmatised as forbidden and evil—much as light is depicted in many spiritual traditions as doing battle with the darkness that seeks to destroy the world.

THE dews drop slowly and dreams gather: unknown spears
Suddenly hurtle before my dream-awakened eyes,
And then the clash of fallen horsemen and the cries
Of unknown perishing armies beat about my ears.
We who still labour by the cromlech on the shore,
The grey cairn on the hill, when day sinks drowned in dew,
Being weary of the world's empires, bow down to you,
Master of the still stars and of the flaming door.

EOIN MACNEILL—*from*:

PHASES OF IRISH HISTORY

(1919)

Born in Glenarm, County
Antrim in 1867, MacNeill
was a co-founder of
the Gaelic League in
1893; editor of its *Gaelic
Journal*; and Professor
of Early Irish History at
University College Dublin
from 1908. He supported
the replacement of the
League's 'no politics'
philosophy by a militant
nationalism in 1915, a
move which led to the
resignation of Douglas
Hyde. Elected to the
First Dáil as a member of
Sinn Féin, he went on to
support the Anglo-Irish
Treaty of 1921. He was
Minister for Education in
the first government of the
Free State. As a scholar
he was an expert on law
and kingship in early Irish
society, and one of the
few commentators to
attempt a thematisation ↗

T HE TERM CELTIC is indicative of language, not of race.
We give the name Celts to the Irish and the Britons
because we know that the ancient language of each
people is a Celtic language.

A certain amount of enthusiasm, culminating in what is
called Pan-Celticism, has gathered around the recognition of
this fact that the Irish, the Gaels of Scotland, the Welsh and
the Bretons are Celtic peoples. So much favour attached to the
name Celtic that in our own time the Irish language was, so
to speak, smuggled into the curricula of the Royal University
and of the Intermediate Board under that name. What ancient
writers called *opus Hibernicum*, 'Irish work', is popularly
known in Ireland as Celtic ornament. In the same way people
speak of Celtic crosses, and there are even Celtic athletic clubs.
There is no small amount of pride in the notion of being Celtic.
It is somewhat remarkable, then, to find that throughout all
their early history and tradition the Irish and the Britons
alike show not the slightest atom of recognition that they
were Celtic peoples. We do not find them acknowledging
any kinship with the Gauls, or even with each other. In
Christian times, their men of letters shaped out genealogical
trees tracing the descent of each people from Japhet—and
in these genealogies Gael and Briton and Gaul descend
by lines as distinct as German and Greek. This absence of
acknowledgement of kinship is all the more noteworthy
because there is little reason to suppose that, before Latin
displaced the Celtic speech of Gaul, the differences of dialect in
the Celtic speech of Gaul, Britain, and Ireland were sufficient
to prevent intercourse without interpreters.

From this ignorance of their Celtic kinship and origin we must draw one important conclusion. The extraordinary vitality of popular tradition in some respects must be set off by its extraordinary mortality in other respects. There must have been a time when the Celts of Ireland, Britain and Gaul were fully aware that they were nearer akin to each other than to the Germans and Italians, but this knowledge perished altogether from the popular memory and the popular consciousness. ▪

→ of Irish history. In *Phases of Irish History* (1919), he sketched a Celtic basis for a distinct Irish nationality, but also challenged the lack of evidential rigour in some romantic nationalist interpretations.

KUNO MEYER—*from*:

'ANCIENT IRISH POETRY'

(1911)

Born in Hamburg,
Germany in 1858, Kuno
Meyer studied there and at
Leipzig, before becoming
a lecturer at University
College Liverpool. In 1904
he founded the journal
Ériu and was appointed
Professor of Celtic
Languages at the Royal
Irish Academy. One of a
galaxy of German Celticists
whose interpretations
powered the Revival, he
was given the freedom of
Dublin and of Cork after
his appointment to a chair
in Berlin in 1911. At the start
of the First World War he
stirred huge controversy
by a pro-German speech
made in the United States.
His studies of *The Vision
of Mac Conglinne* and of
The Voyage of Bran were
influential, but his analyses
of the importance of
concrete detail in ancient
Irish poetry had a palpable
influence on the poets of
Yeats's generation and,
arguably, on the Imagist
movement. He died in 1919
in Leipzig.

RELIGIOUS POETRY RANGES from single quatrains to lengthy compositions dealing with all the varied aspects of religious life. Many of them give us a fascinating insight into the peculiar character of the early Irish Church, which differed in so many ways from the rest of the Christian world. We see the hermit in his lonely cell, the monk at his devotions or at his work of copying in the scriptorium or under the open sky, or we hear the ascetic who, alone or with twelve chosen companions, has left one of the large monasteries in order to live in greater solitude among the woods or mountains, or on a lonely island. The fact that so many of these poems are ascribed to well-known saints emphasises the friendly attitude of the native clergy towards vernacular poetry.

In nature poetry the Gaelic muse may vie with that of any other nation. Indeed, these poems occupy a unique position in the literature of the world. To seek out and watch and love nature, in its tiniest phenomena as in its grandest, was given to no people so early and so fully as to the Celt. Many hundreds of Gaelic and Welsh poems testify to this fact. It is a characteristic of these but rather a succession of pictures and images which the poet, like an impressionist, calls up before us by light and skilful touches. Like the Japanese, the Celts were always quick to take an artistic hint; they avoid the obvious and the commonplace; the half-said thing to them is dearest. ■

J.M. SYNGE

'THE OPPRESSION OF THE HILLS'

(1905)

AMONG THE COTTAGES that are scattered through the hills of County Wicklow I have met with many people who show in a singular way the influence of a particular locality. These people live for the most part beside old roads and pathways where hardly one man passes in the day, and look out all the year on unbroken barriers of heath. At every season heavy rains fall for often a week at a time, till the thatch drips with water stained to a dull chestnut, and the floor in the cottages seems to be going back to the condition of the bogs near it. Then the clouds break, and there is a night of terrific storm from the south-west—all the larches that survive in these places are bowed and twisted towards the point where the sun rises in June—when the winds come down through the narrow glens with the congested whirl and roar of a torrent, breaking at times for sudden moments of silence that keep up the tension of the mind. At such times the people crouch all night over a few sods of turf and the dogs howl in the lanes.

When the sun rises there is a morning of almost supernatural radiance and even the oldest men and women come out into the air with the joy of children who have recovered from a fever. In the evening it is raining again. This peculiar climate, acting on a population that is already lonely and dwindling, has caused or increased a tendency to nervous depression among the people, and every degree of sadness, from that of the man who is merely mournful to that of the man who has spent half his life in the madhouse, is common among these hills.

Not long ago in a desolate glen in the south of the county I met two policemen driving an ass-cart with a coffin on it, and a little further on I stopped an old man and asked

The Famine of the 1840s not only caused great psychological trauma but left many parts of rural Ireland depopulated. The loneliness and silence of many townlands augmented a tendency to melancholy, sometimes leading to depression and even lunacy. The fear of madness (of what 'to let your mind on when the night is down') troubles many of Synge's dramatic characters, as it disturbed many late-nineteenth-century artists. The experience of alienation, about which Synge had learned much in the lecture halls of the Sorbonne in Paris, also afflicted rural people; and the numbers who checked themselves into mental hospitals would remain alarmingly high well into the twentieth century. Some commentators have held that this was not always due to mental illness so much as to →

him what had happened. 'This night three weeks,' he said, 'there was a poor fellow below reaping in the glen, and in the evening he had two glasses of whisky with some other lads. Then some excitement took him, and he threw off his clothes and ran away into the hills. There was great rain that night, and I suppose the poor creature lost his way, and was the whole night perishing in the rain and darkness. In the morning they found his naked footmarks on some mud half a mile above the road, and again where you go up by a big stone. Then there was nothing known of him till last night, when they found his body on the mountain, and it near eaten by the crows.'

Then he went on to tell me how different the country had been when he was a young man. 'We had nothing to eat at that time,' he said, 'but milk and stirabout and potatoes, and there was a fine constitution you wouldn't meet this day at all. I remember when you'd see forty boys and girls below there on a Sunday evening, playing ball and diverting themselves, but now all this country is gone lonesome and bewildered, and there's no man knows what ails it.'

There are so few girls left in these neighbourhoods that one does not often meet with women that have grown up unmarried. I know one, however, who has lived by herself for fifteen years in a tiny hovel near a cross roads much frequented by tinkers and ordinary tramps. As she has no one belonging to her, she spends a good deal of her time wandering through the country, and I have met her in every direction, often many miles from her own glen. 'I do be so afeard of the tramps,' she said to me one evening. 'I live all alone, and what would I do at all if one of them lads was to come near me? When my poor mother was dying, "Now, Nanny," says she, "don't be living on here when I am dead," says she; "it'd be too lonesome." And now I wouldn't wish to go again' my mother, and she dead—dead or alive I wouldn't go again' my mother—but I'm after doing all I can, and I can't get away by any means.' As I was moving on she heard, or thought she heard, a sound of distant thunder. 'Ah, your honour,' she said, 'do you think it's thunder we'll be having? There's nothing I fear like the thunder. My heart isn't

→ a need felt by isolated or elderly persons for institutional care in winter months. Whatever the reasons, once the summer tourists had gone, a deep melancholy pervaded much of the countryside—so much so that people often held hands in the darkness of a kitchen or pub while reciting a ballad or poem. The removal of the landlords, as Synge suggests, led to a bleak sort of freedom, as no new authority had as yet taken their place.

strong—I do feel it—and I have a lightness in my head, and often when I do be excited with the thunder I do be afeard I might die there alone in the cottage and no one know it. But I do hope that the Lord—bless His holy name!—has something in store for me. I've done all I can, and I don't like going again' my mother and she dead. And now good evening, your honour, and safe home.'

Intense nervousness is common also with much younger women. I remember one night hearing someone crying out and screaming in the house where I was staying. I went downstairs and found it was a girl who had been taken in from a village a few miles away to help the servants. That afternoon her two younger sisters had come to see her, and now she had been taken with a panic that they had been drowned going home through the bogs, and she was crying and wailing, and saying she must go to look for them. It was not thought fit for her to leave the house alone so late in the evening, so I went with her. As we passed down a steep hill of heather, where the nightjars were clapping their wings in the moonlight, she told me a long story of the way she had been frightened. Then we reached a solitary cottage on the edge of the bog, and as a light was still shining in the window, I knocked at the door and asked if they had seen or heard anything. When they understood our errand three half-dressed generations came out to jeer at us on the doorstep. 'Ah, Maggie,' said the old woman, 'you're a cute one. You're the girl likes a walk in the moonlight. Whist your talk of them big lumps of childer, and look at Martin Edward there, who's not six, and he can go through the bog five times in an hour and not wet his feet.'

My companion was still unconvinced, so we went on. The rushes were shining in the moonlight, and one flake of mist was lying on the river. We looked into one bog-hole, and then into another, where a snipe rose and terrified us. We listened: a cow was chewing heavily in the shadow of a bush, two dogs were barking on the side of a hill, and there was a cart far away upon the road. Our teeth began to chatter with the cold of the bog air and the loneliness of the night. I could see that the actual presence of the bog had shown my companion the absurdity of her fears, and in a little while we went home.

The older people in County Wicklow, as in the rest of Ireland, still show a curious affection for the landed classes wherever they have lived for a generation or two upon their property. I remember an old woman, who told me, with tears streaming on her face, how much more lonely the country had become since the 'quality' had gone away, and gave me a long story of how she had seen her landlord shutting up his house and leaving his property, and of the way he had died afterwards, when the 'grievance' of it broke his heart. The younger people feel differently, and when I was passing this landlord's house, not long afterwards, I found these lines written in pencil on the door-post:

> In the days of rack-renting
> And land-grabbing so vile
> A proud, heartless landlord
> Lived here a great while.
> When the League it was started,
> And the land-grabbing cry,
> To the cold North of Ireland
> He had for to fly.

A year later the door-post had fallen to pieces, and the inscription with it. ■

Religion

THE EMANCIPATION OF Roman Catholics in 1829 had some slow but lasting effects. A new middle class emerged within the flock, and with it a priesthood intent on producing a more rational theology, less connected with popular beliefs and folk practices (often now dismissed as superstitions). Sir William Wilde noted that the tone of Irish Catholicism was becoming more Protestant with every passing year. The world that recited tales was being replaced by one that read books. In the words of Angela Bourke: 'Fairy belief legend, an elaborate system of fictions through which a significant mode of vernacular thinking is articulated, was clearly in opposition to the modes of literacy, and became increasingly associated with poverty and marginality.'

Yet, even as bourgeois Catholics abandoned oral traditions, many dissident intellectuals from Protestant families began to explore fairy lore and rural beliefs as a way of excavating their buried selves. In some cases (as in that of Oscar Wilde) the repressed dimension turned out to be surprisingly Catholic; in others, the perennial philosophy hidden in peasant culture led artists (such as James and Margaret Cousins) to an encounter with eastern thought; in others again (perhaps a majority) the search for alternative spiritualities generated a mysticism which reconciled Christian ideas with those of Hindu or Buddhist lore.

These various tendencies worked themselves out in creative writing as part of a general attempt to modernise spirituality. A linked set of theological and spiritual debates occurred within the intellectual class. Some teachers at University College Dublin sought to create a lay Catholic intelligentsia (as the university's founder John Henry Newman had always desired). The debate about 'modernism' within European Catholicism in the first decade of the new century found ready local exponents. However, secularists argued that Catholicism, whatever form it took, might itself be a barrier to democratisation and social progress. And, while these discussions gathered fire, large orders of nuns ran schools, hospitals and even industries, with a freedom and audacity which suggested that they did not always feel themselves constrained by the commands of their local bishop.

While many elements of Irish religious practice declined into social decorum and rule-keeping, other elements enjoyed an intellectual and artistic renewal. W.B. Yeats relished the moment, arguing that in his church there would be an altar and no pulpit. Already, he feared that a prim Victorian moralism was extirpating real religious belief. 'The moral impulse and the religious impulse,' he lamented, 'always kill one another in the end.' If Ireland had less morality, he contended, the country might have more religion.

W.B.YEATS

'THE SECRET ROSE'

(1896)

Yeats saw in the symbol
of the Rose the occult
secrets of ancient religions.
The Rose signified both
sacred and profane love
(the love of Christ for the
soul; the desire of lovers
for sexual ecstasy). It was
also the symbol of Ireland
in such figures as Róisín
Dubh (Dark Rosaleen). His
poem opens as a sort of
prayer. It reconciles Celtic
and Christian lore in its
reference to the pagan
king Conor MacNessa,
who was granted a vision
of the crucifixion of Jesus
just before he died. The
notion that Christians know
only 'defeated dreams'
underlies the poem, which
mentions Fergus, the
proud king who gave up
his earthly crown to pursue
poetry, and Oisin who
wandered for hundreds
of years in Tír na nÓg but
lost his youth. These ideas
of 'the triumph of failure'
would resurface in the
philosophy of the Rising
of 1916, which Yeats ↗

Far-off, most secret, and inviolate Rose,

Enfold me in my hour of hours; where those

Who sought thee in the Holy Sepulchre,

Or in the wine-vat, dwell beyond the stir

And tumult of defeated dreams; and deep

Among pale eyelids, heavy with the sleep

Men have named beauty. Thy great leaves enfold

The ancient beards, the helms of ruby and gold

Of the crowned Magi; and the king whose eyes

Saw the Pierced Hands and Rood of elder rise

In Druid vapour and make the torches dim;

Till vain frenzy awoke and he died; and him

Who met Fand walking among flaming dew

By a grey shore where the wind never blew,

And lost the world and Emer for a kiss;

And him who drove the gods out of their liss,

And till a hundred morns had flowered red

Feasted, and wept the barrows of his dead;

And the proud dreaming king who flung the crown

And sorrow away, and calling bard and clown

Dwelt among wine-stained wanderers in deep woods;

And him who sold tillage, and house, and goods,

And sought through lands and islands numberless years,

Until he found, with laughter and with tears,

A woman of so shining loveliness

That men threshed corn at midnight by a tress,

A little stolen tress. I, too, await

The hour of thy great wind of love and hate.

When shall the stars be blown about the sky,

Like the sparks blown out of a smithy, and die?

Surely thine hour has come, thy great wind blows,

Far-off, most secret, and inviolate Rose?

→ would also imagine in terms of a 'right rose-tree'. Here he awaits a 'great wind', portending revolution (and perhaps even the end of the world). This poem reflects the ways in which the aesthetes of the 1890s explored the surfaces of Catholicism. Yeats is different in that he conducts his exploration in a peasant setting, where Catholicism was no mere lifestyle option but the historic faith of a tenacious people.

JOSEPH MARY PLUNKETT

'THE LITTLE BLACK ROSE SHALL BE RED AT LAST'

(1916)

Joseph Mary Plunkett was born in Dublin in 1887. He suffered from tuberculosis throughout his childhood, spending some of it on the shores of the Mediterranean. Scion of a wealthy family, he received a Jesuit education at Belvedere College and Stonyhurst. He joined the Gaelic League and became a close literary collaborator with Thomas MacDonagh. He was a leader and tactician of the Easter Rising. Like all mystics and revolutionaries, Plunkett seeks to express the unknown in the images of what is known. Here the old symbol of Ireland as a rose is joined to the bardic idea of a ruler married to the land. That marriage was usually mediated and interpreted by a poet. In Plunkett's lines, however, the body of the poet bleeds into the earth during a fertility rite which will restore new life even though he dies. Like W.B. Yeats, Plunkett favours an image which both discloses and withholds its many possible meanings.

Because we share our sorrows and our joys

And all your dear and intimate thoughts are mine,

We shall not fear the trumpets and the noise

Of battle, for we know our dreams divine,

And when my heart is pillowed on your heart

And ebb and flowing of their passionate flood

Shall beat in concord love through every part

Of brain and body—when at last the blood

O'erleaps the final barrier to find

Only one source wherein to spend its strength

And we two lovers, long but one in mind

And soul, are made one only flesh at length;

Praise God, if this my blood fulfils the doom

When you, dark rose, shall redden into bloom.

JAMES AND MARGARET COUSINS—*from*:

WE TWO TOGETHER
Worlds Within Worlds
(1950)

HAD BEEN brought up in the belief in two worlds, this
and the next. This world seemed fairly substantial. Yet
it sometimes went off into large pieces that, though
they claimed their own identity, appeared to my mind, in
its early inquisitive stage, to deny a fundamental solidity. I
was aware of a Protestant world that would have no truck
in this world or the next with the Catholic world, and vice
versa. A recently born scientific world threatened what it
regarded as a senile theological world. A not very tidy mass
with which I had some parental association was shaping
itself into a labour world, and trying to focus a red eye on a
bloated capitalist world. All the same, there was 'this world',
which, unless you were very careful of your steps, would
get a hold of you by evil tentacles that the pulpit called
worldliness, and conduct you willy-nilly to an exceedingly
hot section of the 'next world'.

There was also the question whether 'next' had the
meaning of next door or next minute. Prayers for the dead
were, in my circle, called 'popish superstition', it being
obvious that their eternal habitation was unalterable. If so,
I asked myself (I dare not ask anyone else at the time) what
was the use of a day of judgement, seeing that judgement
had already been made. Something in me was quite certain
that 'this world' came from somewhere and was going
somewhere, and that the 'next world' was simultaneous
with this, and accessible anywhere at any moment: it was
both next door and next minute, and was inextricably
mixed up with this world, if one could only get at it.

I had heard the instrument [the planchette] referred to as
a game for getting what were called 'spirit messages' which

James Cousins was born in
1873 to a Protestant family
in Belfast and became
known as a playwright,
actor, poet and teacher.
Margaret (Gretta) Gillespie
was born in Boyle, County
Roscommon in 1878. The
couple met while she
was studying music
in Dublin and married
in 1903, embracing a
vegetarian lifestyle. Theirs
was a companionate
marriage ('the smallest
co-operative society').
They were members of
the Dublin Theosophists,
a movement associated
with occult philosophy but
also with women's rights
and universal peace. In
1915 they went to India,
where as advanced Irish
nationalists they made
common cause with its
independence movement
(and where Gretta wrote
the 1919 music for the
Indian national anthem
and became president
of the All-India Women's
Conference in 1936). →

→ Both were committed
head-teachers of schools.
We Two Together was
published in Madras in
1950, providing valuable
accounts of the Irish
Revival and of the ways in
which Indian intellectuals
looked to Ireland for
inspiration. The following
paragraphs, written by
James, concern their
awakening to theosophy
and to automatic writing,
very similar to that
practised by W.B. Yeats
and Georgina Hyde-Lees
in the early days of
their marriage.

no one took seriously as messages, and no one believed
to come from spirits, since the majority of our friends
consigned spirits to heaven or hell, or an intermediate state
to await judgement, and a small but very superior minority
consigned to nothingness nowhere. I had annexed the
planchette ostensibly as a game, but privately treated it as
an accessory to our enquiry.

In our researches by means of the planchette, Gretta
became the medium, I the observer and recorder. We made
an ideal team. We soon learned that I was of no use on the
mechanical side of the operation: the lightest touch of my
finger would stop the movement of the board. We further
learned that the 'messages' came on the writing block from
the pencil fixed in one end of the small two-wheeled board
on which her right hand lightly rested, no more originated
in the instrument than did a poem in a pen or a drama of
Bernard Shaw's in the shorthand in which he composed it.
Any positive movement of her hand, or any weight beyond
the minimum need to move the planchette, broke the line
of communication. Physical comfort and passivity were the
external essentials of reception. The internal essential was
mental and emotional repose. There was no degree of trance
or renunciation of personal awareness; only a voluntary
cessation of active speculation. My share of the collaboration
was to note every circumstance that reflected light on our
central problem, whether or not demonstrably extraneous
consciousness could operate without the instrumentality
commonly taken to be necessary to it. Happily in this I had
the service of a quick and watchful mind, and a memory
that I had trained in earlier years to a high degree of
certainty and retentiveness, and my observations became

the subject of criticism when she had passed out of the state
of quiescence to her usual mental brightness.

Apart from much material of a metaphysical kind
that had its own literary and intellectual interest, and
prophecies on which we set no score, there were incidents
that indicated a will and intelligence beyond that of the
'medium'. The 'communicator' would stop in search of a
word. I would suggest one, Gretta another; the planchette
would write one different from and better than ours,
and thus impart a decided third-party feeling to the
occasion. Many times, when a communication was in
full flood, it would unexpectedly break off with 'No more
tonight'; the dynamic impulse that had worked vigorously
through Gretta's hand would, for no reason apparent to
us, and contrary to our wish, withdraw itself in a series of
weakening circles, and nothing that we could do would
bring it back. We were constantly on the watch for signs of
possible self-suggestion. Despite the eminent names and
offices of communicators of instructions in occult discipline,
or on the origin and content of the ancient Irish mythology,
we had in the back of our minds the possibility of such
communications being reflections of our interest in these
matters from some as yet unfamiliar stratum of Gretta's
consciousness, through much of the communications were
quite new to us. ■

PATRICK PEARSE

FORNOCHT DO CHONAC THÚ
NAKED I SAW THEE

(1912)

Pearse foresaw the eventual sacrifice of his life for his country in the Rising of 1916. His poem (with his own translation) projects the values of a revolutionary ascetic, renouncing love, family ties and sensual gratification: and it is this power over himself which allows him to claim authority over others. But the poem is also a sort of inversion of the old aisling (vision) conceit: rather than liberate the woman, the hero-poet turns away from her. Like Joseph Plunkett he will liberate her only with his death, which will (better than any material victory) be her ultimate liberation. The lyric grows sumptuous on denial and destitution, much as would the subsequent texts of Samuel Beckett, which also proceeded by a kind of negative theology through a series of renunciations to a self-narrated death.

Fornocht do chonac thú,
a áille na háille,
is do dhallas mo shúil
ar eagla go stánfainn.

Chualas do cheol,
a bhinne na binne,
is do dhúnas mo chluas
ar eagla go gclisfinn.

Bhlaiseas do bhéal
a mhilse na milse,
is do chruas mo chroí
ar eagla mo mhillte.

Dhallas mo shúil,
is mo chluas do dhúnas;
chruas mo chroí,
is mo mhian do mhúchas.

Thugas mo chúl
ar an aisling do chumas,
is ar an ród seo romham
m'aghaidh do thugas.

Thugas mo ghnúis
ar an ród seo romham,
ar an ngníomh a chím,
is ar an mbás do gheobhad.

Naked I saw thee,
O beauty of beauty,
And I blinded my eyes
For fear I should fail.

I heard thy music,
O melody of melody,
And I closed my ears
For fear I should falter.

I tasted thy mouth,
O sweetness of sweetness,
And I hardened my heart
For fear of weakening.

I blinded my eyes
And I closed my ears,
I hardened my heart
And I smothered my desire.

I turned my back
On the vision I had shaped
And to this road before me
I turned my face.

I have turned my face
To this road before me,
To the deed that I see
And the death I shall die.

FREDERICK RYAN—*from*:

'CHURCH DISESTABLISHMENT IN FRANCE AND IRELAND'

(1905)

Frederick Ryan had written his article in *Dana* of 1904 casting some doubt on whether the Gaelic League (by then remarkably popular) was a truly progressive force. His radical and secular philosophy led him to adopt a more internationalist position. When the government of France chose 1905 as the year in which the country would cease to define itself as a Catholic nation, opting instead for the neutrality of a secular space, Ryan went on the attack against Irish clerical critics of the new republican fervour in France. That country had in recent years been harshly divided by the Dreyfus ↗

F ANYONE PERUSES, even cursorily, the comments in the Irish Catholic press on the present political situation in France, he will obtain an interesting and instructive light on the consistency and spirit of justice which the clerical temper connotes. It is not more than a generation since Irish Catholics were loudly calling out for the disestablishment of the Irish Protestant Church. The arguments then used, quite legitimately, were that the Church ministered only to a section of the people, and that in any case it was wrong to take public monies for the endowment of particular creeds. The Irish Catholics were taxed to support a Church in which they did not believe, whilst supporting their own Church voluntarily, and they naturally and properly protested. And the doctrine then in favour in Ireland was that the State, as such, had no right to meddle with religion, which was a private affair that should derive its funds from the free offerings of its own children.

Now observe the case in France. The Catholic Church there is in much the same position as was the Protestant Church in Ireland. There are naturally some slight differences, with which I shall presently deal. But the broad fact remains that under the Concordat, the Church obtains public monies from the public purse; though, of course, she resents public control. For a long time, however, it has been obvious that great numbers of the French people have ceased to believe in this Church or to desire its ministrations. In addition to the large bodies of avowed freethinkers, there are in France vast numbers of indifferentists who resort to their parish church at times of marriage, at burials, and on other occasions of social ceremonial, but otherwise have no living belief in its mission. Between the condition of

the Protestant Church in Ireland and the Catholic Church
in France there are indeed striking resemblances.... Yet
when ... a politician proposes to do in France what, under
very similar circumstances was done by Gladstone in
Ireland, and put an end to a state supported Church, the
Irish Catholics who cheered on Gladstone abuse him as
vile and corrupt. Such, it is to be feared, is the measure of
Catholic and, for that matter, Protestant consistency. One
may fairly describe clerical ethics in the main by altering
the common tag: 'What is sauce for the goose is *never* sauce
for the gander.' Anyone, in fact, who desires a really sane
and really just outlook on any question of politics, especially
if it be one involving ecclesiastical affairs, must seek it
outside the official exponents of clericalism. Certainly, from
those exponents one never obtains anything more than the
enunciation of the commonplace policy of self-interest. In
Ireland at the present moment we see the purely sectarian
and impossible attitude which the ecclesiastical body as a
whole takes up on the University question, it being left to lay
commonsense to suggest any possible or practical scheme. If
the Church in France were anything like the moral exemplar
it is alleged to be, one might have imagined that it would
voluntarily refuse to accept funds collected by the secular
arm from taxpayers who stand outside its pale and only give
on the compulsion of the law. After all, when the Church
relies upon force, it cannot at the same time claim to be
ruling solely through the spirit. ∎

→ case, in which a Jewish
military officer was wrongly
imprisoned for disloyalty.
Irish Catholics had, of
course, gratefully accepted
the disestablishment of
the Anglican Church in
1869, so Ryan pointed to
the inner contradiction in
the thought of bishops
and priests who were
arguing against a similar
development in France.

FATHER MICHAEL O'RIORDAN—*from*:

CATHOLICITY AND PROGRESS IN IRELAND

(1905)

The journal *Dana* stood for unfettered debate and free speech. Some of its contributors, though critical of Catholic clericalism, were equally sardonic about Protestant values, questioning whether their application in Ireland had always been conducive to personal freedom or industrial enterprise. The Penal Laws against Catholics in the seventeenth and eighteenth centuries had hardly promoted democratic rights or sound business methods. Yet some contributors to the debate, notably Horace Plunkett in *Ireland in the New Century* (1904), argued that Catholicism, with its focus on the 'next world', had prevented people from developing agriculture and industry to anything like their full potential. This analysis went clean against the celebration of peasant ↗

THIS, THEN, IS the process of his [Plunkett's] reasoning. Individuality and self-reliance are necessary for industrial progress. But the reliance of Catholics on authority represses individuality, and checks self-reliance. Therefore, the religion of Roman Catholics is essentially an impediment to industrial progress. Moreover, industrial progress demands the development of the qualities of this life. But Catholicism completely shifts the moral centre of gravity to the other life. Hence the absence of those qualities in Catholics which makes for industrial progress.

Now, I might admit all that, and pass it by as being outside the business of the Catholic Church. Even though I granted that Catholicism is an obstacle to industrial progress, there would be no ground for complaint unless it professed, or ought to have professed, to promote the temporal interests of man....

The want which Sir Horace Plunkett finds in Catholicism, any Roman citizen would have found in the teaching of Christ. Any economist of old Rome might object that He made no provision for commercial enterprise, said nothing about the copper or corn trade in the Sermon on the Mount, in fact that His principles tended to tear up by the roots the very idea of Roman citizenship...

Modern times can show nothing to compare with the social work which Catholicism did in those days. Protestant nations started with the capital which Catholicism had made. No non-Catholic nation—neither of Protestantism which took its share and went its own way, like the Prodigal Son, nor of naturalism which is begotten of it, with the 'pig philosophy' which it picked up in its wanderings—has ever civilised itself from within, as the Christian Commonwealth of Europe arose from the bosom of the Catholic Church. How can any man, with such a history before him, think of doubting that the tendency of Catholicism is to human progress? No modern instances of national decadence can disprove the evidence of a thousand years. I am now neither admitting nor denying that decadence; but, in any case, the social structure which Catholicism had raised out of ruins and rubbish is a *fact* which should make us seek some other cause than Catholicism for that decadence.

It may be said to me that the moral and divine law, or the Catholic Church which I suppose to be their official interpreter, have nothing to do with politics or economics: I reply—with politics or economics as such, certainly not. But, may Parliament then justly revive the Penal Laws, make laws of distributive injustice, legalise a system of slavery by which human beings may be bought and sold and become the property of their purchaser? Is an economic system right which sanctions usury, or finds a place for trusts and monopolies which place the public at the mercy of a grinding industrialism? If not, why not? What is the criterion according to which they are wrong? Not surely the politics or the economics which sanction them. Then we must seek the source of their injustice in a higher law, namely, the moral and the divine, whose official interpreter is the Church of Christ. It will be asked, what has the Gospel of Christ to do with factories or the Stock Exchange? I reply, no more than a professor of mathematics has to do with the building of railway bridges, or a professor of chemistry with the sowing of potatoes or oats, and yet, let a railway bridge be built

→ virtue in much Revival writing, but Plunkett's credentials in making the point were telling, since he was a successful leader of the Co-Operative Movement. Father Michael O'Riordan's book, *Catholicity and Progress in Ireland* (1905), provided an answer. Born in Limerick in 1857, O'Riordan studied in Rome and became rector of the Irish College there in 1905. From this influential post he engaged in many controversies concerning education, science and the Revival itself, before his death in 1919.

irrespective of the principles taught in mathematics, and it will be shattered and broken down by the first goods train that passes over it; let potatoes or oats be sown in a soil not suited to them, and the crop will be a failure. In like manner, society, either in its political or economic action, cannot go on irrespective of the moral and divine law.

We must not identify human or social progress with mere material or industrial progress. They are quite separable, and are often found apart. They are neither necessarily opposed nor necessarily united. One is found without the other, for instance, in the millionaire who has no higher notion than making money, and he makes it; whose highest aspirations are on a level with the luxury which wealth can minister.

I have already pointed out the mistake which Sir Horace Plunkett has made in representing the Catholic Church as 'completely shifting the moral centre of gravity to the future existence.' I now recall his argument, that its reliance on authority is an impediment to progress, inasmuch as it checks initiative and self-reliance.

If reliance on authority be a check to individual initiative and an obstacle to progress, how is progress possible at all? Authority is an essential element in every society. It is authority which gives unity and stability to society and is the safeguard of the liberty of its members. Society is the offspring of human intelligence and liberty. Civil authority unifies millions of individuals of different personal interests and passions, and makes them act with common national interest and purpose. It guards the rights and liberties of each, protecting each from the injustice or the despotism of the selfish and strong. Any society, from a municipal corporation to a nation, is simply inconceivable without an authority to rule it.

Every Catholic knows, unless those 'Catholics' who are outside everything Catholic except the name, that he is as free as air in all his political and economic, in his temporal activities and relations of all sorts, as long as he does not run counter to the teaching or discipline of that Church which he believes to have been instituted by Christ to expound the moral and divine Law, and to guard their observance by the necessary discipline of life. And the doctrine and discipline of the Catholic Church gives every member of it plenty of scope for all the economic activity he wishes to put forth. ■

'We must not identify human or social progress with mere material or industrial progress.'

ELIZABETH BURKE-PLUNKETT—*from*:

SEVENTY YEARS YOUNG

(1937)

Elizabeth Burke was born in Moycullen, County Galway in 1866 and married Arthur Plunkett, Earl of Fingall and one of the few Catholic peers in Ireland. She was a co-founder of Horace Plunkett's Co-Operative Movement and first president of the Irish Countrywomen's Association, but was also a keen supporter of theatrical and suffragist movements. Despite remaining a life-long unionist she became a president of the Irish Camogie Association. She was an advocate for native industries and this work brought her into contact with the Irish Sisters of Charity who ran the Foxford Woollen Mills in County Mayo. In the following passage, which may be a coded answer to ↗

ONE OF OUR expeditions was to Foxford in the County Mayo, for the Connacht Exhibition, organised by that great woman and wonderful Sister of Charity, Mother Morrogh Bernard. She had built up at Foxford, within a few years, an industry that, with its many offshoots and wide embracing roof of Christian charity, was like a guild of the Middle Ages. The Exhibition was designed primarily to advertise the woollen goods being produced at the Foxford mills. But the side sections indicated the width and imagination of Mother Morrogh Bernard's work in her district for the better living, towards which we were all, in our different ways, trying to help the people. There were prizes for gardening, domestic science, poultry, dairy products, even for the most humble and necessary trade of mending. The great business woman, who was responsible for all this, forgot nothing, organised everything. And then, when the grand party of influential people whom she had collected to assist her travelled to the County Mayo for the Exhibition, she hid herself away as she always did on such occasions.

The net of this great little nun was as wide as her charity and the most surprising people got caught in it and were safely landed on the Foxford shore—where they might sometimes have been surprised to find themselves!

When she had first thought of establishing the Providence Woollen Mills on the Moy River, which should work under the eye of God and by direction of the Sisters of Charity, she had written to the man who, she was told, could help her more than any other man in Ireland, for his advice. That man happened to be Mr. Smith of the Caledon Mills, Tyrone, who replied to her letter: 'Madam! Are you aware that you have written to a Protestant and a Freemason?'

I do not know Mother Morrogh Bernard's answer. But
in due course the Protestant and Freemason travelled at
his own expense to Foxford, was met at the station by the
parish priest and his curate and accompanied to the convent.
Having surveyed the proposed site and gone into other
details, he advised Mother Morrogh Bernard to abandon her
scheme. When that had no effect he placed himself 'and his
twenty-years experience at her disposal.' He kept his word.
And what a good alliance—the Protestant Freemason from
the North and the Southern Catholic nun, both filled with
the same spirit of charity.

Her courage was unwavering—'always a wonderful
champion of the poor and outcast,' writes one of her sister
nuns,—her justice absolute. There had been an incident during
the height of the fever following the Parnell divorce case and
split. Some employees of the Woollen Mills had hissed the local
priests at a political demonstration, and the Bishop's orders were
conveyed to the Reverend Mother. The men were to be dismissed.
She refused. She could not excuse the men for what they had
done, she said. But neither could she dismiss them. She gave her
reasons to her own superior authority. Politics had no place in
their industry. The Sisters of Charity had no politics. She had left
all that in the world. If she allowed the men to be dismissed it
would mean—that like so many other things in Ireland—politics
would enter the mills disastrously. It would come in time that
only those of a certain way of thinking need apply. She stood firm.
A second request came from the Bishop. She refused. But she
guaranteed an apology from the men and read it herself in public
on a Sunday morning, standing between the two priests who had
been insulted. Her first and last public appearance. The following
Sunday, the Bishop came and said Mass at the convent. ▪

→ her friend Plunkett's
strictures on Catholicism,
she praises the pragma-
tism and independent-
mindedness of the nuns,
as well as their diplomatic
skills. She died in 1944.

JOHN EGLINTON—*from*:

'THE WEAK POINT OF THE CELTIC MOVEMENT'

(1905)

John Eglinton believed that the literary renaissance provided an opportunity for debate not only between Catholic and Protestant but also between clergy and laity within all denominations. The tendency of most writers to take a position 'above the fray' struck him as a form of intellectual cowardice. Yet Horace Plunkett had received a cool enough response for articulating a rather Protestant critique of what he saw as Catholic stoicism and resignation to poverty. By way of contrast, the popularity of a Protestant intellectual like Douglas Hyde, who went out of his way to placate Catholic priests, was soaring. Nationalist Ireland, through the nineteenth century, had often gladly submitted to leadership by charismatic Protestants from Davis to Parnell, but generally on the implicit condition that no religious issues be raised—the ⟶

PERHAPS ONE OF the most genuine signs of the new awakening in Irish life of late is the recrudescence among us of religious bigotry. That we are a little behind the times in this respect is a subject about which we must make up our minds to be chaffed by foreign visitors, as well as by our own countrymen who return out of the dazzling enlightenment of the twentieth century in the United States and elsewhere, to find us here just emerging out of the seventeenth century. We make a mistake in not taking up the intellectual history of our country at the point where it was stereotyped by the Battle of the Boyne, and in recommending tolerance prematurely, and so perhaps destroying the potentialities of a really promising because spontaneous religious situation.

If our fathers thought these questions worth killing each other for, we surely need not mind a few nasty personal insinuations being made about us. We do wrong, then, to neglect what may be called the doctrinaire side of the Celtic renaissance, for, rightly considered, the advantage we have in this country lies in the practically inexhaustible reservoir of intellectual energy which may be generated in an effort to bring Ireland into the inheritance of liberating ideas. What would be thought of an English or French literature which professed a lofty unconcern with national religious movements? Yet in Ireland we are asked to believe in the nationality of a literature of which the main canon is that it must not give offence by any too direct utterance on the central problem of Irish life— the religious situation. The only chance, one is tempted to think, which the Celtic school has of becoming really national, and ceasing to be merely a sodality of ladies and gentlemen, of more or less Irish extraction, with an amiable penchant for writing verses and tales, lies in bringing thought and criticism to bear on that 'religious question' which meets us at every turn in Ireland. Our litterateurs should not be content to witness these brawls between parish priests and colporteurs, these mobbings of street preachers, or the closing of the Protestant ranks against a Catholic association, without stepping down, like the Greek gods, from their Olympus, and championing their favourites. It is only in those countries whose writers concern themselves with popular movements that, on the one hand, national thought is raised to a higher plane, and, on the other, that the history of literature is woven in with the history of the nation.

It is said indeed, why try to disturb the beliefs of the people? Or, is it plain that Ireland is going to remain a Catholic country whatever you may do. But this is only the petulance of that indifferentism of which we complain, or perhaps sometimes of the literary artist annoyed at any threatened disturbance in the pose of his model. What lies before humanity, whether in this island or the world at large, no one can prophesy, but we may feel pretty sure that the acquisition of Christianity, real or nominal, has not exhausted the potentialities of development in any intelligent branch of the human race.

Every nation has, from time to time, to throw over its Jonahs, and sometimes, it is true, pitch on the wrong victim. The Russian bureaucracy, for example, have thrown out the Stundists and the Jews, yet foul weather continues, and the workers at the oar of the Russian ship of state begin to

→ destruction of Parnell when the question of his private life convulsed the country seemed confirmation of the wisdom of that approach. So Eglinton was asking for a lot. Many Revival debates would eventually take the form of controversies within the Protestant communities, north and south, as to what form self-election and self-determination might ideally take—but these debates only became clear years after Eglinton's plea and especially in the wake of the Ulster Covenant of 1912.

cast determined eyes on what they suspect to be the true Jonah. In France they have thrown out the religious orders. In Ireland we have lately thrown out landlordism, and yet, after a century of mutinous discontent with landlordism, we are surprised to find that its abolition has made very little difference in Irish life. Perhaps we shall only discover the true Jonah experimentally, that is to say, when the crew of the Irish ship of state assumes command of its own vessel, and then Jonah, like the gentleman he is, will, no doubt, be the first to suggest what should be done with him.

Meanwhile it is clear that, however odious they may be, theological questions count for nearly as much in Ireland now as in seventeenth century, and that the new literary movement, if it would make itself 'national', must not quite ignore the fact. ■

'Yet in Ireland we are asked to believe in the nationality of a literature of which the main canon is that it must not give offence by any too direct utterance on the central problem of Irish life—the religious situation.'

The Wider World

THE IDEA OF 'Ireland' was invented not only at home but across the world. Being islanders, the Irish could have been forgiven for thinking themselves unique, like no other race on earth: but the tradition of migration to other lands encouraged comparison and study. There had always been a link in the popular mind between writing and exile: Saint Colmcille had, after all, been banished in the sixth century for copying a sacred book. In subsequent centuries missionaries from the Island of Saints and Scholars had spread across Europe, founding centres of prayer and learning. Again, after the defeat of Gaelic princes at Kinsale in 1601, exiled writers such as Seathrún Céitinn (Geoffrey Keating) studied at continental seminaries and universities, Europeanising the Gaelic tradition in all kinds of new ways.

By the later nineteenth century, German and French scholars had defined the outlines of a Celtic identity. In the same years emigrants to the United States, encountering the culture of Poles and Italians, began by reflex to sketch what values a modern Irish nation could embody. If exile was the cradle of nationality, they would (as Benedict Anderson has suggested in a striking image) take a white-on-black negative photograph based on these vitalising contacts, before bringing the process back home to print the positive in the dark-room of cultural and political struggle.

The United States provided the example of a successful young republic. Yeats, as early as the 1890s, was already creating himself as a national bard by sedulous imitation of Walt Whitman as much as by modelling himself on the Gaelic filí. France also provided a crucible in which elements of a modernised Irish identity might be forged. If Synge rediscovered elements of Latin Quarter anarchism on the Aran Islands, then Yeats himself could shape his own anti-naturalist dramas at the Abbey Theatre along Parisian lines. Nor did the leaders of the Revival confine themselves to these more obvious points of reference. If James Joyce took inspiration from the Norwegian Ibsen, or Arthur Griffith from the political example of Hungary, then the young Patrick Pearse could find on a visit to Belgian schools a child-centred form of bilingual schooling which might point the way ahead.

Such comparisons, though challenging, had a derivative aspect. Ultimately, however, the Revivalists wished to self-invent, to derive finally from themselves. The years of being an imitation-England had led Ireland down a cul-de-sac: now the people decided to become metropolitan and interesting to themselves. The result was that Revival Ireland soon became a model for other peoples—in fact, a test-case of the modern—whose leaders sought 'alternative modernities' beyond the reach of imperial systems. Intellectuals overseas began to read into Ireland a version of their own ideal aspiration—religious conservatives saw a spiritual nation, while political radicals identified a rebel paradise. French and German commentators repeatedly celebrated the avant-garde qualities of Irish art. In India intellectuals looked for example to the insurgents of 1916 and to the writings of Yeats, and the Irish reciprocated—their sailors carried secret messages in transcontinental ships for Indian insurgents, and the Friends of the Freedom of India were featured at St. Patrick's Day celebrations in New York. The colonial-servant-turned-rebel Roger Casement, in his speeches and texts before his execution in 1916, defined notions of human rights which would eventually be enshrined in the charter of the United Nations. The critique of empire offered by Revival writers had a world-historical dimension. The Irish were the first English-speaking people in the twentieth century to decolonise, the first to walk in darkness and bafflement down what would become a much more familiar road.

MAUD GONNE AND THE BOER WAR—*from*:

A SERVANT OF THE QUEEN

(1938)

T HE BOER WAR was on. 'England's difficulty is Ireland's opportunity.' How often I had heard those words! I was determined to put them into acts.

Though Cecil Rhodes was distributing fortunes in the lobbies of the House of Commons chiefly in the form of Stock Exchange advice, the Irish parliamentary party were pro-Boer.

The *United Irishman* started a vigorous campaign. Griffith had worked with John MacBride in the Langlaarte mine in the Transvaal until homesickness brought him back to Ireland. He wrote well-informed articles under different pseudonyms and in different styles. Few knew that they came from the same pen.

It was in this year that I at last succeeded in founding Inghinidhe na hÉireann (the Daughters of Ireland).

I called a meeting of all the girls who, like myself, resented being excluded as women from national organisations. Our object was to work for the complete independence of Ireland.

Willie Rooney and Arthur Griffith helped us; the sisters of both and Willie Rooney's fiancée, Maire Kileen, were on the committee. Among others were Mary, Bridget and Julia Maher, Marcella Cosgrave, Maggie Quinn, Mary Macken, while Mary Quinn became our very active and efficient secretary.

Besides organising free classes in history, the Irish language, music and dancing for children, we started an intense campaign against enlistment in the British army. To make recruiting easier, the Army authorities altered their rule of obliging the men to sleep in barracks, and O'Connell Street at night used to be full of redcoats walking with their girls. We got out leaflets on the shame of Irish girls consorting with the soldiers of the enemy of their country

Maud Gonne had studied in a French boarding school, where she developed a patriotic conviction that the country must recapture Alsace-Lorraine, lost to Germany in 1870-1. She was soon also supporting jailed leaders of Irish nationalism. In 1889 she met W.B. Yeats, who fell deeply in love with her—but she did not reciprocate. She became instead the consort of the conservative French politician Lucien Millevoye and the mother of two children by him. Drawn ever further into Irish agitation, she organised protests against the English Queen Victoria's jubilee celebrations in 1897. She founded the radical women's society Inghinidhe na hÉireann (Daughters of Ireland) in 1900. She became fascinated by Major John MacBride, who led the Transvaal brigade against the British, fighting for →

→ the Boers against
annexation of their land.
A close collaborator with
Arthur Griffith, Gonne
encouraged his writing
in support of the Boers.
Having converted to
Roman Catholicism
in 1902, she married
MacBride a year later.
The couple had one son,
Sean. MacBride was
executed for participation
in the Easter Rising.
Gonne's autobiography,
A Servant of the Queen
(1938) vividly recalls,
among much else, her
work with Griffith and
MacBride during the
Boer War.

and used to distribute them to the couples in the streets, with the result that almost every night there were fights in O'Connell Street, for the brothers and the sweethearts of Inghinidhe na hÉireann used to come out also to prevent us being insulted by the English soldiers and the ordinary passers-by often took our side. The Dublin police were slow to interfere, for we managed to get some clergymen to denounce the danger to the morals of young innocent working girls consorting with the military, and persuaded the Dublin Guardians to raise the question of illegitimate babies in the workhouses, for which there was enough justification to make it unwise for Dublin Castle to allow cases where such issues would get publicity in the police courts. Fighting soldiers became quite a popular evening entertainment with young men, in which Arthur Griffith and Mary Quinn's brother used to take part—though Griffith I think hated it. Our girls used bravely to follow the recruiting sergeants even into the public houses, distributing thousands of leaflets written by a courageous priest, the Rev. Father Cavanagh of Limerick, setting forth Catholic teaching to the effect that anyone taking part in a war, knowing it to be unjust, and killing anybody, was guilty of murder.

'Have you notes on the work of the Brigade?' Griffith asked. 'I want them for the *United Irishman* and you had better prepare a lecture, for you will have to lecture in America.'

'You will have to write the lecture for me, then,' he answered.'

It was so late that it was not worthwhile for MacBride to go to his lodgings, so he shared Griffith's bed. Next

morning, seated at my writing table, Griffith wrote the
lecture, supplementing the sparse notes from MacBride's
memory. I sat in an armchair, smoking cigarettes and
listening. It was great to hear of Irishmen actually fighting
England. The capture of General Buller's guns near the
Tugeela was thrilling; the capture of English officers
delighted me; the English have imprisoned so many
Irishmen that it was good at last to have it the other
way round.

'I hope you treated your prisoners decently to give them
a good example and show how much more civilised we are
than they?'

'Yes,' said MacBride. 'We took possession of their arms,
but we fed them well, same as ourselves, and they thanked
us and said it was the fortune of war when we handed them
over to the Boers, who treat their prisoners quite well in the
prison camps near Pretoria. They had quite a lot of English
prisoners, a tremendous lot of Irishmen among them. I
wanted Kruger to let me pick some of these to join the
Brigade. A lot of these Irish lads would have gladly joined;
some of them told me they had let themselves get captured
in the hope of joining us, but old Kruger wouldn't allow it—
said it was not done. The Boers are queer people; they may
not have trusted them, though I said I would be answerable
for them.'

I told him of the scenes I had witnessed in Limerick
when the police were rounding up militia men for the war
and putting them on the boats in handcuffs, and I showed
him our leaflet with Father Cavanagh's words on Catholic
teaching and the sin in taking part in an unjust war. 'We got
these well circulated among the Irish regiments.'

John laughed: 'Well, a good many deserted and if Kruger had only consented we would have had the Brigade up to full strength.'

I felt that little band of Irishmen in the Brigade had done more for Ireland's honour than all of us at home, for it is action that counts. MacBride said the flag sent out by Inghinidhe na hÉireann had been greatly appreciated.

'We had it up at our camp and at night I often saw one or other of our lads go up and kiss its folds. When the fighting got livelier we had to send it back with the rest of our belongings to a man in Johannesburg to keep it safe for us.'

Years after, when the fighting was on for the Republic in Ireland, I got a letter from a man called Burke in the Transvaal, asking if he should send me the flag of the Brigade, but as all the Republican houses were then being constantly raided by the Free State soldiers, I felt it would not be safe and wrote asking him to keep it a little longer. When things were quieter, I wrote to him to send it to me, but never received an answer.

People said the Boer War was nearing its end. De Wet and President Steyn of the Orange Free State were still gallantly holding their own. President Kruger was in Europe, making a vain appeal for belated assistance. The German Emperor, probably from family feelings for his grandmother Victoria, refused to allow him to go to Berlin. I loved the French people for the magnificent reception they accorded him. However pro-English the French government might be, it could not stand against the tremendous surge of popular enthusiasm, but the great welcome was from the people and hardly official. Cheering crowds thronged the boulevards and stood all day round the Grand Hotel where he was staying. It was with difficulty that I and a few members of the Paris Young Ireland Society pushed our way through to present the address from Ireland. Some French students recognised me and cheers for Ireland mingled with the cheers for the Boer Republics and way was made for us.

President Kruger was a tragic, broken-hearted old man, with rugged dignity. He looked very weary. He put his hand on my shoulder, as he took the scroll on which the address was written, and kept me near him awhile though the rooms were crowded with delegations waiting to present addresses. He said:

'The Irish have proved their sympathy by fighting for us. The Irish Commando has done fine work.'

I answered: 'There are thousands of Irishmen waiting to get out and join.'

He shook his head: 'It is a different kind of war now. No more big battles; only guerrilla war; to be of use men must know the country and speak our language, but we will wear the English down, we will not give in.'

A year later the peace of Vereeniging was signed and two years later President Steyn, slowly recovering in Paris from a paralytic stroke due to the terrible hardships of the campaign, told me:

'Thank God this hand of mine was paralysed so I could not sign that treaty; when I signed the order for the Orange Free State to go into the war I was very sad, knowing the suffering it would entail on our people, but I was far sadder when that peace treaty was signed, for I knew then that if we had held out a little longer—and we could have done it—we would have won. De Wet was a great general; he would have worn the British out.'

Some months later in Dublin, I got a letter from MacBride. He was returning to France and asked me to meet him in Paris. He had asked me to marry him in America and I had replied that marriage was not in my thoughts while there was a war on and there was always an Irish war on. I feared it might be that personal reason that was bringing him to France, but I hoped there might be a more interesting reason. When I met him he was very disheartened. The Boer Was was almost over and, except for the Irish Brigade and Luke Dillon's gallant attempt on the Welland Canal, Ireland had done nothing.

'What are you going to do in Paris?' I asked him.

'Earn my living, I suppose,' he answered, and 'wait for the chance of a fight.' ■

W.B. YEATS IN AMERICA—*interview*:

'WE ARE UNLIKE THE ENGLISH IN ALL EXCEPT LANGUAGE'

(1904)

A tour of the United States became a frequent rite of passage in the period for political leaders in search of funding or for artists in need of recognition and support. Oscar Wilde had gone there while still a very young man, achieving immediate fame by his exotic lecturing style and clever manipulation of newspaper reporters. He soon learned how to appeal in speeches to the sympathies of Irish-Americans. In 1882, after the killing of government officials in the Phoenix Park, he said that England was 'reaping the fruit of seven centuries of injustice.' Wilde was followed on American tours by Douglas Hyde and Patrick Pearse (who praised the egalitarian teacher-student relationship in American classrooms), and later ↗

I MUST SAY that I shall leave this great country and its hospitable people with sincere regret. The warmth of the welcome given me wherever I went—and I have covered a good deal of ground during the three months I have been here, going as far west as the Pacific coast—has far outstripped anything I could have hoped for or had a right to hope for. I landed a total stranger I may say, and I go back to my beloved Dublin feeling as though I had known America and Americans all my life.

The only similarity between Americans and Englishmen that I have been enabled to discover is that they speak the same language. For the rest, they are as unlike as any two peoples you can think of. Their habits of thought, their forms of expressions, their shops, their methods of travel, their hotels, their homes, the clothes they wear, the food they eat, the current of daily talk, the newspapers they print by the million, and scan with such devouring assiduity—all, all remind one of America and of no other country under the sun. Solid, massive and splendid surely is this republic. And it is unique at the same time.

While standing alone as a whole, certain phases of life in America bear a marvellous resemblance to those of her great sister republic of France. The enthusiasm of the two peoples is very much alike. The American has an imagination not alone lively but palpable as well—exactly as has the Frenchman, and he has unrestrained enthusiasm at the proper moment. This I feel impelled at times to describe as a God-given inheritance.

An American not alone sees the point , but also seizes the point of an argument with lightning speed, or, to use one of your own clever phrases, 'quick as a wink'. You don't need to draw a diagram to furnish him with a key to a joke which, I am afraid, is more or less the case in the land where the Saxon dwells. The American may jump to conclusions now and again, it is true, but his conclusions are in the main correct, being based, for the most part, like those of the French and Irish, on natural impulse rather than the crabbed waywardness of conventional laws. And so, as I've heard New Yorkers often declare, he 'gets there every time.'

Well, good luck to him, I say! The great interest in education has surprised me more than all else. In England, the cultivated class is, in the main, confined to London, and those who compose it are by no means numerous. I found it different in America, where you have, not one, but many centres of thought diffused throughout the land—New York, Philadelphia, Boston, Chicago, Baltimore, Washington, Indianapolis, St. Paul, St. Louis, and San Francisco.

And how wonderful are your seats of learning—and as numerous as they are wonderful. Indeed, it was inspiring to witness all this. How generous, too, appear the rich among you in supporting these institutions, vying with each other in their lavish distribution of money both in cash and endowments.

And what a democratic spirit is over all! The president of the republic I found less pretentious than many a little village Dogberry of an English official in Ireland, who sits on a tuppenny throne. Mr. Roosevelt has a fine memory and a fine mind, and is I should judge, an omnivorous reader.

Much of the poetry written by women here I would describe as organised sentiment. The women themselves—and I have met many types in many places—are adorable and inspiring. It is a delight to talk to them and a happiness little less than enduring to hear them talk. I hope to renew my recollections of all this by making a return visit to the United States at no distant day. ∎

→ by politicians such as de Valera. Yeats's first speaking tour of great cities lasted from November 1903 until March 1904. Just before departure, he was interviewed by a journalist from the *New York Daily News* on 4 March. The reporter captured the poet's ideas but 'translated' them into a 'breezy American style'.

JOHN EGLINTON ('OSSORIAN')
to SIR HORACE PLUNKETT—*from*:

'THE IRISH IN AMERICA'

(1904)

John Eglinton spent
some months in New
York and St. Louis, which
he wrote up for *Dana* in
October 1904. Horace
Plunkett, who had
extensive experience of the
co-operative movement
among homesteaders in
Wyoming, was curious
to learn what opinions
Eglinton had formed on
his visit, and whether
they corresponded with
Plunkett's own analysis
offered in *Ireland in the
New Century*. Eglinton
formulated these in an
'open letter' to Plunkett.
He praised the energy,
ambition and success of
Irish-Americans, while
seeking to explain their
relative reticence in
the political and literary
spheres by reference
to their Catholicism. ↗

My Dear Sir Horace Plunkett,...

You are right, I think, in saying that the Irish have not signally
distinguished themselves as politicians, in the higher sense of
the term. They have not as yet been leaders of thought in that
sphere. They hardly could, in a country whose institutions
are so essentially Protestant as those of America. But the
things they have done, and done well, seemed to me to bulk
much bigger than those they have not. Instead of the curse
of unsuccess pursuing them into America, it appeared to
me that in crossing the Atlantic they did really, to a great
extent, leave it behind them, and that there is a great deal
of justification for the popular view as to what their history
in America reveals about Ireland and Irish problems. The
career of the Irish race in America (using, as I mean to do,
the word 'Irish' in the special sense in which it is used in your
book) is a very big subject indeed, and is full of features of the
deepest interest for the student of sociology, ethnology, etc.
Moreover, it is one which, so far as I know, no one has ever
attempted to handle in a philosophic and critical spirit. Your
own references to it are slight and few—they form merely a
subordinate feature in one of your chapters, and are of course
not to be taken as a full account of your views on the subject.
But I think it might have been better not to treat of it at all
unless you were in a position to do so more adequately, and to
give at least a broad outline picture of the whole range of facts.
As it is, it seems to me that even if every individual sentence
of yours could be defended—and perhaps it might—the total
effect is misleading—much is left untouched that goes to the
make-up of the Irish in America, and prominence is given to
elements which count for less in reality than they seem to in
your book.

I have not noticed any great distinction, as you appear to do, between the Irish who emigrate to the United States of America and those born in the States of Irish parentage. In both cases I am quite unable to resist the impression of an elastic human force released from some external pressure and springing at once into its natural position. *The Irishman finds his level in the States,* and it seems to me impossible to deny—in spite of the criminal statistics on which I shall touch later on—that this is, on the whole, a far higher level than he reaches at home. I do not see him confined to any one field of distinction. He is to be found at the head of affairs in finance, organisation of labour, management of business concerns, law, journalism, and of course political campaigning. Perhaps literature is the field in which he is least in evidence, and here, no doubt, his religion stands in the way. An important Catholic literature, in days when literature means an attempt to sound the depths of moral and social problems long ago dogmatically settled, or open to dogmatic settlement, by the Church, seems hardly possible. But elsewhere he seems to me fully to hold his own in the States, and to contribute to them some of their very best elements. I have met Irishmen, natives of Ireland and American-born, who have verified the highest ideal one could form of the ennobling influence of freedom and equality, and who have raised my idea of human nature.

The case I am about to refer to is not exactly one of these, but it is very typical and it seems, as we shall see, to lead us straight to the heart of the Irish problem.

Larry Harrigan was Chief of Police in St. Louis before the present very able occupant of that post, also an Irishman named Kiely. In Harrigan's time St. Louis was one of the

→ Catholics, he feared, were still suspect in a white Anglo-Saxon Protestant polity (though this was already beginning to change as he wrote). Plunkett in his reply questioned whether the Anglo-Irish ascendancy were still the blockage to native enterprise of which Eglinton continued to complain. Plunkett argued shrewdly that the energies which now animated Irish-Americans might, by a sort of back-formation, help in turn to unleash a phase of social and cultural confidence in Ireland.

'toughest' towns in the United States. The east and the west met there—forgers and swindlers learned the ways of desperadoes. Harrigan was picked out to cope with this state of things. He was a man of genius in his way, and a man born to command and lead. He had endless fertility of resource and dauntless courage. He attacked gang after gang of criminals and broke them up. On one occasion, in getting on the track of an association of counterfeiters, he had a running fight with four men who attempted his life, and he killed every one of them. During his tenure of office I am told that no less than sixteen criminals fell by Harrigan's own hand. This will give an idea of the sort of situation he had to deal with, but in the end law and order came to the top in St. Louis, and it was Larry Harrigan who put them there, as the citizens gratefully remember.

I do not of course refer to this career in order to show how the Irish succeed in the States, but because it seems to throw a ray of light on the position of the Irish at home. Harrigan began life as a shoemaker in the town of Tipperary. Just think what his probable career would have been if he had stayed in Ireland! What is the sort of social outlook that would present itself to the eyes of Larry Harrigan, shoemaker, of Tipperary? I think it very doubtful if law and order would have found a champion in him. His natural abilities would have probably made him a man of mark in some more or less limited sphere, but barriers very strong, though invisible on the surface of things, would have kept him from rising to any position of dignity and usefulness such as he occupied in the States. The Ascendancy, who represent the combined force, the concentrated exclusiveness and bigotry, of a social caste, a political party,

a religion, and a race, are in possession of the strong places
in Ireland, not only in the public service, but also, owing
to the action of the penal laws, in commerce, industry, and
education. The moment Harrigan began to rise in Ireland
he would have come into the atmosphere of this class, and it
would have repelled him. 'This is no place for me', he would
have felt, and they would have felt the same about him. It is
not easy for a man of the class and type of Larry Harrigan to
avoid feeling himself in Ireland either a helot or a rebel.

Compare this with the reception which America gave
him, judging him simply on his merits, and the career which,
on that basis, it opened to him. We get by such a comparison
a vivid conception of one at least of the great forces which
keep down the Irishman in Ireland. It is that stiff, coagulated
crust in Irish social life which we call the Ascendancy.
Abolished long ago in law, it is mighty to the present day in
practical life, and just as surely as in the days of the Wild
Geese, when it worked by legal proscription, it sends the
flower of the Irish race to give their best qualities to the
service of another country wherein many important respects
they are more truly 'at home' than in their own.

I do not suppose that you by any means ignore in your
own thought the existence of this repressive force, but you do
not give it in your book anything like the recognition which it
seems to me it ought to have in any survey of the conditions
of Irish life and progress. This crust has got to be thoroughly
dissolved, broken up, done away with in one fashion or
another before the Irishman in Ireland can come to his own.

There is another crust which has also to be broken up
and that is the crust of mental apathy and inertness which
has spread over a great mass of the people. To this feature

you have given, and rightly, a good deal of notice, and probably one of the best results of your book, as more than one Irish-American reader has said to me, is that it will help powerfully to break up this crust and to make way for the passage of thought. But you have not noticed the extent to which the Irish-American mind is free from it. Undoubtedly the Roman Catholic Church or its representatives in Ireland are the main power in keeping this crust of inertia intact. The Cardinal who recently told his people that he felt obliged to warn them against your book because he had read a letter in the papers from a parish priest who objected to it, was helping to put another layer to that crust, and so does everyone who tries to substitute vituperation for thought, or authority for argument. Now, whether the Irish in America are really less Catholic than the Irish at home is a question I have no means of answering, but unquestionably they are far less 'clerical'. A prelate in the United States who should warn his flock in a pastoral address against a serious book by an eminent public man—one notorious too for his sympathy with Catholic claims—and tell them plainly that he had not thought it worthwhile to read the book, but judged it solely on the evidence of a stupid and violent letter written to the papers by some obscure cleric, would excite no feeling but one of amazement or ridicule. He simply *could* not do such a thing—it would never occur to him to treat the Irish-American laity with such contempt, such a reckless straining of authority as this episode implies, and if it did, they would very soon find means to bring him to his senses.

In fact, if it were possible to sum up the whole question in a sentence, I should say that all my observations point to

one conclusion, namely that the Irish at home are living in
an abnormal condition, and are hemmed in by forces which
leave them scarcely any opportunity for natural growth
and expansion. In America they are free and if many go
downwards, there is more assurance and more significance
in the fact that so many rise. In Ireland, whatever some may
hope and others fear there seems little doubt that an era of
the loosening of bonds in all directions has set in. The results
may not be wholly admirable, but the process means life, and
if it is checked the nation will die. That your book will help
the Irish people to a fuller and worthier life is a conviction
of mine which of course you will understand is in no way
weakened by the American observations, of which I have
tried to give you some brief account in this letter.

I am, my dear Sir Horace,
Yours faithfully,
Ossorian

from: SIR HORACE PLUNKETT
to JOHN EGLINTON

My Dear Ossorian,

Thanks for your 'open letter' which you are quite welcome to
publish if you so desire....

In my study of the dominant influences upon the Irish mind
and character at home I could not omit politics. My main
contention was that political agitation, while essential to
legislative reform, was carried on in Ireland in a manner

calculated to suppress independent political thought. It
is commonly said that the pre-eminent services of our
countrymen to the political life of the great Republic
demonstrate that they are not lacking in the qualities of
statesmanship, but only in the opportunity for their display.
My object was, of course, here, as in every other part of
my argument to put in a plea for social and economic
work, under existing conditions at home, and to deprecate
the sacrifice of all progress to the ideal of a political
millennium. In this connection I gave it as the result of my
own experience, observation, and reflection that, taking
the mass and not the brilliant exceptions into account, our
countrymen have not themselves profited by their politics,
nor made any important contribution to the political thought
of the United States, but, on the contrary that their too
great addiction to that pursuit has handicapped them in the
less exciting paths where nations find the surest means to
material, social and even political advancement. Compared
with what he could have done at home, the success of the
Irish immigrant is great, especially when full account is taken
of the depressing conditions which led to the expatriation of
vast numbers of them. I regard the relative unimportance
of the Irish factor in the pending presidential campaign
as a sign of growth of their real power. Viewed in relation
to the record of other immigrants, and of their own moral,
intellectual, and physical qualities, the question whether the
Irish-American record is all that it might have been, remains
for your philosophic critic to decide. I personally feel that
the Irishman is only now beginning to 'find his level in the
United States,' and that when he has found it there will set in
a reflex action which will help him to find it in Ireland.

Another very interesting feature in your letter is the deductions you draw from the career of Larry Harrigan. You are quite right in saying that the moment he began to rise in Ireland he would have felt 'this is no place for me.' His 'endless fertility of resource and dauntless courage' would have availed him little as soon as he went beyond his last. Probably before he had accounted for one of his sixteen desperadoes the minions of the law would have checked his further usefulness. But I wonder it did not occur to so agile and brilliant an imagination as yours that a moral Larry Harrigan is just what we most need in Ireland at the moment. We have had leaders of men of almost every type except this moral Larry Harrigan. Not long ago I thought one such had appeared, but, alas! He soon himself joined the shouting crowd of intellectual bullies. It would be too much to say that there is no country in Europe where there is so little liberty as in Ireland, but if freedom to express honest conviction be the test applied, and if public opinion be taken as the arbiter in the matter, then such a proposition would be hard to disprove.

The Irish question would be more than half solved if some of the effort which is squandered in belabouring the old Ascendancy were directed against the intellectual tyranny which threatens to stifle with its rank growth the tender shoots of a nascent nationality.

Yours very truly,
Horace Plunkett

ARTHUR GRIFFITH—*from*:

'THE RESURRECTION OF HUNGARY'

PREFACE TO THE FIRST EDITION

(1904)

Born in Dublin in 1872,
Arthur Griffith initially
worked as a printer but
would achieve fame as a
crusading journalist. In 1897
he visited South Africa
(in hopes of a cure for his
tuberculosis) and became
a staunch supporter of
the Boer resistance to
British imperial expansion.
With William Rooney he
set up the weekly paper
United Irishman in 1899.
In its columns in 1904 he
suggested that resistance
to oppression need not
take a violent form, but
simply required of a people
that they turn their backs
on the British Parliament,
creating alternative
structures of their own. He
cited the dual monarchy of
Austria-Hungary as a viable
model. Denouncing the Act
of Union of 1800 as illegal,
he argued that Ireland
should share a monarch
with Britain but enjoy
a separate government.
The articles were published
as *The Resurrection of* A

THE SERIES OF articles on the 'Resurrection of Hungary' originally appeared in the *United Irishman* during the first six months of the present year [1904]. The object of the writer was to point out to his compatriots that the alternative of armed resistance to the foreign government of this country is not acquiescence in usurpation, tyranny, and fraud.

A century ago in Hungary a poet startled his countrymen by shouting in their ears: 'Turn your eyes from Vienna or you perish.' The voice of Josef Karman disturbed the nation, but the nation did not apprehend. Vienna remained its political centre until, years later, the convincing tongue of Louis Kossuth cried up and down the land: 'Only on the soil of a nation can a nation's salvation be worked out.'

Through a generation of strife and sorrow the people of Hungary held by Kossuth's dictum and triumphed gloriously. The despised, oppressed, and forgotten province of Austria is today the free, prosperous, and renowned Kingdom of Hungary.

Sixty years ago, and more, Ireland was Hungary's exemplar. Ireland's heroic and long-enduring resistances to the destruction of her independent nationality were themes the writers of Young Hungary dwelt upon to enkindle and make resolute the Magyar people. The poet precursors of Free Hungary—Bacsanyi and Vorosmarty—drank in Celtic inspiration, and the journalists of Young Hungary taught their people that Ireland had baffled a tyranny as great as that which threatened death to Hungary. Times have changed, and Hungary is now Ireland's exemplar.

It is in the memory of men still living when Hungary had not five journals in which a word of the Hungarian language was permitted to appear, when she had no modern literature save a few patriotic songs; when she had no manufactures of moment, and no commerce, save with her enemy, Austria; when she was cursed with an atrocious land system and rule by foreign bureaucrats; when her whole revenue did not reach £6,000,000 yearly, and her finances were robbed to perpetuate her oppression.

Today the revenue of Hungary is £42,000,000. 800 newspapers and journals are printed in the Hungarian language. She possesses a great modern literature, an equitable land system, a world-embracing commerce, a thriving and multiplying people, and a national government. Hungary is a nation.

She has become so because she turned her back on Vienna. Sixty years ago Hungary realised that the political centre of the nation must be within the nation. When Ireland realises this obvious truth and turns her back on London the parallel may be completed. It failed only when, two generations back, Hungary took the road of principle and Ireland the path of compromise and expediency. ■

→ *Hungary* (1904). They became the basis of Griffith's 'Sinn Féin' (Ourselves) policy of self-reliance after 1905. The abstention principle was adopted by Sinn Féin following success in the 1918 election, but the dual-monarchy idea was trumped by the republic proclaimed in the 1916 Proclamation. Griffith served as acting president during de Valera's visit to the United States from 1919 to 1921 (and spent a period in jail). He was a leading negotiator of the Anglo-Irish Treaty of 1921. But the strain of years, followed by de Valera's decision to lead a dissident anti-Treaty movement, wore him down. He died in 1922, aged only 50.

PATRICK PEARSE—*from*:

'BELGIUM AND ITS SCHOOLS'
In Belgium
(1905)

In 1905 Pearse visited Belgium in order to study the workings of bilingualism in schools, but also to familiarise himself with its modern, child-centred approach to pedagogy. He was impressed by the thoughtful way of introducing children to ideas of colour, intellectual comparison, object study and collective creative activity. Most of all he was interested in its direct method of teaching French as a second language to the children of Flemish speakers. He wrote an extensive series of articles for *An Claidheamh Soluis* on these themes. Pearse had an extensive range of educational contacts in Denmark, France, Wales, Scotland and ↗

THE REVIVAL

Such a movement as this could not and did not long continue a literary movement pure and simple. Flemings, now that they had poets, and dramatists, and journalists amongst them, began to demand official recognition for their speech. Forming a majority of the population, and intellectually as vigorous as their Walloon fellow-citizens, their demands could not long be resisted. By successive steps Flemish established itself in the law courts, in the civil service, in the Houses of Parliament. Fifty years ago the whole administration of public affairs in Belgium was as French in tone as the administration of public affairs in this country is English. Today a knowledge of Flemish is compulsory for every civil servant, for every municipal official (at least in the Flemish country), for every post-office clerk. No judge who does not know Flemish may sit on the bench in Belgium, and no advocate ignorant of Flemish need hope for a lucrative practice. In the Walloon country French is the language of the courts, in the Flemish country Flemish. In the High Courts in Brussels cases are conducted in French or Flemish according as the one or the other is the vernacular of the litigants. In the Chambers, French is still heard oftener than Flemish, but many of the Flemish deputies and senators uniformly speak in their native language. All public documents are bilingual. In the churches, Flemish is used as the vernacular in Flemish districts, French in Walloon. In the large cities both French and Flemish-speaking priests are attached to every parish. Briefly, Flemish has gained substantive equality with French—in five or ten years more it will have gained absolute equality. It has taken the Flemings exactly three-quarters of a century to accomplish this. How long will it take Ireland to reach a corresponding stage? We do not know, but this we do know, that in twelve years we have travelled well-nigh as far as the Flemings—notwithstanding the immense initial advantage of a Flemish-speaking population which actually outnumbered the non-Flemish-speaking population—had travelled in twenty-five.

→ the United States, whose republican philosophy of an egalitarian teacher-student relationship would inform his policies as headmaster of St. Enda's School, a school run also on Gaelic lines. In the following essays he compares and contrasts the Flemish revival with that of the Irish language.

'IN FLANDERS FLEMISH'

In many respects the Flemish language movement has developed on lines parallel with those pursued by our own. But it must always be remembered that the two movements differed widely in scope. In Belgium there is not, and there never has been, a question of preserving a language from almost eminent extinction. When the Flemish movement began the speakers of Flemish were actually a majority of the population of Belgium. They still remain a majority, having neither gained nor lost in relative numerical strength during the seventy-five years that have elapsed. The aims of the movement have simply been, first, the creation of a modern Flemish literature, and secondly, the securing for Flemish of official recognition as full and ample as that accorded to French. Let it be frankly realised that Ireland's problem is vastly more difficult. We have to rescue a language from the very brink of the grave. We have to instil a spirit of national pride and self-reliance into a people broken by political conquest and demoralised by a system of education designed and administered in the interest of foreign civilisation. We have to fight against the apathy of public opinion at home, and against the avowed and secret opposition of an alien government and its agents. The Flemings were citizens of a free state and their whole task was merely to convince their non-Flemish-speaking fellow citizens of the reasonableness of admitting their language to equal rights with French in school and state. There was no question of *restoration*; no question of prevailing on non-Flemish speakers to learn Flemish; no French-speaking territory to be evangelised; it was simply a matter of securing fair play for that one of the two national vernaculars which an historical accident had placed in a subordinate position in the commonwealth.

The fact that the Flemish movement differs thus widely in scope from our own explains why its organisation is so different. In Belgium there is no body corresponding to the Gaelic League. That is to say, there is no vast popular organisation, with its headquarters in the capital and branches ramifying throughout the country, taking charge of a national movement for the rehabilitation of a national language. There is no need for such a body. No campaign having for its end the inducing of Flemish speakers to speak Flemish has to be carried on in the Flemish-speaking districts. No teaching work has to be done in the non-Flemish districts. The literary interests of the language are looked after by the Flemish Academy. The teaching is done in the schools. Flemish clubs and 'cercles' exist everywhere, but their objects are social and religious as much as linguistic. The actual fighting is carried on in Parliament by the Flemish deputies and senators, and outside Parliament through the medium of the Flemish press. There are at least six Flemish dailies, and a host of Flemish weeklies, whilst there are also Flemish reviews, literary, social, and religious. The Flemish press is in reality the first fighting line of the movement. I met at Louvain Emile Vlieberghe, the editor of the leading Flemish review—*De Dietsche Warande en Belfort*—and a pillar of the movement. Of him, and of his views on the Flemish and Irish questions—for he has studied the Irish movement—I may write hereafter.

I have said that the Flemish movement simply sought to secure for Flemish absolute equality of treatment with French in every department of national life, and that this object has now been substantively attained. Let us see how matters work out linguistically in the Belgium of today. Belgium is often referred to as a bilingual country.

If by 'bilingual country' we mean a country in which two
languages are spoken side by side, then the description
is accurate enough, but if we mean a country whose
inhabitants are bilingualists the description is far from
accurate. The Belgians, as a people, are not yet bilingualists:
in a generation or two, however, their system of bilingual
education will have made them so.

THE BILINGUAL PRINCIPLE IN PRACTICE

In our École Froebel at Antwerp we have seen the
Belgian child entering on his school life. We have duly noted
that his very first steps are taken in his mother tongue—that,
in fact, as long as he remains in the infant school he hears no
other. We have seen, however, that the teaching of the second
language is commenced almost as soon as the primary school
is reached—that is to say, at the age of six or seven. We have
further seen that the teaching of the second language is
conducted on the Direct Method from the outset, and that in
such up-to-date schools as that of M. de Cleene at Etterbeck,
special devices of a very attractive and interesting kind are
made use of by the teacher.

From this point on the second language enters ever
larger and more largely into the scheme of school work.
Let us say that three hours per week are devoted to it
during the first school year. In the second school year
this time will have been increased to four or four-and-a-
half hours; in the fourth or fifth school year, to five or six.
Furthermore, the second language is after the first year and
(as will have appeared from my account of my experiences
at Etterbeck), in many cases from the very first moment,
freely employed in giving instructions in other branches:
mathematics, geography, manual training, etc. Either of
two plans may be adopted, according as circumstances or
the inclination of the teacher may suggest: either *all* the
lessons may be given bilingually, as is done by M. de Cleene,
or in the alternative certain lessons may be set apart to be
given in the vernacular, and certain others to be given in
the second language. Thus, it is common to find geography,
history, and manual training dealt with in Flemish, whilst

mathematics and science are taught in French. The plan of bilingualism all through seems preferable, provided always that the teacher is skilful and conscientious enough to avoid the temptation to have his French lesson a mere translation of his Flemish lesson and *vice versa*. Yet another device would be to use the languages on alternative days, but I do not remember to have seen this employed. I need hardly add that there is no such thing, at least in the more progressive schools, as bilingual *language* lessons. French, as a set subject, is taught *through French*. This applies also to foreign languages like German and English when they come to be taken up in the higher standards.

It will be seen that a child commencing at the age of six such a course as I have described will, at the end, have acquired a thorough mastery over the two languages, both as written and as spoken tongues. It has been doubted whether a language can really be learned at school: I have satisfied myself by observations both in Ireland and in Belgium that it can. A child who spends half his school time for six years thinking in and speaking a language must of necessity know that language at the end of the six years. It is all a matter of getting him really *to think in* the language, and this again is all a matter of good teaching. ∎

RABINDRANATH TAGORE—*from*:

THE POST OFFICE

(1911)

MADHAV (*Whispering into Amal's ear*): ... Beg for a gift from him. You know our humble circumstances.

AMAL: Don't you worry, Uncle—I've made up my mind about it.

MADHAV: What is it, my child?

AMAL: I shall ask him to make me one of his postmen that I may wander far and wide, delivering his message from door to door.

MADHAV (*Slapping his forehead*): Alas, is that all?

AMAL: What'll be our offerings to the King, Uncle, when he comes?

HERALD: He has commanded puffed rice.

AMAL: Puffed rice! Say, Headman, you're right. You said so. You knew all we didn't.

HEADMAN: If you send word to my house then I could manage for the King's advent really nice—

PHYSICIAN: No need at all. Now be quiet all of you. Sleep is coming over him. I'll sit by his pillow; he's dropping into slumber. Blow out the oil-lamp. Only let the star-light stream in. Hush, he slumbers.

MADHAV (*Addressing Gaffer*): What are you standing there for like a statue, folding your palms.—I am nervous.— Say, are they good omens? Why are they darkening the room? How will star-light help?

GAFFER: Silence, unbeliever.

(SUDHA *enters*)

'Yeats thinks *The Post Office* a masterpiece', wrote a friend of the poet in a letter to Rabindranath Tagore in 1912. One year later Yeats encouraged the staff and students of St. Enda's School to stage a production of the play on the boards of the Abbey Theatre. It presents the plight of Amal, a child confined to his uncle's home by a mortal disease: he wonders whether the building of a new post office nearby means that he'll receive a letter from the king, but is mocked for presumption by the village headman. The king himself does come, with his physician in train, along with a girl named Sudha bearing promised flowers— but it is already too late, for Amal has fallen into a sleep, perhaps even a coma. The suggestion in the final scene, reproduced here, is that redemption can never come from a monarch or parliament—only from a supernatural king. →

→ Yeats strongly supported
the successful campaign
to have Tagore awarded
the Nobel Prize in 1913,
and he wrote a glowing
introduction to the Indian's
book of poems *Gitanjali* in
1916. Tagore, born into an
aristocratic family in 1861,
had already reinvented
Bengali literature, music
and dance, achieving
global fame also as a
sage. He often asserted
that political freedom
was meaningless
without cultural liberty
too. His play's dream of
freedom led to its being
performed in the Warsaw
ghetto in 1942 and in the
concentration camps of
World War Two. Tagore
died in 1941.

SUDHA: Amal!

PHYSICIAN: He's asleep.

SUDHA: I have some flowers for him. Mayn't I give the
into his own hand?

PHYSICIAN: Yes, you may.

SUDHA: When will he be awake?

PHYSICIAN: Directly the King comes and calls him.

SUDHA: Will you whisper a word for me in his ear?

PHYSICIAN: What shall I say?

SUDHA: Tell him Sudha has not forgotten him. ■

ROGER CASEMENT

HUMAN RIGHTS

(1903–1916)

from: LETTER *to* THE MARQUESS OF LANSDOWNE
30 SEPTEMBER 1903

I am amazed and confounded at what I have both seen and heard; and if I, in the enjoyment of all the resources and privileges of civilized existence, know not where to turn to, or to whom to make appeal on behalf of these unhappy people whose sufferings I have witnessed, and whose wrongs have burnt into my heart, how can they, poor, panic-stricken fugitives, in their own forest homes, turn for justice to their oppressors? The one dreadful, dreary cry that has been ringing in my ears for the last six weeks has been, 'Protect us from our protectors.'

from: LETTER *to* SIR CHARLES DILKE
17 FEBRUARY 1904

It is this aspect of the Congo question—its abnormal injustice and extraordinary invasion, at this stage of civilised life, of fundamental human rights, which to my mind calls for the formation of a special body and the formulation of a very special appeal to the humanity of England.

from: *THE AMAZON JOURNAL of ROGER CASEMENT*
JOURNAL ENTRY, 6 NOVEMBER 1910

Just as this thought raised itself, I looked up from the verandah to the eastern sky—and saw, to my amazement, an arc of light across the dark, starless heaven. For a moment I did not realise what it was—then I saw it—a lunar rainbow— a perfect arch of light in the night. The moon was in the West— with stars and a clear sky round her in the East, obscure sky

Roger Casement was born in Dublin in 1864. He was orphaned by the age of 13. He was knighted in 1911 for his services as a British consul who had exposed abuses of native workers in Peru and in the Congo. Like Joseph Conrad, whom he met in the Congo in 1890, he had gone there in the belief that European codes would help Africans to achieve freedom; but soon came to a different valuation. He retired from the diplomatic service in 1913, devoting more and more time to Irish republican activity. He went to Germany in search of assistance for the Rising of 1916 but was arrested on return, stripped of his knighthood and executed for high treason. Bernard Shaw made a strong case for clemency, arguing that such rebel leaders should be treated as prisoners-of-war rather than traitors. →

→ The government circulated excerpts allegedly from Casement's journals recording homosexual activity, and these so-called Black Diaries weakened public support. Casement's sense of being an outsider probably heightened his sympathy for victims of empire: but his writings on the rights of exploited peoples anticipated the United Nations charters developed after World War Two. His remains were returned to Ireland in 1965.

and coming rain—and this wondrous, white, perfect bow spanning the dark. I called Fox, Bell, all of them—everyone came—none had ever before seen such a sight. It was about 7.30—as near as could be—and as we looked at the perfect arch, curving from forested hill to forested hill right across the Eastern heavens, the rain began to gather over it. It was slowly dissipated—broadening and fading away. We watched it for nearly ten minutes—I take it to be a good omen—an omen of peace and augury of good—that God is still there—looking down on the sins and crimes of the children of men—hating the sin and loving the sinner. He will come yet to these poor beings—and out of the night a voice speaks. I shall not sell the great question of the Indians and their hopes of freedom for this mess of pottage for the handful of blackmen. These shall get their rights, too—but they shall come as rights—freely granted—and I shall not be the agent of silence, but I hope of the voice of freedom.

from: ROGER CASEMENT'S BERLIN DIARY
DIARY ENTRY UNDATED

Poor Indians, you had life – your white destroyers only possess things. That is the vital distinction I take it between the 'savage' and the civilised man. The savage *is* – the white man *has*. The one lives and moves to *be*; the other toils and dies to *have*. From the purely human point of view the savage has the happier and purer life – doubtless the civilised toiler makes the greater world. It is 'civilisation' versus the personal joy of life. ■

EOIN MACNEILL

IMPERIALISM

(C. 1919)

IMPERIALISM IS SOMETHING more than the glory of dominating over lands and seas and subject peoples. To the pride of life, it adds the lust of the flesh and the lust of the eyes, the appetite for luxury and gain. Its pride, being contemplative, needs to be sustained, by these active forces; and wherever you find the Imperialist spirit, you will find that it take to itself a body made up of predatory feudalism and predatory capitalism, of oligarchies seeking to dominate the earth given to the millions to inhabit and the industry exerted by the millions to make the earth inhabitable—in short, to enslave the world.

It has been the destiny of this small nation of ours to make an age-long stand against imperialism and its forces of predatory feudalism and predatory capitalism. All savage peoples are imperialistic, and imperialism is the survival of the savage instinct under the forms of civilisation. Our heathen forefathers were just as predatory as the Romans, the Anglo-Saxons, the Franks, and the Normans, but with their heathenism they left their imperialism behind, and from the time when they became Christian, Irish people have never sought domination or any partnership in domination over other lands or other peoples. Imperialism of necessity includes militarism. Ireland, becoming Christian, ceased to be militarist and, paradoxical though it may appear, with all their 'fighting qualities' the Irish people are anti-militarist.

It is impossible to reconcile the Irish nation with imperialism. The late Mr. Redmond, in the plenitude of his influence failed in the attempt, and that attempt will not again be made by any leader of Irish public opinion in our time. It is not merely that this nation has no attraction towards the evil thing. Our own history for centuries has been the history of

The critique of imperialism is as old as empire itself, but it took on a particular urgency after 1900 as radicals within Europe began to question the scramble for land and materials in Africa, Asia and Latin America. The importance of the Irish contribution was identified even earlier. 'Ireland lost', wrote Karl Marx in the 1850s, 'the empire is gone.' Socialists believed that such a blow might lead to mutinies against the aristocracy by the working class in Britain. 'A pin in the hands of a child', said James Connolly, the Irish labour activist, 'could pierce the heart of a giant.' In the years after 1918 the minutes of the cabinet in London record repeated fears that if the Irish case were conceded, India, Egypt and a dozen other holdings would fall. →

→ Some of the more
conservative leaders of
the Revival (such as Arthur
Griffith) believed that an
independent Ireland could
in time found colonies of
its own; but others drew
from Ireland's experience
the lesson that the imperial
project was a barbarous,
outdated concept. Eoin
MacNeill's essay, with
its caustic reference to
the recent death of John
Redmond (who had
supported the British war
effort) is representative;
and it also offers an
interesting sidelight by a
native of County Antrim on
the 'unionist difference'.

an unbroken struggle against imperialism, and in imperialism we recognise the cause of our national calamities.

In English politics, it is possible for a reactionary class to pose for decades before itself and the world as a body of progressives. In Irish politics, the attitude is not so easily sustained. The lords of industry in north-eastern Ireland needed no Parnell to clear up their position, and they were generations earlier than their British *confrères* in accomplishing a political fusion with feudalism. This was partly an affect of Irish national conditions, partly the fruit of that enlightened self-interest which is described as the 'business capacity' of the Ulster unionist employer. With a skill unrivalled in political history, the landlords and the business lords of Ulster manipulated in their own favour a most unfavourable set of conditions. They had little difficulty indeed in securing the sympathy and support of the English government of Ireland for that government from its earliest beginnings had been consecrated to the same aim and policy that united the two classes, the exploitation of Ireland and its people.

The interests of the Irish democracy are naturally identical and undivided. In such a case the predatory oligarchies of all ages have had two principles of management, reduced by the ancients to two simple statements: *Populus vult decipi* and *Divide et impera*: 'the democracy is willing to be humbugged' and 'divide and conquer'. What was the line of division? It did not occur, even to the astute, until quite recently, to pretend that Irish democracy consisted of two distinct races. Even yet, the false pretence is made mainly for outside consumption.

My belief has often been stated that, where Ireland or any other alien nation is concerned, the two great British parties are one. However, their policies may often seem to differ, their principle is the same. In the word's of Gladstone's chief governor in Ireland, 'the government of Ireland is a continuity' and the basis of that continuity is that Ireland must be governed in the interest of Great Britain, more particularly in the interest of England. From that basis, since the days of Henry II, English statecraft has never departed. The rest of the history of the Irish Volunteers I leave to unfold itself in evidence. The Irish Volunteer movement has been an episode in Ireland's secular resistance to the glorified piracy that is called imperialism. ▪

Education and Popular Culture

THE ENGLISH IDENTITY proposed for every citizen of Ireland in the later nineteenth century was considered unproblematic by the authorities: a natural inheritance of 'freedom'. English culture and history became core elements of the national school curriculum, which paid no heed to the Irish language or to the nation's history (except as errata in the grand narrative of empire). Tens of thousands of children recited at the start of each school day:

I thank the goodness and the grace
Which on my days have smiled;
And made me in these Christian days
A happy English child.

The fact that the English were—as a result of trying to run an empire and adjust to industrial society—among the most stressed peoples of Europe was never considered. As far as the educational authorities were concerned, 'England' represented the ideal human norm. Children's books offered poems and pictures of the English Home Counties, and this had the effect of making the children's own settings seem unvital, second-rate, derivative. Reality was to be found elsewhere.

If Ireland were ever again to become interesting and metropolitan to itself, all that would have to be challenged in a

revised national pedagogy, and so the leaders of the Revival set
to work. Sometimes, there was an element of abject imitation, at
other times of subversive parody, about the re-education process.
When the authorities offered sweets to children in celebration of
Victoria's half-century on the throne in 1897, Maud Gonne, not to be
outdone, marked the Queen's visit to Dublin in 1900 by distributing
treats to schoolchildren. If the English told their children stories
of King Arthur and the Knights, Augusta Gregory could rediscover
the boy-deeds and man-deeds of Cuchulain. If the English looked
for leadership to a Parliament, the Irish might one day have their
own Dáil. For every approved English institution, there must be
an equivalent but opposite Irish institution—for soccer, Gaelic
football; for the wearing of trousers, the donning of kilts. There was
a danger in all this of producing Ireland as a not-England, a zone
based on neurotic negation. Anything English was by definition un-
Irish, as to possess such things might weaken the claim to separate
nationhood, but all valued cultural practices of the English were
shown to have Gaelic equivalents—English law was long preceded
by Brehon law; hockey by hurling (played by the boy Cuchulain);
the Prime Minister by a Taoiseach. These latter three equivalents
did long exist, but others had to be invented in astonishing examples
of instant archaeology. Gaelic football was a creation of the late

nineteenth century. To this very day the procedures of the Dáil (the native Irish Parliament) are based on those of Westminster.

Unlike other colonised peoples administered by London, the Irish looked almost identical to the English, a fact which often distressed the imperialists, especially in the years after they had been unhinged by the evolutionary theories of Darwin. It followed, as night followed day, that the Irish with their lower-set brows and prognathous jaws must be far closer to apes on the biological spectrum—and so the novelist Charles Kingsley could call them 'white chimpanzees'. The Irish answer was to assert a dignified difference through a 'national' formula in clothing: Hyde, Synge, and a galaxy of Revivalists got caught up in the debate, which always had an element of strain about it. The kilt had never been Irish, being an invention of Lancashire industrialists cashing in on Walter Scott's popularity to unload over-supplies of tartan, but this did not prevent many earnest young men from ending speeches with the cry 'Down With Trousers.'

The Yeats sisters were on surer ground in reconnecting native arts and crafts. The modern English musical composer, Arnold Bax, morphed for a time into 'Dermot O'Byrne', attempting to create a national opera on the story of Deirdre. The debate about dancing was almost as fraught as that about kilts: nobody could say for certain whether set or céilí dances really were pure Irish. Yeats attempted to solve the question by founding a ballet school at the Abbey.

Few of these ambiguities troubled those who sang or listened to popular songs (some insurrectionary, some imperial, some simply devoted to a love of landscape). In the years when sheet music and phonograph records sold in tens of thousands, these versions were influential indeed.

One surprising absence from most discussions of popular culture was the question of a national cuisine: there was such a thing (soda bread; fish soups; potato cakes; bacon and cabbage; colcannon) but memories of the Great Famine were perhaps still too distressing to permit its codification by Revivalists in a country where many still went hungry.

The most radical of all theorists of a new pedagogy was Patrick Pearse, who sharply contested the notion that the school syllabus offered 'freedom'. He called it instead a 'murder machine', designed to manufacture the consent of polite automatons rather than free thinkers. He sketched an alternative in essays which seem uncannily to anticipate current fears about the sell-out of education to market forces.

MARY E.L. BUTLER—*from*:

'IRISH WOMEN'S EDUCATION'

(1899)

MOST OF OUR boys and girls in fashionable circumstances are sent to school in England. Those who are educated at home are not much better off. The atmosphere of many Irish educational institutions is almost as Anglicising as that of English ones. 'Wearing English clothes, reading English books, speaking the English language, imbibing English sentiments, consciously or unconsciously, in every way, how are Irish children to be distinguished from English ones?' as a public speaker asked the other day. We have many schools and colleges, both for boys and girls, at which instruction on a variety of subjects is imparted, but at how many of these places is what might be described as a truly Irish education instilled into the hearts and minds of the rising generation?

The writer has in mind a college for the higher education of women—an institution which evokes the tender recollections ever inspired by one's alma mater, but mingled with the affection and gratitude felt is a deep regret. A true centre of liberal education in other respects, it was lacking in one particular, and that the most essential—national knowledge. The curriculum was certainly comprehensive— science, literature and art, political economy, and domestic hygiene, mathematics and logic; the classics and cookery, were studied in turn, but one branch of knowledge was excluded. Everything relating to the country to which they belonged was a sealed book to the students. In after life some of them grew to learn by accident the things which they had not been told, and having learned them, they grew to know and love their country. Their teachers marvelled when they heard that their former pupils, having passed out of their control, had become imbued with this new, strange, inspiring knowledge.

Born in 1874, Mary Butler was educated at Alexandra College, Dublin. A reading of John Mitchel's *Jail Journal* made a nationalist of her and soon she was learning Irish on the Aran Islands (having renamed herself Máire de Buitléir). She wrote essays for women, as well as a children's page, in the *Irish Weekly Independent*, promoting Revival values to the chagrin of her famous relation, Edward Carson (tormentor of Oscar Wilde in the witness box in 1895 and future leader of militant unionism). She wrote novels and stories, as well as pamphlets and essays, the latter often featuring in *An Claidheamh Soluis*. She suggested the name Sinn Féin (Ourselves) to Arthur Griffith for the self-help movement he proposed. She married Thomas O'Nolan in 1907 but he died just six years later. She died in Rome in 1920.

Those who formed independent opinions of their own were
unfortunately the exception. Most were content to continue in
the groove in which their steps were first directed. And this is
not to be wondered at. As the twig is bent, so will it grow. Few
are found prepared to work out their salvation on their own
lines—to think and act for themselves.

But this is what our people must accustom themselves
to doing. They must determine to be 'self-respecting, self-
relying, self-advancing.' They must inculcate these principles
in the rising generation, and see that they come equipped to
the battle of life with a stock of national knowledge. Hourly
training and education are of paramount importance. Let
Irish parents see that their children get them of the right
kind. Let them insist that patriotic principles and information
on national subjects are inculcated at the educational
establishments to which they send them. If they are not, the
remedy is in their own hands. ■

MAUD GONNE—*from*:

A SERVANT OF THE QUEEN

Children's Treats

(1938)

S HE ARRIVED IN Dublin and was received and duly presented with the keys of the city of Dublin by a grovelling unionist fishmonger who had succeeded in getting elected as Lord Mayor of Dublin with the assistance of one of the foremost members of the IRB, Fred Allan. This pure-souled revolutionist had come to the '98 centenary committee with cheques of £10 from Alderman Pile, the fishmonger, and £5 from Councillor Jones, his henchman. I had moved that the cheques be returned, as neither of the donors stood for Irish independence, and I had been outvoted on Fred Allan declaring he had converted them both to the national cause. There was so much joy over the sinner that repenteth that these cheques led to the election of Alderman Pile to the mayoralty and the pure-souled revolutionist became his secretary and sat in the gilded mayoral coach which, escorted by foot and horse police, drove through the streets lined with military to present the keys of the city to Victoria. The Dublin crowd had no chance of getting near the ceremony, but on its way back, when returning from the royal procession, the gilded coach was sorely battered and its glass broken by the infuriated crowd on the quays and, white and trembling, the Lord Mayor and his revolutionary secretary were barely saved by the police from a dip in the Liffey.

At the Viceregal Lodge in the Phoenix Park, Victoria the Famine Queen gave a treat to 15,000 schoolchildren. Convent schools vied with the Protestant ascendancy in sending the largest contingents of children, shepherded by holy nuns. Obviously we could not interfere with nuns and children, and the unionist papers revelled in picture and print descriptions of this spontaneous display of loyalty.

The 1890s was a decade of commemorations but also a period in which the ghosts of victims of the Great Famine featured increasingly in folk legends. There was a palpable nervousness about the approach of the new century, the last of the second millennium, as people began to project their anxieties onto symbolic dates. 1896 was the anniversary of an ill-fated French naval expedition. 1897 was the fiftieth anniversary of the worst year of the Famine, but in London it was celebrated as the near-miraculous jubilee of the reigning queen Victoria. Not to be outdone, the Irish countered with a memorial in the following →

→ year to the rebels of 1798.
England was experiencing
beneath its gaiety the
sense of an ending (of
the Victorian era, of
male power, of imperial
expansion), but in Ireland it
was a time of beginnings,
of self-help, cultural
renewal and a strong
Celtic womanhood. If
Victoria's arrival in Dublin in
1900 on a state visit was a
signal for the Viceroy again
to ply Irish children with
sweets, Maud Gonne as a
not-very-loyal subject (who
had once been presented
to Victoria as a debutante)
could do much the same.

Inghinidhe na hÉireann got out posters announcing a patriotic children's treat to all children who had not participated in Queen Victoria's treat, and some twenty thousand responded. We opened a subscription list to defray expenses and all our time, for two days and nights before it, was spent in cutting up hams and making sandwiches in a big store we had secured in Talbot Street. Headed by beflagged lorries piled with casks of ginger beer and twenty-thousand paper bags containing sandwiches, buns and sweets, that wonderful procession of children carrying green branches moved off from Beresford Place, marshalled by the young men of the Celtic Literary Society and the Gaelic Athletic Association on the march to Clonturk Park. Mary Quin and I, on an outside car, drove up and down the line, for the safety of such a huge concourse of children was a fearful responsibility, but there was no hitch. When the last child had left the Park I drove round to all the city hospitals. 'We have never had a Sunday so free from child accidents,' was the reply everywhere, and one enthusiastic young doctor said: 'You should organise a children's treat every week.'

The Patriotic Children's Treat became legendary in Dublin and, even now, middle-aged men and women come up to me in the streets and say: 'I was one of the patriotic children at your party when Queen Victoria was over.' ▪

PERCY FRENCH

'THE QUEEN'S AFTER-DINNER SPEECH'

(1900)

Sez she

Me loyal subjects sez she
Here's my best respect, sez she
And I'm proud this day, sez she
Of the elegant way, sez she
That you gave me the hand, sez she
When I come to the land, sez she
There was some people said, sez she
They were greatly in dread, sez she
I'd be murdered or shot, sez she
As like as not, sez she
But it's mighty clear, sez she
That it's not over here, sez she
That I have cause to fear, sez she
It's them Belgiums, sez she
That's throwing the bombs, sez she
And frightening the life, sez she
Out of the son and the wife, sez she
But in these parts, sez she
They have warm hearts, sez she
And they all like me well, sez she
Barring the Honour Parnell, sez she
I don't know Earl, sez she
What's come over the girl, sez she
And that other one, sez she
That Maud Gonne, sez she
Dressing in black, sez she
To welcome me back, sez she
Now Maud'll write, sez she
That I'd brought the blight, sez she

Probably the most famous
comical poem of the
Revival, this text was
written by a man with a
keen ear for Dublinese,
and it confirms that
Hiberno-English existed
in urban forms many years
before Sean O'Casey
would make it famous
on the Abbey stage. The
sub-title of the work is
'As Overheard and Cut
into Lengths of Poetry by
Jamesy Murphy, Deputy-
Assistant-Waiter at the
Viceregal Lodge'. Its author
Percy French was born
into an Anglo-Irish family in
1854 and worked as a civil
engineer after graduation
from Trinity College Dublin.
He was a respected
landscape painter but →

→ won his greatest fame as
composer and performer
of comic songs. His
send-up of Maud Gonne's
symbolic funeral-wear
here is accompanied by
a sly deflation of the self-
importance of W.B. Yeats.
Already the poses of the
thirty-five-year-old poet
were provoking a counter-
thrust. It is interesting, also,
that French could imagine
a waiter in the viceroy's
lodge harbouring his own
private reservations about
those who affected to
own the world.

Or changed the season, sez she
For me own private reason, sez she
And I think there's a slate, sez she
Off Willie Yeats, sez she
He should be at home, sez she
French polishing his poems, sez she
Instead of writing letters, sez she
About his betters, sez she
And parading me crimes, sez she
In The Irish Times, sez she
Ah, but what does it matter, sez she
All this magpie chatter, sez she
When I heard the welcoming roar, sez she
Coming up from the shore, sez she
Right over the foam, sez she
Sure it was like coming home, sez she
And me heart fairly glowed, sez she
Along the "Rock Road", sez she
And into Butterstown, sez she
And be Merrion Round, sez she
Until I come to the ridge, sez she
Of the Leeson St Bridge, sez she
And was greeted in style, sez she
By the beautiful smile, sez she
Of me Lord Mayor Pyle, sez she
Fate if I'd done right, sez she
I'd a made him a knight, sez she
And I need not repeat, sez she
How they cheered in each street, sez she
Till I come to them lads, sez she
Don't you know them undergrads, sez she

Oh, and indeed and indeed, sez she
I got many a God Speed, sez she
But nothing to compare, sez she
With what I've got here, sez she
So pass the jug, sez she
And I'll fill each mug, sez she
And I'll give you a toast, sez she
At which you may boast, sez she
Now I have a power of sons, sez she
All sorts of ones, sez she
Some as quiet as cows, sez she
Some always in rows, sez she
And the one that causes the most trouble, sez she
Sure the mother loves double, sez she
So here's to the men, sez she
That's gone into win, sez she
That's clearing the way, sez she
To Pretoria today, sez she
And the gap of danger, sez she
There's a Connaught Ranger, sez she
And a fusilier not far, sez she
From the heart of the war, sez she
And I'll tell you what, sez she
They may talk a lot, sez she
And them foreign baboons, sez she
May drawn their cartoons, sez she
But there's one thing they'll never draw, sez she
And that's the lion's claw, sez she
For before our flag is furled, sez she
We'll own the world, sez she

AUGUSTA GREGORY

'THE BOY-DEEDS OF CUCHULAIN'

(1902)

Augusta Gregory
published *Cuchulain*
of Muirthemne in 1902
in London, because no
Irish publisher would
take it on. Some had
advised that only a trained
scholar should do the
work, but she cheerfully
set herself to what she
called 'man's work',
rebuking the professors
of Trinity College Dublin
for their lack of interest
in the manuscripts which
they hoarded. One of
these academics, Robert
Atkinson, had decried 'the
smallness of the element
of idealism' in the tales,
but Gregory wished to
reconnect the people to
their signature stories.
She welded the disparate
materials of legend
into a unity and was
congratulated by the Celtic
scholar Eoin MacNeill, who
joked in a letter that 'the
Gaelic League will want

NOW, AS TO the boys at Emain, when they were done playing, everyone went to his father's house, or to whoever was in charge of him. But Setanta set out on the track of the chariots, shortening the way for himself as he was used to do with his hurling stick and his ball. When he came to the lawn before the smith's house, the hound heard him coming, and began such a fierce yelling that he might have been heard through all Ulster, and he sprang at him as if he had a mind not to stop and tear him up at all, but to swallow him at the one mouthful. The little fellow had no weapon but his stick and his ball, but when he saw the hound coming at him, he struck the ball with such force that it went down his throat, and through his body. Then he seized him by the hind legs and dashed him against a rock until there was no life left in him.

When the men feasting within heard the outcry of the hound, Conchubar started up and said: 'It is no good luck brought us on this journey, for that is surely my sister's son that was coming after me, and that has got this death by the hound.' On that all the men rushed out, not waiting to go through the door, but over walls and barriers as they could. But Fergus was the first to get to where the boy was, and he took him up and lifted him on his shoulder, and brought him in safe and sound to Conchubar, and there was great joy on them all.

But Culain the smith went out with them, and when he saw his great hound lying dead and broken there was great grief in his heart and he came in and said to Setanta: 'There is no good welcome for you here.' 'What have you against the little lad?' said Conchubar. 'It was no good luck that brought him here, or that made me prepare this feast for yourself,

King,' he said, 'for from this out, my hound being gone, my substance will be wasted and my way of living will be gone astray. And, little boy,' he said, 'that was a good member of my family you took from me, for he was the protector of my goods and my flocks and my herds and of all that I had.' 'Do not be vexed on account of that,' said the boy, 'and I myself will make up to you for what I have done.' 'How will you do that?' said Conchubar. 'This is how I will do it: if there is a whelp of the same breed to be had in Ireland, I will rear him and train him until he is as good a hound as the one killed, and until that time, Culain,' he said, 'I myself will be your watchdog to guard your goods and your cattle and your house.' 'You have made a fair offer,' said Conchubar. 'I could have given no better award myself,' said Cathbad the Druid. 'And from this out,' he said, 'your name will be Cuchulain, the Hound of Culain.' 'I am better pleased with my own name of Setanta, son of Sualtim,' said the boy. 'Do not say that,' said Cathbad, 'for all the men in the whole world will someday have the name of Cuchulain in their mouths.' 'If that is so, I am content to keep it,' said the boy. And this is how he came by the name Cuchulain.

It was a good while after that, Cathbad the Druid was one day teaching the pupils in his house to the north east of Emain. There were eight boys along with him that day and one of them asked him, 'Do your signs tell of any special thing this day is good or bad for?' 'If any young man should take arms today,' said Cathbad, 'his name will be greater than any other name in Ireland. But his span of life will be short,' he said.

Cuchulain was outside at play, but he heard what Cathbad said, and there and then he put off his playing suit,

→ to suppress you on a double indictment, to wit: depriving the Irish language of her sole right to express the innermost Irish mind, and, secondly, investing the Anglo-Irish language with a literary dignity it has never hitherto possessed.' Cuchulain, epitomising pagan energy and Christ-like suffering, seemed rather like an English public schoolboy in the drag of a muscular Christian. The book, with its near-novelisation of epic heroes, became a minor cult classic, revered by Synge who told Gregory it 'is part of my daily bread.' It replaced Standish O'Grady's rather stiff retellings. Its account of the childhood of Cuchulain made it a firm favourite among English as well as Irish schoolboys.

and he went straight to Conchubar's sleeping room and said: 'All be good with you, King!' 'What is it you are wanting?' said Conchubar. 'What I want is to take arms today.' 'Who put that into your head?' 'Cathbad the Druid,' said Cuchulain. 'If that is so, I will not deny you,' said Conchubar. Then he gave him his choice of arms, and the boy tried his strength on them, and there were none that pleased him or that were strong enough for him but Conchubar's own. So he gave him his own two spears, and his swords and his shield.

Just then Cathbad the Druid came in, and there was wonder on him, and he said. 'Is it taking arms this young boy is?' 'He is indeed,' said the king. 'It is sorry I would be to see his mother's son take arms on this day,' said Cathbad. 'Was it not yourself bade him do it?' said the king. 'I did not surely,' he said. 'Then you have lied to me boy,' said Conchubar. 'I told no lie, King,' said Cuchulain, 'for it was he indeed put it in my mind when he was teaching the others, for when one of them asked him if there was any special virtue in this day, he said that whoever would for the first time take arms today, his name would be greater than any other in Ireland, and he did not say any harm would come on him, but that his life would be short.' 'And what I said is true,' said Cathbad, 'there will be fame on you and a great name, but your lifetime will not be long.' 'It is little I would care,' said Cuchulain, 'if my life were to last one day and one night only, so long as my name and the story of what I had done would live after me.' ■

PATRICK PEARSE—*from*:

'THE MURDER MACHINE'

(1912)

THEY HAVE PLANNED and established an education which more wickedly does violence to the elementary human rights of Irish children than would an edict for the general castration of Irish males. The system has aimed at the substitution for men and women of mere things. It has not been an entire success. There are still a great many thousand men and women in Ireland. But a great many thousand of what, by way of courtesy, we call men and women, are simply things. Men and women, however depraved, have kindly human allegiances. But these things have no allegiance. Like other things, they are for sale.

When one uses the term education system as the name of the system of schools, colleges, universities, and whatnot which the English have established in Ireland, one uses it as a convenient label, just as one uses the term government as a convenient label for the system of administration by police which obtains in Ireland instead of a government. There is no education system in Ireland. The English have established the simulacrum of an education system but its object is the precise contrary of the object of an education system. Education should foster; this education is meant to repress. Education should inspire; this education is meant to tame. Education should harden; this education is meant to enervate. The English are too wise a people to attempt to educate the Irish, in any worthy sense. As well expect them to arm us.

Professor Eoin MacNeill has compared the English education system in Ireland to the systems of slave education which existed in the ancient pagan republics side by side with the systems intended for the education of freemen. To the children of the free were taught all noble and goodly

Pearse was a gifted teacher at both secondary and university level. His classes, like his writings, were characterised by an insistent lucidity and a visionary intensity. He founded St. Enda's School in 1908 to provide a bilingual education, for he was convinced (perhaps naively) that Irish could be saved in the nation's classrooms. The language projected alternative structures of thought and feeling. At St. Enda's, in the words of one pupil (Desmond Ryan), 'Cuchulain was an important if invisible member of the staff', which included also Willie Pearse and Thomas MacDonagh (as well as visits from such luminaries as W.B. Yeats and Douglas Hyde). →

→ The motto of the school
was Cuchulain's 'I care
not if I live but a day and
a night so long as my
deeds live after me.' For all
this emphasis on manly
discipline (and some of
the boys became rebels in
1916), St. Enda's had much
in common with the sort of
'alternative' English schools
supported by liberals like
Bertrand Russell and
A.S. Neill: an emphasis
on nature-study as well
as classical literature, on
science as well as arts and
crafts, and on a thoroughly
democratic practice. In
his 'child republic', Pearse
encouraged an open vote
among boys on whether
they should play cricket
or hurling in the summer
term. His anti-imperial
philosophy—really a
denunciation of a crass ↗

things which would tend to make them strong and proud and valiant; from the children of the slaves all such dangerous knowledge was hidden. They were taught not to be strong and proud and valiant, but to be sleek, to be obsequious, to be dexterous: the object was not to make them good men, but to make them good slaves. And so in Ireland. The education system here was designed by our masters in order to make us willing or at least manageable slaves.

I do not know how far it is possible to revive the old ideal of fosterer and foster-child. I know it were very desirable. One sees too clearly that the modern system, under which the teacher tends more and more to become a mere civil servant, is making for the degradation of education, and will end in irreligion and anarchy. The modern child is coming to regard his teacher as an official paid by the state to render him certain services; services which it is in his interest to avail of, since by doing so he will increase his earning capacity later on, but services the rendering and acceptance of which no more imply a sacred relationship than do the rendering and acceptance of the services of a dentist or a chiropodist. There is thus coming about a complete reversal of the relative positions of master and disciple, a tendency which is increased by every statute that is placed on the statute book, by every rule that is added to the education code of modern countries.

Against this trend I would oppose the ideal of those who shaped the Gaelic polity nearly two thousand years ago. It is not merely that the old Irish had a good education system; they had the best and noblest that has ever been known among men. There has never been any human institution more adequate to its purpose than that which, in pagan times, produced Cuchulain and the Boy Corps of Eamhain Macha and, in Christian times, produced Enda and the companions of his solitude in Aran. The old Irish system, pagan and Christian, possessed in pre-eminent degree the thing most needful in education: an adequate inspiration. Colmcille suggested what that inspiration was when he said, 'If I die it shall be from the excess of the love that I bear the Gael'. A love and a service so excessive as to annihilate all thought of self, a recognition that one must give all, must be willing always to make the ultimate sacrifice—this is the inspiration alike of the story of Cuchulain and of the story of Colmcille, the inspiration that made the one a hero and the other a saint.

… What the teacher should bring to his pupil is not a set of readymade opinions, or a stock of cut-and-dry information, but an inspiration and an example, and his main qualification should be, not such an overmastering will as shall impose itself at all hazards upon all weaker wills that come under its influence, but rather so infectious an enthusiasm as shall kindle new enthusiasm. The Montessori system, so admirable in many ways, would seem at first sight to attach insufficient importance to the function of the teacher in the schoolroom. But this is not really so. True, it would make the spontaneous efforts of the children the main motive power, as against the dominating will of the teacher which is the main motive power in the ordinary schoolroom. But the teacher must be there always to inspire, to foster. If you would realise how true this is, how important the personality of the teacher, even in a Montessori school, try

→ commercial schooling and celebration of a child-centred education— was spelled out in 'The Murder Machine' (1912). He was appalled at the pressure on teachers, paid less than the colonial police, to produce a tractable, biddable type. A free child would not be a copy of the teacher but become his or her destined innermost self. By the time of the Rising in 1916 Pearse's school was in financial difficulties, despite money raised by him on an American lecture tour.

to imagine a Montessori school conducted by the average teacher of your acquaintance, or try to imagine a Montessori school conducted by yourself!

The first thing I plead for, therefore, is freedom: freedom for each school to shape its own programme in conformity with the circumstances of the school as to place, size, personnel, and so on; freedom again for the individual teacher to impart something of his own authority to his work, to bring his own peculiar gifts to the service of his pupils, to be, in short, a teacher, a master, one having an intimate and permanent relationship with his pupils, and not a mere part of the educational machine, a mere cog in the wheel; freedom finally for the individual pupil and scope for his development within the school and within the system. And I would promote this idea of freedom by the very organisation of the school itself, giving a certain autonomy not only to the school, but to the particular parts of the school: to the various sub-divisions of the pupils. I do not plead for anarchy. I plead for freedom within the law, for liberty, not licence, for that true freedom which can exist only where there is discipline, which exists in fact because each, valuing his own freedom, respects also the freedom of others.

Well-trained and well-paid teachers, well-equipped and beautiful schools, and a fund at the disposal of each school to enable it to award prizes on its own tests based on its own programme—these would be among the characteristics of a new secondary system. Manual work, both indoor and outdoor, would I hope, be part of the programme of every school. And the internal organisation might well follow the models of the little child-republics I have elsewhere described, with their own laws and leaders, their fostering of individualities yet never at the expense of the common wealth, their care for the body as well as for the mind, their nobly-ordered games, their spacious outdoor life, their intercourse with the wild things of the woods and wastes, their daily adventure face to face with elemental life and force, with its moral discipline, with its physical hardening. ∎

JOHN E. KENNEDY

'THE DEBATE ON NATIONAL DRESS'
(1902)

THE PHYSICS THEATRE was the scene of a violent debate on Irish national dress on the 18th of January. Mr. Fournier, who looked pretty in yellow and green, took the chair, as there was nothing else about worth taking. The speeches were enthusiastic. Some said we should wear one thing; another, another; some, too, that we should not wear anything at all, because Englishmen did. When young men dressed in London 'ready-mades', reproached us in bitter words and scraps of poetry for not being attired as Brian Boru or King Roderick, our tears flowed to such a degree that the ceiling of the room below was near being ruined. Mr. Fournier in a final speech outrivaled even Surgeon Dwyer in his explanations of the terrible diseases of the knee which might be produced if we wore kilts like his rival, Mr. Gibson.

We cheered, howled, and asked so many questions about his costume that Mr. Fournier left, evidently thinking to see three-fourths of the students stalking Grafton Street next day in a robe of that pattern.

Alas for the fickleness of man! Mr. Fournier was deceived. We determined that if we were to have a national costume we would invent or discover one ourselves.

So, some days after, by the aid of an O'Growney and a Cook's interpreter, we ordered Klankey and Clanshemus (two wild Irishmen from the Kildare Street Museum) to hie to Tara and dig for manuscripts.

As a keeper, a guide, and one who understands (or stands over) Irish barbarians, we borrowed from Trinity a celebrated Greek Professor and his dog, and sent him also. The day at Tara passed pleasantly, Alcibiades whiling away the time with stories of the lords, counts, and dukes of his acquaintance, and relating how he had explained to the Lord

What follows is an account from *St. Stephen's*, the students' magazine of University College Dublin, of a meeting at which the Literary and Historical Society discussed the question of national dress. The ironical tone, characteristic of most L and H activities, indicates a fair degree of youthful cynicism about such debates. In England George Bernard Shaw was promoting the wearing of sandals and brown woollen stockingette suits (promoted by the health-conscious Dr. Jaeger). His nearest Irish equivalent was Francis Sheehy Skeffington, mocked for →

→ his lush beard ('meigioll'
in Irish) in the report, which
mischievously proposes
it as the most appropriate
dress. Sheehy Skeffington,
himself a recent Auditor of
the L and H in 1897, was
Registrar from 1902 to
1904 but resigned after a
dispute over the rights of
women in college. In 1901
he had published an essay
on the theme, called 'A
Forgotten Aspect of the
University Question', which
appeared in pamphlet-form
with James Joyce's 'The
Day of the Rabblement'.
UCD students tended
to laugh at Sheehy
Skeffington for his idealism
(Joyce dubbed him 'Hairy
Jaysus') but they greatly
respected him too.

Lieutenant the Irish play at Dublin Castle, and how the Duke of Connaught complimented him on his brogue, and how pretty the Princess Patricia looked in Irish tweed.

The excavations succeeded beyond all expectations. I shall not weary you with descriptions of mouldy fashion papers and time-worn records of ancient colleges that the learned excavator and his assistants brought back with them. But one very important result has been gained, which has occasioned this paper.

At last we have solved a difficulty that long puzzled the College authorities—how to dress the College Registrar. Reading an ancient prospectus we discovered a drawing of a famous cosmopolitan Registrar who, we see, also wore the meigioll, and we hope the authorities will adopt his dress, which differs in little from the costume now in use. We see no reason also why there should not be a portrait of the Registrar on the heading of the present-day prospectus.

We also made several discoveries of costumes for college students, male and female, but we may add that, piquant and interesting as they undoubtedly were, they hardly exceeded in beauty that of the ancient College Registrar. We have only been able to reproduce for the benefit of the readers of *St. Stephen's* a few of the types, but we feel sure they are sufficient to create a general longing for the immediate adoption of Irish national dress. ∎

DOUGLAS HYDE—*from*:

'THE NECESSITY FOR DE-ANGLICISING IRELAND'

Irish Clothing

(1892)

WHEREVER THE WARM striped green jersey of the Gaelic Athletic Association was seen, there Irish manhood and Irish memories were rapidly reviving. There torn collars and ugly neckties hanging awry and far better not there at all, and dirty shirts of bad linen were banished, and our young hurlers were clad like men and Irishmen, and not in the shoddy second-hand suits of Manchester or London shop boys. Could not this alteration be carried still further? Could we not make that jersey still more popular, and could we not, in places where both garbs are worn, use our influence against English second-hand trousers, generally dirty in front, and hanging in muddy tatters at the heels, and in favour of the cleaner worsted stockings and neat breeches which many of the older generations still wear? Why have we discarded our own comfortable frieze? Why does every man in Connemara wear homemade and home-spun tweed, while in the midland counties we have become too proud for it, though we are not too proud to buy at every fair and market the most incongruous cast-off clothes imported from English cities, and to wear them? Let us, as far as we have any influence, set our faces against this aping of English dress, and encourage our women to spin and our men to wear comfortable frieze suits of their own wool, free from shoddy and humbug. So shall we de-Anglicise Ireland to some purpose, foster a native spirit and a growth of native custom which will form the strongest barrier against English influence and be in the end the surest guarantee of Irish autonomy. ∎

If language is the garb of thought, it was logical that Douglas Hyde should link his call for a return to Irish with a restoration of national dress and of traditional music. He lamented the decline of harp and pipe music and their replacement by the German band and barrel organ, and the displacing of old melodies like 'Róisín Dubh' or 'Eibhlín a Rúin' with English music-hall ballads. Hyde's call for native clothes had echoes of the 'free movement' modes of dress favoured by radicals in the aftermath of the French revolution, but it led to some strange reactions. Confronted by the allegation that the kilt never was Irish, George Moore invited guests to wear tartan trousers to his 'Gaelic lawn party' at Ely Place. *An Claidheamh Soluis* had attempted to clarify matters in 1901: 'We condemn English-made dress, but evening dress of Irish manufacture is just as Irish as a Donegal cycling suit.'

J.M. SYNGE—*from*:

THE ARAN ISLANDS

(1907)

Synge usually wore tweeds in preference to more conventional business suits. Like all dramatists, he understood that clothes reveal a lot—that people may be at their most naked when they have their clothes on. He insisted that Abbey Theatre productions of a play such as *Riders to the Sea* use only authentic flannels and pampooties (leather shoes) from the islands. His characters, whenever they change clothes or adopt those of another person, undergo massive transformations: and sometimes, in rejecting an article of clothing, they seem to be rejecting a false version of the self. It may be no accident that one factor which contributed to the disturbances at the *Playboy of the Western World* was the use in the script of the word 'shift' (an item of female under-clothing). Synge shared Hyde's belief that country people looked more graceful when wearing their traditional clothes and that the adoption of modern suits by males degraded clothing to the level of mere costume. The subject of clothing is one to which he returns again and again, as in these passages from *The Aran Islands*.

THE SIMPLICITY AND unity of the dress increases in another way the local air of beauty. The women wear red petticoats and jackets of the island wool stained with madder, to which they usually add a plaid shawl twisted round their chests and tied at the back. When it rains they throw another petticoat over their heads with the waistband round their faces, or, if they are young, they use a heavy shawl like those worn in Galway. Occasionally other wraps are worn, and during the thunderstorm I arrived in I saw several girls with men's waistcoats buttoned round their bodies. Their skirts do not come much below the knee, and show their powerful legs in the heavy indigo stockings with which they are all provided.

The men wear three colours: the natural wool, indigo, and a grey flannel that is woven of alternate threads of indigo and the natural wool. In Aran Mór many of the younger men have adopted the usual fisherman's jersey, but I have only seen one on this island.

As flannel is cheap—the women spin the yarn from the wool of their own sheep, and it is then woven by a weaver in Kilronan for four pence a yard—the men seem to wear an indefinite number of waistcoats and woollen drawers one over the other. They are usually surprised at the lightness of my own dress, and one old man I spoke to for a minute on the pier, when I came ashore, asked me if I was not cold with 'my little clothes.' ■

LILY YEATS, LOLLIE YEATS,
EVELYN GLEESON—*from*:

THE DUN EMER
INDUSTRIES PROSPECTUS

(1903)

A WISH TO FIND work for Irish hands in the making of beautiful things was the beginning of Dun Emer. In the autumn of 1902 a house on the side of the mountain near Dundrum was taken, and with village girls as workers three distinct industries were started. These are the printing of books by hand, embroidery on Irish linen and the weaving of tapestry and carpets. Bookbinding will soon be added.

The idea is to make beautiful things; this, of course, means materials honest and true and the application to them of deftness of hand, brightness of colour, and cleverness of design.

Everything, as far as possible, is Irish: the paper of the books, the linen of the embroidery and the wool of the tapestry and carpets. The designs are also of the spirit and tradition of the country.

The education of the work-girls is also part of the idea; they are taught to paint and their brains and fingers are made more active and understanding; some of them, we hope, will become teachers to others, so that similar industries may spread through the land.

Things made of pure materials, worked by these Irish girls, must be more lasting and more valuable than machine-made goods which only serve a temporary purpose. All the things made at Dun Emer are beautiful in the sense that they are instinct with individual feeling and have cost thought and care.

There is no limit to the number and kind of things that could be well-made in Ireland if designers and workers could depend upon a certain market. It is indisputable that the talent for artistic handwork is widely spread amidst the Irish people.

Lily and Lollie Yeats (sisters of the poet) were keen to promote traditional hand-crafts and in 1902 they joined with Evelyn Gleeson to commence the project. Gleeson's father, although a doctor, had set up a woollen mills in Athlone and sent his daughter to study painting in London. While there she became interested in the arts and crafts movements of the 1890s; her particular passions were weaving and tapestry. She took a house near Dundrum in County Dublin, with the name Dun Emer (The Fort of Emer) in Gaelic characters on the gate-posts. The weaving and tapestry were done in a bright room facing south, and the printing press occupied another room. By 1905 the company employed thirty young women. Its tapestries were shown at exhibitions in the United States →

→ and among the first
books from the hand-
press were works by
W.B. Yeats, George
Russell, John Eglinton,
Augusta Gregory and
Katharine Tynan. In 1908
Lollie Yeats moved to
Churchtown in County
Dublin to set up the Cuala
Press, leaving Gleeson to
continue working in the
Dun Emer studio.

The Dun Emer Industries have been working now for over a year, and they have been well supported by friends and strangers. Ecclesiastical artwork has until now been mainly supplied from continental workshops, and it is with great satisfaction that we record the support given to us by a large order from Loughrea Cathedral, where embroidered banners from Dun Emer depicting Irish saints can now be seen. The embroidery is in the medieval style which was revived by William Morris. It is worked from original designs supplied by well-known artists, and carries with it a note of individuality and distinction, and is applicable to church banners, vestments and altar cloths; to hangings, cushions, and other decorative purposes.

The tapestry and carpets are equally suitable for decoration, and use in churches; some are at present being made for this purpose. ■

'The idea is to make beautiful things...'

AN FEIS CEOIL/ AN tOIREACHTAS

(1897)

In 1894, following the publication of Douglas Hyde's comments on the neglect of traditional instruments by the elite musical groups in Ireland, there was a prolonged debate on the subject in the *Evening Telegraph* through the month of December. A committee drawn from the Irish Literary Society and Gaelic League was mandated to found an annual festival. Among those involved were Dora Sigerson, P. J. McCall and A.P. Graves. At the same time it was agreed that a separate festival, with a focus on literature, language and cognate arts be founded under the presidency of Douglas Hyde. The Gaelic League sent members to the Welsh Eisteddfod with a mandate to examine its competitions in drama, poetry, prose, recital, singing, art and dancing. Both of these new organisations (feis ceoil meaning music festival, oireachtas indicating a convocation) held their first events in May 1897, with concerts, competitions and lectures. Here follows an extract from the 'syllabus' of the Feis Ceoil of 1897.

THE WORD FEIS is associated with the ancient gathering of Tara, described in the *Book of Leinster* and surrounded by a halo of romantic traditions which date its origin back into prehistoric times. The modern Feis Ceoil, first established in May, 1897, is a musical festival, and aims at the cultivation of Irish music, and its presentation to the public in a becoming manner. It also includes among its objects the advancement of musical education and activity in Ireland generally, so as to regain for this country, if possible, its old eminence among musical nations.

The constitution of the Feis Ceoil Association today includes the following aims: (A) to promote the study and cultivation of Irish music; (B) to promote the general cultivation of music in Ireland; (C) to hold an Annual Musical Festival, or Feis Ceoil, consisting of prize competitions and concerts, similar to that held in 1897; (D) to collect and preserve by publication the old airs of Ireland. ■

PATRICK PEARSE

'ÓRÓ 'SÉ DO BHEATHA ABHAILE'

(1912)

This became a favourite song among choirs competing at the Feis Ceoil. The chorus is ancient and it was sung to welcome home a bride after a wedding, and later it was recast during the 1740s as a rebel song to welcome Bonnie Prince Charlie during the Jacobite uprising. It was rewritten by Patrick Pearse and rendered frequently as a marching song by Irish Volunteers between Easter 1916 and the War of Independence (sometimes titled 'Dord na bhFiann' – 'The Warrior Hum of the Fianna'). ↗

'Sé do bheatha, a bhean ba léannmhar
Dob' é ár gcreach do bheith i ngéibheann,
Do dhúthaigh bhreá i seilbh méirleach,
'S tú díolta leis na Gallaibh.

CHORUS:

Óró, 'sé do bheatha abhaile,
Óró, 'sé do bheatha abhaile,
Óró, 'sé do bheatha abhaile,
Anois ar theacht an tsamhraidh,

A bhuí le Dia a bhfeart go bhfeiceam,
Muna mbímid beo ina dhiaidh ach seachtain,
Gráinne Mhaol is míle gaiscíoch
Ag fógairt fáin ar Ghallaibh.

CHORUS

Tá Gráinne Mhaol ag teacht thar sáile,
Is Fianna Fáil 'na mbuidhin gharda,
Gaeil féin 's ní Francaigh ná Spáinnigh,
Is ruagairt ar na Gallaibh!

CHORUS

'Sé do bheatha, O woman that wast sorrowful,
What grieved us was thy being in chains,
Thy beautiful country in the possession of rogues,
And thou sold to the foreigners,

CHORUS:

Óró, 'sé do bheatha abhaile,
Óró, 'sé do bheatha abhaile,
Óró, 'sé do bheatha abhaile,
Now at summer's coming!

Thanks to the God of miracles that we see,
Altho' we live not a week thereafter,
Gráinne Mhaol and a thousand heroes
Proclaiming the scattering of the foreigners!

CHORUS

Gráinne Mhaol is coming from over the sea,
The Fenians of Fál as a guard about her,
Gaels they, and neither French nor Spaniard,
And a rout upon the foreigners!

CHORUS

→ Pearse's lyrics replace a reference to Prince Charlie with a celebration of Gráinne Mhaol, the pirate queen Grace O'Malley, who fought and (according to legend) faced down Elizabeth the First of England; and the accompanying lines, emphasising self-help, insist that the rebels against empire are neither French nor Spanish but the Irish people themselves.

JACK JUDGE

'IT'S A LONG WAY TO TIPPERARY'

(1912)

The most beloved marching song among soldiers of the British army in World War One, it was written as a music-hall ditty in 1912. The Connaught Rangers sang it as they marched through Boulogne in August 1914 and a report of this in the *Daily Mail* helped its rapid dissemination among the forces. A recording by the Irish tenor John McCormack later that year made it a worldwide hit, capturing the homesickness of soldiers and the intent of couples separated by war to keep in touch. An earlier version, written with Harry Williams, had been called ↗

Up to mighty London
Came an Irishman one day.
As the streets are paved with gold
Sure, everyone was gay,
Singing songs of Piccadilly,
Strand and Leicester Square,
Till Paddy got excited,
Then he shouted to them there:

CHORUS
It's a long way to Tipperary,
It's a long way to go.
It's a long way to Tipperary
To the sweetest girl I know!
Goodbye, Piccadilly,
Farewell, Leicester Square!
It's a long long way to Tipperary,
But my heart's right there.

Paddy wrote a letter
To his Irish Molly-O,
Saying, 'Should you not receive it,
Write and let me know!'
'If I make mistakes in spelling,
Molly, dear,' said he,
'Remember, it's the pen that's bad,
Don't lay the blame on *me*!'

CHORUS

Molly wrote a neat reply
To Irish Paddy-O,
Saying 'Mike Maloney
Wants to marry me, and so
Leave the Strand and Piccadilly
Or you'll be to blame,
For love has fairly drove me silly:
Hoping you're the same!'

CHORUS

→ 'It's A Long Way to Connemara'. By locating a nostalgic Irishman dreaming of home in the city of London, the lyric repeats a manoeuvre made famous some years earlier by W. B. Yeats in 'The Lake Isle of Innisfree'—the national poet had been moved to write his exile's lament by the sight of a water fountain in a clay dish of a London shop window. The words of this song also have, however, a slightly stage-Irish element, which was quickly picked up in soldiers' parodies.

PERCY FRENCH

'THE MOUNTAINS OF MOURNE'

(1896)

Just six years after the publication of Yeats's 'The Lake Isle of Innisfree'—arguably the most famous poem of the Revival—Percy French wrote one of its most popular songs of exile. Apart from being an engineer and comic songster, French was a landscape artist with a deep feeling for the hills and valleys of his native land. Although at moments the song shades into his characteristic stage-Irish whimsy, that jocularity is kept in balance with a genuine lyric intensity (so that the humour, if anything, increases and completes the longing for home). ↗

Oh, Mary, this London's a wonderful sight,
With people all working by day and by night.
Sure they don't sow potatoes, nor barley, nor wheat,
But there's gangs of them digging for gold in the street.
At least when I asked them that's what I was told,
So I just took a hand at this digging for gold,
But for all that I found there I might as well be
Where the Mountains of Mourne sweep down to the sea.

I believe that when writing a wish you expressed
As to know how the fine ladies in London were dressed,
Well if you'll believe me, when asked to a ball,
They don't wear no top to their dresses at all.
Oh I've seen them meself and you could not in truth,
Say that if they were bound for a ball or a bath.
Don't be starting such fashions, now, Mary Macree,
Where the Mountains of Mourne sweep down to the sea.

I've seen England's king from the top of a bus
And I've never known him, but he means to know us.
And tho' by the Saxon we once were oppressed,
Still I cheered, God forgive me, I cheered with the rest.
And now that he's visited Erin's green shore
We'll be much better friends than we've been heretofore;
When we've got all we want, we're as quiet as can be
Where the mountains of Mourne sweep down to the sea.

You remember young Peter O'Loughlin, of course,
Well, now he is here at the head of the force.
I met him today, I was crossing the Strand,
And he stopped the whole street with a wave of his hand.
And there we stood talkin' of days that are gone,
While the whole population of London looked on;
But for all these great powers he's wishful like me,
To be back where the dark Mourne sweeps down to the sea.

There's beautiful girls here, oh never you mind,
With beautiful shapes nature never designed,
And lovely complexions all roses and cream,
But let me remark with regard to the same:
That if of those roses you venture to sip,
The colours might all come away on your lip,
So I'll wait for the wild rose that's waiting for me
In the place where the dark Mourne sweeps down to the sea.

→ Its appeal grew all the greater in the years after independence, when many families were broken by emigration and when letters home from some of the more sardonic departees hinted that the promised land had not turned out to be all that it was cracked up to be. French, whose own life was shadowed by the tragic death of his young wife and daughter in childbirth, died of pneumonia at the age of sixty-six in 1920.

J. M. SYNGE—*from*:

THE ARAN ISLANDS
The Grief of the Keen
(1907)

Poor health dogged
J. M. Synge through his
short life. He may have
projected his own sense
of mortality onto the
fishermen of the Aran
Islands. In talking with
them, he often felt as
if he were talking to a
man 'under a judgement
of death'. The beauty of
Aran life was connected
in his mind with its
precariousness as a
subsistence economy,
whose sponsors felt
battered by wind and
sea. In sensing that this
ancient way of life might
soon be doomed, Synge
was also projecting onto
it a sense of the imminent
death of his own social
class: but he was careful
also to note that wild jests
and loud laughter allowed
the people to express a
full emotional range. His
account of the caoine, a
formal lament by women
wailing over a dead body,
captures the ambiguity
of an island life caught
between pagan energy and
Christian resignation: but it
also shrewdly recognises
that every tradition lives on
in the very lament for its
passing.

THE MORNING HAD been beautifully fine, but as they lowered the coffin into the grave, thunder rumbled overhead and hailstones hissed among the bracken.

In Inishmaan one is forced to believe in a sympathy between man and nature, and at this moment when the thunder sounded a death-peal of extraordinary grandeur above the voices of the women, I could see the faces near me stiff and drawn with emotion.

When the coffin was in the grave, and the thunder had rolled away across the hills of Clare, the keen broke out again more passionately than before.

This grief of the keen is no personal complaint for the death of one woman over eighty years, but seems to contain the whole passionate rage that lurks somewhere in every native of the island. In this cry of pain the inner consciousness of the people seems to lay itself bare for an instant, and to reveal the mood of beings who feel their isolation in the face of a universe that wars on them with winds and seas. They are usually silent, but in the presence of death all outward show of indifference or patience is forgotten, and they shriek with pitiable despair before the horror of the fate to which they are all doomed.

Before they covered the coffin an old man kneeled down by the grave and repeated a simple prayer for the dead.

There was an irony in these words of atonement and Catholic belief spoken by voices that were still hoarse with the cries of pagan desperation.

A little beyond the grave I saw a line of old women who had recited in the keen sitting in the shadow of a wall beside the roofless shell of the church. They were still sobbing and shaken with grief, yet they were beginning to talk again of the daily trifles that veil from them the terror of the world. ■

DERMOT O'BYRNE/ARNOLD BAX

MUSIC IN IRELAND

(1952)

I LIKE TO dally with the fancy that the creative mind in mountainous and hilly countries tends to express itself almost exclusively through the medium of literature, leaving the arts of music and painting to the plains. Certainly during the last hundred years or more there has been a ceaseless and phenomenal outpouring of books of all kinds in Ireland and Norway, both of them small and hilly lands. The casual stroller in Dublin or Oslo, in Cork or in Bergen, might reasonably expect to collide with a poet or dramatist round every street corner, whilst hitherto neither country has—with a few notable exceptions, e.g. Jack Yeats—achieved very much of outstanding merit in the other arts. Norway, of course, is rightly proud of her *petit maître* Edvard Grieg, incidentally one of the most truly national composers who was ever born (though whether nationalism in art is a desirability can be a matter for non-stop debate). But Grieg is an isolated figure. The Irish for their part can point to C.V. Stanford, Charles Wood, and Hamilton Harty. Unhappily, these three undoubtedly proficient musicians were assiduous and dutiful disciples of the nineteenth-century German tradition, even whilst clothing their native melodies in all too conventional dress. They never penetrated to within a thousand miles of the hidden Ireland.

This lack of individuality is the more curious since of all countries in the world Ireland possesses the most varied and beautiful folk music, though even now it cannot be fully appreciated in its strange and startling richness until the great collection of gramophone records enshrined in the library of the Irish Folklore Commission is made accessible to the general public. Here is folk music in splendid barbaric nudity (much of it coming from Connemara) and despite

Born into a wealthy family in London in 1883, Arnold Bax studied composition, clarinet and piano at the Royal Academy of Music. An early encounter with the poems of Yeats prompted him to learn Irish (often on visits to Glencolumbkille, County Donegal). He adopted the pseudonym 'Dermot O'Byrne', under which he wrote poetry and short stories derived from Irish folk tales, as well as a 1913 novel *Children of the Hills*. He said that even in music he 'began to write Irishly, using figures and melodies of a definitely Celtic curve.' He attempted an Irish national opera on the Deirdre theme. His impressionistic strain combined with Celtic themes in such tone-poems as 'Cathleen Ni Houlihan' (1905) and 'Rosc-Catha' ('Battle-Hymn' 1910). After the 1916 Rising he composed a lament →

more decent 'arrangements' by Stanford, Harty, Hughes, and others 'there's more enterprise in walking naked.' This music derives from the heart and core of Ireland.

I have known Ireland intimately for forty-five years and love her better than any land 'beneath the visiting moon.' Indeed since the National University was generous enough to confer an honorary degree upon me in 1947 I feel delightedly that I have become a naturalised Gael! This is sufficient reason that the desire for the country's musical awakening lies very near my heart.

In my early Dublin days I moved in an almost wholly literary circle. There was no talk of music whatever; indeed AE never tired of relating time after time how I had lived in the city for two or three winters before he discovered that I was a musician at all. Both AE and W.B. Yeats were tone deaf, though on one rare occasion the former expressed admiration for *Tristan and Isolde* (of all things!). Other than this the only comment upon music I heard from him was at an evening gathering in Rathgar Avenue when apropos of nothing in particular he suddenly remarked, 'There is a composer named Brahms. He aims at intense profundity, but all he achieves is an impenetrable fog!' I cannot recall anything of musical activity in Dublin at that time except a recital by Cortot, a week of Pavlova at the Gaiety (as regards music this was negligible, for the great dancer's taste was very indifferent) and the visit in 1912 of Thomas Quinlan's operatic company giving for the first time in Dublin *Tristan* and *Die Walküre*. It seemed strange indeed that a capital city had never before heard these world-famous and almost hoary masterpieces.

Perhaps the best regular institution at that period was the tiny chamber orchestra performing at the intervals of the Abbey plays. Directed by J.F. Larchet, the music was always of a high standard and carefully prepared by its gifted conductor. That was very long ago, but I do not think there was much more liveliness in the musical life of Ireland until quite recently—indeed, until the foundation of the Radio Éireann Orchestra. ■

W. B. YEATS

AN ABBEY SCHOOL OF BALLET

(1934)

BEGAN WRITING little dance plays, founded upon a Japanese model, that need no scenery, no properties, and can be performed in studio or drawing-room, thinking that some group of students might make a little money playing them and gradually elaborate a technique that would respect literature and music alike. Whenever I produced one of these plays I asked my singers for no new method, did not even talk to them upon the subject. When the Abbey School of Ballet was founded I tried these plays upon the stage where they seemed out of place. Why should musician or actor fold and unfold a cloth when the proscenium curtain was there, why carry on to the stage drum, gong, and flute when the orchestra was there? *Fighting the Waves* and the present play so far imitate the Japanese model that they climax in a dance, substitute suggestion for representation, but like the Japanese plays themselves they are stage plays.

The orchestra brings more elaborate music and I have gone over to the enemy. I say to the musician 'Lose my words in patterns of sound as the name of God is lost in Arabian arabesques. They are a secret between the singers, myself, yourself. The plain fable, the plain prose of the dialogue, Ninette de Valois' dance are there for the audience. They can find my words in the book if they are curious, but we will not thrust our secret upon them. I can be as subtle and metaphysical as I like without endangering the clarity necessary for dramatic effect. The Elizabethan singer, according to Edmund Spenser—and his music was simpler than yours—read out his song before he sang it. We will adopt no such arbitrary practice; our secret is our religion.'

Purists in the Gaelic League repeatedly in the early years of the Revival denounced four- and eight-hand reels as un-Irish. But since some of the dances had come via England from France, nobody was sure exactly what an Irish form of dance might be. In March 1906 Eoghan Brioscu said in a letter to *An Claidheamh Soluis* that 'an Irishman is not the less Irish because he waltzes or joins in a set of lancers.' At about this time W. B. Yeats, inspired by Oscar Wilde's *Salomé*, began to explore ways in which the body might express the spirit, much to the chagrin of Augusta Gregory who found in explicit sensuality 'a degradation of our stage.' But Yeats persisted in using dance in many plays, eventually inviting Ninette de Valois to found a →

→ school of ballet at the
Abbey at 1927. This ran
with about sixteen students
until 1933, using traditional
melodies but shunning
the rather rigid forms of
céili dancing for a more
full-body experience. In his
preface to *The King of the
Great Clock Tower* (1934),
Yeats explained his interest.

The dance with the severed head, suggests the central idea of Wilde's *Salomé*. Wilde took it from Heine who has somewhere described Salomé in hell throwing into the air the head of John the Baptist. Heine may have found it in some Jewish religious legend for it is part of the old ritual of the year; the mother goddess and the slain god. In the first edition of *The Secret Rose* there is a story based on some old Gaelic legend. A certain man swears to sing the praise of a certain woman, his head is cut off and the head sings. A poem of mine called 'He Gives His Beloved Certain Rhymes' was the song of the head. In attempting to put that story into a dance play I found that I had gone close to Salomé's dance in Wilde's play. But in his play the dance is before the head is cut off. ■

Social Conditions

ALTHOUGH THE IRISH Revival is widely thought of as a high-minded intellectual affair, many of the most significant literary figures were anxious to change the social conditions and material realities of the poorest of the Irish people. A poet such as George Russell, for example, invested considerable energy cycling around Ireland, preaching the gospel of rural reform and agricultural co-operation to small farmers. On the other side of the coin, social organisers and political activists took a healthy interest in literary matters, and had much to say about the role of culture in the fight to change Irish society. Not only did Maud Gonne agitate against appalling poverty in the west of Ireland but she also acted in rousing revolutionary plays. As a result, the period produced a rich ferment of intellectual debate on the relationship between culture and politics. Literary figures like Yeats critiqued social agitators for their programmatic thinking and adherence to rigid ideological models. Activists like James Connolly responded by pointing out that the literary pursuits of the leisured classes were far removed from the day-to-day realities of Dublin's poor. Synge reconciled these two perspectives by suggesting that the best kind of analysis was produced 'where the dreamer is leaning out to reality, or where the man of real life is lifted out of it.' This aphorism sums up very well a Revival movement in which the best creative minds were constantly confronted with the abrasive pressures of political agitation, and the most skilled activists worked in the backwash of extraordinary artistic innovation.

The richness of such cultural debates, however, could never compensate for the social conditions that afflicted the poorest sections of the Irish population in country and city. As late as 1898 people were dying from famine conditions in County Mayo. The eyewitness accounts of the period testify to the ill-thought-out 'relief' measures that often compounded the suffering of the poor, and stifled local enterprise. Roads were built which led nowhere, and government policy often exacerbated the poverty that it was supposed to relieve. Meanwhile, an emerging elite of middlemen shopkeepers regularly profited on the misfortune of the vulnerable people who were most beholden to them. In a similar fashion, government land reforms often concentrated holdings in the hands of the better-off rather than effecting radical redistribution of property. It was to counter such aggrandising tendencies in rural Ireland that the co-operative movement was set up. Small farmers were encouraged to combine to achieve economies of scale, and modern agricultural methods were introduced. A central element of the programme promoted in the *Irish Homestead* was the improvement of the social and cultural life of the rural districts. This was an attempt to neutralise the tendency of the younger generations to flee from the sheer boredom, as well as the poverty, of country life.

For those escaping subsistence conditions in rural districts, city life provided little comfort. In Dublin, unscrupulous landlords squeezed entire families into single rooms. Over 20,000 families lived in slum conditions in the crumbling grandeur of Georgian townhouses on the city's northside. Medical statistics ranked the city among the unhealthiest of the British empire with shameful death rates, infant mortality, and levels of disease. Those lucky enough to find jobs were often brutally treated by their employers, working long hours in dangerous environments for poor wages. In 1913, as the workforce mobilised for better conditions in response to the leadership of James Larkin, strikers were locked out by the employers, and were violently

abused by the police. Despite the setbacks, James Connolly
urged workers to unite in the cause of socialism against their
capitalist oppressors. He broadly supported the revival of Irish
culture and traditions of radical action but, like Sean O'Casey,
was wary of the bourgeois aspirations of some Revivalists.
Connolly also bemoaned the self-centred insularity often
evident in the Gaelic movement. Yet he was critical, too, of the
industrial processes of capitalism which homogenised cultural
experience everywhere and destroyed local distinctiveness.
In this respect, he anticipated later critiques of the culture
industry promoted by prominent European Marxists.

Much of the social commentary of the day laid the blame
for Irish poverty and suffering on British misrule, with
initiatives such as the relief works and the Poor Law system
being singled out for particular criticism. As Irish society
made the uncertain shift from colony to independence,
expectations gathered that these failed ideas and institutions
would be replaced by the more enlightened and socially aware
thinking of the 1916 generation.

MAUD GONNE—*from*:

THE DISTRESS IN THE WEST

(1898)

Returning from a lecture tour in America, Maud Gonne was distressed to hear of new outbreaks of famine in the west of Ireland. She travelled to the congested districts of County Mayo to survey the situation and publicise the hardship she encountered. She was outraged by the inadequacy of the official response to widespread starvation and circulated a leaflet, jointly written with James Connolly, urging the starving people to seize supplies of food necessary for survival. Gonne used her influence, and funds she had raised, to organise nursing for those sick with famine fever. She also supported the building of a fish-curing plant at Belderrig, County Mayo to make available a food source other than the potato. In this letter published in the *Freeman's Journal* on 30 March 1898, she gives an eye-witness account of the appalling suffering taking place in Belderrig, describing in detail the distress of mothers and children and the unjust nature of official 'relief' measures.

D EAR SIR—I have been travelling in Mayo for the last month, where I have been distributing the little sums kindly contributed by the readers of *L'Irlande Libre*. I am powerless to describe the suffering I have witnessed. The famine as usual is accompanied by a terrible amount of sickness. In Belderrig, a village in Killala Union, composed of some twenty houses, eighteen people have died from measles; they are terrible, these famine measles; killing people in less than three days and leaving the corpses black and dreadful. In many other places I hear the influenza is proving as fatal. If we would look facts honestly in the face and call things by their right names we should say that these unfortunate peasants died not of measles or influenza, but of starvation. If they had proper food and nourishment they would, like the rest of us, have strength to resist these ailments. I saw mothers with nothing to give their dying children but Indian corn, stirabout and no milk.

... It is true the government has granted a loan to the guardians to buy seed for the people, but the conditions of this loan are so unpractical that in many places where potato seed can be bought in the ordinary market for 3s a hundred weight, the guardians are charging the people actually as much as 9s the hundred weight. They have two years in which to repay it.

Three years ago this same sort of relief was given, and I am told that in many places the potatoes thus supplied, at three times the market prices, were so bruised and rotten that not one-third were available for seed, though the unfortunate people had to pay for them just the same. As if to emphasise the mockery of this so-called assistance, at the beginning of this winter, when the pinch of hunger was already keenly felt, the last instalment of this old seed rate was collected. People who had saved a few pounds of this money earned in England and Scotland to buy seed had to give it up to pay the old debt, while those who had no money saw their last cow driven off, which meant no milk for the children, and in some cases even the flannel spun by the women to make clothes for the young ones was seized to repay the British government's last charity. What wonder if this year the people, though entirely without seed, should refuse such onerous help? ▪

J.M. SYNGE—*from*:

'THE INNER LANDS OF MAYO'

(1905)

In 1905 Synge was commissioned by the *Manchester Guardian* newspaper to write a series of articles on the economic and social condition of the 'congested districts' of the west of Ireland. He was accompanied on this trip by the artist, Jack B. Yeats, who illustrated the articles. These essays are stark in their reportage of acute poverty experienced by the most vulnerable of the rural population. They are pointed, too, in attributing blame for the dire state of rural Ireland. Synge was critical of the misguided government relief schemes that created a culture of abject dependency and stifled enterprise. He was most disparaging, however, of the dubious practices of the publican-grocers or 'gombeen men', who wielded disproportionate power in the poorest regions of the country. In his view, the cosy alliance between publicans, politicians, the clergy and the professions exerted as malign an influence on the peasantry as the colonial administration.

THERE IS A curious change in the appearance of the country when one moves inland from the coast districts of Mayo to the congested portion of the inner edge of the county. In this place there are no longer the Erris tracts of bog or the tracts of stone of Connemara; but one sees everywhere low hills and small farms of poor land that is half turf-bog, already much cut away, and half narrow plots of grass or tillage. Here and there one meets with little villages, built on the old system, with cottages closely grouped together and filled with primitive people, the women mostly in bare feet, with white handkerchiefs over their heads. . . . we walked on for a few miles, and then turned into one of the wayside public-houses, at the same time general shop and bar, which are a peculiar feature of most of the country parts of Ireland. An old one-eyed man, with a sky-blue handkerchief round his neck, was standing at the counter making up his bill with the publican, and disputing loudly over it. Here, as in most of the congested districts, the shops are run on a vague system of credit that is not satisfactory, though one does not see at once what other method could be found to take its place. After the sale of whatever the summer season has produced—pigs, cattle, kelp, etc.—the bills are paid off, more or less fully, and all the ready money of a family is thus run away with. Then about Christmas time a new bill is begun, which runs on till the following autumn—or later in the harvesting districts—and quite small shopkeepers often put out relatively large sums in this way. The people keep no pass-books, so they have no check on the traders, and although direct fraud is probably rare it is likely that the prices charged are often exorbitant. What is worse, the shopkeeper in out-of-the-way places is usually the only buyer to be had for a number of home products, such as eggs, chickens, carragheen moss, and sometimes even kelp; so that he can control the prices both of what he buys and what he sells, while as a creditor he has an authority that makes bargaining impossible: another of the many complicated causes that keep the people near to pauperism!

'The people keep no pass-books, so they have no check on the traders, and although direct fraud is probably rare it is likely that the prices charged are often exorbitant.'

IRISH HOMESTEAD COMPETITION

(1901)

The *Irish Homestead* was the journal of the Irish Agricultural Organisation Society founded by Horace Plunkett in 1894. Although dedicated to promoting modern farming methods and the ethos of agricultural co-operation, this remarkable publication also took an interest in the social life of rural Ireland. Edited by George Russell (AE), it published work by many of the leading literary figures of the period, including James Joyce, whose first short story, 'The Sisters', was published in its pages. Joyce's attack on 'paralysis' in that story was appropriately in line with the editorial policy of the journal. On 9 November 1901, the *Homestead* advertised a competition to encourage co-operative societies to improve the cultural and civic life of Ireland's towns and villages. The prize went to the Dromahair society in County Leitrim for establishing a library and setting up a feis ceoil.

HOMESTEAD COMPETITION
IMPORTANT NOTICE

The *Irish Homestead* has been enabled, through the generosity of Mr. Horace Plunkett, whose interest in Irish things is not confined solely to economics, to initiate A COMPETITION OF UNIQUE CHARACTER.

A FIRST PRIZE OF £25
A SECOND PRIZE OF £15
and
A THIRD PRIZE OF £10

to the co-operative society which shall have done most during the six months ending the 31st March next, to make their parish a place where no Irishman would like to emigrate from.

The particular form of social amelioration which the societies may undertake is left altogether to themselves but, for their guidance, the following suggestions are made:

a) Revival of national sports, Gaelic pastimes, and other outdoor games.

b) Establishment of classes for Gaelic, Irish literature and poetry.

c) Organisation of village libraries.

d) The revival of the Céilithe.

e) Encouragement of Irish music and song by local concerts or classes.

f) The formation of village choirs.

g) Dances, jigs and recitations.

h) Crusade against badly kept and dirty homesteads. ∎

JAMES CONNOLLY—*from*:

'THE LANGUAGE MOVEMENT'

(1898)

TALKING OF GAELIC scholars brings me by an easy and natural transition to speak of the great Celtic renascence of late years.

I think it has its bad and its good points. Its bad points are, in my opinion, only accidental to the movement and were well got rid of. *largely uncritical*

They consist in the attempt to exclude all other methods of culture, to deny the value of all other literature and the worth of all other peoples and, in general, to make our Irish youths and maidens too self-centred. *necessary in establishing national identity*

I believe the Gaelic movement has great promise of life in it, but that promise will only be properly fulfilled when it naturally works its way into the life of the nation, side by side with every other agency making for a regenerated people.

The chief enemy of a Celtic revival today is the crushing force of capitalism which irresistibly destroys all national or racial characteristics, and by sheer stress of its economic preponderance reduces a Galway or a Dublin, a Lithuania or a Warsaw to the level of a mere second-hand imitation of Manchester or Glasgow. *national freedom as 2nd w cos becoming economic freedom as*

In the words of Karl Marx, 'capitalism creates a world after its own image,' and the image of capitalism is to be found in the industrial centres of Great Britain.

A very filthy image indeed.

You cannot teach starving men Gaelic; and the treasury of our national literature will and must remain lost forever to the poor wage-slaves who are contented by our system of society to toil from early morning to late at night for a mere starvation wage.

Therefore, I say to our friends of the Gaelic movement— your proper place is in the ranks of the Socialist Republican

how can occur new when Bri wiped out?

James Connolly, the son of Irish immigrants, was born on 5 June 1868 in Edinburgh. He had little formal education but a love of reading and a belief in workers' rights led him to the socialist literature and ideas of the time. Influenced by the British labour leader, James Keir Hardie, he moved to Dublin in 1896 as a socialist organiser and set up the Irish Socialist Republican Party. Over the next two decades, Connolly emerged as the major voice of Irish socialism writing for journals such as the *Workers' Republic* and the *Shan Van Vocht*. Although critical of bourgeois forms of parliamentary nationalism, Connolly's socialism was deeply informed by the radical ideas of the Irish republican tradition. In this article, published on 1 October 1898 in the *Workers'* →

→ Republic, he criticises the lofty aestheticism that characterised literary circles during the Revival. As a self-educated intellectual, Connolly was well aware of the transformative power of high ideas but was keen to emphasise the harsh realities of working-class life—'you can't teach starving men Gaelic,' as he puts it. Although he attended the Abbey Theatre, Connolly did not contribute to the enterprise as a playwright. Instead he involved himself in 'street theatre' and orchestrated protests to advance his class-based analysis of the Irish question.

Party, fighting for the abolition of this accursed social system which grinds us down in such a manner; which debases the character and lowers the ideals of our people to such a fearful degree, that to the majority of our workers the most priceless manuscript of ancient Celtic lore would hold but a secondary place in their esteem beside a rasher of bacon.

Help us to secure to all our fellow-countrymen, a free, full, and happy life; secure in possession of a rational, human existence, neither brutalised by toil nor debilitated by hunger, and then all the noble characteristics of our race will have full opportunity to expand and develop. And when all that is good in literature, art, and science, is recognised as the property of all—and not the heritage of the few—your ideals will receive the unquestioned adhesion of all true Irishmen.

I do not ask you to cease for a moment your endeavours on your present lines of education, but only to recognise in us your natural allies, as you should recognise that those who, under any pretext, however specious, would ask you to help them to perpetuate that British capitalism—which now thwarts you at every turn—is your enemy and the enemy of your cause.

The success of our cause is certain—sooner or later. But the welcome light of the sun of freedom may, at any moment, flash upon our eyes and with your help we would not fear the storm which may precede the dawn. ■

SEAN O'CASEY—*from*:

DRUMS UNDER THE WINDOWS

(1949)

S EAN HOPED NO-ONE who knew him would come along this way, especially any Gaelic League friend or a Republican brother. Not that he cared a lot, of course, but it was just as well to keep a few things hidden from the sneaking world. And didn't he remember well good-natured Peader O'Nuallain catching his arm one day, and drawing him aside to whisper—what d'ye think now?—nothing less than 'Why don't you wear a collar and tie, Sean, and not come to the Branch with a muffler around your neck?' Of course, that remark ringed his neck with a muffler for the rest of his days, for he wasn't the one to germinate into unaccustomed grandeur of clothing so that Gaelic snobs of school teachers, civil servants, and customs officers shouldn't shiver with shame when he was near them. When I was dry with rage, and extreme toil, breathless and faint, leaning upon my sword, came there a certain lord, neat and trimly dressed, and perfumed like a milliner. Ay, indeed, there's a lot of fretful popinjays lisping Irish wrongly. Fight for Irish—no, fight for collars and ties, and it's these boyòs that have handed Michael O'Hickey to humiliation, limping lonely through the streets of Rome.

Here he was, up every morning at five, bar Sunday, home again at six in the evening, after a hard day's work with hack, shovel, sledgehammer, or hod; out again at seven to work even harder for the Gaelic League or Republican Brotherhood till he heard the bells chime at midnight; and, in between, after much agony, fear, and heart-searching, he had pulled out the jewelled pins of thought keeping together the coloured and golden Gospel-pictures of prophet, saint, apostle, martyr, and virgin singing laughingly hand in hand with the sons of the morning, so that they came all asunder,

Although Sean O'Casey lived in tenements and endured acute poverty, he did not suffer the worst conditions of the northside slums. In his Dublin plays and autobiographical writings, however, he drew attention to the poverty-ridden and unsanitary conditions endured by large sections of Dublin's population. In 1880, the year O'Casey was born, the *Medical Press* reported that no other city in Britain, Europe or Asia 'approaches Dublin in unhealthiness'. At this time, the death-rate stood at 44.8 per 1000 of the population; by 1958, the figure was 12.5. O'Casey's parents, in fact, had suffered the tragic loss of eight children before he was born. His first-hand experience of these dire conditions, together with his deep interest in socialism, led him to →

→ take a more sober view
of nationalist cultural
activities. He was
particularly critical of
the evangelical zeal and
bourgeois ethos palpable
in certain Gaelic League
circles. Some clerks and
young professionals, it
seemed to him, became
interested in the language
revival as a way of
furthering their own social
mobility rather than out of
any genuine commitment
to speaking Irish.

and fell into the dust and rain and cold appraisal of a waxing world, their colours dimmed, the glittering figures forced into fading, the gold between them losing its reverence, and turning an ashen grey in the red glow of all life's problems. And all this, and more, they tell me should be respectably circled by a collar and a tie!

He was leaning against a railing outside a tenement house in Summerhill on a damp November day, a cold core in the moist air that looked dark under the leaden sky that panelled the heavens. His sister, with her five youngsters, had been hunted from their home for non-payment of rent, her worldly goods had been carried out and deposited in the street just beyond the sidewalk, to do with as she would, but to take them somewhere soon, as a policeman had told her, because she couldn't be let leave an obstruction in the street to impede the passage of law-abiding citizens.

His sister's husband had died in the asylum, and a sight he was when he was placed in the coffin. Practising on him they were, said Mick. One could see the marks round his head where, said Mick, the skull had been lifted, and the brain removed, so that it could be watched for developments later on in the day. Sean had pressed his hand over the poor body, and was shocked to find nothing there but flat bone. And the knee of one leg was embedded deep in the breast just under the chin. They tried, said Mick, with a block and tackle, to get it to lie down decently, but it wouldn't budge. Sean was very glad when the pitying earth covered it kindly up forever. His sister and her young were sheltering with him and his mother for the time being, and he had taken a day off to take care of the Benson property now collected before him in the street. He was tired and sleepy, having worked for forty-eight hours without a break as a member of a gang repairing a bridge that had shown signs of wanting to sit down and have a rest itself. Poor as the things were, they couldn't afford to let any be pinched, for they were all the Bensons had, and so he was waiting for a one-eyed friend to come with an ass and car to take them to the shelter and safety of his own home.

He glanced over them again to tick them off, for he had dozed several times in spite of a continuous effort to keep awake: a kitchen table—the one whole thing among the little heap of goods; three chairs, with slats of rough wood nailed across where the seats used to be; a sofa, with a few rags of false leather still cleaving to it, and bunches of hairy fibre oozing through holes in the sacking that vainly tried to keep it under cover; a wash-hand stand with a tin basin on the top of it; the frame and laths of a wide iron bedstead; a broken, rusty iron fender; an old dresser, with two drawers that held two knives, one fork, and three spoons; two metal saucepans and a kettle; the tin bowl of a one-wicked lamp; an iron lath to do the work of a poker whenever they had a fire; a sweeping brush that was almost bald; a butter-box with the seat painted red, two sides white, and the other sides blue; a frying-pan with a patch on its bottom; a rug, tawny now with dirt and stains, once a brilliant thing of red, white, and blue wool, with a Union Jack in its centre, that Drummer Benson had made on a frame for Ella before they were married—and two others, of blue and red cloth, made of strips torn from old soldiers' trousers, and the red stripes that streaked each leg of them. ∎

---

from:

'THE GREAT REVIVAL: A WAVE OF TEMPERANCE'

(1910)

The weakness for alcohol had been a concern within nationalist Ireland from the end of the eighteenth century. A drinking culture that promoted a vibrant tradition of storytelling and informing was also blamed for the failure of numerous revolutionary plans and activities. Fr. Theobald Mathew successfully led a national temperance crusade in the decade preceding the Famine. Such was his influence that William Wilde (father of Oscar) could remark wryly in 1852: 'Well honoured be the name of Theobald Mathew but, after all, a power of fun went away with the whiskey.' ↗

A WONDERFUL THING is happening in Ireland. Ireland itself does not seem to properly appreciate how great and wonderful this thing is. A mighty wave of temperance is sweeping over the land, though very many people may not realise the extent of it.

This mighty movement of Temperance Reform is already great in power. It has assumed magnificent proportions. It is being attended with glorious results. Day by day it is becoming more 'live' and achieving greater effort. It is in no sense a class movement. It is not confined to any particular section of our people. It is general. It is national. That is an aspect of the movement I would like to emphasise—its national aspect.

Of course, there is nothing new in a temperance movement. No more is there anything new in a language movement or in an industrial movement. But whereas it seems to be generally recognised that our language movement and our industrial movement have been attended with great success, the same knowledge does not seem to be as widely shared in respect of the Temperance movement. Yet the Temperance cause is making splendid headway—sure and steady headway.

EDUCATING PUBLIC OPINION

Then look at the splendid demonstrations that are being held through the country. His Eminence Cardinal Logue presided last Sunday at Dundalk over a mighty gathering of twenty thousand followers of the Total Abstinence Movement. Twenty trainloads of people poured into the town for the occasion. They came from Down, Armagh, Tyrone, Monaghan, Cavan, Louth, and Dublin. A mighty

HANDBOOK OF THE IRISH REVIVAL

muster of earnest, enthusiastic total abstainers. Next
Sunday, Longford will be the venue of another monster
demonstration and on the 9th of July there will be
witnessed in Ulster the first great organised public
demonstration of those associated with the new form of
Temperance propaganda classically denominated by the
Catch-my-Pal movement. It is of recent origin, yet it claims
150,000 adherents. Its leader is Rev. Mr. Patterson, and it
might be said to be the first really great organised effort on
the part of Protestant Ulster in which the drink traffic is
confronted and fought by aggression. It might also be said
that the idea of this Catch-my-Pal movement was inspired
by the practical work done by Rev. P. Sheerin, now Parish
Priest of Crossmaglen, who while in Armagh city never lost
a chance of winning over a recruit to Total Abstinence and
of stimulating others to do the same.

SPREADING THE LIGHT

What has caused this public feeling? I asked the question of
one of the best-known authorities. He told me. The present
flourishing state of the Temperance Cause, he said, is
entirely due to the splendid earnest co-operation amongst
people and clergy of all denominations, in season and out of
season, in creating and fostering a sound and enlightened
public opinion on the evils of intemperance.

The Gaelic League puts Temperance in the forefront of
its propaganda. Its main plank is patriotism. Its teaching
is that every man who labours for the betterment of his
country and its people is so far a patriot, and it emphasises
the point that Ireland for the Irish would avail us naught
if we remain fettered by what is described a national

→ The great successor to the earlier movement was the Pioneer Total Abstinence Association of the Sacred Heart founded by Fr. James Cullen S.J. in 1898; although Protestant churches, too, consistently promoted temperance. It caught on quickly and by 1917 recorded a membership of over 250,000. This article published in the *Irish Independent* on 29 June 1910 compares the growing temperance movement to the movements for language revival and development of Irish industries.

curse, calamity, and scandal. Milk and minerals and light refreshments may be had at feiseanna and industrial exhibitions. No alcohol. A branch of the League may not have its meeting on licensed premises. Even now there is a movement to do away with the custom that prevailed of holding athletic sports and Gaelic pastimes in the near vicinity of public houses. Crossroad orgies are no longer countenanced. ▪

'Crossroad orgies are no
longer countenanced.'

SUSANNE R. DAY—*from*:

'THE WORKHOUSE CHILD'

(1912)

O F ALL THE thousands of men and women who daily pass the great gates of our Irish workhouses, how many, we wonder, give a thought to the child life within? To how many does the term 'the workhouse child' conjure up a vision of Oliver Twist, empty porridge cup in hand, asking for more, and to how many, an army of young boys and girls, the citizens of tomorrow, thrust through no fault of their own into surroundings shadowed by failure and disgrace?

The passer-by, if he thinks at all about these little derelicts, will find a thousand questions thronging upon his mind. How are they housed, how fed, how trained; is their education one that will secure for them economic independence by and bye, will it give them a fair start in life, develop their resources, and teach them independence and self-reliance, or is it a machine-made system turning out machine-made animated images, without ambition, without initiative, without individuality?

Within its four walls everything that is or has been of evil may be found in its symptoms or its effects, embodied in men and women whose souls are seared with the brand of vice, and whose standard of life is sometimes scarcely higher than that of the brute. And there, too, are the children, daily exposed to sights and sounds which cannot but have a deteriorating effect, and learning to look upon the Workhouse as a home to which in times of stress and struggle they will return in later life as surely as the homing pigeon returns to its loft.

Susanne Rouvier Day was born in Cork in 1876 and is best known as a suffragist, social activist and writer. She was a co-founder of the Munster Women's Franchise League and was also a member of the Cork branch of the Irishwomen's Suffrage Federation. With fellow Corkonian, Geraldine Cummins, she wrote two plays for the Abbey Theatre that reflected their interest in suffragist issues. *Broken Faith* (1913) tackles the question of spousal abuse while *Fox and Geese* (1917) pokes fun at the rituals of marital courtship. Day travelled to France in 1916 to work as a nurse during the First World War. Her memoir, *Round about Bar-le-Duc*, is based on her wartime experiences during the battle of Verdun. Another volume *Where the Mistral Blows* was published in 1933. In 1911 she became one of the first women to be elected a poor-law guardian →

→ in Cork and thereafter campaigned for reform. This article published in the *Irish Review* in 1912 is a scathing critique of the maltreatment of children under the poor law regime. In language that echoes Pearse's analysis of education, she draws attention to 'a machine-made system' that crushes the individuality of the children in its care. Social commentary of this nature informed the aspiration of the 1916 Proclamation to cherish all the children of the nation equally. Indeed, the aim to abolish the 'odious, degrading and foreign Poor Law System' was explicitly stated in the Democratic Programme of the First Dáil in 1919. The new Irish state offloaded these responsibilities largely on the Catholic Church, which retained many of the structures of the old system while remaining democratically unaccountable.

Few people seem to realise that the teacher who instructs a boy in the school probably oversees his conduct in the playground, watches him during mealtimes, superintends him during evening hours, and may even be on duty in the dormitory at night. And still fewer seem to understand what effect such constant intercourse may have upon the nerves of teacher and taught. Even though the former has his annual holiday, for many pupils there is no such respite. All over the country there may be found children who have spent years within the cheerless precincts, imprisoned as surely as any convict in his cell, leading dreary, monotonous existences filled with dreary, monotonous duties, day in day out practically without interruption—a day in the country or a treat at Christmas being the sum total of their amusements.

From every workhouse in the country the cry of the children goes up; under every workhouse roof pathetic tragedies of unhappy child-life unfold themselves day by day. Our responsibility can no longer be denied or shirked; we cannot, like Pilate, wash our hands and say that the fault is not ours, nor can we choose the coward's path and say that the fault is theirs. For the children are innocent. They suffer for the sins of others, and it lies with us to decide whether the burden of that suffering is to continue on its intolerable way, or to be lifted from shoulders too weak to carry it, too innocent to deserve it and too helpless to remove it. ▪

JAMES LARKIN—*from*:

'LARKIN'S SCATHING INDICTMENT OF DUBLIN SWEATERS'

(1913)

THE FIRST POINT I wish to make is that the employers in this city, and throughout Ireland generally, think they have a right to deal with their own as they please, and to use and exploit the workers as they please. They assume all the rights and deny any to the men who make their wealth. They are men who say they are of paramount intelligence; they say they are able in organising abilities as 'captains of industry'; that they can always carry out their business in their own way. They deny the right of the men and women who work for them to combine and try and assist one another to improve their conditions of life. While denying the men and women who work for them the right to combine, these men not only take unto themselves this right, but they also intimidate the men—a matter upon which I shall enlarge later on.

Will these gentlemen opposite accept responsibility? They say they have the right to control the means by which the workers live. They must, therefore, accept responsibility for the conditions under which the workers live. Twenty-one thousand families living in the dirty slums of Dublin, five persons in each room, with, I suppose, less than one thousand cubic feet. Yet it was laid down that each sleeping room should at least have 300 cubic feet space. In Mountjoy Jail—where I have had the honour to reside on more than one occasion—criminals (but I am inclined to believe that most of the criminals were outside and innocent men inside) were allowed 400 cubic feet. Yet men who slave and work, and their women—those beautiful women we have among the working classes—are compelled to live, many of them, five in a room, with less than 300 cubic feet. They are taken from their mother's breasts at an early age and are used up as material is used up in a fire. These are some of the conditions that obtain in this Catholic city of Dublin, the most church-going city, I believe, in the world.

James Larkin was born in Liverpool on 28 January 1874 to recent Irish immigrants. He developed a deep interest in labour activism at an early age and would play a crucial role in the development of trade union politics in Ireland. Sent to Belfast as a union organiser in January 1907, he called a general strike in Belfast port some months later, and proved his capabilities as a leader and charismatic speaker. Shortly afterwards, Larkin founded the Irish Transport and General Workers' Union out of the belief that Irish workers needed to be represented by Irish unions. The epic stand-off between labour and capital that took place in Dublin in 1913 was caused by the refusal of the major employers to allow their workers to join Larkin's union. In September of that year, over 20,000 workers →

→ were locked out of their places of work in an attempt to break the union. This passage is taken from Larkin's evidence, on 2 October 1913, before a commission of inquiry into the circumstances that led to Lock-Out. In an earlier contribution, William Martin Murphy requested that the employers be represented by the barrister, Tim Healy, as they lacked the ability to present their own case. Larkin was chosen to reply on behalf of the workers.

Mr. Healy has drawn a picture from the employers' viewpoint. I want to show the other side, the true side. I will use other pigments and more vivid colours. Go to some of the factories in Dublin. See some of the maimed men, maimed girls, with hands cut off, eyes knocked out, eyes punctured, bodies and souls seared, and think of the time when they are no longer useful to come up to the £1 a week or some other standard. Then they are thrown on the human scrapheap.

See at every street corner the mass degradation controlled by the employers, and due to the existing system. Their only thought was the public house, and, driven to death, they made their way thither to poison their bodies and get a false stimulant to enable them, for a time, to give something more back to the employer for the few paltry shillings thrown at them. These are the men whom the employers called loafers. Mr. Murphy has agreed with me that in the main the Dublin worker is a good, decent chap, but Mr. Murphy and others of his class deny the Dublin men the right to work on the Dublin trams, on the Dublin quays, and in the Dublin factories. They deny Dublin men the right to enjoy the full fruit of their activities. Why? Because they want to bring up in their place poor, uncultured serfs from the country, who know nothing of Dublin or city life—to bring these men into a congested area, so that they would bring down the wages of the men already here. The employers do this because their souls are steeped in grime and actuated only by the hope of profit-making, and because they have no social conscience. But this lock-out will arouse a social conscience in Dublin and in Ireland generally. I am out to help to arouse that social conscience and to lift up and better the lot of those who are sweated and exploited. But I am also out to save the employers from themselves, to save them from degradation and damnation. ■

JAMES JOYCE—*from*:

A PORTRAIT OF THE ARTIST AS A YOUNG MAN

(1916)

H E PUSHED OPEN the latchless door of the porch and passed through the naked hallway into the kitchen. A group of his brothers and sisters was sitting round the table. Tea was nearly over and only the last of the second watered tea remained in the bottoms of the small glass jars and jampots which did service for teacups. Discarded crusts and lumps of sugared bread, turned brown by the tea which had been poured over them, lay scattered on the table. Little wells of tea lay here and there on the board, and a knife with a broken ivory handle was stuck through the pith of a ravaged turnover.

The sad quiet grey-blue glow of the dying day came through the window and the open door, covering over and allaying quietly a sudden instinct of remorse in Stephen's heart. All that had been denied them had been freely given to him, the eldest; but the quiet glow of evening showed him in their faces no sign of rancour.

He sat near them at the table and asked where his father and mother were. One answered:

—Goneboro toboro lookboro atboro aboro houseboro.

Still another removal! A boy named Fallon in Belvedere had often asked him with a silly laugh why they moved so often. A frown of scorn darkened quickly his forehead as he heard again the silly laugh of the questioner.

He asked:

—Why are we on the move again if it's a fair question?

—Becauseboro theboro landboro lordboro willboro putboro usboro outboro.

The spectre of poverty haunts the work of James Joyce. The reality of the fall of his family from the ranks of the secure middle classes to the condition of near penury informs nearly everything he wrote. This slippage down the social ladder mirrors the decline of the Irish nation throughout the nineteenth century. Dublin, once the second city of the empire, had become a provincial backwater. Joyce's father, whose financial failings and profligate lifestyle created so much hardship for his family, seemed to exemplify the wider condition. In this passage from *A Portrait*, Stephen Dedalus becomes →

→ acutely aware of the effect of the family's decline on his younger siblings as they are faced, once again, with the prospect of eviction. Their singing of 'Oft in the Stilly Night' heightens the pathos of a moment of family solidarity in dismal poverty.

The voice of his youngest brother from the farther side of the fireplace began to sing the air 'Oft in The Stilly Night'. One by one the others took up the air until a full choir of voices was singing. They would sing so for hours, melody after melody, glee after glee, till the last pale light died down on the horizon, till the first dark night clouds came forth and night fell.

He waited for some moments, listening, before he too took up the air with them. He was listening with pain of spirit to the overtone of weariness behind their frail fresh innocent voices. Even before they set out on life's journey they seemed weary already of the way. ■

PADRAIC COLUM—*from*:

THE ROAD ROUND IRELAND

(1926)

AT THE OUTSKIRTS of the town there is a building of a kind that is to be seen in each of the two or three important towns of an Irish county. It is as big as the convent and as massive as the military barrack; it is the building that, until just now, was known as 'The Workhouse', 'The Poorhouse', 'The Union'.

. . . I go in through the massive gateway. Between the gateway and the house entrance there is a garden that was once well cared-for: in it are lilacs in blossom and fuchsias; beyond is a great patch of cabbages. And in the garden are the three men I had come to talk with—the Editor, the Curate, and the young Doctor.

They are going to a conference in the boardroom; what is to be done with the building is to be decided at it. I look towards a group of old men who are standing or moving about at the other side of the garden. Are these all of the inmates of the County Home, I ask.

There are others too, I am told. Unmarried mothers. I hear how many there are in the place: thirty. The number is surprisingly high. Twenty years ago, I say, there would not have been so many here.

Not half so many, the Editor says.

The Curate holds the guerrilla warfare was responsible; it broke down the old restraints—boys on the run, girls carrying despatches. 'We were prepared for it,' he says; 'we are not so harsh about it as we used to be a few years ago.

Public opinion is not so harsh about it, either, the Editor says. A girl no longer runs out of the country or hides herself away. The child is born in a place like this and the whole affair is noticed. He didn't think that there was much of an increase in illegitimate births; it was that they were less concealed.

Padraic Colum, a central figure during the first decade of the theatre movement, was born in County Longford in 1881. He joined the Gaelic League in 1901 and befriended a number of key individuals of the period including George Russell, Arthur Griffith and James Joyce. His early plays include *The Saxon Shillin'* (1902), *Broken Soil* (1903), *The Land* (1905) and *Thomas Muskerry* (1910). Greatly influenced by Ibsen, Colum's plays were heavily invested in the gritty realism of the small farmer. He married the writer Mary Catherine Gunning (Mary Colum) in 1912 and joined the Irish Volunteers the following year. Having moved to America in 1914, he missed the revolutionary years of the Irish conflict and gained a reputation in the US as an accomplished →

→ writer of books for
children. Colum is probably
best known today as the
author of the lyrics of the
well-known song, 'She
Moved Through the
Fair'. His travelogue, *The
Road Round Ireland*, was
published in 1926 and
offers an astute analysis
of an Irish society making
an uneasy transition
from British colony to
independent state. In
the passage below, he
demonstrates the powerful
influence of the journalist,
the priest and the doctor
in shaping the future of the
new Ireland. The concerted
effort to rein in the radical
energies unleashed during
the revolutionary period is
unmistakable. So, too, is
the missionary zeal of the
re-Gaelicising project that
characterised the early
decades of the new state.

But the Curate assured us that there was a breakdown in the old restraints; it was temporary, he thought; the old restraints would once again be observed.

The young Doctor was glad that the Curate did not think that the morale of the people was going down a bit. He did not think it was himself. He knew that the standard of living was higher than it used to be—the young people were better dressed, they insisted upon having surroundings somewhat better than their elders had been satisfied with. The women had more insistence upon this higher standard of living than the men had. But the men were more sober than used to be the case in that part of the country, and that sobriety was helping to raise the standard. The health of the people was good, he thought.

The Curate thought that the language movement would come to dominate the mind of the country. The Editor was doubtful if Gaelic could be spread, even with the aid that was not being give to it—the teaching of it in the schools of the Free State. The Curate was very sure that there would be a revival, and with that revival the language would be spread and would be made current. He based this certainty on a mysticism that is often in Irish political thought—without the Gaelic language Ireland would become assimilated to England and America. That would be the end of the Irish nation. But the Irish nation could not come to an end. Therefore, the language would be spread and would be made current.

He went on to say something that was true and that was enlightening. The Irish people, he said, were above everything else a missionary people. In the days of their greatest intellectual vitality, in the eighth-and-ninth centuries, missionary work was what they were drawn to. All the successful Irish movements have been missions, carried on with missionary zeal. Sinn Féin originally was carried on as a mission to the country. All this was revealing. And then he went on to say that it was only the language movement that could arouse this missionary zeal.

I thought that the spreading of Gaelic and the making of it current through the country was a task as difficult as any country ever undertook. I had been in an Irish-speaking district, and I thought that economic conditions in it were so bad and the people had so much self-distrust that it was hard to think of the place becoming a centre for the spread of a language and a culture. Most of the other Gaelic-speaking districts, according to what I had heard, were in the same condition. His reply was, at least, heroic. 'The Gaelic-speaking districts are not the cradles of the language; they are the vestibules to its tomb. Gaelic can only be spread, as English was spread through Ireland, from the centres of power and population. We must use the schools and all the agencies of the government to spread the language. And when the missionary zeal of the country rises on behalf of the language, it will spread it and make it current through these agencies.'

The protagonists of the Gaelic idea talk as if the language meant everything. Bound up with the language, however, there is in their minds the idea of a social order—a national life in which there will be a distinctive and varied culture. They have been spoken about as backworldsmen, but they have a vision of a new social order in Ireland. Those who are striving to realise the idea of a co-operative organisation are planning for a new social order too. But they have not done anything like as much as the protagonists of the Gaelic idea have done already. And the reason, perhaps, is that the idea of co-operation is being handed down to the people from above, whereas the idea of re-Gaelicising the country belongs to men and women who are really of the people.

But what does one mean by a social order? By a social order I mean an establishment in which every member may receive a portion of the social well-being—some share of the education, the culture, the comfort, the security which have been attained to and to which additions are always being made. And the establishment should not be a copy of an establishment somewhere else; it should have the distinction of its locality and the distinction of the race that has built it up and that uses it. Take this little town—or rather, this heaped-up village—that we are in now. Such social well-being as there is here is only grudgingly shared. No attempt is being made to add to it, or to give what there is of it any original or distinctive cast. There is no park here; there is no public music; there is no library, no collection of pictures. The education to be got here is only elementary, and there is no one here who would strive to make it wider, deeper, or more interesting. Those who have acquired money here would never think of benefitting anyone except an immediate relation; they would never think of doing something for the community, of giving something to the community (Ireland is woefully wanting in the public-benefactor class). And because the social order there is so rudimentary, so much a bad copy of another social order, so filled with pettiness and exclusiveness, the possibilities for recreation, education, culture, advancement of any kind, for any individual here are at a minimum. ■

Women and Citizenship

BY THE LATE nineteenth century, Ireland was pervaded by male values. The numbers of women working on farms and in industry had dropped markedly, and this in the decades when the Catholic Church extended its control of education. The very spread of literacy was an ambiguous gift, since it reinforced a common male view of womanhood as passive, domestic, retiring. This may have made the attractions of anti-colonial activism all the greater; in an age when British women lacked the right to vote, the case for political independence seemed all the stronger. Partners, sisters and daughters of incarcerated nationalist men often had to find ways of supporting a family and began in consequence to assume equality with men as a right. The family thus became in many cases not just a haven in a heartless world but also the model of an alternative modernity.

When Charles Stewart Parnell was arrested in 1882, his sister Anna took over the campaigns of the Land League, but her uncompromising 'no rent' policy annoyed her brother so much that he had her movement wound up and he blocked its bank account. Yet she and her friends persisted in the belief that they had every right to break laws which women had no part in making.

Literacy may have propagated ideas of Victorian gentility among the women of an emerging Catholic middle class, but it also fed the demand of women for equal rights to university education (supported by the radical Francis Sheehy Skeffington, who resigned as registrar of the Royal University in 1904 as a protest against the slow pace of reform). Mary Hayden ran such a skilful campaign, however, that by 1909 the new National University was treating women on a basis of equality with men and she herself became a professor in the institution. Other intrepid women, such as Agnes O'Farrelly (Úna Ní Fhaircheallaigh), who had given lectures to Gaelic League classes before 1909, also got posts and professorships. They recognised an intrinsic link between women's and nation's rights. James Connolly, however, while convinced that women laboured under a double colonialism, warned suffragists that the vote might not heal all disabilities of an oppressed, often impoverished, womanhood. He foresaw that some women might cast their vote for conservative groups and so he urged suffragists to get involved in programmes for the abolition of bad housing and childhood poverty. Socialists like Constance Markiewicz and Hanna Sheehy Skeffington further developed this critique.

The tactics adopted by suffragists were so original that they
would later be emulated by male nationalists. In 1912 Hanna
Sheehy Skeffington went on hunger strike in Mountjoy Jail with
three other women, a tactic soon to be repeated by imprisoned
men during the War of Independence, and later by Gandhi in
India. In prison, she abandoned her attempt to read novels
of Dickens, because of their repeated accounts of sumptuous
meals, preferring the more famished world of Emily Bronte's
Wuthering Heights, with its treatment of hunger-striking as a
psychological weapon.

Markiewicz questioned the logic of Irishwomen seeking
the vote from an oppressive foreign power. She urged women
to ignore English politics altogether and instead to join
organisations such as Sinn Féin and the Gaelic League in
which women had equality with men. She wanted an Ireland
not just free but feminist, not just feminist but free—if women
were not free, men would not be either. The rediscovery by
scholars of the strong women of the Celts and of the legal
rights which some enjoyed had the effect of buttressing this
analysis, but Hanna Sheehy Skeffington warned that the
militarist element gaining traction in the Irish Volunteers after

1914 was leading to a subordination of woman. As if to prove her point, Skeffington was named two years later as the first female minister in the provisional government which would meet if the Rising were successful, but none of the male leaders thought fit to alert her to this possible appointment. (She would thus have been the first female government minister anywhere in the world, a full year before Alexandra Kollontai won that honour in Moscow). Nevertheless, many women took part in the rebellion (sixty from Cumann na mBan as nurses and messengers; the remainder from the Citizen Army as combatants)—and the Proclamation of the Republic addressed itself equally to women and to men, guaranteeing social rights and a welfare state for all. Two years before British women won the right to vote in 1918, the rebel leaders recognised that women volunteering for the republic were taking the same risks as men.

ANNA PARNELL

'THE JOURNEY'

(1898)

Born in 1852, Anna Parnell,
along with her sister Fanny,
organised a Ladies' Land
League when their brother
Charles was imprisoned
in 1881. The women's
branch of the movement
proved remarkably active
in boycotts, picketing of
evictions and in pursuing
a 'no rent payment'
policy. They created
shelters for families left
homeless after evictions
and collected money for
prisoners' dependents.
By the following year
there were by some
counts five hundred
branches, which drew
large numbers of women
into politics for the first
time. But Charles Stewart
Parnell, once out of prison,
chose to concentrate on
constitutional issues rather
than land agitation. His
sister Anna, by contrast,
supported an alliance with
the more impoverished
sections of the community
as the natural option of
women who despaired of
ever receiving justice ↗

When I first began my journey
My step was firm and light,
And I hoped to reach a shelter
Before the fall of night.

But a band of thieves beset me
Quite early in the day;
They robbed me and then they cast me
All bleeding by the way.

And since that hour I have crawled,
A cripple, blind with tears;
While each step I've made has cost me
The pain and strain of years.

I've had no shelter from the storm,
No screen against the heat;
The sun has beat against my head,
The shards have cut my feet.

My fellow-travellers on the road
Bound for the selfsame goal
With purse and staff and scrip equipped
And limbs and raiment whole.

All point at me with scorn, and say:
'Why does he choose to roam?
For travelling he is not fit;
Cripples should stay at home'.

Alas! They do not know that I
Was once as fit as they
And that there is no turning back
For those who go this way.

The long dark shadows of the night
Are closing on me now,
And its clammy dews are lying
Heavily on my brow.

I see the light of the City
Where I may never win
And I know there's warmth and comfort
For those who are within.

And alone in the cold and darkness
I know that I must die,
And unburied in the desert
My bones will always lie.

→ from Westminster. The fear of 'unmanageable revolutionaries', which dogged conservative forms of nationalism thereafter, was probably an after-effect of the radical politics of the Ladies' Land League. Following the breach between them in 1882, Anna never again spoke to Charles, saying 'it would never be possible for me to believe that any body of Irishmen meant a word of anything they said.' Foreseeing the collapse of the nationalist parliamentary party at Westminster, she astutely predicted 'armed rebellion'. Exiled in England and near-destitute for years, she nonetheless sent money contributions towards Maud Gonne's Patriotic Children's Treat in 1900. She drowned while swimming in choppy waters off the coast of Cornwall in 1911. 'The Journey' captures that sense of anticlimax which shadowed her later life.

MARY HAYDEN—*from*:

'WOMEN CITIZENS – THEIR DUTIES AND THEIR TRAINING'

(1912)

Born in 1862 in Dublin,
Mary Hayden attended
Alexandra College, where
her teachers such as
Isabella Mulvany alerted
her to the suffrage
question. She graduated
from the Royal University
with degrees in modern
languages and became
an activist for Irish
language and women's
rights. She and Agnes
O'Farrelly masterminded
a successful campaign for
the inclusion of women
on an equal footing with
men in University College
Dublin. She was also a
prominent suffragist and
Gaelic Leaguer. Elected to
the Senate of the National
University in 1911, she was
a charismatic professor
of history at University
College Dublin. Despite
a friendship with Patrick
Pearse, she disapproved
of the Rising. In 1921, with
George Moonan, she
published *A Short History
of the Irish People*, which
remained a standard ↗

'**A**ND THEN, TOO, opportunities should be afforded
for training the boys in the duties of citizenship and
the girls in domestic science.' Thus spoke a reverend
gentleman some time ago, when setting forth at a public
meeting his ideal of education, and amongst his hearers no
one was found to suggest that with 'the duties of citizenship'
the girl, too, had some concern. Evidently the capacity to
cook a chop, to make, wash and iron a shirt were to their
minds, if they considered the matter at all, the feminine
equivalents for patriotism, municipal virtue and public
spirit generally.

'Home is a woman's province, let her confine her
attention to it.' How often do we hear these words: almost
as often as those others—'The hand that rocks the cradle
rules the world.' But each home is part of a municipality, a
district, a county, a whole world, and with the interests of
these larger entities its interests are bound up. In these
homes, and by those rockers of their cradles mainly, are
trained the men who, in future years, will sway the destinies
of village, town, county and country, and to a great extent
they will be, for bad or for good, what their mothers
made them. If the mothers, then, are blind or indifferent,
ignorant or narrow or careless, how can they teach young
eyes to see clearly, young feet to walk on boldly, cost what it
may, in the path of public duty?

'If she be small, slight-natured, miserable,
How shall men grow?'

Will the best ironed shirt, the best cooked chop, make
up for prejudices early imbibed, enthusiasm early crushed
or wrongly directed?

'George, be a king,' advised his narrow-minded mother to the child who was one day to be the Sovereign of England. George III grew up and strove to carry out her counsels, to be a king indeed, to have his own way in defiance of everyone — and the American colonies were lost.

At present women play a not inconsiderable part in public life. They exercise, both directly and indirectly, an influence which cannot be ignored. It behoves us, then, to consider how they should be trained to play this part and exert their influence most usefully and most conscientiously.

So far as I know, little has yet been done in Ireland in this direction. The average Irish girl, no matter to what social class she belongs, no matter whether she be town or country-bred, leaves school, especially if she has been educated at a boarding school, ludicrously—perhaps one had better say pitiably—ignorant of public affairs and wholly indifferent to them. She knows a good deal probably about William the Conqueror and Henry VIII, perhaps something about the Statute of Kilkenny or Poyning's Law—dead men and dead ordinances—but question her about the Local Government Act, ask her to name the present Prime Minister of England, inquire what she understands about the Congested Districts' Board, and you will find that, concerning these living actualities, she is, as a rule, entirely ignorant, and perfectly content to remain so.

While at school, she has practically never an opportunity of reading a newspaper, and so has never been accustomed to follow the course of passing events. Therefore, when she grows up and returns home, she generally contents herself with skimming over the notices of social functions and reading the lists of births, deaths and marriages; unless

→ textbook on school courses for many decades and which offered a frankly nationalist view of the long historical basis of the state which had emerged in the years of the book's gestation between 1917 and 1922. Hayden, though a supporter of the Anglo-Irish Treaty of 1921, was highly critical of the new state's treatment of women—their restriction from almost all forms of jury service and their compulsory retirement from the civil service on the occasion of their marriage. She died in 1942. This essay appeared in The Irish Citizen.

indeed, as too often happens, she turns her attention to those more sensational items on account of which she was debarred from newspaper-reading during her school days. When politics, under which heading she classes public concerns of all sorts, are discussed, she generally keeps silence and looks bored, or sometimes utters a silly remark.

With ignorance of public affairs comes, almost of necessity, indifference to public duties, and an incapacity to pass, even in thought, beyond the narrow circle of personal or family concerns. Some persons will probably consider that this is as it should be, and will tell you that the essential thing for a woman is to be a good housewife and a good mother; that, until this is secured, we should defer the less-important work of trying to make her a good citizen. By a similar course of reasoning, it might be argued that we should defer teaching a boy Latin or mathematics until we had trained him in such a manner as to ensure that he should be a good Christian, which is certainly more important. But in truth the mind is not composed, as this seems to imply, of a number of watertight compartments. One thing re-acts on another, and an all-round moral development will be found best in the long run if thoroughness in any one branch only is to be secured. The woman who is truly patriotic, public-spirited, philanthropic, will not be less, but more efficient when she turns her attention to the care of that household which has been committed to her special charge. To such a woman, her home is a part of a great national whole, and every home duty is ennobled in her eye, because she looks beyond its actuality, and sees its place in the scheme of things.

We have all read in comic publications of the 'advanced' woman who spends her time in addressing public meetings and neglects her husband and children; we probably have seen pictures in which she is represented as reading some pamphlet on 'Woman's Rights' while her partner parades the room with the baby, but which of us has met this strange creature in the flesh? The deserted homes and the forlorn unmothered children usually belong to the social butterflies, who would consider it quite unbecoming to take an interest in public questions.

Again, we often hear it lamented that, up to the present, the majority of women have been very lukewarm supporters of the Irish industrial movement. In this their power is almost supreme, so it is all the more regrettable that it is not more generally exercised. 'What do I care where the stuff was made, so that it is pretty?' a young girl will say. 'Yes, I'd like to buy Irish jam, but, you see, my grocer does not keep it,' a matron will tell you. If it had been explained to them in their school-days why they should patronise native goods; if they had been taught to consider such questions as emigration, want of employment, ruin of industries; perhaps the one would make another effort to please herself in an Irish cloth, and the other would insist on her grocer's stocking Irish jams, or else would take her custom elsewhere. ∎

JAMES CONNOLLY—*from*:

'THE RECONQUEST OF IRELAND'

(1914)

N IRELAND, THE women's cause is felt by all Labour men and women as their cause; the Labour cause has no more earnest and whole-hearted supporters than the militant women. Rebellion, even in thought, produces a mental atmosphere of its own; the mental atmosphere the women's rebellion produced, opened their eyes and trained their minds to an understanding of the effects upon their sex of a social system in which the weakest must inevitably go to the wall, and when a further study of the capitalist system taught them that the term 'the weakest' means in practice the most scrupulous, the gentlest, the most humane, the most loving and compassionate, the most honourable, and the most sympathetic, then the militant women could not fail to see, that capitalism penalised in human beings just those characteristics of which women supposed themselves to be the most complete embodiment.

Thus the spread of industrialism makes for the awakening of a social consciousness, awakes in women a feeling of self-pity as the greatest sufferers under social and political injustice; the divine wrath aroused when that self-pity is met with a sneer, and justice is denied, leads women to revolt, and revolt places women in comradeship and equality with all the finer souls whose life is given to warfare against established iniquities.

The worker is the slave of capitalist society, the female worker is the slave of that slave. In Ireland that female worker has hitherto exhibited, in her martyrdom, an almost damnable patience. She has toiled on the farms from her earliest childhood, attaining usually to the age of ripe womanhood without ever being vouchsafed the right to claim as her own a single penny of the money earned by her labour, and knowing that all her toil and privation would not earn her that right to the farm which would go without question to the most worthless member of the family, if that member chanced to be the eldest son.

The daughters of the Irish peasantry have been the cheapest slaves in existence—slaves to their own family, who were, in turn, slaves to all social parasites of a landlord and gombeen-ridden community. The peasant, in whom centuries of servitude and hunger had bred a fierce craving for money, usually regarded his daughters as beings sent by God to lighten his burden through life, and too often the same point of view was as fiercely insisted upon by the clergymen of all denominations. Never did the idea seem to enter the Irish peasant's mind, or be taught by his religious teachers, that each generation should pay to its successors the debt it owes to its forerunners; that thus, by spending itself for the benefit of its children, the human race ensures the progressive development of all. The Irish peasant, in too many cases, treated his daughters in much the same manner as he regarded a plough or a spade—as tools with which to work the farm. The whole mental outlook, the entire moral atmosphere of the countryside, enforced this point of view. In every chapel, church or meeting-house the insistence was ever upon duties—duties to those in superior stations, duties to the Church, duties to the parents. Never were the ears of the young polluted by any reference to 'rights', and, growing up in this atmosphere, the women of Ireland accepted their position of social inferiority. That, in spite of this, they have ever proven valuable assets in every progressive movement in Ireland, is evidence of the great value their co-operation will be, when to their self-sacrificing acceptance of duty they

→ Ireland were often exploiters of female labour and not much different from those upper-class drones denounced by Mary Hayden. Connolly warned that Celtic Studies of itself risked 'crystallising nationalism into a tradition, glorious and heroic indeed, but still only a tradition'— unless they engaged their themes and analyses with contemporary social questions. Thirty women (including Constance Markiewicz) fought as soldiers in the Citizen Army in 1916; nobody, he said, was better fitted to break chains than those who wore them.

begin to unite its necessary counterpoise, a high-minded assertion of rights.

. . . In Ireland, the soul of womanhood has been trained for centuries to surrender its rights, and as a consequence the race has lost its chief capacity to withstand assaults from without, and demoralisation from within. Those who preached to Irish womankind fidelity to duty as the only ideal to be striven after, were, consciously or unconsciously, fashioning a slave mentality, which the Irish mothers had perforce to transmit to the Irish child.

The militant women who, without abandoning their fidelity to duty, are yet teaching their sisters to assert their rights, are re-establishing a sane and perfect balance that makes more possible a well-ordered Irish nation.

The system of private capitalist property in Ireland, as in other countries, has given birth to the law of primogeniture under which the eldest son usurps the ownership of all property to the exclusion of the females of the family. Rooted in a property system founded upon force, this iniquitous law was unknown to the older social system of ancient Erin and, in its actual workings out in modern Erin, it has been and is responsible for the moral murder of countless virtuous Irish maidens. ■

HANNA SHEEHY SKEFFINGTON

'SINN FÉIN AND IRISHWOMEN'

(1909)

W E ALL, UNIONISTS and nationalists alike, live overmuch on our past in Ireland. Our great past condones our empty present, and seems to deprecate, instead of stimulating endeavours. Living thus in our past, one is apt to overdraw one's bank account. This tendency is nowhere more aptly illustrated than with regard to the position of Irishwomen in the Ireland of today. Nowhere in the pitiful tangle of present-day life does the actual more sadly belie the far-off past. It is barren comfort for us Irishwomen to know that in ancient Ireland women occupied a prouder, freer position than they now hold even in the most advanced modern states, that all professions, including that of arms, were freely open to their ambitions (indeed 'open' is scarcely the word, for it implies concession, whereas the right seems never to have been questioned), that their counsel was sought in all affairs of state, that 'in the humane ideal of Irish civilisation' (to quote from Mrs. Green's *Making of Ireland and its Undoing*), 'women were called to public duties of conciliation and peace.' Let the Irishwoman who doubts herself turn to these records for inspiration, but nor for mere complacency, for if ever the theory of *noblesse oblige* held good in its best sense it is here it ought to be vindicated by the descendants of such ancestresses. Our ancestresses were the state-recognised arbiters in matters under dispute between rival factions, forming a final court of appeal, a permanent Hague Tribunal.

'Where is it now, the glory and the dream?' Does the vision of the past mitigate the abject present? Is the degradation of the average Irishwoman the less real, her education sacrificed to give her brothers ampler opportunities of having a good time loitering through their examinations

Revivalist radicals took the view that there could be no free nation without free women, and no free women in an enslaved nation. Yet, noticing the casual sexism of many males in the national movement, some worried about whether their ascent to power would bring beneficial changes for women. Hanna Sheehy Skeffington was not fully convinced by the theory that sexual oppression was due entirely to the British presence: she knew the wide world (and Irishmen) too well to accept such a naïve and sentimental reading of the past. And she knew also the truth often observed by socialists: that in Ireland the worship of the past can become an excuse for not addressing the mediocrity of the present and for refusing thus to open up a challenging future.

in the capital, her marriage a matter of sordid bargaining, broken maybe because an over-insistent prospective father-in-law demands a cow or a pig too much, her 'fortune' (the word is significant and the fortuneless had better never have been born) instead of being, in French fashion, sensibly settled on her and her children, handed over blindly to her husband to dispose of it as he may think fit, it may be to pay his racing debts, or, if he is a generous brother, to endow a sister for the matrimonial market, or to equip an aspiring brother for the priesthood? Whatever its uses, the bride's portion belongs irrevocably to the husband's family.

I have chosen a few salient examples to illustrate the disabilities Irishwomen suffer today. The result of Anglicisation? This is partly true; much of the evil is, however, inherent in latter-day Irish life. Nor will the evil disappear, as we are assured, when Ireland comes to her own again, whenever that may be. For until the women of Ireland are free, the men will not achieve emancipation. It is for Irishwomen, therefore, to work out their own 'Sinn Féin' on their own lines, for with the broader, non-party aspect of Sinn Féin—namely, the reformation from within, outwards all nationalists have always been in agreement.

The Irishwoman has far to go before achieving her destiny. At present she counts for less in her own land than does the Englishwoman in hers (time and again the Englishwoman has forced her point of view on reluctant legislators, and we may expect her one of these days to wrest the vote similarly from her countrymen). First, as the Englishwoman counts less to the nation than the Frenchwoman, and as the Frenchwoman is a harem-slave compared with her American sister, so in the scale of civilisation the Irishwoman comes somewhere between the oriental woman and her more advanced western sisters.

Many vested interests (notably that of the publican) are openly opposed to any broadening of woman's horizon in Ireland. Public opinion, educational fallacies, convention militate against her assuming her rightful place in public life. In the Gaelic movement, in the industrial revival and in the Sinn Féin organisation, she has undoubtedly made her power felt. So much the better for the movement. The reason, however, is obvious; it is not due, as many would have us believe, to a reversion to the older Irish (for the individual in all these movements is as narrow as his presumably less enlightened brother), but rather because of the nature of the work involved. The Gaelic League must make its final appeal to the young, unless those to whom the very beginnings are entrusted take up Irish it will surely perish. So too with the industrial revival—it is the woman who looks after the domestic budget, her voice can make or mar Irish industrialism. Therefore, it is primarily in her capacity as mother and housekeeper, not as individual citizen, that these movements have of necessity recognised her importance. After all, as a wag has put it, 'woman is matchless as wife and mother.' No male has ever denied her these onerous privileges, and for that very reason the average male would see her confined to these purely incidental avocations. That is why, doubtless, many worthy Gaelic Leaguers get restive at the thought of women having places on the Executive Body, that is why, too, in spite of theoretical equality, some Sinn Féiners have not yet rounded Cape Turk where women are concerned. One of the leaders afforded an interesting object-lesson to his women colleagues in the movement by founding university scholarships from which girls were expressly excluded. Irishwomen may be excused, therefore, if they distrust all parties in Ireland, for what I have said of the Sinn Féin organisation applies with far greater force to the parliamentarian movement which, since the extinction of the Ladies' Land League in the eighties, has steadily ignored Irishwomen, hitherto indeed with impunity. It is for Irishwomen of every political party to adopt the principle of Sinn Féin in the true sense of the word, and to refuse any longer to be the camp-followers and parasites of public life, dependent on caprice and expediency for recognition. It is for Irishwomen to set about working out their political salvation. Until the parliamentarian and the Sinn Féin women alike possess the vote, the keystone of citizenship, she will count but little with either party, for it is through the medium of the vote alone that either party can achieve any measure of success. This is a fact of which we parliamentarians have long been aware to our cost, but which Sinn Féin women have yet to learn. ■

MARY MCSWINEY—*from*:

'SUFFRAGISTS AND HOME RULE: A PLEA FOR COMMON SENSE'
(1914)

Socialists were frequently told that 'Labour must wait' until the national question was resolved. Similarly, Irish suffragists were often lectured on the evils of delaying Home Rule by making additional demands. The situation was further complicated by the determination of certain English suffragists to campaign in Ireland. Some radical feminists took the view that 'Home Rule will not be Home Rule' i.e. it would do nothing for the cause of female suffrage. Here, in an essay published in the *Irish Citizen*, Mary McSwiney argues for a sort of 'stages theory'—only when the Home Rule question is resolved can Irishwomen expect progress on other fronts, and it is unfair of suffragists ↗

T O PLEAD WITH suffragists for a little common sense and political insight may be looked upon nowadays as a request for a despatch of coals to Newcastle, and yet it seems to be true that many Irish suffragists are rather losing their heads, and by their present tactics injuring their own cause. This does not apply to militants only, but to all those whose views are expressed in recent 'leaders' of the *Irish Citizen*.

In England, convinced suffragists rightly place votes for women above and before all other reforms, and this policy expresses itself in consistent and continual opposition to the Government, while the Government, as such, is opposed to woman suffrage. No question of party—no reform of any kind—social, fiscal, agrarian—can in any way compare with the dominant need in England today—the woman's voice—backed by the power of the vote—in all questions of reform. But in Ireland, even those who place suffrage first must take the special circumstances of the country into consideration if they wish to win adherents to their cause. Ireland is struggling to settle not a party question, but a national one, and opposition to the government in the present crisis means opposition to Home Rule.

The fact that many Irish suffragists play the political ostrich and refuse to recognise the essential difference between this and English party questions, does not minimise that difference; it simply blinds their political intelligence and injures the cause they wish to promote.

Let us take England in an analogous position. Suppose her in thrall to Germany, and that after many fruitless struggles she is at length on the road to receive a measure of freedom. Can we imagine England refusing that measure because it only enfranchised half her people, but left her to enfranchise the other half within a few years? It is thinkable that English women would try to ruin that measure because for a few years they would have to be governed by Englishmen instead of Germans? Can you fancy Chistabel Pankhurst herself hesitating, even if she honestly believed that by clinging to Germany she would get the women's vote sooner? Even if such an unpatriotic course were possible to Englishwomen, it would be none the more acceptable to Irishwomen. It is idle to pooh-pooh this point of view; it is the actual point of view of the vast majority of Irish people, and it has to be reckoned with. If, then, suffragists do not wish to alienate the sympathy of the Irish people—women as well as men—they must not hail with delight the prospect of the destruction of the Home Rule Bill.

To maintain that Home Rule is not Home Rule, and should not be accepted unless women are included, is puerile. The point for Irish suffragists to note is this: that no question but the Home Rule one will turn a single vote at an Irish election until Home Rule is finally attained. Therefore, it is an absurdity to write that 'In Ireland the opposing parties are not yet fully convinced of the importance of the suffrage movement or the need to make terms with it.' The suggestion made lately that Irish suffragists should help to 'drum Asquith out of Fife' shows so little grasp of the situation in Ireland that one almost asks if we are supposed to be content to be cats-paws for English suffragists. In consequence of such deplorable partisan tactics, the suffrage cause is rapidly becoming synonymous with the unionist cause, and is losing

→ in Ireland to criticise John Redmond and parliamentary nationalists for not supporting English suffragists at Westminster. In the event, when women over thirty won the vote in 1918, many contributed to the victory of Sinn Féin.

McSwiney, born in London and educated at Cambridge University, moved to Cork in 1904, working for the Munster Women's Franchise League, the Gaelic League and, later, Cumann na mBan. She was arrested in 1916 and on release founded St. Ita's, a female version of Pearse's St. Enda's School. She was first elected for Sinn Féin in 1921 and opposed the Treaty, speaking for over three hours against it. She refused to enter the Dáil in 1923, and remained a staunch republican until her death in 1942.

day by day many nationalist supporters.

Englishwomen want the vote for themselves first and foremost. That is natural, and we applaud and sympathise with their efforts. But in order to hasten their political enfranchisement—even by a year—they would not hesitate to wreck the cause of suffrage in Ireland for a generation or more. The sooner Irishwomen open their eyes to that fact, the sooner they will get back to sane methods. What is good for England is *not* good for Ireland in suffrage tactics, and more than in other matters and, as Irishwomen, we are concerned with our own country first. ■

CONSTANCE MARKIEWICZ

'EXPERIENCES OF A WOMAN PATROL'

(1915)

O N A GLORIOUS MORNING like this, with the sun shining so brightly, and, apparently, everything around one in such a peaceful condition, one can hardly realise the horrors and disgrace in which one found the city of Dublin last night. Where are most of those poor creatures, men and women, who loitered around the neighbourhood of Sackville Street and along the quays? Some of the men we know are in barracks, others scattered throughout the city. As to the other half of the community—our sisters—many of them are in that filthy—Street. Street is a very dignified name for a place that is more like a ditch with ruins on one side of it. In this awful street one can hire a 'furnished' room for 6d. a night. I think few Dubliners know that this locality (Coombe district) is so bad. One should see it to realise all its horrors. Here one can pick up vermin as easily as one can get one's boots muddy on a rainy day, and this is where many of our girls go back to in the early hours of the morning, and sleep well on into the day, till their horrid trade begins again.

Many of the inhabitants of this street did not begin life in this way. Some of them were domestic servants, and in various other callings of life, and from many causes they sank to this degradation. We, who have not been put in the way of this particular temptation, ought to make strenuous efforts to see that the conditions in Dublin shall in every way be improved, and that our young girls shall not have the chance of being thrown in such awful depravity. We have no right to blame them.

Some of our girls in paper factories are earning 4s. 10d. a week, their hours being from 8 to 6, with one hour for dinner. The whole mode of life and upbringing of the less privileged classes is too horrible. We give them low wages, and provide

Prostitution was common in the streets of Revival Dublin. Many young women, known among the sympathetic poor as 'unfortunate girls', could find no other work. With marriage out of the question for many poor men, and conventional sexual activity policed by the Catholic Church, there was a thriving red-light district in the area called Monto (from Montgomery Street to Gloucester Diamond) and also near the Coombe. After independence, a concerted effort was made by the Free State government and the Legion of Mary (a Catholic lay apostolate) to close the whorehouses and find a better life for the women. There was a widespread belief, echoed in this essay by Markiewicz, that the soldiers of the British army had kept some brothels in business. Sean O'Casey, however, caused a riot with *The Plough and the Stars* (1926) by featuring a →

→ prostitute in a pub alongside the flag and soldiers of the Citizen Army. 'There are no prostitutes in Dublin', shouted one protester, only to be told by O'Casey 'I was accosted by one last night.' 'Well', came the reply, 'there were none until the British soldiers brought them over.' Markiewicz's account of her patrol suggests that socialist republicans always admitted their existence and were anxious to address the underlying poverty which usually lay behind it.

very bad living accommodation at high rents, with no relief from work or any simple kind of entertainment for them. One hears a small talk of starting clubs, but one of the great difficulties is the lack of funds. A large club with plenty of room should immediately be opened in the heart of the city, where the girls and men can amuse themselves and meet in decent surroundings. Of course, it would be impossible to bring into the club the girl who has already fallen a victim to the streets. Something else must be done for her. We have no right to shirk this duty: we must face at once the problem of our streets at night, and face it squarely. Just now it is easy enough to get women volunteer workers, who are dying to make munitions, wait on the wounded soldiers, drive motors, etc., etc. Why should not some of them come forward to help cure this open sore that has been in their midst all their lives? Now is the time, while public interest is being roused.

Working among factory girls is really very interesting, and one gets back plenty of reward for any little inconvenience one may be put to. The girls respond so quickly to any little sympathy and kindness, and the more one sees of them the better one loves them. Who will start a fund to collect money for a club for our girls and men? ■

Markiewicz - aristocratic. Priveleged background. Poor almost Othered + seen as something almost subhuman??

CONSTANCE MARKIEWICZ—*from*:

'THE WOMAN WITH A GARDEN'

(1915)

WE HAVE HAD such a dry, hot May this year that the garden is in rather an abnormal condition; roses in damp, hot corners are in full flower, while those in dry windy places are barely in leaf. Many apple trees have been very late in blossoming, from which I should prophesy a good show of fruit in the autumn, as they have escaped the usual May frost; but we must not be too confident, for our enemies in the insect world have also escaped its ravages, and it is full time now that you should turn your attention to the various 'pests', slugs, snails, green fly, etc.

It is very unpleasant work killing slugs and snails, but let us not be daunted. A good nationalist should look upon slugs in a garden much the same way as she looks on the English in Ireland, and the only regret that she cannot crush the nation's enemies with the same ease that she can the gardens, with just one tread of her fairy feet. True the garden's enemies are as hard to find, and as subtle in their methods as the nation's. You must creep about in the dusk, with a lamp, and catch them in the act, or make traps by placing little heaps of bran near the plants that are most attacked—for no slug can resist bran—and then when you come round with your lamp you will find a goodly company of yellow, brown, and black gluttons who will fall easy victims to the zealous gardener. If you do not feel inclined for the work by lamplight, strew around cabbage or hemlock leaves or orange peel, and when you come in the morning you will find many a foe resting replete under their cool shade.

Green fly may be syringed with soapsuds, but I should advise my readers to go or to write to a good professional rose grower and get advice if her rose trees are unhealthy. There are so many pests and diseases with which a rose tree can be attacked that I have not the space in these short notes to enter into them at all. The same advice may be given with regard to the fruit trees and bushes. ∎

Markiewicz (like her sister Eva) was an early environmentalist. She wrote a gardening column for *Bean na hÉireann* (*Woman of Ireland*), the journal published intermittently by Inghinidhe na hÉireann under the editorship of Helena Molony, as a successor to Maud Gonne's *Irlande Libre* journal (1896-7) and *The Shan Van Vocht* (edited by Alice Milligan and Anna Johnston 1896-7). *Bean na hÉireann* was keen to highlight the blind-spots of men in the national movement, to which it nonetheless gave strong support. Gonne crusaded in it for the provision of free meals for the poor schoolchildren of Dublin. Markiewicz used her gardening column, in the judgement of C.L. Innes, in a rather subversive style parodic of other women's magazines of the time, since her commentaries combined 'discourses of warrior-hood and stereotyped feminisation.'

A Sovereign People

ONE OF THE notable features of the Revival period is the frequency
and intensity of debate over the visits of British monarchs to Ireland,
and in relation to the recruitment of Irishmen to the British army.
These public disputes generated much protest and acrimony
precisely because they involved important issues fundamental to
the idea of political sovereignty. In a country like Ireland, where the
constitution of the nation was hotly contested, attitudes to royal visits
and foreign wars revealed much about the thinking of established
politicians and radical activists in relation to the national question.

If political sovereignty is the supreme power by which an
independent state is governed, that power became incarnate
whenever the British monarch walked on Irish soil. Such moments
were often greeted with enthusiasm by a large proportion of the Irish
people, who welcomed the celebratory occasion and relished the
opportunity to catch a glimpse of the king or queen. It also reinforced
the idea that Ireland was part of the wider configuration of empire.
Historically speaking, however, these public displays of loyalty were
often followed by protracted periods of revolutionary action against
the crown. Royal visits, it seems, could unmask the rigid hierarchies
underpinning the ruling system. In such deferential moments,
ordinary people were reminded that they were subjects of a monarch
rather than citizens of a republic. Subject status brought with it a

vulnerability to the exercise of arbitrary power. As Maud Gonne reminded her readers, many cruelties had been carried out in the name of Queen Victoria—the 'Famine Queen'.

It was largely to counteract the mystique of the British monarch with an Irish equivalent, that Yeats and Lady Gregory exhumed the old Gaelic sovereignty goddess, Cathleen Ní Houlihan. This figure, much beloved of the Gaelic *aisling* poets, embodied the nation in the form of a woman who could inspire the loyalty of the people, and the bravery of young men. If the aging Victoria came to Dublin in 1900 to recruit Irishmen to fight in the Boer War, the Sean Bhean Bhocht made an appearance on the Dublin stage shortly afterwards to impel Irishmen to reclaim her 'four beautiful green fields'. While Cathleen Ní Houlihan was suggestive of the existence of the Irish nation in the abstract, a new generation of political activists sought to define the borders of the nation by rejecting British foreign policy. A key feature of sovereignty, after all, is the power to regulate internal affairs without foreign influence. In this regard, decisions not to participate in British war efforts made clear statements that Ireland's destiny lay outside the empire, as an independent sovereign nation. Nonetheless, thousands of Irish men chose to enlist in the ranks of the British army. Whether out of loyalty, economic necessity or thirst for adventure, a high proportion of these recruits paid the ultimate price with their own lives.

What form Irish sovereignty would take was widely debated and hotly contested within the broad nationalist movement. John Redmond favoured Home Rule within the empire; Arthur Griffith proposed an Irish assembly based loosely on the restoration of Grattan's Parliament; William Rooney and Patrick Pearse advocated the republicanism of Tone and Emmet; and James Connolly worked for a socialist republic inspired by his reading of Marx. In all these disputations the arguments moved steadily away from the abstract and mystical notions of Cathleen Ní Houlihan and focused instead on the actual constitution of a putative Irish sovereign state.

When John Redmond broke from the Irish Volunteers and lent his support to the British war effort during World War One, he held true to his belief that Ireland's destiny lay within the United Kingdom, with a self-governing assembly. The Volunteers who stayed at home, however, assumed the authority of the army of the sovereign Irish nation, which put them on an inevitable collision course with British forces. The actions of Easter 1916 were initiated by men and women who regarded themselves as equal citizens but who, paradoxically, lacked elected authority. These actions were justified in their minds by the fact that in Ireland no elected national authority was permitted to exist, or could come into being, without the use of force.

WILLIAM ROONEY—*from*:

'THE DEVELOPMENT OF THE NATIONAL IDEAL'

(1900)

SWIFT'S CAMPAIGN HAD in it rather more of nationality, for it united all the elements of Irish society for the first time for centuries, and frightened the British minister into the possibilities of Irish union. But it was also narrow, for it did not look beyond the mere legislative freedom demanded by Molyneux. Lucas, Grattan, the Volunteers—their ideals were all more or less patriotic, but recognising the claim of an English king on Irish loyalty, their views cannot be accepted as marking the ideal of an Irish nation. The first men who adequately voiced the truest and fullest conception of an independent Irish state were Tone and the United Irishmen. We can honour the patriots of Confederate and Williamite days; we can be proud of Molyneux, Swift and Lucas for their courage and persistence in the face of all the opposition of their times. Flood and Grattan and the Volunteers may remind us of the opportunities which English difficulties afford to Ireland. But our whole hearts can go out unreservedly, enthusiastically, to the United Irishmen who banded all classes of Irishmen—the Gael and the Gall, the Protestant, Catholic, and the Dissenter—into one great united body, and who sealed their convictions with their blood at Antrim, at Ballynahinch, in Kildare, in Wexford, in Wicklow, and in almost every county from Mayo to the streets of Dublin. 'I made what was to me a great discovery—though I might have found it in Swift and Molyneux—that the influence of England was the radical vice of our government, and consequently Ireland would never be either free, or happy until she was independent and that independence was unattainable while the connection with England lasted.' Thus, Tone and his words must ever remain for the Irish

nationalist, the cardinal feature of his political faith. An
Irish state self-supporting, self-defending; her flag respected
in every port; her welcome and her sympathy for the
oppressed of every race and colour; her voice in the councils
of the nations; her language, her laws, and her achievements
the pride of all her people—such is a national ideal, and
to Tone do we owe the fact that any of its most militant
features still recommend themselves to the vast bulk of
our countrymen. It outlived the terrors of '98, it survived
the sacrifice of 1803 and, though it showed not its head
during O'Connell's years of work, it lived and stirred in all
the cabins of the country. No one can claim the Catholic
agitation as a national one, though of its necessity there
is no question, and, while we must regard O'Connell as a
man devoid of all national ambition, we give him credit
for what he did. He probably wielded more power during
his prime than any Irishman gone before. Finding the
Irish Catholic on his knees, he lifted him to his feet, and
taught him the power that lay within him. What he must be
blamed—eternally blamed—for, is that he endeavoured to
confound religious freedom with national liberty. His slavish
loyalty to the British crown, his bitter enmity to the United
Irishmen, and his horror of the very name of revolution, all
contributed to make his influence hurtful to the ideal of his
immediate predecessors, and consequently injurious to the
nation in general. ∎

MAUD GONNE

'THE FAMINE QUEEN'

(1900)

Maud Gonne published
this essay in protest
against the visit of Queen
Victoria to Ireland in April
1900. Prior to this, she
and Arthur Griffith had co-
founded the Irish Transvaal
Committee to discourage
Irishmen from joining the
British army to fight in
the Boer War, which they
regarded as an unjust
conflict. When the royal
visit was announced, the
feeling within nationalist
Ireland was that the aging
monarch was being sent
on a recruitment drive to
bolster British forces after
heavy casualties in South
Africa. On this occasion
a fault-line opened up
within nationalism, with
John Redmond pledging
to respect the visit while
separatists vowed to
protest against it. Gonne
reminded her readers that
Victoria had been on the
throne during the darkest
days of the Famine and
that every eviction had
been carried out in her ↗

'THE QUEEN'S VISIT to Ireland is in no way political,' proclaims the Lord Lieutenant, and the English ministers. 'The Queen's visit has no political significance, and the Irish nation must receive her Majesty with the generous hospitality for which it is celebrated,' hastens to repeat Mr. John Redmond, and our servile Irish members whose nationality has been corrupted by a too lengthy sojourn in the enemy's country. 'The Queen's visit to Ireland has nothing at all to do with politics,' cries the fishmonger, Pile, whose ambitious soul is not satisfied by the position of Lord Mayor and who hankers after an English title.

'Let us to our knees, and present the keys of the city to her Most Gracious Majesty, and compose an address in her honour.'

'Nothing political! Nothing political! Let us present an address to this virtuous lady,' echo 30 town councillors, who when they sought the votes of the Dublin people called themselves Irishmen and nationalists, but who are overcome by royal glamour. Poor citizens of Dublin! Your thoughtlessness in giving your votes to these miserable creatures will cost you dear. It has already cost the arrests of sixteen good and true men, and many broken heads and bruised limbs from police batons, for you have realised—if somewhat late—the responsibility of Ireland's capital, and, aghast at the sight of the men elected by you betraying and dishonouring Ireland, you have, with a courage which makes us all proud of you, raised a protest, and cried aloud, 'The visit of the Queen of England is a political action, and if we accord her a welcome we shall stand shamed before the nations. The world will no longer believe in the sincerity of our demand for national freedom.'

And in truth, for Victoria, in the decrepitude of her eighty-
one years, to have decided after an absence of half-a-century
to revisit the country she hates and whose inhabitants are
the victims of the criminal policy of her reign, the survivors
of sixty years of organised famine the political necessity *sarcasm*
must have been terribly strong; for after all she is a woman,
and however vile and selfish and pitiless her soul may be,
she must sometimes tremble as death approaches when she
thinks of the countless Irish mothers who, sheltering under
the cloudy Irish sky, watching their starving little ones, have
cursed her before they died. *magical element*

Every eviction during sixty-three years has been carried
out in Victoria's name, and if there is a Justice in heaven,
the shame of those poor Irish emigrant girls whose very
innocence renders them an easy prey and who have been
overcome in the terrible struggle for existence on a foreign
shore, will fall on this woman, whose bourgeois virtue is so
boasted and in whose name their homes were destroyed. If
she comes to Ireland again before her death to contemplate
the ruin she has made, it is surely because her ministers
and advisors think that England's situation is dangerous *growing nationalism*
and that her journey will have a deep political importance.
England has lived for years on a prestige which has had *colonisation*
no solid foundation. She has hypnotised the world with
the falsehood of her greatness; she has made great nations
and small nations alike believe in her power. It required
the dauntless courage and energy of the Boers to destroy
forever this illusion and rescue Europe from the fatal
enchantment. Today no one fears the British empire; her
prestige has gone down before the rifles of a few thousand
heroic peasants.

→ name. She portrayed
the British monarch in
menacing terms as a
vampiric crone seeking
the blood sacrifice of her   *Cathleen*
young Irish subjects—
suggestive, in some
ways, of the Cathleen
Ni Houlihan figure that
Gonne herself would
play on the Dublin stage
exactly two years later. The
publication of the essay
in the *United Irishman*
(7 April 1900) led to the
suppression of that issue
of the newspaper by order
of the Lord Lieutenant.

If the British empire means to exist she will have to rely on real strength, and real strength she has not got, England is in decadence. She has sacrificed all to getting money, and money cannot create men, nor give courage to her weakly soldiers. The men who formerly made her greatness, the men from the country districts have disappeared; they have been swallowed up by the great black manufacturing cities; they have been flung into the crucible where gold is made. Today the giants of England are the giants of finance and of the Stock Exchange, who have risen to power on the backs of a great struggling mass of pale, exhausted slaves. The storm approaches; the gold which the English have made out of the blood and tears of millions of human beings attracts the covetousness of the world. Who will aid the pirates to keep their spoils? In their terror they turn to Victoria, their Queen. She has succeeded in amassing more gold than any of her subjects; she has always been ready to cover with her royal mantle the crimes and turpitude of her empire, and now, trembling on the brink of the grave, she rises once more at their call. Soldiers are needed to protect the vampires. The Queen issues an appeal in England, the struggling mass of slaves cry 'Hurrah'; but there is no blood in their veins, no strength in their arms. Soldiers must be found, so Victoria will go herself to fetch them; she will go over to Ireland—to this people who have despised gold, and who, in spite of persecutions and threats, have persisted in their dream of freedom and idealism, and who, though reduced in numbers, have maintained all the beauty and strength and vitality of their race.

Taking the shamrock in her withered hand she dares to ask Ireland for soldiers— for soldiers to protect the exterminators of their race! And the reply of Ireland comes sadly but proudly, not through the lips of the miserable little politicians who are touched by the English canker but through the lips of the Irish people. *d i choť emy*

'Queen, return to your own land: you will find no more Irishmen ready to wear the red shame of your livery. In the past they have done so from ignorance, and because it is hard to die of hunger when one is young and strong and the sun shines, but they shall do so no longer; see! Your recruiting agents return unsuccessful and alone from my green hills and plains, because once more hope has revived, and it will be in the ranks of your enemies that my children will find employment and honour! As to those who today enter your service to help in your criminal wars, I deny them! If they die, if they live, it matters not to me, they are no longer Irishmen.' *ireland speaking*

'England is in decadence. She has sacrificed all to getting money...'

W.B. YEATS—*from*:

'NOBLE AND IGNOBLE LOYALTIES'

(1900)

I HAVE WRITTEN a couple of letters to the Irish papers on the visit of Queen Victoria to Ireland, but they have been very short, for I do not find that I have much to say upon such matters. Kings and queens come and go, and men wear emblems in their button-holes, and cannons fire and we all grow excited, and forget how little meaning there is in the cheers that such things buy.

She came in 1849 and though we had the Great Famine to forget, and though Mitchel and Meagher and Smith O'Brien had been transported a few months before she came, she was met by cheering crowds. The streets were as full as they were a couple of weeks ago, and yet she had scarce gone when the Tenant League was founded and the Land War in its modern shape began. She came again in 1853 and opened an exhibition, amid cheering crowds, and five years later the Fenian organisation was founded. In August 1861, she paraded the streets again amid cheering crowds and two years later, after she had gone, the *Irish People* was founded, and after that came state trials, and insurrection, and suspension of constitutional law. Her visits to Ireland have indeed been unfortunate for English power, for they have commonly foreshadowed a fierce and sudden shaking of English power in Ireland. I do not think this last visit will be more fortunate than the others, for I see all round me, among the young men who hold the coming years in their hands, a new awakened inspiration and resolve. It is for the best that they should have the two loyalties—loyalty to this English Queen, loyalty to her we call Cathleen Ní Houlihan—called up before them, that they may choose with clear eyes the harder way, for man becomes wise alone by deliberate choice and deliberate sacrifice. . . . *no influence?*

Is it, then, that although this royalty, that England sends as her messenger is vulgar, the loyalty it would have from us is so ennobling that we should close our eyes and do it reverence? No, for this royalty comes among us with all the bribes of the world upon its knees, and a shopkeeper has but to cheer loudly enough, and to fly flags enough, and he will fill his shop. And if a man has some half shame-faced hope to sit at rich men's tables, he has but to cheer loudly enough and to fly flags enough and he will find the way made easy before him. . . . *easier option?*

Contrast this loyalty with the loyalty that has been the supreme emotion of so many thousands of poor Irishmen *national loyalty* and women. It gave them nothing, but the peace of heart that comes to those who serve high things, and for its sake they have gone to prison and exile and death, and endured the enmity and the scorn of the great and the wealthy. What can these royal processions mean to those who walk in the procession of heroic and enduring hearts that has followed Cathleen Ní Houlihan through the ages? Have they not given her their wills and their hearts and their dreams? What have they left for any less noble royalty? ∎

Queen less noble than Cathleen

J.M. SYNGE—*from*:

'POSSIBLE REMEDIES'

(1905)

Having studied the congested districts of Connemara and Mayo in the company of Jack Yeats, Synge wrote a final article in a series for the *Manchester Guardian* in which he drew his conclusions about the condition of Ireland. Although he gave much consideration to economic problems and possible solutions, it was his view that economic measures alone would never solve Ireland's problems. Ireland would never retain its most talented and ambitious citizens, he argued, until some measure of political autonomy was secured and national life restored.

ONE OF THE chief problems that one has to deal with in Ireland is, of course, the emigration that I have mentioned so often. It is probably the most complicated of all Irish affairs, and in dealing with it, it is important to remember that the whole moral and economic condition of Ireland has been brought into a diseased state by prolonged misgovernment and many misfortunes, so that at the present time normal remedies produce abnormal results. For instance, if it is observed in some neighbourhood that some girls are going to America because they have no work at home, and a lace school is started to help them, it too often happens that the girls merely use it as a means of earning money enough to pay for their passage and outfit, and the evil is apparently increased. Further, it should not be forgotten that emigrants are going out at the present time for quite opposite reasons. In the poorest districts of all they go reluctantly, because they are unable to keep themselves at home, but in places where there has been much improvement the younger and brighter men and girls get ambitions which they cannot satisfy in this country, and so they go also. Again, where there is no local life or amusements they go because they are dull, and when amusements and races are introduced they get the taste for amusements and go because they cannot get enough of them. They go as much from districts where the political life has been allowed to stagnate as from districts where there has been an excess of agitation that has ended only in disappointment. For the present, the Gaelic League is probably doing more than any other movement to check this terrible evil, and yet one fears that when the people realise in five—or perhaps in ten—years that this hope of

restoring a lost language is a vain one, the last result will be
a new kind of hopelessness and many crowded ships leaving
Queenstown and Galway. Happily in some places there is
a counter-current of people returning from America. Yet
they are not very numerous, and one feels that the only real
remedy for emigration is the restoration of some national
life to the people. It is this conviction that makes most Irish
politicians scorn all merely economic or agricultural reforms,
for if Home Rule would not of itself make a national life
it would do more to make such a life possible than half-a-
million creameries. With renewed life in the country, many
changes of the methods of government and the holding of
property would inevitably take place, which would all tend to
make life less difficult even in bad years in the worst districts
of Mayo and Connemara. ■

JAMES JOYCE—*from*:

'HOME RULE COMES OF AGE'

(1907)

Joyce wrote a number of essays for the Italian press in which he attempted to explain Irish history and politics to an outside audience. These essays oscillate between pride in distinctive Irish achievements, and exasperation at the failure of his countrymen to break free from the oppression of the Catholic Church and British rule. He also lamented the fact that the economic and intellectual conditions of his homeland did not allow the individual to prosper. In this extract, which concludes an essay on Home Rule, he comments on the reasoning behind the Irish separatist position, and excoriates the politicians of the Irish Parliamentary Party for failing the people they represent while they lined their own pockets. The article was originally published as 'Home Rule Maggiorenne' in *Il Piccolo della Sera* (Trieste) on 19 May 1907.

NOW, EVEN FROM a cursory study of the history of Home Rule, it seems that we may draw two conclusions. The first is this: the most powerful weapons that England may use against Ireland are no longer those of conservatism, but of liberalism and the Vatican. Conservatism, for all that it may be tyrannical, is a frank and openly hostile doctrine. Its position is logical; it does not want a rival island to arise beside Great Britain, or Irish factories to compete with English ones, or tobacco and wine once again to be exported from Ireland, or the Irish ports to become an enemy naval base, whether under a foreign protectorate or a native government. This position is logical, just as the Irish separatists' position, which contradicts it point by point, is also logical. It takes little intelligence to see that Gladstone has done Ireland greater damage [to] Ireland than Disraeli did, and that the fiercest enemy of the Catholic Irish is the leader of English Vaticanism, the Duke of Norfolk.

The second conclusion is even more obvious. It is this: the Irish Parliamentary Party is bankrupt. For twenty-seven years it has been agitating and talking. In that time, it has drawn 35 million from its supporters, and the fruits of its agitation are that Irish taxes have increased by 88 million, while the Irish population has decreased by one million. The deputies themselves have improved their lot, aside from such small discomforts as a few months in prison or a few lengthy sittings. From being peasants' sons, street traders and clientless lawyers, they have become salaried administrators, factory and company bosses, newspaper owners and large landholders. Only in 1891 did they give proof of their altruism when they sold Parnell, their master, to the pharisaical conscience of the English nonconformists without exacting the thirty pieces of silver. ∎

JOHN REDMOND —*from*:

'SPEECH AT WOODENBRIDGE'

(1914)

FELLOW COUNTRYMEN, IT was indeed fortunate chance that enabled me to be present here today. I was motoring past, and I did not know until I arrived here that this gathering of the Volunteers was to take place at Woodenbridge. I could not deny myself the pleasure and honour of waiting to meet you, to meet so many of those whom I have personally known for many long years, and to see them fulfilling a high duty to their country. I have no intention of making a speech. All I desire to say to you is that I congratulate you upon the favourable beginning of the work you have made.

You have only barely made a beginning. You will yet have hard work before you can call yourselves efficient soldiers, and you will have to have in your hand—every man—as efficient weapons as I am glad to see in hands of some, at any rate, of your numbers. Looking back as I naturally do, upon the history of Wicklow I know that you will make efficient soldiers. Efficient soldiers for what?

Wicklow Volunteers, in spite of the peaceful happiness and beauty of the scene in which we stand, remember this country at this moment is in a state of war, and your duty is a twofold duty. The duty of the manhood of Ireland is twofold. Its duty is, at all costs, to defend the shores of Ireland against foreign invasion. It is a duty more than that of taking care that Irish valour proves itself: on the field of war it has always proved itself in the past. The interests of Ireland—of the whole of Ireland—are at stake in this war. This war is undertaken in the defence of the highest principles of religion and morality and right, and it would be a disgrace for ever to our country and a reproach to her manhood and a denial of the lessons of her history if

On the 20 September 1914, John Redmond made an historic speech at Woodenbridge, County Wicklow, in which he called on the Irish Volunteers to enlist in the British army for service overseas during World War One. This was perhaps the first time that a leader of nationalist Ireland encouraged Irish men to join the British forces. Redmond regarded this demonstration of loyalty as a means of applying moral pressure on the British to deliver Home Rule in a new post-war era. Senior republicans were outraged and renounced Redmond's strategy, causing a split in the Volunteer movement. They regarded the Volunteers as a *de facto* Irish army and viewed the British army as an enemy force of occupation.

young Ireland confined their efforts to remaining at home to defend the shores of Ireland from an unlikely invasion, and to shrinking from the duty of proving on the field of battle that gallantry and courage which has distinguished our race all through its history. I say to you therefore, your duty is twofold. I am glad to see such magnificent material for soldiers around me, and I say to you—go on drilling and make yourself efficient for the work, and then account yourselves as men, not only for Ireland itself, but wherever the fighting line extends, in defence of right, of freedom and religion in this war. ■

'I am glad to see such magnificent material for soldiers around me, and I say to you—go on drilling and make yourself efficient for the work, and then account yourselves as men, not only for Ireland itself, but wherever the fighting line extends, in defence of right, of freedom and religion in this war.'

PATRICK PEARSE—*from*:

'THE SEPARATIST IDEA'

(1916)

I HAVE NAMED Tone and Davis and Lalor and Mitchel as the four among us moderns who have chiefly developed the conception of an Irish nation. Others, I have said, have for the most part only interpreted and illustrated what has been taught by these; these are the fathers and the rest are just their commentarists. And I need not repeat here my reasons for naming no other with these unless the other be Parnell, whom I name tentatively as the man who saw most deeply and who spoke most splendidly for the Irish nation since the great seers and speakers. I go on to examine what these have taught of Irish freedom. And first as to Tone. He stands first in point of time, and first in point of greatness. Indeed, he is, I believe, the greatest man of our nation; the greatest-hearted and the greatest-minded.

We have to consider here Tone the thinker rather than Tone the man of action. The greatest of our men of action since Hugh O'Neill, he is the greatest of all our political thinkers. His greatness, both as a man and as a thinker, consists in his sheer reality. There is no froth of rhetoric, no dilution of sentimentality in Tone; he has none even of the noble oratoric quality of a Mitchel. A man of extraordinarily deep emotion, he nevertheless thought with relentless logic, and his expression in exposition or argument is always the due and inevitable garb of his thought. He was a great visionary but, like all the great visionaries, he had a firm grip upon realities, he was fundamentally sane.

One is now in a position to sum up Tone's teaching in a series of propositions:

1. The Irish nation is one.

2. The Irish nation, like all nations, has an indefeasible right to freedom.

Pearse's thinking developed significantly during his two decades of involvement with the Irish Revival. He began as an enthusiastic member of the Gaelic League with moderate Home Rule views, and ended up leading the insurrection in 1916. The shifting phases of his personal interests broadly mirror the trajectory of the period from cultural activities to political organisation to revolutionary action. Pearse was a key figure in the development of a modern Gaelic literature and an influential educationalist. In earlier writings he embraced the idea of the spiritual nation but in advance of the Easter Rising he began to embrace more overtly the republican revolutionary tradition of Wolfe Tone.

3. Freedom denotes separation and sovereignty.
4. The right to national freedom rests upon the right to personal freedom, and true national freedom guarantees true personal freedom.
5. The object of freedom is the pursuit of the happiness of the nation and of the individuals that compose the nation.
6. Freedom is necessary to the happiness and prosperity of the nation. In the particular case of Ireland, separation from England is necessary not only to the happiness and prosperity but almost to the continued existence of Ireland, inasmuch as the interests of Ireland and England are fundamentally at variance, and while the two nations are connected, England must necessarily predominate.
7. The national sovereignty, implied in national freedom holds good both externally and internally, i.e. the sovereign rights of the nation are good as against all other nations and good as against all parts of the nation. Hence:
8. The nation has jurisdiction over lives and property within the nation.
9. The people are the nation.

All this Tone taught, not in the dull pages of a treatise, but in the living phrases that dropped from him in his conversation, in his correspondence, in his diaries, in his impassioned pleas for his nation to the Executive Directory of France. . . .

That God spoke to Ireland through Tone and through those who, after Tone, have taken up his testimony, that Tone's teaching and theirs is true and great and that no other teaching as to Ireland has any truth or worthiness at all, is a thing upon which I stake all my mortal and all my immortal hopes. And I ask the men and women of my generation to stake their mortal and immortal hopes with me. ▪

JAMES CONNOLLY

'THE IRISH FLAG'

(1916)

THE COUNCIL OF the Irish Citizen Army has resolved, after grave and earnest deliberation, to hoist the green flag of Ireland over Liberty Hall, as over a fortress held for Ireland by the arms of Irishmen.

This is a momentous decision in the most serious crisis Ireland has witnessed in our day and generation. It will, we are sure, send a thrill through the hearts of every true Irish man and woman, and send the red blood coursing fiercely along the veins of every lover of the race.

It means that in the midst of and despite the treasons and backslidings of leaders and guides, in the midst of and despite all the weaknesses, corruption and moral cowardice of a section of the people, in the midst of and despite all this there still remains in Ireland a spot where a body of true men and women are ready to hoist, gather round, and to defend the flag made sacred by all the sufferings of all the martyrs of the past.

Since this unholy war first started we have seen every symbol of Irish freedom desecrated to the purposes of the enemy, we have witnessed the prostitution of every holy Irish tradition. That the young men of Ireland might be seduced into the service of the nation that denies every national power to their country, we have seen appeals made to our love of freedom, to our religious instincts, to our sympathy for the oppressed, to our kinship with suffering.

The power that for seven hundred years has waged bitter and unrelenting war upon the freedom of Ireland, and that still declares that the rights of Ireland must forever remain subordinate to the interests of the British empire, hypocritically appealed to our young men to enlist under her banner and shed their blood 'in the interests of freedom.'

In this article published in the Workers' Republic on 8 April 1916, Connolly announced that the Irish flag would fly over Liberty Hall in a symbolic act to reclaim Irish sovereignty. This political gesture was a harbinger of the storming of the GPO a matter of weeks later. Some of the language and ideas expressed here informed the Proclamation read by Pearse on Easter Monday. Connolly rails against cynical British appeals to religion and liberty, and criticises the use of Irish symbols such as the shamrock, to persuade Irishmen to fight in World War One. Sovereignty, according to Connolly, is vested in the Irish people rather than in a monarch or in an abstract idea of nation. As he succinctly put it: 'The cause of labour is the cause of Ireland, the cause of Ireland is the cause of labour. They cannot be dissevered.'

The power whose reign in Ireland has been one long
carnival of corruption and debauchery of civic virtue, and
which has rioted in the debasement and degradation of
everything Irish men and women hold sacred, appealed to
us in the name of religion to fight for her as the champion
of christendom. (Christian world) territory)
    The power which holds in subjection more of the world's population than any other power on the globe, and
holds them in subjection as slaves without any guarantee
of freedom or power of self-government, this power that
sets Catholic against Protestant, the Hindu against the
Mohammedan, the yellow man against the brown, and
keeps them quarrelling with each other whilst she robs and
murders them all—this power appeals to Ireland to send
her sons to fight under England's banner for the cause of
the oppressed. The power whose rule in Ireland has made of
Ireland a desert, and made the history of our race read like
the records of a shambles, as she plans for the annihilation
of another race appeals to our manhood to fight for her
because of our sympathy for the suffering, and of our hatred
of oppression.
    For generations, the shamrock was banned as a national
emblem of Ireland, but in her extremity England uses the
shamrock as a means for exciting in foolish Irishmen loyalty
to England. For centuries the green flag of Ireland was a
thing accurst and hated by the English garrison in Ireland,
as it is still in their inmost hearts. But in India, in Egypt, in
Flanders, in Gallipoli, the green flag is used by our rulers to
encourage Irish soldiers of England to give up their lives for
the power that denies their country the right of nationhood.
Green flags wave over recruiting offices in Ireland and
England as a bait to lure on poor fools to dishonourable
deaths in England's uniform.
    The national press of Ireland, the true national press,
uncorrupted and unterrified, has largely succeeded in
turning back the tide of demoralisation, and opening up
the minds of the Irish public to a realisation of the truth
about the position of their country in the war. The national
press of Ireland is a real flag of freedom flying for Ireland

despite the enemy, but it is well that also there should fly in Dublin the green flag of this country as a rallying point of our forces and embodiment of all our hopes. Where better could that flag fly than over the unconquered citadel of the Irish working class, Liberty Hall, the fortress of the militant working class of Ireland.

We are out for Ireland for the Irish. But who are the Irish? Not the rack-renting, slum-owning landlord; not the sweating, profit-grinding capitalist; not the sleek and oily lawyer; not the prostitute pressman—the hired liars of the enemy. Not these are the Irish upon whom the future depends. Not these, but the Irish working class, the only secure foundation upon which a free nation can be reared. *Removes aristocracy from ma[...] discourse. Adds women*

The cause of labour is the cause of Ireland, the cause of Ireland is the cause of labour. They cannot be dissevered. Ireland seeks freedom. Labour seeks that an Ireland free should be the sole mistress of her own destiny, supreme owner of all material things within and upon her soil. Labour seeks to make the free Irish nation the guardian of the interests of the people of Ireland, and to secure that end would vest in that free Irish nation all property rights as against the claims of the individual, with the end in view that the individual may be enriched by the nation, and not by the spoiling of his fellows.

Having in view such a high and holy function for the nation to perform, is it not well and fitting that we of the working class should fight for the freedom of the nation from foreign rule, as the first requisite for the free development of the national powers needed for our class? It is so fitting. Therefore, on Sunday, 16 April 1916 the green flag of Ireland will be solemnly hoisted over Liberty Hall as the symbol of our faith in freedom, and as a token to all the world that the working class of Dublin stands for the cause of Ireland, and the cause of Ireland is the cause of a separate and distinct nationality.

In these days of doubt, despair, and resurgent hope we fling our banner to the breeze, the flag of our fathers, the symbol of our national redemption, the sunburst shining over an Ireland reborn. ■

SEAN O'CASEY—*from*:

THE STORY OF THOMAS ASHE

(1918)

Thomas Ashe was born in Lispole, County Kerry in 1885. In 1908 he was appointed as principal of Corduff National School, near Lusk in North County Dublin. An influential figure in GAA and Gaelic League circles in Fingal, Ashe was a founding member of the Black Raven Pipe Band in Lusk. He led the Fingal Brigade of the Irish Volunteers in the Battle of Ashbourne on Easter Week, and was the only commandant in the Rising to achieve military success. He died on 25 September 1917 after being forcibly fed while on hunger strike in Mountjoy Jail. His death was a pivotal moment that registered increasing public support for the actions of the insurgents of 1916. His funeral (the biggest since Parnell's) was a massive republican demonstration and an early indication of the electoral sea change that would take place in 1918.

O PPRESSION HAS BROKEN Thomas Ashe, but she could not bend him. His brave soul has overflowed into the soul of the Irish people. He is dead: his ideals are alive and flourishing.

Oppression of the bloody hands, you cannot put a rope around the neck of an idea, you cannot put an idea up against a barrack-square wall and riddle it with bullets; you cannot confine it in the strongest prison cell that your slaves could ever build.

Thomas Ashe's body, today, is covered with Irish mould, but his principles are surging into stronger life within the minds of the Irish proletariat, the Irish scholar, and the Irish worker. Death has won a poor victory! Labour has lost a champion; Irish-Ireland had lost a son; militant Ireland has lost a soldier, but all have gained a mighty and enduring inspiration. Ashe died that human liberty might be vindicated and that Ireland might live. ■

Militarism/
Modernism

IT IS HARDLY surprising that Ireland produced so much gothic literature in the nineteenth century. During that period, the country was a dark place of almost medieval privations, which challenged even modernising leaders. A largely illiterate and landless peasantry endured feudal government and tolerated the dire consequences of cruel natural processes that could wipe out its main source of sustenance overnight. The great project of enlightenment promised by the United Irishmen in 1798 had been well and truly defeated. What remained of that republican impulse was driven underground into the clandestine world of the Irish Republican Brotherhood and eclipsed by O'Connell's drive for Catholic Emancipation. Although we associate the period with the rise of mass democracy in Ireland, the force of the various nationalist movements rested largely on the ability of charismatic leaders to manipulate and mobilise the threat of an unruly, uneducated peasantry. This may explain why so much of Irish nationalist analysis in that troubled century was heavily invested in traditions of physical force, and remained intellectually underdeveloped beyond the ballad tradition of the Young Irelanders.

In contrast, a radical shift in cultural and political ambition can be detected as the Irish Revival begins to take hold after the death of Parnell. This complex moment of reconnection with the submerged traditions of the Irish past, in many ways, reignites the stalled enlightenment project of 1798 and adds a cultural inflection. If anything distinguishes this period of extraordinary achievement, it is the combination of deep civic participation and brilliant artistic accomplishment—not always coterminous, needless to say. In Ireland at this time the transformative energy of the moment comes out of a creative rapprochement with newly discovered pre-colonial traditions at a time when old cultural moorings were being severed across Europe. If modernist experiment elsewhere was being driven by the revolutionary shock of the new, in Ireland a new cultural epoch was being inaugurated by the revolutionary shock of the old.

Imperial modernity, after all, had had a catastrophic effect: colonial policies fed the machine of empire but denuded the country of its most valuable resource—its people. Those who turned to tradition often registered a prudent scepticism of a particular form of imperial modernity, but many were happy to use the innovations of the modern world to spread an alternative message. The latest technologies of printing and the easy availability of newspapers greatly facilitated intellectual exchange and activism of all sorts. The involvement of women in the politics of advanced nationalism, and even as soldiers in the 1916 Rising, was but another example of a modernity which often expressed itself in the imagery of 'tradition': such women could discover in the example of Maeve and Deirdre empowering precursors to their own liberation from the restrictions of the modern world.

The rebels of 1916 fought for a republic constructed as a welfare state (years before such a system was generated elsewhere in Europe), yet they first met in the meeting rooms of the Celtic Literary Society and the Gaelic League. In a land that had lost many of its traditions, the rediscovery of the old often unleashed newer, radical energies that offered alternatives to the oppressive orthodoxies of Victorianism. W.B. Yeats and Maud Gonne, for example, could abandon conventional Christianity and rediscover alternate spiritualities in the Celtic world. James Joyce deployed similar tactics in his retelling of Homer's Odyssey, although his concerns about the insular tendencies of a purely Irish tradition were expressed in his preference for Greek over Irish myth.

The Rising, when it came, seemed arbitrary, capricious, even irrational. Appalled at the time by its polarising effect, cultural leaders such as Yeats and Gregory felt at first that the achievements of the Revival had been overturned at a stroke. Others were not so sure: to some the Rising appeared as an early example of 'modernism in the streets'. Yeats would, like many others, come to recognise that he had forged many links in the causal chain. His heroic poems and plays, like Hyde's talk of de-Anglicisation or even Maud Gonne's speeches on self-reliance, might seem to have been consummated in the revolutionary action (though it could also be argued that the Democratic Programme of the 1919 Dáil was an even fuller fulfilment of those ideals). At any rate, many of the key texts of the preceding decades seemed after 1916 to have been somehow anticipating this action, either as rich potential, dire possibility or plunge into the unknown.

Every artist who creates an idea yearns to give it form. Every thinker likewise wishes to incarnate central intuitions in embodied action. Some of the rebel leaders have been described as *artistes manqués*, figures who failed to achieve greatness in art or thought and so were tempted, like many others in their European generation, by the fatal lure of action. Equally, figures like Yeats and O'Casey, who had in youth been activists (Yeats in the Irish Republican Brotherhood, O'Casey in the Citizen Army), must have felt pangs at their non-involvement when so many friends and associates were putting their lives on the line. But it would be too simple to treat the artists as frustrated rebels, the rebels as frustrated artists. Some writings of major artists contributed directly to the actions: and some of the rebels were brilliant artists, thinkers, educationalists. The object of most was not redemption through violence but rather to take Ireland out of the carnage of World War One.

The Rising still represented what Ernie O'Malley would later ruefully look back on as 'the lyric phase' of a revolution which had been going on for over two decades. In the years of guerrilla war that followed, it seemed, in Ireland as well as in the wider theatre of Europe, that militarism was beginning to trump modernism. Experiment in art continued in the 1920s and 1930s, but the hope that artists could connect their work with the struggles of ordinary people towards fuller self-expression began to wane. Mass suffrage came to many places but soon declined into mere electoralism, as political leaders whose consciousness had been formed more through soldiering than through cultural action, offered ever more dogmatic, ever less thoughtful analyses. It was a bleak fact that even as the democratic franchise spread, political leaders spoke in a language that was more coercive than consensual. Yet in a country still excited by the challenge of dismantling imperial structures and perfecting native forms, the hope lingered that people might together create a more democratic society.

JAMES CONNOLLY—*from*:

'ERIN'S HOPE'

(1897)

Men make the world, said Karl Marx, but not in conditions of their own choosing. James Connolly was always a socialist but one who believed that the labour movement in Ireland would prosper through an identification with the claim to separate nationhood. He believed that the cause of labour and the cause of Ireland were one. In this he followed Marx who said that the Irish had a duty to be as national as possible, in order to be international in their effect: a blow against the imperial state in Ireland would have knock-on effects not only in other countries across the world but within Britain itself, whose working class might emulate such an insurrection by striking against their own rulers.

[L] ET THE CO-OPERATIVE organisation of the workers replace the war of classes under capitalism and transform the capitalist himself from an irresponsible hunter after profit into a public servant fulfilling a public function and under public control. Recognise the right of all to an equal opportunity to develop to their fullest capacity all the powers and capabilities inherent in them by guaranteeing to all our countrymen and women, the weak as well as the strong, the simple as well as the cunning, the honest equally with the unscrupulous, the fullest, freest, and most abundant human life intelligently-organised society can confer upon any of its members.

'But,' you will say, 'this means a socialist republic; this is subversive of all the institutions upon which the British empire is founded—this cannot be realised without national independence.' Well, I trust no one will accuse me of a desire to fan into flame the dying embers of national hatred when I state as my deliberate and conscientious conviction that the Irish democracy ought to strive consistently after the separation of their country from the yoke that links her destinies with those of the British crown. The interests of Labour all the world over are identical, it is true, but it is also true that each country had better work out its own salvation on the lines most congenial to its own people.

The national and racial characteristics of the English and Irish people are different, their political history and traditions are antagonistic; the economic development of the one is not on a par with the other; and, finally, although they have been in the closest contact for seven hundred years, yet the Celtic Irishman is today as much of an insoluble problem to even the most friendly English as on the day when the

two countries were first joined in unholy wedlock. No Irish
revolutionist worth his salt would refuse to lend a hand to
the social democracy of England in the effort to uproot the
social system of which the British empire is the crown and
apex, and in like manner no English social democrat fails to
recognise clearly that the crash which would betoken the fall
of the ruling classes in Ireland would sound the tocsin for the
revolt of the disinherited in England.

But on whom devolves the task of achieving that
downfall of the ruling classes in Ireland? On the Irish people.
But who are the Irish people? Is it the dividend-hunting
capitalist with the phraseology of patriotism on his lips and
the spoil wrung from sweated Irish toilers in his pockets; is
it the scheming lawyer—most immoral of all classes; is it the
slum landlord who denounces rack renting in the country
and practises it in the towns; is it any one of these sections
who today dominate Irish politics? Or is it not rather the
Irish working class—the only secure foundation on which
a free nation can be reared— the Irish working class which
has borne the brunt of every political struggle, and gained
by none, and which is to-day the only class in Ireland which
has no interest to serve in perpetuating either the political
or social forms of oppression—the British connection or the
capitalist system? The Irish working class must emancipate
itself, and in emancipating itself it must, perforce, free
its country. The act of social emancipation requires the
conversion of the land and instruments of production from
private property into the public or common property of the
entire nation. This necessitates a social system of the most
absolute democracy, and in establishing that necessary social
system, the working class must grapple with every form of

government which could interfere with the most unfettered
control by the people of Ireland of all the resources of their
country.

On the working class of Ireland, therefore, devolves the
task of conquering political representation for their class
as the preliminary step towards the conquest of political
power. This task can only be safely entered upon by men and
women who recognise that the first action of a revolutionary
army must harmonise in principle with those likely to be
its last, and that, therefore, no revolutionists can safely
invite the co-operation of men or classes whose ideals are
not theirs, and whom, therefore, they may be compelled to
fight at some future critical stage of the journey to freedom.
To this category belong every section of the propertied
class, and every individual of those classes who believes in
the righteousness of his class position. The freedom of the
working class must be the work of the working class. And
let it be remembered that timidity in the slave induces
audacity in the tyrant, but the virility and outspokenness of
the revolutionists ever frightens the oppressor himself to
hide his loathsomeness under the garb of reform. And thus
remembering, fight for your class at every point.

Our people are flying to the uttermost ends of the earth;
seek to retain them at home by reducing the hours of labour
wherever you have the power and by supporting every
demand for legislative restriction. Your Irish railways employ
thousands of men, whose working hours average twelve per
day. Were they restricted to a forty-eight-hour week of labour,
employment would be provided for thousands of Irishmen
who at present are driven exiles from their native land.
Pledge every Irish representative to support an eight-hour

bill for railways; if he refuses you will know that he considers profits as more sacred than patriotism, and would sacrifice his country on the altar of greed. Our Irish municipalities and other public bodies controlled by popular vote employ also many thousands of men. What are their hours of labour? On the average, ten, and their wages just above starvation point. Insist upon Irish corporations establishing the eight-hour day in all their works. They at least do not need to fear foreign competition. If you have no vote in the corporation you can at least help to hound off the political platform elsewhere every so-called patriot who refuses to perform this act of justice. Every Irish corporation which declines to institute an eight hours' working day at a decent wage for its employees has virtually entered into a conspiracy with the British government to expatriate the Irish people, rather than pay an additional halfpenny in the pound on the rates. In all our cities, the children of the labouring class are dying off before their time for lack of wholesome nourishing food. As our municipalities and public trusts provide water for the people free of direct payment and charge the cost upon the rates, let them also provide at our schools free breakfasts, dinners and teas to the children in attendance there, and pay for it from the same source. ∎

HELENA MOLONY—*from*:

'NATIONAL ACTIVITIES'

(1950)

Born in Dublin in 1883, Helena Molony was a feminist, socialist and writer. She joined Inghinidhe na hÉireann in 1903 and became the first editor of *Bean na hÉireann* in 1908. She supported Maud Gonne's crusade to provide free meals for the poor schoolchildren of Dublin. Molony acted for the Abbey Theatre. She was a friend of both Constance Markiewicz and James Connolly, becoming secretary of the Irish Women Workers' Union founded during the Lock-Out of 1913. Molony described the leaders of the Revival as selfless patriots: 'In such a manner is the real aristocracy of a country born.' She fought as a soldier of the Citizen Army in the attack on Dublin Castle in 1916 and was imprisoned. ⁊

THE INGHINIDHE GREW out of that [the Patriotic Children's Treat], and formed itself into a permanent society of Irishwomen pledged to fight for the complete separation of Ireland from England, and the re-establishment of her ancient culture. The means decided upon for the achievement of this object was the formation of evening classes for children, for Irish language, Irish history—social as well as political—the restoration of Irish customs to everyday life, Irish games, dancing and music. The chief work of the society was the teaching of children's classes in the above subjects. The children were mostly recruited from the poorer quarters of the city, where, at that time, the British army got its most valuable recruits.

As well as the work of teaching children, the Inghinidhe were always active in opposing any expression of the loyal flunkeyism which was so rampant at that time—it was a sort of hangover from the visit of Queen Victoria, when, in spite of all the efforts of our people who held national views, and who were then dubbed 'extremists', Queen Victoria got an official 'Address of Welcome, on behalf of the Citizens of Dublin' from the Corporation, many parliamentary nationalists voting for it. However, this disgrace was wiped out in 1903 when King Edward VII came, and no address was presented by the Corporation. This was in no small measure due to the very active canvassing by Inghinidhe of the aldermen and councillors, at their homes, their places of business, and by their attendance in force at the Corporation meetings where a loyal address was mooted. The senior members can give a better account of these activities than I can.

Another important work of the Inghinidhe was the continuous anti-recruiting campaign, which was carried on year by year up to the First World War. Our President [Maud Gonne] was always very keen that we should keep up this work, and was mainly responsible for the many leaflets we issued. They were in all cases addressed to Irish girls appealing to them not to consort with the armed and uniformed enemies of their country, telling them that we were at war with England, and that all our political and social ills were due to her occupation of our country.

It is difficult for people today to realise the atmosphere of our capital city in the early years of this century. The uniformed soldiery were not then the pampered darlings they are today. They were considered (even by the English) good enough to fight, but not fit to mix with civilians in peace time. In Dublin, for instance, they were confined to one side of O'Connell Street, i.e. GPO side. No respectable person—man or woman—would dream of walking on that side of the street after twilight. But many thousands of innocent young country girls, up in Dublin, at domestic service mostly, were dazzled by these handsome and brilliant uniforms, with polite young men with English accents inside them—and dazzled often with disastrous results to themselves, but that is another side of the matter, and we were only concerned with the national political side. These young girls had not the faintest idea of the moral, social, or political implications of their association with the redcoats.

Of course the publication and distribution of these bills was illegal, in fact any statement derogatory to the forces of the crown was regarded seriously by the authorities. There may be some of these handbills in existence, but unfortunately I have not got any, as my dwelling was raided many dozens of times in the following years, and all my

→ After a long career as a republican activist, Molony died in 1967. This description of the state of feeling in the main thoroughfare of Dublin in the first years of the twentieth century is taken from Molony's deposition to the Bureau of Military History in 1950. British soldiers, who sought to fraternise with female nationalist activists, were sometimes waylaid and beaten up by the women's male comrades. Arthur Griffith denounced republican militants for precipitating such scenes but Molony's account suggests that the city centre was already a contested space, simmering on the brink of insurgency.

belongings scattered from time to time. The danger of distributing these bills was not only from the police, but from the troops themselves and their sympathisers. A group of us would set out about eight o'clock in the evening and start from the Rotunda hospital, walking rapidly as far as the Bank of Ireland. We walked in twos some twenty or thirty yards apart, and managed in that way to 'paper' the whole promenade, before these young people had time to grasp the contents of their handbill. Sometimes the girls thought they were religious tracts, and would display some hostility. The soldiers, when they became aware of this campaign against them were, of course, offensive and threatening. The leaflets had to be concealed in handbags or hand-muffs (which were then worn) and delivered surreptitiously. Any hesitation or delay would lead to a mobbing, and soldiers at that time had the habit of taking off their belts and attacking civilians with them if they thought there was any hostility to them. This was a very crowded thoroughfare at this time, but only by soldiers and their girlfriends. Ordinary civilians did not walk on that side of the street. If they managed to locate any of us we would have got a rough passage, so naturally it was considered dangerous work for the Inghinidhe and many of our friends disapproved, as it was not thought 'becoming'. At that time, the military 'suffragette' movement had not been heard of and women and girls were still living in a semi-sheltered Victorianism. The hurly-burly of politics, particularly the kind which led to the risk of being involved in street rows, was certainly not thought 'becoming'. However, we managed to avoid any real unpleasantness. Only on one occasion did we come near it. Misses E. O'Farrell and Sighle Grenan and myself were spotted by police. We took to our heels, and were chased through Henry Street, Mary Street and right up to the markets in Capel Street. We got away clear, as we were young and swift, and the police were hampered by long heavy overcoats. On the whole, we feared more the soldiers with their canes. We desired above all to avoid any fracas, and we succeeded. This campaign led to a prolonged newspaper controversy which showered us with abuse and called us all sorts of names, and we individually got a constant supply of anonymous letters of the foulest nature. It was not pleasant, but it did raise a volume of opinion and we had our defenders too. ■

PEADAR KEARNEY—*from*:

'THE SOLDIERS' SONG'
'AMHRÁN NA BHFIANN'

(1907)

Written in English by
Peadar Kearney to music
by Kearney himself and
Patrick Heaney, this lyric
was published in *Irish
Freedom* in 1912 and used
as a marching song by
volunteers during the
Rising and Anglo-Irish
war. In the years after
independence, some
members of the national
army argued for its
adoption as the national
anthem but members of
the government thought it
inappropriate. Tom Moore's
'Let Erin Remember' was
an unofficial anthem until
1926, when the Free State
adopted Kearney's lyric,
which by then had been
translated into Irish by
Liam Ó Rinn. It was played
nightly by Radio Éireann
and later in theatres, at
public events and on
sporting occasions. It is
used instrumentally as a
formal salute to Uachtarán
na hÉireann, the Irish
President. The Irish-
language version is the one
most often sung.

Soldiers are we,
Whose lives are pledged to Ireland;
Some have come
From a land beyond the wave;
Sworn to be free,
No more our ancient sireland,
Shall shelter the despot or the slave.
Tonight we man the 'bearna baoil',
In Erin's cause, come woe or weal,
'Mid cannon's roar and rifles' peal,
We'll chant a soldier's song

Sinne Fianna Fáil,
Atá faoi gheall ag Éirinn;
Buíon dár slua
Thar toinn do ráinig chughainn.
Faoi mhóid bheith saor
Seantír ár sinsear feasta,
Ní fhágfar faoin tíorán ná faoin tráill.
Anocht a théam sa bhearna baoil,
Le gean ar Ghaeil, chun báis nó saoil,
Le gunna scréach faoi lámhach na bpiléar,
Seo libh canaídh amhrán na bhfiann

GEORGE RUSSELL—*from*:

'PHYSICAL FORCE
IN LITERATURE'

(1904)

THE THEORY OF physical force has been gradually ebbing away from politics in Ireland. It required men to be brave, and for those who are willing to risk their lives we always have respect. When a man is ready to shoulder pike or rifle for an idea, he regards his ideal as more important than life, and however he may pervert those ideals in expression, I have never felt a doubt but that in such a case the man's heart has been made holy by some sacred fire. There are nobler ways of settling the right or wrong of a question, but the heroes of gentleness and love *ineffogiox* are few, and if a man is unable to live this life, it is better he should take some course which at least demands of him a sacrifice. But while much may be said for the man who, seeing no higher way, decides to establish his right by force, there is nothing at all to be said for the physical force theory in literature which has come to be accepted by so many journalists in Ireland. To adopt it in life shows courage. To bring it into literature or argument shows that the man is *poify?* a coward. He runs away from the battle while seeming to take a sword. It never stays in the least the march of the conquering idea, for an idea once put forward can only be overcome by a superior beauty or truth.

It seems to be the way for many in Ireland, either through hatred of thought, or through incapacity to think, to content themselves with abuse. They shout 'bigot', 'sourface', continually, and at any attempt to reason out the right or wrong of a question, the chorus of abuse grows more vehement and angry, until the shouters are at last stupefied and happy, having deafened themselves to anything but their own voices. . . . It is amazing to hear these cries of 'bigot' from people who refuse to argue, and of 'shallow' *hypocrites*

The opening sentence of Russell's essay in *Dana* might strike a later generation as naïve, but his diagnosis of a violent dogmatism in many of the responses to Horace Plunkett's *Ireland in the New Century* is expressed in a language which is remarkably alert to the tensions simmering beneath the surface calm of Irish public life in 1904. In particular, he detects a growing rift between Ulster papers and the journals of Catholic nationalism in more southern latitudes of the island. As a native of Portadown, a resident of Dublin and an activist for agricultural co-operation across the country, Russell was well placed to comment. Equally interesting is the suggestion that the 'physical force' element which has been subsumed from politics into literature may yet assert itself and unite the country in 'facile orthodoxy' and 'forceless platitude'.

from people who do their thinking by proxy. The criticism of *Ireland in the New Century* illustrates the physical force element in argument. The most eminent critic never found it necessary to read the book, . . . The criticism was as bad on one side as the other. The Ulster papers selected and quoted with delight the same sentences which the Catholics condemned. All they wanted was to find some empty echo of the prejudices of their readers, for no Irish paper, paying a dividend, can bring itself to tell the really unpleasant truth to its readers. While the party man listens to the shouts of his audience and enjoys his paltry triumph of an hour, he forgets his defeat in the everlasting battle between good and evil, between nobility and littleness, which is the only real battle to be fought in life. It is a sad truth that in Ireland every cause is injured more by its adherents than by its opponents.

It is possible for a party or creed to gain the letter and lose the spirit of their hope. It may be that we shall have a Catholic or Protestant country without any religion, or self-government and a people not worth governing. Everything is howled down here except a facile orthodoxy. I would rather see four millions of Irish people disunited and thinking out policies for themselves, than an Ireland united under any policy at present known to them. The latter would only unite them in some forceless platitude. Through independent thought there is some hope that a policy with the will of many people behind it might finally emerge. It is because they are not allowed to think, that Irishmen are so apathetic in matters of national importance. The country is strewn with the wrecks of leagues and societies of one kind or another, and they all fell through or are falling through because independent thought is forbidden. ■

JOHN FREDERICK MACNEICE

'ON REFUSING TO SIGN THE ULSTER COVENANT'

(1912)

'OUR VIEWS,' SAID the Rector, 'seem to be taken of it (the Covenant).'

'First, there is the view of those who take it to mean a policy of physical force, and who are persuaded that the circumstances justify such a policy. Secondly, there's the view of those who say it does not mean a policy of physical force, and who sign it in the belief that it does not. Thirdly, there's the attitude of those who look at it simply as a resolution against Home Rule, and a demand for an appeal to the nation. Those who view it in any of these three ways can, of course, sign it with a clear conscience. And lastly, there's the attitude of those who try to study the Covenant primarily from the Church's standpoint. Amongst these are some who think that it means a call to arms, and who also think that as the Church of Christ is in this land to interpret the life of Christ and to exhibit the mind of Christ, she cannot sound that call. They do not censure or criticise those who take a different view—far from it. All they say is—"Let each man be fully persuaded in his own mind." But they do feel strongly that the Church as a Church, fighting for her own life, must fight under Christ's banner, and in Christ's way, and need not borrow the weapons of the kingdoms of the world. . . . They believe the Church is here by God's appointment to publish the Gospel of Peace; to be a reconciler, a healer, to be a city set on a hill with the message of Christ's love light and life for all the people of this land. Furthermore, they think that Ireland's greatest interest is peace, and they shrink from a policy which, as is avowed, in the last resort, means war and worse still, civil war. They fear that even the avowal of such a policy may add to the dissensions that are already too characteristic of Irish life, and intensify the bitterness that

Born in Connemara in 1866, MacNeice was Church of Ireland rector at Carrickfergus in County Antrim when the Ulster Covenant was proposed, but (along with some other Protestant clergymen) he refused to sign. This report of his subsequent sermon in the *Carrickfergus Examiner* of 4 October 1912 contains a cogent summary of his reasoning. He thought it contradictory for loyalists to pronounce themselves rebels against the law; had a Christian objection to militarism; and feared a war between Irish people. The politicising of religion disturbed him. He saw in Protestant tradition the opportunity for 'self-election', for the right of the individual voice to be raised against group-thinking. Aware that the Irish Revival had generated a debate among →

→ Protestants about
the different forms
which self-election and
self-determination might
assume, he took the view
that a common Christian
heritage unites rather than
divides Irish people. He
died in 1942, by which time
one of his children, Louis,
was a famous poet.

many of them hoped was fast dying away. This is the attitude of a minority, possibly a small minority. This is my own attitude. . . . I do not ask anyone to adopt my view. I may, of course, be mistaken in my interpretation of Christ's life and of the Church's duty, but I am entitled to hold the opinion I have expressed, and I make no apology for holding it. . . . May God be with us, may He give to us, and to all our fellow-countrymen, the blessing of peace, may He draw together in Christ those who have been too long apart and may He, even through our troubles, help us, wherever we live, north, south, east, west—to hear the voice—"Sirs, ye are brethren." ■

EOIN MACNEILL—*from*:

'THE NORTH BEGAN'

(1913)

THE ULSTER VOLUNTEER movement is essentially and obviously a Home Rule movement. It claims, no doubt, to hold Ireland 'for the empire', but really it is no matter whether Ireland is to be held for the empire or for the empyrean, against the pope, against John Redmond, or against the man in the moon. What matters, is *by whom Ireland is to be held*. Lord Lansdowne, speaking recently against Home Rule, spoke fine old medieval worlds, 'We have Ireland and we mean to keep her.' The Ulster Volunteers reply, '*We* are going to hold Ireland—of course for your lordships.'

The true meaning of this extraordinary development is dawning painfully on English unionists. They are beginning to understand that Sir Edward Carson has knocked the bottom out of unionism. To add to their comfort, a Mr. Arnold White has been proving in elaborate detail that the present available resources of the British army are not sufficient to put down the Volunteer movement in four of the thirty-two Irish counties. In any case, it appears the British army cannot now be used to prevent the enrolment, drilling, and reviewing of Volunteers in Ireland. There is nothing to prevent the other twenty-eight counties from calling into existence citizens' forces to hold Ireland 'for the empire'. It was precisely with this object that the Volunteers of 1782 were enrolled, and they became the instrument of establishing self-government and Irish prosperity. Their disbanding led to the destruction alike of self-government and of prosperity, and the opportunity of rectifying a capital error of this sort does not always come back again to nations.

This essay in *An Claidheamh Soluis* on 1 November 1913 led directly to the creation of the Irish Volunteers later that month. During the previous year, the Ulster Volunteer Force had resolved to resist Home Rule by military force, if necessary—the idea of a 'covenant betrayed' had a biblical resonance for Protestant militants. MacNeill, however, saw in this idea a model of that self-reliance which the rest of Ireland might emulate (although, as a native of Antrim, he must have recognised that the movements might ultimately be on a collision course). The analogy with the Irish Volunteers of 1782 pleased him and he was installed as leader. For a time the authorities tolerated this militarisation and the Volunteers represented a broad →

→ coalition of nationalists from Redmond's constitutionalists to insurrectionists, but by 1914 the Irish Republican Brotherhood outflanked MacNeill and assumed control. MacNeill here is perhaps more troubled than he admits by the possible emergence of a separate northern state— his jocular reference to the new UVF title of George Richardson, a retired British army lieutenant-general, does not fully conceal that underlying worry.

English unionists realise, explicitly or instinctively, that the Ulster Volunteers have scuttled the ship; some of them, sooner than admit their discomfiture, are hankering after the separation from Ireland of what they are pleased to call 'homogenous Ulster', namely, the four eastern counties. Not a single responsible man and no assembly of men in Ireland has authorised this proposal. All nationalist opinion and any unionist opinion that has been expressed is strongly hostile to it. And for a very good reason.

There is no 'homogenous Ulster'. It is impossible to separate from Ireland the city that Saint Patrick founded, the city that Saint Columba founded, or the tombs of Patrick, Brigid and Columba. They would defy and nullify the attempt. It is impossible to separate from Ireland the frontier town of Newry, the men of south Down, Norman and Gael, the Gaelic stock of the Fews that hold 'the Gap of the North', the glensmen of south Derry, or north Antrim. If there were any possibility of civil war, if civil war were assured, not to speak of its being insured, these districts alone would hold immovable all the resources of General—I believe—Richardson. There are, besides, the 100,000 nationalist Home Rulers of Belfast, and others, Protestants, Catholic, Orange and Presbyterian, in every corner of the four counties, who under any change of government are certain to 'revert to type'. With what facility they have fallen in with the idea of holding Ireland—for the empire!

It is evident that the only solution now possible is for the empire either to make terms with Ireland or to let Ireland go her own way. In any case, it is manifest that all Irish people, unionist as well as nationalist, are determined to have their own way in Ireland. On that point, and it is the

main point, Ireland is united. It is not to follow, and it will
not follow, that any part of Ireland, majority or minority, is
to interfere with the liberty of any other part. Sir Edward
Carson may yet, at the head of his Volunteers, 'march to
Cork'. If so, their progress will probably be accompanied
by the greetings of ten times their number of national
Volunteers, and Cork will give them a hospitable and a
memorable reception. Some years ago, speaking at the
Toome Feis, in the heart of 'homogenous Ulster', I said that
the day would come when men of every creed and party
would join in celebrating the defence of Derry and the battle
of Benburb. That day is nearer than I then expected. ■

'... all Irish people, unionist as well
as nationalist, are determined to
have their own way...'

FRANCIS SHEEHY SKEFFINGTON

'THE WRITING ON THE WALL'

(1914)

THE TERRIBLE WAR into which we are now plunging marks the Nemesis and the doom of the man-made state and of the purely male idea of government and polity. Blind to spiritual forces, devoting themselves to the building of a civilisation on a purely material basis, making property their god and cultivating a steady disregard, in comparison, of the value of human life, the rulers of Europe have gone on complacently in the belief and confidence that their system of society was destined to endure, and that they represented the final triumph of civilisation. Amid all the outward splendour, all the conquests of commerce, of science and of industry, the penetrating eye of the seers of this and the last generation have long foretold collapse. At the top, excessive arrogance, boundless ambition, unscrupulous exploitation; at the bottom, destitution, crime, and shame—thus did the Cassandras of our day depict the fabric of civilisation, permeated, in spite of its overwhelming appearances, by a rottenness that sprang ultimately from one cause—an insufficient appreciation of the sacredness of human life and personality—that is to say, a lack of precisely those thought-elements which it is the special function of women, in public as in private life, to supply. It has long been predicted that the sex-bias of the modern civilisation would lead to its overthrow; that the anti-feminist canker in its heart would fester, breeding war or revolution, ruin from above or ruin from below. These predictions, scoffed at so long, are on the verge of fulfilment. War has come; revolution, at least in the countries which suffer most heavily, cannot be long delayed. All that delicate network of civilisation, of human brotherhood and international amity, which artists and

scientists and philosophers have been patiently weaving by
their accumulated work for decades, has been swept aside
at one blow at the command of the unreasoning blood
lust and thirst for domination. Those who, yesterday, were
horror-stricken at the destruction of a stained-glass window,
a racecourse stand, or a picture, are today contemplating,
without protest and in some cases with joy, the wholesale
destruction of ships of war, the bombarding of cities, the
burning of thousands of houses, accompanied by the
inevitable loss of millions of human lives—lives every one of
which has cost some woman the agonies of the Valley of the
Shadow to produce. Bombs dropping from the sky, tearing
up the ground, hurling hundreds to death, destroying
blindly the most precious products of human industry and
artistic skill, as well as the human beings themselves; great
ships, the work of thousands of hands and brains, manned
by hundreds more, ramming each other in the deep, and
plunging together to annihilation; blazing cities, thousands
of destitute wanderers, mobs fiercely fighting for bread,
soldiers aflame with passion wreaking their cruelty and
their lust on the defenceless—these are some of the horrors
that are now, in the true sense of a much-abused word
inevitable; for once the war demon has been unleashed,
nothing can control him.

We are clearly of opinion that the root cause of this
appalling dissolution of society is to be found in the same
spirit that engenders contempt for women and denies them
a place in the state. War and anti-feminism are branches
of the same tree—disregard of true life values. It is not a
coincidence that all the countries concerned in the war are
countries which do not recognise women as citizens, and

→ the pacifist Francis Sheehy Skeffington published an open letter to Thomas MacDonagh in the *Irish Citizen* of May 1915, claiming that an insurrection could never be more than 'militarism'. Why, he asked, were arms glorified by the kind of men who kept women marginal in the nationalist movement? Skeffington had already given a full account of his reservations in this article in the *Irish Citizen* after the outbreak of World War One.

that those which are most aggressively and unscrupulously war-like are precisely those in which women are held in least regard. It is no mere coincidence that it is those who support women's claim to freedom who are, in every country, the most active in trying to prevent war or to limit its consequences. And the one ray of hope in the darkest international situation within living memory is, that when the lurid and unimaginable sequel has burnt itself into the brains and bodies of humanity, a new Europe may arise, with a new spirit, determined to build no more on unstable and lopsided foundations, but to erect a new society based on the divinity of humanity, without distinction of physical sex. But before that day can dawn, Europe will go through the valley of agony. ■

'War and anti-feminism are branches of the same tree— disregard of true life values.'

DIARMUID COFFEY

THE OUSTING OF DOUGLAS HYDE, GAELIC LEAGUE, DUNDALK

(1915)

THIS WAS THE position when the Ard Fheis for 1915 met at Dundalk. Meanwhile the malcontent element in the Gaelic League, though checked at Galway in 1913, was glad of a new opportunity of attacking Hyde. The tide had set towards uniting the League with the new political revolution, and it is doubtful if anything could have stopped it, though Pearse, O'Rahilly, MacNeill, and others of the leaders of Sinn Féin were still sufficiently strong supporters of Hyde to oppose a change in its official policy.

Motions to bring politics into the League had occasionally been moved at previous annual meetings but had never been passed. An abuse had crept into the Ard Fheis in the form of proxies. Poor branches of the Gaelic League, in order to avoid the expense of sending a representative, used to give their delegates cards in blank to members of other branches to find delegates to speak for them. At the Ard Fheis held in Dundalk in 1915, this abuse was rampant. The malcontents took full advantage of it, and it was said that one member had fifty delegates' cards in his pocket.

A resolution was moved that to the objects of the Gaelic League should be added a clause stating that the League was working for an 'Independent Ireland'. This was a clear issue, and many who were present thought the motion would have been defeated.

The issue was obscured by substituting the vague word 'free' for the definite word 'independent'. In this form, the motion was carried out and next day Hyde resigned.

His position with the new rule in force would have been impossible. The word 'free' is incapable of interpretation between two bodies, one wishing to be political, the other non-political. It was obvious that the majority of active

The 'no politics' rule in the Gaelic League was causing increasing strain after 1912. When an ever-more-radical Pearse made a speech in favour of Dublin workers during the Lock-Out the following year, Douglas Hyde rebuked him for prejudicing the independence of the League. Hyde himself had refused tempting offers from John Redmond to become a leader of the parliamentary party at Westminster—and Pearse admired him for that refusal. As the Volunteers gathered members and force, Redmond was compelled (somewhat reluctantly) to urge his followers to join. The Volunteers duly split between a large constitutional majority and a small but resourceful 'physical force' faction, some of whose leaders were key members of the Keating Branch of the →

→ Gaelic League. With the
outbreak of war in 1914,
the Redmondites and
radicals split. Diarmuid
Coffey, born in Dublin
in 1888 and a graduate
of Trinity College, was a
Protestant intellectual
who ran guns for the
Volunteers and was asked
by Hyde to act as his
biographer in 1917. This is
his account of how Hyde
ceased to be president
of the Gaelic League.

Gaelic Leaguers had determined to throw the weight of the League on to the extreme political side, and any further attempt on Hyde's part to stop this would have simply meant a fight which he was certain to lose. Hyde had not changed his views since he had made his presidential address to the National Literary Society in 1892, but the background had changed. He had fought for a literary and linguistic revival, but now his followers had gone far beyond this and were embarking on what developed into a five years' war; textbooks were being exchanged for rifles, and Hyde was a scholar and a literary man, not a military commander. He had to resign the leadership into the hands of men of a different type, though they were men whose outlook had been formed largely by Hyde's own teaching.

So great was the personal respect with which Hyde was regarded that for a year no president was elected to the Gaelic League. ■

'Motions to bring politics into the League had occasionally been moved at previous annual meetings but had never been passed.'

PATRICK PEARSE

SPEECH AT THE GRAVE OF O'DONOVAN ROSSA

(1915)

I T HAS SEEMED right, before we turn away from this place in which we have laid the mortal remains of O'Donovan Rossa, that one among us should, in the name of all, speak the praise of that valiant man, and endeavour to formulate the thought and the hope that are in us as we stand around his grave. And if there is anything that makes it fitting that I, rather than some other, rather than one of the grey-haired men who were young with him and shared in his labour and in his suffering, should speak here, it is perhaps that I may be taken as speaking on behalf of a new generation that has been re-baptised in the Fenian faith, and that has accepted the responsibility of carrying out the Fenian programme. I propose to you then, that, here by the grave of this unrepentant Fenian, we renew our baptismal vows; that, here by the grave of this unconquered and unconquerable man, we ask of God, each one for himself, such unshakable purpose, such high and gallant courage, such unbreakable strength of soul as belonged to O'Donovan Rossa.

Deliberately here we avow ourselves, as he avowed himself in the dock, Irishmen of one allegiance only. We of the Irish Volunteers, and you others who are associated with us in today's task and duty, are bound together and must stand together henceforth in brotherly union for the achievement of the freedom of Ireland. And we know only one definition of freedom: it is Tone's definition, it is Mitchel's definition, it is Rossa's definition. Let no man blaspheme the cause that the dead generations of Ireland served by giving it any other name and definition than their name and their definition.

We stand at Rossa's grave not in sadness but rather in exaltation of spirit that it has been given to us to come

Jeremiah O'Donovan Rossa, born in County Cork in 1831, was a legendary leader of the Irish Republican Brotherhood, sentenced in 1865 for plotting the Fenian uprising. His election to represent Tipperary at the House of Commons was declared null because he was in prison, where at various times he was manacled and put in solitary confinement. He was released in 1870 on condition that he leave Ireland, taking up residence in New York. He masterminded a bombing campaign in English cities, becoming a hate-figure in the London press. He died in 1915 and his body was returned for burial at Glasnevin. The vast funeral procession, during which the streets of Dublin were effectively taken over and controlled by Thomas MacDonagh and the Irish Volunteers, represented →

→ a rehearsal of the Rising
which would happen just
a few months later; and
Pearse's speech, with
its reference to being
re-baptised in the 'Fenian
faith', constituted a
clear challenge to those
Catholic bishops who
regarded physical force
as sinful. The large funeral
procession of Michael
Collins, seven years later,
would also provide an
occasion—this time for
the government of
the Free State—to
demonstrate its control
of a contested space.

thus into so close a communion with that brave and splendid Gael. Splendid and holy causes are served by men who are themselves splendid and holy. O'Donovan Rossa was splendid in the proud manhood of him, splendid in the heroic grace of him, splendid in the Gaelic strength and clarity and truth of him. And all that splendour and pride and strength was compatible with a humility and a simplicity of devotion to Ireland, to all that was olden and beautiful and Gaelic in Ireland, the holiness and simplicity of patriotism of a Michael O'Clery or of an Eoghan O'Growney. The clear true eyes of this man almost alone in his day visioned Ireland as we of today would surely have her: not free merely, but Gaelic as well; not Gaelic merely, but free as well.

In a closer spiritual communion with him now than ever before or perhaps ever again, in a spiritual communion with those of his day, living and dead, who suffered with him in English prisons, in communion of spirit too with our own dear comrades who suffer in English prisons to-day, and speaking on their behalf as well as our own, we pledge to Ireland our love, and we pledge to English rule in Ireland our hate. This is a place of peace, sacred to the dead, where men should speak with all charity and with all restraint; but I hold it a Christian thing, as O'Donovan Rossa held it, to hate evil, to hate untruth, to hate oppression and, hating them, to strive to overthrow them. Our foes are strong and wise and wary but, strong and wise and wary as they are, they cannot undo the miracles of God who ripens in the hearts of young men the seeds sown by the young men of a former generation. And the seeds sown by the young men of '65 and '67 are coming to their miraculous ripening

today. Rulers and defenders of realms had need to be wary
if they would guard against such processes. Life springs
from death, and from the graves of patriot men and women
spring living nations. The defenders of this realm have
worked well in secret and in the open. They think that they
have pacified Ireland. They think that they have purchased
half of us and intimidated the other half. They think
that they have foreseen everything; think that they have
provided against everything, but the fools, the fools, the
fools!—they have left us our Fenian dead, and while Ireland
holds these graves, Ireland unfree shall never be at peace. ∎

[handwritten marginalia: sacrifice; gendered sacrifice remove; negative attitude toward pacifists; Yeats; cannot be sacrifices for nothing]

'...a new generation...has been
re-baptised in the Fenian faith...'

FRANCIS SHEEHY SKEFFINGTON—*from*:

'IRELAND AND THE WAR'

(1916)

At the outbreak of war, British recruiting officers asked Ireland to support 'Catholic Belgium'. Sheehy Skeffington, however, scoffed at the idea that the war was being fought to aid small nationalities. Ireland's need after centuries of despoliation and de-population, he countered, was for peace and the development of resources. Belgium had 'not yet suffered a tithe of what has been endured by Ireland at the hands of England' and Britannia's domination of the seas had been used to smother Irish trade. The mainstream press had been bribed into a pro-war stance: 'our books and papers cannot get out; the books and papers of other nations cannot get in'. The government he accused of using the emergency to imprison radicals without trial or to send them into exile. This was the last ↗

BOTH REGIONS PROMPTLY started gun-running. In April 1914, the biggest gun-running operation up till then was carried out by the Ulstermen. The *Fanny*, the yacht which brought the guns, was talked about in the press for a fortnight before it reached Ulster; the patrols of the English navy were watching the coasts; yet somehow the *Fanny* reached Larne, unloaded its cargo, and got away without any interference from the gunboat patrols. At Larne, it was met by a host of automobiles, which took away the rifles. To facilitate the operation, the Ulster Volunteers seized Larne harbour, imprisoned the harbour master and police, and took the entire control of the town into their hands. Another shipload was disembarked on the same night at another Ulster port. Here a too-zealous customs official offered resistance; *he died of heart disease.* Nobody was identified, punished, or even prosecuted for this flagrant defiance of the law, although the episode was described by Mr. Asquith in the House of Commons as an 'unprecedented outrage', and pledges were given that due punishment would be meted out to its perpetrators. Nothing was done. After all, these were the faithful 'English garrison in Ireland'; for the moment the politicians must pretend to oppose them, but in reality they were doing England's work and helping to make more difficult, or perhaps impossible, any measure of Home Rule for Ireland.

Very different was the attitude of the government and its officials towards nationalistic gun-running. Here the utmost vigilance was displayed. Gunboats patrolled the shores of Dublin and Wicklow, as well as the western coast, unceasingly. Even when Mr. Redmond, by order of the English government (as is generally believed in Ireland) asserted his right to command the Irish Volunteers, which he had not founded; even when the founders of the organisation yielded to Mr. Redmond and gave his nominees half the seats on their committee, still, Mr. Redmond could not persuade the government to relax the ban on the importation of arms. Perhaps he did not try very hard. He was as much afraid of the Volunteers as the Government was; his only wish was to keep them under his control, lest they might become an instrument for those nationalists who looked beyond parliament's sham battles to the complete liberation of Ireland.

This portion in the Volunteers continued gun-running under the double disadvantage of having to deceive both the government and their own Redmondite colleagues on the Joint Executive Committee. On July 26, just after the Austrian ultimatum to Serbia, the famous gun-running exploit of Howth took place. The Dublin Volunteers made a Sunday route march to Howth (nine miles), none but a few leaders knowing the object. As they entered the village, a yacht, steered by a woman, came alongside the pier. The English patrol boat was not in the neighbourhood, a conveniently disseminated rumour of gun-running in Wexford having sent it off on a false scent. This yacht's arrival had not been boomed in advance, like the *Fanny's*, otherwise the vigilance of the patrol would not have been so easy to elude as the Ulstermen had found it. The Volunteers, following strictly the Ulster precedent, took possession of the pier, excluded the police and harbour officials—they did not go so far as to imprison them in their own offices and barracks as had been done, with only a shadow of resistance, at Larne—disembarked with guns, and marched off to Dublin with them. Meantime the wires had been humming and Dublin

→ essay by Sheehy Skeffington in the February 1916 issue of *Century Magazine* in the United States. Four months later, it would report his murder by a British officer as he tried to stop looting. The essay records Sheehy Skeffington's disapproval of the British and unionist war machines: the government was caught in the double bind of suppressing Irish mutiny and of pretending to the outside world that it didn't exist.

Castle was on the alert. At Clontarf, in the outskirts of the city, the Volunteers, marching with unloaded rifles, were met by a combined force of police and soldiers. A parley took place. The government's official, Harrel, demanded the surrender of the rifles; the Volunteer leaders refused. Harrel ordered the police to take the rifles. Some of the police refused, and the remainder acted with evident reluctance, an unheard-of thing in Ireland, but a symptom of the general perception of the deliberate favouritism shown by the government to the Ulstermen as compared with the Irish Volunteers. The soldiers, a company of the King's Own Scottish Borderers, were then ordered to charge the Volunteers with fixed bayonets. Some Volunteers were stabbed, and a massacre seemed inevitable, when a fresh parley was entered upon. By the time it was over, Harrel discovered that only the front rank of the Volunteers still stood their ground in front of him; the remainder, in obedience to a rapidly disseminated order, 'Save the guns', had executed a strategic retirement. Harrel then drew off his force, and the remnant of the Volunteers completed their march unmolested, no guns having been lost.

As the soldiers marched back to the barracks, the Dublin populace assailed them with curses and later with stones. The troops retaliated with a series of bayonet charges which further enraged the crowd, in which wild rumours of the fight at Clontarf had spread. The soldiers were undoubtedly peppered pretty severely with stones, but the assailants were all unarmed and were largely composed of women and children. There was no justification whatever for the action taken by the soldiery. They turned and fired at the crowd without giving any warning, without even firing a preliminary volley over their heads. Four people were killed, one man, two women, one boy. Several others were wounded, of whom one subsequently died. *Nobody* was punished; a whitewashing enquiry was held, but meantime the Scottish Borderers had 'distinguished themselves' by getting wiped out in the retreat from Mons, and no disciplinary measures were taken. Harrel, the assistant commissioner of the Dublin police, who had taken it upon himself to call out the soldiers in the first instance, was made a temporary scapegoat, but he is now again in the service of the government in Ireland, helping in the secret service department, which looks after political affairs.

I have dwelt upon this incident of the struggle at Clontarf and the shooting at Bachelors Walk because it happened before the war. Some people in America, I find, think that England's present severity to Ireland is merely a result of the state of war. When the anniversary of Bachelors Walk came round this year, the people proposed to put up a commemorative tablet, but the military forbade.

A week after the Bachelors Walk massacre (the Irish Zabern as we call it) the war against 'German militarism' broke out. Mr. Redmond, in the House of Commons, had the incredible audacity to commit the Irish people to the support of this war. He and his party were returned to parliament for one object only—to secure Home Rule. At no Irish election did any other question become an issue. Repeatedly had Mr. Redmond, when called upon to help some progressive cause, sheltered himself behind his lack of 'mandate'; his mandate, he declared, was for Home Rule only. Yet without any mandate he ventured to commit Ireland to the support of England in a European war. By doing so, he missed the greatest opportunity that has ever come to an Irish statesman. Had he, on August 3, 1914, spoken as follows in the imperial parliament: 'I have no mandate from the Irish people as to what our attitude should be in the event of a European war; the question has never been discussed between us. My colleagues and I are now going home to Ireland to consult our constituents as to what Ireland's attitude should be'—had he spoken thus, and followed up such a speech by walking out of the House and returning to Ireland, the English government would have been on its knees to him within a fortnight, and he would have been able to command, as the price of his and Ireland's aid, something much better than a mutilated Home Rule act on the statute book, which can never come into operation. He should, in short, have acted after the fashion of those Balkan statesmen, who care nothing for either of the warring parties, but look with a single eye to the interest of their own country. ∎

AUGUSTINE BIRRELL—*from*:

THINGS PAST REDRESS

(1937)

Augustine Birrell, born
in Liverpool in 1850, was
a lawyer and academic,
who won fame also as
an essayist and MP for
the Liberals. He became
chief secretary for Ireland
in 1907 and successfully
guided the Universities
Act into law in 1908. He
encouraged the Home
Rule Bill of 1914 but it was
suspended, owing to the
war. By then, constitutional
nationalists were being
eclipsed by a more radical
element in the movement,
but Birrell, while noting
a sense of 'exaltation'
among cultural nationalists,
did not believe that this
would translate into an
insurrection. ↗

IRISH LITERATURE AND the drama, Messrs. Maunsell's list of new Irish publications, and the programme of the Abbey Theatre became to me of far more real significance than the monthly reports of the RIC. The plays of John Synge and Lady Gregory, the poems of Mr. Yeats, AE, and Dora Sigerson, the pictures of Orpen, Lavery, and Henry, the provocative genius of Mr. Bernard Shaw, the bewitching pen of Mr. George Moore, the penetrative mind of Father Tyrrell (the list could easily be prolonged) were by themselves indications of a veritable renaissance—a leap to the front rank of thought and feeling altogether novel.

The intelligence of England, never over-represented in parliament, at last took cognisance of the change, and the sister island began no longer to be regarded as a dreary, dingy, disreputable politico-religious problem but a land with a literary and poetical tradition of her own, a 'point of view' all her own, and a genius of expression not confined to stale jokes and specimens of 'so-called' Irish humour invented to gratify the crude tastes of the English traveller.

In this Revival, which included all classes, high and low, rich and poor, the Gaelic League, with its enthusiasm for the Irish language, played a great part. If asked, as was often the case, 'Was the Gaelic League a "disloyal association"?' there could be but one reply: 'It was intensely disloyal to the English connection.' But then, nobody in Ireland, north or south, save a handful of officials, was or ever had been, 'loyal' to England, in the true sense of that noble word.

Irish 'loyalty' has always been a conditional, hypothetical loyalty; that is to say, no loyalty at all. Mr. Redmond and Lord Carson were both either potential or actual rebels, and recognised each other at once in those characters and liked each other all the better for being able to do so.

The Ulster rebellion preceded the Easter rising in Dublin.
The famous 'gun-running' exploit in the spring of 1914, though an overt act of rebellion, did not excite in southern Ireland the same laudable feelings of indignation as it did in constitutional bosoms in England. So far as I could observe, the 'victory' at Larne gave universal satisfaction in Ireland. Was it not an affront to England? Was it not boldly conceived and well executed? Was it not an excellent example? The 'national' volunteers had no better recruiting sergeant.

There will always be a difference of opinion as to the whether the leaders of this Ulster rebellion against the supremacy of the law should have been prosecuted. As to the offence, the law officers had no doubt. Where or how the rebels were to be tried, and how many of them should be put in the dock, were more difficult questions to answer. The consequences of not doing anything were obvious to everybody, but politics often consists of balancing one set of grave evils against another set, and after consideration, the Cabinet, with my concurrence, decided to leave it alone, although by doing nothing they almost negatived their right to be called a government at all. But then how long had there been a government in Ireland dealing out even-handed justice between one set of Irishmen and another? ■

→ When the Rising occurred, he immediately offered his resignation and the subsequent commission of enquiry rebuked him for failing to curb militant nationalists in the lead-up to it. He died in London in 1933 and his autobiography, in which he sought to explain his conduct, appeared three years later.

SEAN (JOE) KEEGAN

THE COUNTERMANDING ORDER

(1916)

On Easter Sunday Eoin MacNeill published a statement in the *Sunday Independent* calling off manoeuvres of the Irish Volunteers and in effect countermanding the planned uprising. He had been trumped by the more radical conspiratorial leadership of the Irish Republican Brotherhood, who used him as a convenient front-man for the Volunteers and had then secured his support for rebellion by showing him a document which suggested that the authorities were about to arrest him and other leaders. The arrest of Roger Casement at Banna Strand and the loss of German arms then re-awakened MacNeill's conviction that the uprising was ill-advised. ↗

MY WIFE (reading the paper) said 'this is a very dangerous business I think, and you will need to mind yourself, I hope everything will be all right. Remember dinner is at 2 o'clock.'

I set out for the city on a bicycle at 8.55 a.m. Twenty-five minutes later I was knocking and ringing at the hall door of 27 Mountjoy Square. The door opens and I said, 'Good morning nurse, I called to see Mr. Plunkett.' 'Oh dear she replied, Mr. Plunkett is gone away bag and baggage about one hour ago, it's really too bad.' 'No harm done nurse,' I said, then 'good morning and thank you.' Nurse said 'good morning.'

A couple of minutes later I was knocking at 44 Mountjoy Square. A young lady in black answered the door. I enquired—'I wonder if I could see Mr. Pearse?' The young lady remarked: 'Mr. Pearse, that's strange, there was another man here this morning looking for him also. Is he a clergyman?' I thought for a moment and said, 'well yes he could be as far as I am concerned. I have only a message for him.' The young lady then said, 'there is no one of the name here and there never has been, so you are disappointed.' I said, 'I am sorry for troubling you so early but this was the address given to me. Good morning and thanks.' 'Good morning.'

I am now thinking hard, nothing but disappointment, where am I going to turn to next? Yes, I will go down to Tom Clarke's shop, one never knows how luck goes. I enter, I was looking for Mr. Clarke, or Mr. Pearse, or even Mr. Plunkett—are any of them here?

I sensed that I was diagnosed as a policeman and so got a very poor showing from Mrs. Clarke (this was not to be wondered at, for I looked the part and she had never seen me before).

I thought if only Kitty were here I would be all right, but there you are, just luck. Where for next? I will try 41 Parnell Square, I might just hit it off. This house is generally crowded out on Sunday mornings with clubs of one sort or another, but now there is no one to be seen, not even the caretaker. I suppose it's too early for anyone to be here.

Well now, suppose I try the Gaelic League at 25, on chance. No luck here either—the only occupant of this big house is a solitary cat. Am I beaten, no, not yet. I will try go over to Whelan on the quay. If I find him at home, he will put me right on to Arthur Griffith or Sean T. O'Kelly.

I enter Mr. Whelan's shop. A volunteer in uniform is at the counter conversing with the lady assistant. I said, 'good morning Miss, is Mr. Whelan in?' She said, 'No, Mr. Whelan is out.' 'Will he be back soon?' I enquired. 'No, I don't think so,' she replied. I then asked was Mrs. Whelan in and she said, 'Oh, yes Mrs. Whelan is in but you can't see her, she is bathing the baby.' I then said, 'Oh look here I don't mind, I've seen babies bathed before.' She then said, 'But . . .' 'But what?' (Mrs. Whelan in the room off the shop hears the conversation and comes to the door, baby in arms). Mrs. Whelan said, 'Well, well, but you are an early visitor from the hills.' I replied 'Yes, yes I am looking for himself and your assistant says he is not in.' Mrs. Whelan said, 'He is upstairs, go up and see him.' Mr. Whelan is on his way down as we meet. Mr. Whelan said, 'What's the news, anything strange? You are early in town.' I replied, 'Well as you know from the morning papers, everything is off for the present.' 'Yes, it's too bad.' I continued, 'Well I'm in town trying to locate Mr. Pearse or Mr. Plunkett, with corroboration of the press notice in Mr. MacNeill's own handwriting. I got the address 27 Mountjoy Square and 44 Mountjoy Square and I have failed

→ He met Volunteer Joe Keegan after eight o'clock mass at Rathfarnham church and asked him to cycle into Dublin, bearing a letter confirming the newspaper advertisement to Pearse and comrades. Keegan took no part in the Rising but his brother Edward, a printer at the *Irish Times* and former actor of the Abbey Theatre, was one of the first rebels shot in the fighting.

to make contact.' Mr. Whelan remarked, 'Oh that must be
44 Mountjoy Street, you should try there. Just ask for Sean
T. And there you are. Wait, I shall come with you—there are
usually G. Men knocking around there.' Mr. Whelan brings
out a bike and sticks a revolver in his pocket, remarking 'You
never know.'

We are going up Capel Street now and at Dominick
Street corner he says, 'you go up this way and I'll go round
Blessington Street and we will meet accidentally at 44.' That
plan worked out but it brought no result from 44. There was
no Sean T. there. The G. Man was outside all right and there
were a good many lads inside in the parlour if one was to
judge by the revelry. Mr. Whelan suggests to go down to Sean
T.'s address at Belvedere Avenue and I part with him, wishing
him 'God Speed', and I am away again.

Arrived at Belvedere Avenue—Sean T. is not living there
now. 'He has moved to the corner of Mountjoy Square and
Charles Street,' I am informed by a local volunteer whom I
questioned. Back again to the corner of Mountjoy Square
where I knock and a woman answers the door. 'Is Mr. O'Kelly
in?' I ask. 'No', came the reply, 'Mr. O'Kelly is gone to half-
eleven mass and won't be back. Can I take any message for
him? I am his wife.' 'Pardon me, if I may say so but I don't
think your Mr. O'Kelly is the man I'm seeking. I am looking
for Councillor Sean T. O'Kelly and I don't think you are his
wife.' She said, 'That is so, but I know the Councillor: he lives,
I think, at the corner of Charles Street and Rutland Street.'
I thank her very much and said, 'I must be away, I am in a
hurry.' A few seconds later, I am knocking at the hall door in
Rutland Street. Knock. Knock. A volunteer in uniform opens
the door (it is Mr. O'Kelly's brother). I said, 'I want to see Mr.
O'Kelly if he is in—I mean Councillor O'Kelly.' He replied,
'He is in all right but you can't see him.' 'Why?' I said. 'There
is no why about it, you can't see him,' and with that remark
he thrusts the point of a bayonet towards my chest. 'Oh, look
here man', I said: 'Just put that thing round at my back, it is
just as effective that way, but I must see Sean T.' 'Well, if you
are so persistent,' he said, 'go on in front of me up the stairs,
first door on the left, but be careful and knock easy.' I knock.

'Who's there?' said a voice. 'Keegan from Rathfarnham' said I. 'Come in Sean,' said the voice and right there in the bed was the Councillor, resting awhile as he said himself, after being out all night raiding Brittas Camp. 'Well Sean,' he said, 'what's your trouble?' 'I am looking for Comdt. Pearse', I replied, 'and I am sure you can help me. I have here Mr. MacNeill's cancellation order for him.' 'Oh that can't be,' he interjected, 'it must go on now.' 'Well,' I said, 'I am not going to argue with you at all, where can I see Comdt. Pearse?' Sean T. then said, 'he was here up to a half-hour ago and he has gone down to Liberty Hall, but I say it must go on.' I then said, 'goodbye and thanks and the best of luck no matter what happens.' 'The best of luck to yourself,' he rejoined, 'but I say it must go on.'

Very soon after I arrived in Beresford Place where there appears to be thousands assembled. I try to cycle through the crowd towards the Hall. Several voices shouted. 'Pull him off, don't let him in there.' 'Easy on there, friend, I'll get off.' 'But you can't go in there', shouted my interrupter. 'And why not?' I enquired. 'What's the objection?' 'You are a policeman, a spy,' he repeats. 'Now do you think if I were a policeman', I said, 'that I was going to rush this place all by myself? Have a little sense,' I added, and kept moving forward. 'All right then', he said, 'go on but look out for yourself'. I am now on the steps of Liberty Hall. I make up my mind that I cannot ask for Comdt. Pearse right away, so I decide to ask for Councillor P.T. Daly, but before doing so I see Countess Markiewicz on the stairs landing, so I decide to approach her which I do with a military salute, saying, 'I have a despatch here for Comdt. Pearse, where can I see him?', to which she replied, 'I know nothing about him.' I am in a quandary to know what to do next when a voice rings out from the top stairs. 'Hello Sean.' It was a voice that I knew well for I had known it for close on twenty-five years. It was Capt. Sean Connolly who spoke. I hastened up the stairs towards him and we shook hands, had a few friendly words about old acquaintances and in answer to my enquiry for Comdt. Pearse, he opened the door of the Council Chamber and I went in and there, sure enough, was Comdt. Pearse coming towards the door. I saluted him and handed him my despatch. Before he read it, he asked me did I want any answer to it, to which I replied 'I don't think it requires any answer. It is, as far as I know, the commands of the Chief of Staff.' He then said, 'Tell him it shall be so.'

I got one hurried glance around that Council Chamber and at the further end of the room from me I saw MacDonagh, Clarke, McDermott, and Plunkett with a few others whose backs were towards me. And so I left Liberty Hall with another few words to my friend Sean Connolly, thanking him for making my visit so easy. I returned with all speed to Woodtown, Rathfarnham where Mr. MacNeill apparently was anxiously awaiting my return. Round about there were a lot of people, motor cars and bicycles. I communicated to him Comdt. Pearse's decision and he expressed 'thanks to God for that same.' ■

JAMES STEPHENS—*from*:

THE INSURRECTION IN DUBLIN

(1916)

A SULTRY, LOWERING day, and dusk skies fat with rain. I left for my office, believing that the insurrection was at an end. At a corner I asked a man was it all finished. He said it was not, and that, if anything it was worse.

On this day the rumours began, and I think it will be many a year before the rumours cease. The *Irish Times* published an edition which contained nothing but an official proclamation that evilly-disposed persons had disturbed the peace, and that the situation was well in hand. The news stated in three lines that there was a Sinn Féin rising in Dublin, and that the rest of the country was quiet.

No English or country papers came. There was no delivery or collection of letters. All the shops in the city were shut. There was no traffic of any kind in the streets. There was no way of gathering any kind of information, and rumour gave all the news.

It seemed that the military and the government had been taken unawares. It was bank holiday, and many military officers had gone to the races, or were away on leave, and prominent members of the Irish government had gone to England on Sunday.

It appeared that everything claimed on the previous day was true, and that the city of Dublin was entirely in the hands of the Volunteers. They had taken and sacked Jacob's biscuit factory and converted it into a fort which they held. They had the Post Office, and were building barricades around it ten feet high of sandbags, cases, wire entanglements. They had pushed out all the windows and sandbagged them to half their height, while cartloads of food, vegetables and ammunition were going in continually. They had dug trenches and were laying siege to one of the city barracks.

James Stephens, born in 1890, became a language revivalist and republican socialist. He published variations on Celtic legend (including *The Crock of Gold* and *The Charwoman's Daughter*). This eyewitness account appeared six months after the Rising. Stephens's close personal knowledge of many of the protagonists and his solidarity with the poor of Dublin (in whose streets the conflict was conducted) imbue his narrative with a depth of feeling. Like the narrative of Father Aloysius Travers, this diaristic account captures the climate of rumour and uncertainty which pervaded Dublin all through Easter Week (with reports of German guns advancing on the city); and it conveys a sense of how everyone caught up in the event, →

It was current that intercourse between Germany and Ireland had been frequent, chiefly by means of submarines, which came up near the coast and landed machine guns, rifles and ammunition. It was believed also that the whole country had risen, and that many strong places and cities were in the hands of Volunteers. Cork Barracks was said to be taken while the officers were away at the Curragh races, that the men without officers were disorganised, and the place easily captured.

→ whether army leaders or unemployed labourers, felt themselves at the mercy of the immediate moment. Stephens, tiny of stature, was somewhat bedazzled by men of action. The *Irish Times*, whose emergency edition is mentioned, advised citizens to stay indoors and study the writings of Shakespeare, the tercentenary of whose death was being celebrated.

It was said that Germans, thousands strong, had landed, and that many Irish-Americans with German officers had arrived also with full military equipment.

On the previous day, the Volunteers had proclaimed the Irish Republic. This ceremony was conducted from the Mansion House steps, and the manifesto was said to have been read by Pearse, of St. Enda's. The Republican and Volunteer flag was hoisted on the Mansion House. The latter consisted of vertical colours of green, white and orange. Kerry wireless station was reported captured, and news of the republic flashed abroad. These rumours were flying in the street.

It was also reported that two transports had come in the night and had landed from England about 8,000 soldiers. An attack reported on the Post Office by a troop of lancers who were received with fire and repulsed. It is foolish to send cavalry into street war.

In connection with this lancer charge at the Post Office it is said that the people, and especially the women, sided with the soldiers, and that the Volunteers were assailed by these women with bricks, bottles, sticks, to cries of:

'Would you be hurting the poor men?'

There were other angry ladies who threatened Volunteers, addressing to them this petrifying query:

'Would you be hurting the poor horses?'

Indeed, the best people in the world live in Dublin.

The lancers retreated to the bottom of Sackville Street, where they remained for some time in the centre of a crowd who were caressing their horses. It may have seemed to them a rather curious kind of insurrection—that is, if they were strangers to Ireland.

In the Post Office neighbourhood the Volunteers had some difficulty in dealing with the people who surged about them while they were preparing the barricade, and hindered them to some little extent. One of the Volunteers was particularly noticeable. He held a lady's umbrella in his hand, and whenever some person became particularly annoying he would leap the barricade and chase his man half a street, hitting him over the head with the umbrella. It was said that the wonder of the world was not that Ireland was at war, but that after many hours the umbrella was still unbroken. A Volunteer night attack on the quays was spoken of, whereat the military were said to have been taken by surprise and six carts of their ammunition captured. This was probably untrue. Also, that the Volunteers had blown up the arsenal in the Phoenix Park.

There had been looting in the night about Sackville Street, and it was current that the Volunteers had shot twenty of the looters.

The shops attacked were mainly haberdashers, shoe shops, and sweet shops. Very many sweet shops were raided, and until the end of the Rising sweet shops were the favourite mark of the looters. There is something comical in this looting of sweet shops—something almost innocent and child-like. Possibly most of the looters are children who are having the sole gorge of their lives. They have tasted sweet stuffs they had never toothed before, and will never taste again in this life, and until they die the insurrection of 1916 will have a sweet savour for them.

I went to the Green. At the corner of Merrion Row a horse was lying on the footpath surrounded by blood. He bore two bullet wounds, but the blood came from his throat which had been cut.

Inside the Green railings four bodies could be seen lying on the ground. They were dead Volunteers.

The rain was falling now persistently and, persistently from the Green and from the Shelbourne Hotel, snipers were exchanging bullets. Some distance beyond the Shelbourne I saw another Volunteer stretched out on a seat just within the railings. He was not dead, for, now and

again, his hand moved feebly in a gesture for aid; the hand
was completely red with blood. His face could not be seen.
He was just a limp mass, upon which the rain beat pitilessly,
and he was sodden and shapeless, and most miserable to
see. His companions could not draw him in for the spot was
covered by the snipers from the Shelbourne. Bystanders
stated that several attempts had already been made to
rescue him, but that he would have to remain there until
the fall of night. ■

'... until the end of the Rising
sweet shops were the favourite
mark of the looters.'

LOUISE GAVAN DUFFY

KITCHEN DUTY IN THE POST OFFICE
Easter Week 1916
(1949)

I WAS BROUGHT INTO the Post Office and I saw Mr.
Pearse. He was as calm and courteous as ever. I now
think it was very insolent of me because I said to him
that I wanted to be in the field but that I felt that the
rebellion was a frightful mistake, that it could not possibly
succeed and it was, therefore, wrong. I forget whether he
said anything to that or whether he simply let it go. He
certainly did not start to justify himself. I told him that
I would rather not do any active work; I suppose what I
meant was that I would not like to be sent with despatches
or anything like that, because I felt that I would not be
justified. He asked me would I like to go to the kitchen. I
could not object to that, and I went up to the kitchen at the
top of the back of the building. He was at the bottom of the
main building, in front. I suppose it was the public room,
but I did not recognise it, it looked so different.

I suppose I began to wash up, or cut bread and butter: then I
did not see very much. We came down once or twice during
the week perhaps, but we were very busy and we did not
get invitations to come down. When we were not working
we were resting. We did go to sleep, but I forget how it was
arranged— whether we took shifts or not. I remember going
to sleep on a mattress in one of the corridors.

There were a couple of prisoners there. One was a British
officer, who just sat there looking glum. He was not asked to
do any work but the Tommies were washing up. There were
two or three Tommies who were quite cheerful. I think they
were in uniform; they were taken prisoners in the street.

I probably did not know one day from another. We did know
when Friday came, but the other days were all the same.

Louise Gavan Duffy was
a daughter by his third
marriage of Charles Gavan
Duffy, Irish rebel and
subsequent prime minister
of the Australian state of
Victoria. Born in Nice in
1894, Louise Gavan Duffy
first visited Ireland for her
father's burial in 1903 (at
which she was fascinated
to hear Irish spoken). After
settling in Ireland in 1907,
she joined Sinn Féin and
graduated from University
College Dublin in 1911. She
taught at St. Ita's Girls'
School, which Pearse
asked her to take over in
1912, but her family did
not want her to take on
its debts. She was active
in the Gaelic League
and taught in a teacher
training college after 1914,
becoming secretary of
Cumann na mBan at its
foundation in the autumn
of that year. She drilled
with other women but
was never taught the use
of firearms. When the
Rising began, she went to
the Post Office to see →

→ Pearse, as related in
this deposition written
for the Bureau of Military
History in 1949. She was
one of those who managed
to escape from the GPO
through Jervis Street
hospital. She founded
Scoil Bhride, Earlsfort
Terrace, a girls' school run
on Pearsean principles, in
1917 and many leaders of
the new state sent their
daughters to it. She died
in 1969.

There was nothing outstanding until the fire came in front
and we saw the flames out of the windows. From the back
top windows we could see right across to the front because
we were high upon the roof. We must have been above the
main roof some way. We saw the fire on Friday morning,
or it may have been Thursday evening. The flames were
coming from the front of the G.P.O. but all the width of
the building was between us and the flames and we did
not feel hot. We did not feel that the fire was in the same
house as ourselves, and we did not feel any sense of danger.
I suppose we thought in a vague way that it would probably
come nearer, but it seemed a good way off. There were some
explosions, I think, they also were in the street and seemed
a long way off. We really were not in any danger where we
were; I suppose we would have been in danger if we had
stayed for a long time.

I thought we were going to stay in the building until we
died. I thought we were going to retire into the cellars, but I
did not ask and nobody told me.

We were told to evacuate the buildings on Thursday
evening; that all the women were to go out under a Red
Cross flag. Peggy Downey said she was not going, and the
others said they did not want to go. Peggy Downey was
from Liverpool. We went to Mr. Pearse and said that we
did not want to go, that we wanted to stay. I think that was
Thursday afternoon, because the girls were to go out in
the daytime. We went back and resumed our occupations,
because Pearse said we could stay. He said he did not think
he had any right to prevent anybody taking part in the
rebellion who wanted to stay.

On Friday morning, we heard that they were evacuating the building and that we were to go with the wounded.

Before we left the Post Office we were in a front room downstairs taking messages from the men to bring to their friends and relatives. I had a notebook, but I was afraid to write anything in it, I only wrote their names and addresses. The messages were not exactly goodbyes, but that they were all right; that they had been in the Post Office all week, and that they were leaving now and not to worry about them. These were all the rank and file soldiers, and they did not know much more than I did. I remember with great admiration an elderly man named Turner. He was perhaps about fifty or sixty years of age, and he had three sons in the fighting, some of them were in the Post Office with him. He gave me his address in Summerhill. I do not think he was a Citizen Army man, he might have been, but he was not in uniform as far as I can remember. I admired him because he was quite cheerful and pleasant, and I admired his wife when I brought her the message. She was not a bit perturbed, although all her men-folk were out. She was a great little woman and did not make a scene. Most of the women said when I called, 'What do you mean? My husband or son was not in the rebellion. He had nothing to do with the Volunteers.' That is what they had been told to say, but Mrs. Turner did not say that. She was rather proud of them.

I did not get any instructions before we left the Post Office. Desmond FitzGerald, I suppose, got the instructions which appeared to be that we were to go to Jervis Street hospital with the wounded men, and do the best we could. I do not know who told them to go out through Henry Street. There were holes broken through the walls. There is a yard at the back of the GPO, I think, and some men must have gone out beforehand and prepared the way. They must have climbed up the wall at the back, on to some low roofs, then on to the gable end and smashed a way into the nearest house, from that to the next house and from that to the next house. They went through about three houses, and these houses were in Henry Street. There was a tiny little theatre in Henry Street, with a stage. I think it was the Coliseum. There was a refreshment room there too. I think Nancy Wyse Power said that was the first or second house.

I was not helping with the wounded man but it must have been a struggle getting him over the roofs. I think his name was Conroy. He was a big man, wounded in the stomach, and he was being carried in a sheet. I think we were in front of him, and there were four boys with cut fingers or sprained wrists there, who were not very much use as soldiers any more.

There was somebody carrying a Red Cross flag in front of our procession. We went into the variety hall, I think it was in Henry Street. We went into this place; it was supposed to be a place where we could rest, and went up to the refreshment room, which was all shut up. Somebody lit a light. We must have had Father Flanagan with us—they would not let him go back. He and Desmond FitzGerald and whoever else was responsible got afraid that the men would partake of the innumerable bottles that were there, which would have been an awful catastrophe.

I think we were the last to leave the Post Office. We thought the men had left before us. We were so long waiting for the holes to be broken that we thought we were to last to leave on Friday evening.

We went through from Prince's Street to Abbey Street. We went through a very narrow passage that is there still, and down Abbey Street. It was in this lane, Williams's Lane, that we met a detachment of British soldiers with an officer, and they stopped us. I think it was Father Flanagan who pointed out the Red Cross flag, and the wounded men, and said that we were taking these men to Jervis Street hospital.

The British accompanied us to the hospital. We went into the hospital and the nurses received us very well. They immediately took the wounded men away and we saw no more of them. They were put to bed. The officer said that we, the women, could go in and lie on the floor in the waiting room for the night. I think there were seven or eight women.

Next morning, we got a meal, a cup of tea and bread and butter, and we were told to go.

Somebody told us about the surrender. I do not know if there was a paper that morning, Saturday morning. I do not remember how we heard, but I was quite certain of the news so that it must have been given by somebody. We never communicated with the men after we left the Post Office. I did not know when we were leaving that they were going to surrender; I thought that they were evacuating the Post Office and going somewhere else. I certainly did not have the impression that it was all at an end.

When I was going home I walked along Leeson Street, and it was getting late in the afternoon. This is Saturday. It was then that Paddy McGilligan and Charlie McCauley saw me and announced that I was wounded, because I had a swollen foot and I was limping. I was very dirty, and was wearing neither hat nor coat. I must have been a very beautiful object.

I went to Haddington Road to my digs, washed, had a meal and slept there that night. The landlady came to my room with hot water for me and stayed talking to me. She was excited and kept saying, 'Do you think will Martin lose his pension?' Martin was a retired policeman. I thought she really meant 'Why did you come back to stay here?', but she was very nice. I said to her, 'There is no reason why he should lose his pension. He had no connection with anything.' The landlady kept talking, and interrupting herself to say, 'Wasn't it grand that they held out for the week! Wasn't it lovely!' That was as much in her heart as the pension. She was thrilled with delight about the Rising, but Martin was the life and soul of her existence and was very important to her. He was like a child. He was a great, big, half-stupid ex-policeman, and she was a little bit of a thing, but her word was law. She could twist him round her little finger and she adored him. The thought that he was going to lose his pension was nearly too much for her, but she was too thrilled to say much.

Next morning I went up to Min Ryan's place to see if they had any news there. . . . Min Ryan and I decided we would go to Jacobs to see Thomas MacDonagh. This was about eleven or twelve o'clock on Sunday morning. We had been at mass and had our breakfast.

When Thomas MacDonagh came back I said to him that it was all over, that it should not have taken place, that it was wrong and could not have succeeded. He said to me, 'Don't talk to my men if that is the way you are feeling. I don't want anything to be putting their spirits down.' We left Jacob's then and took Máire Nic Shiubhlaigh with us.

We went up by Stephen's Green, and the men out of the College of Surgeons were just being rounded up to be marched off. That was Sunday morning, before dinner time. These were the people who were looking so depressed and deplorable. Including the women, I doubt if there were forty in it. There might have not have been more than twenty. I remember a small group standing four deep in the street outside Surgeons. We did not go as far as Surgeons, we went towards Harcourt Street. We saw a large crowd of loafers gazing at the people out of Surgeons; they were murmuring against them, but when the order was given to set off a cheer was raised. ∎

FATHER ALOYSIUS TRAVERS—*from*:

DIARY OF EASTER WEEK 1916

(1941)

MONDAY MAY 1ST

Early in the morning the son of Superintendent Dunne (DMP), a sub-deacon, called to me and said that Father Murphy, the military chaplain, had sent him to ask if I could call to the Castle during the afternoon. James Connolly, who was a prisoner and a patient there, had expressed a wish to see me. I called, and saw Father Murphy. He told me he had arranged for the necessary permissions. With Captain Stanley, RAMC, I went to the ward. At the door the sentry challenged Captain Stanley and informed him he had orders to allow no one to see the prisoner without special instructions. Captain Stanley was obliged to return for his permit. The sentry asked me if I were Father Aloysius and, on my replying in the affirmative, said: 'You can go in.' However, as the nurses were engaged with Connolly, I delayed outside until they had finished and Captain Stanley had returned.

I entered with Captain Stanley, but I remarked that two soldiers with rifles and bayonets were on guard and showed no intention of leaving. I pointed out this to Captain Stanley, but he said it was necessary that they should remain; that he had no power to remove them. Then I said: 'If that is so I cannot do my work as a priest. I have never before, to my knowledge, spoken to James Connolly. I cannot say if he may not be hard of hearing. Confession is an important and sacred duty that demands privacy and I cannot go on with it in the presence of these men.' I had given my word that I would not utilise the opportunity for carrying political information or as a cover for political designs, and if my word was not sufficient or reliable they had better get some other priest. But I felt quite confident

William Patrick Travers was born in Cork in 1870 and became a Capuchin priest in 1894, taking the name Aloysius. A crusader for temperance, he was in charge of the Father Mathew Hall in Dublin, where he ran the Feis Maitiú and promoted 'buy Irish' campaigns. From 1913 to 1916, he was provincial of the Irish Capuchins. The 1916 Feis Maitiú was to be conducted in the days after Easter but a boy was shot on the Monday and the hall became a refuge centre for endangered local people and for the wounded. Father Aloysius was a trusted go-between in the truce negotiated at the week's end; Prime Minister Asquith appeared to place more trust in Travers's analysis of the on-the-ground situation than in that of General Maxwell. He remained active in work on behalf of Dublin's poor and →

→ was summoned by
Jim Larkin to minister to
him on his death-bed
in 1947. He himself died
in 1957. This eyewitness
account of events after the
surrender appeared in the
Capuchin Annual of 1941,
marking the twenty-fifth
anniversary of the Rising.

I would have my way. I suggested that we go to seek Father Murphy. On the way we met General Lowe. He greeted us warmly and said he had spoken to General (Sir John) Maxwell of the work we had done on the previous day for peace and the prevention of bloodshed, and that he had expressed a wish to see us and would be pleased if we could call to headquarters the following day. Hoping it might afford an opportunity for speaking a word on behalf of the prisoners and securing fair and lenient treatment for them, I consented. Then General Lowe, after some discussion, acceded to my demand for privacy for the purpose of attending the prisoner Connolly.

I returned to the ward or room where Connolly lay. The soldiers left and I was alone with Connolly. I told him I had given my word I would act only as a priest and not in any political capacity. 'I know that, Father,' he said. 'You would not get this privilege otherwise, and it as a priest I want to see you. I have seen and heard of the brave conduct of the priests and nuns during the week and I believe they are the best friends of the workers.' I then heard Connolly's confession.

Captain Stanley met me again after I had left the ward, and said it would be a consolation if one of the priests would drop into the 'Sinn Féin' ward in which the other prisoner-patients were, and say a word to those in it, and let their friends know they were alive. I said I would do so with pleasure and I was permitted to go round to each bed and speak to the patients. Some of them said they would be grateful if I would send them prayer books. Captain Stanley said he we would distribute them with pleasure if I sent them, and he did very kindly distribute the books which were sent. I cannot refrain from saying here that Captain Stanley showed himself, all through, a Christian and humane man, and James Connolly spoke to me of his very great kindness to him, although Stanley was politically and in religion at variance with the prisoners . . .

Called to the Castle for permit to visit prisoners and others needing my services; the permit 'to pass through the streets of Dublin by day or night' was signed by Lord Powerscourt. Referring in my presence to the events of the preceding days, Lord Powerscourt and some officers paid a tribute to the bravery of the Volunteers, one of the officers remaking that 'they were the cleanest and bravest lot of boys he had ever met.'

Lord Powerscourt, who was, I understand, Asst. Provost-Marshal, proved courteous and anxious to relieve the sufferings and anxieties of the prisoners. He asked me if I could get one of the fathers to visit the wife of one of the Volunteers. The poor fellow, he said, had been taken down from a chimney in an exhausted state and was worrying about his wife who was in a delicate condition of health when he left home. He would be glad if I could reassure him. I undertook to visit the woman, and Lord Powerscourt said I could see the prisoner afterwards, or at any time I wished.

TUESDAY 2ND

In the morning I gave holy communion to James Connolly. Later in the day I went with Father Augustine to Headquarters, Infirmary Road, and met General (Sir John) Maxwell.

At night a military car came to the gates of the friary and a letter was handed in:

Kilmainham Detention Barracks,
2-5-'16

Sir,

The prisoner H.T. Pearse desires to see you and you have
permission to visit him. Failing you he would be glad to see
any of the Capucines (sic).

I am, sir,
Your obedient servant,
W.S. Kinsman,
(Major)
Commandant.

To Rev. Father Aloysius

The name of the Major and the initials before 'Pearse'
were not very legible.

Accompanied by another Father I went with the soldiers.
We drove through the city in the direction of Charlemont
Bridge. We were told that the soldiers had a couple of calls to
make. The sniping from the roofs, however, was so bad that
when we got as far as Charelmont Bridge we were obliged
to turn back. Later, I heard the calls the military proposed
making were to Mrs. Pearse and Mrs. MacDonagh, in order to
bring them to the prison before the executions.

When I reached Kilmainham Jail I was informed that
Thomas MacDonagh also wished for my ministrations. I was
taken to the prisoners' cells and spent some hours between the
two. 'You will be glad to know that I gave holy communion to
James Connolly this morning,' I said to Pearse when I met him.
'Thank God,' he replied. 'It is the one thing I was anxious about.'

Pearse assured me he was not in the least worried or
afraid, and that he did not know how he deserved the privilege
of dying for his country. He was anxious that his mother
should get a letter he had just written. He knew that I could
not take anything out, and he would not wish it, but he would
be glad if I would speak to the officer in charge and make the
request to him. The officer assured me that the papers would
be given to Mrs. Pearse.

Then I heard the confessions and gave holy communion
to Pearse and MacDonagh, and I cannot easily forget the

devotion with which they received the most blessed sacrament. They assured me they were happy. They spent the time at their disposal in prayer. I told them I should be very near at the last moments although they would probably be blindfolded and unable to see me and I exhorted them to make aspirations and acts of contrition and love. I left them in a most edifying disposition sometime between 2 a.m. and 3 a.m.

To my astonishment I heard that orders were given that all the friends were to leave the prison and that the orders referred to me too. I protested that I was present not merely as a friend but in the capacity of a priest, and held that I should be permitted to remain with the prisoners to the end. The officer in charge said that he had to carry out his instructions. I asked him to communicate with the Provost-Marshal and put my views before him. He 'phoned and then told me he was instructed I could not remain. I had no option. Leaving the jail I saw a little company of soldiers approach. Afterwards I was told they were bringing Willie Pearse. I returned to Church Street and said Holy Mass for their souls.

In the morning about 9.30 a.m. I called back to Kilmainham to ask the officer for a rosary beads which Sister M. Francesca had left with her brother (Thomas MacDonagh) the previous night. I availed myself of the occasion to make a protest. I said that in every civilised community the clergy were permitted to remain with the prisoner and administer the last rites of the Church. I had not been permitted to remain to administer Extreme Unction, as I was not permitted to be present at the execution. I requested him to convey my protest officially to the authorities. I am glad to say that at the later executions the priest was allowed to remain to the end and that when I attended James Connolly in the Castle a week later, I was taken with him in the ambulance at the execution.

WEDNESDAY MAY 3RD

I went to Mrs. MacDonagh and Mrs. Pearse to break the sad news to them. I told Mrs. Pearse that I believed Willie would be spared; that I could not conceive them executing her second son. 'No,' she said. 'I believe they will put him to death, too. I can't imagine Willie living without Pat. They were inseparable. It was lovely to see the way they bade goodnight to each other every night. Willie would never be happy to live without Pat.' Indeed she had a strong conviction from the day when they said goodbye and walked out of St. Enda's that she would never see them alive again . . .

WEDNESDAY NIGHT

Message to say that some of the fathers were wanted to attend executions—Plunkett, Daly, O'Hanrahan, and Willie Pearse executed in early hours of Thursday—fathers Albert, Augustine, and, I think, Sebastian attended.

FRIDAY MORNING MAY 5TH

John McBride executed, attended by one of the fathers.

SUNDAY MAY 7TH

Called on John Nugent, MP, at Phibsboro' to urge action to put stop to executions. Nugent undertook to visit John Dillon immediately. Later Nugent called to Church Street to say that John Dillon would like very much if I could see him. Consultation with John Dillon at North Great George's Street. Dillon said that although he disagreed heartily with the policy of the men and believed that they had put back the Home Rule movement, still he admired their courage and respected their convictions. He said that he always had an admiration for Patrick Pearse. He would do everything in his power to put an end to the executions. He took my car and went to [the] Castle to send telegraphic message to John Redmond. Returning, he called to Church Street to inform me that he had succeeded in sending the telegram.

MONDAY MAY 8TH

To Drumcondra with message from General Maxwell to His Grace the Most Rev. Dr. Walsh, Archbishop.

MONDAY EVENING

Message that four or five executions were to take place and that the services of some of the fathers would be required.

Went to John Dillon to tell him and to urge him to cross to
London and raise the matter in Parliament. Dillon regretted
he could not cross in [the] morning but would go at the
earliest opportunity.

TUESDAY 9TH

Papers report that previous night John Redmond asked
the Prime Minister to put a stop to executions.

THURSDAY MORNING 11TH

Papers report that John Dillon had crossed and moved
adjournment of House to discuss continuance of the
executions in Ireland. Asquith undertook to give opportunity
for debate on 11th, and, on the understanding that no further
executions would take place meantime. Mr. Dillon withdrew
his motion.

THURSDAY AFTERNOON

Called to [the] Castle to see Connolly. Connolly had
not slept and seemed feverish. I said that I would let him
rest and would call in [the] morning to give him holy
communion. Uneasy about him I tried to get [in] contact
with Captain Stanley, but he could not be found. Reached
Castle gates and, still uneasy, decided to return and make
another attempt to see Stanley. Saw him and was assured
that there was no danger of any steps being taken: he
reminded me that Asquith had given to understand that no
executions would take place pending debate which was on
that night. Got back to Church Street some time near 7 p.m.
About 9 p.m. Captain Stanley called and told me that my
services would be required about 2 a.m. He was not at liberty
to say more but I could understand.

FRIDAY MORNING 12TH

About 1 a.m. [a] car called and Father Sebastian
accompanied me to [the] Castle. Heard Connolly's confession
and gave him holy communion. Waited in [the] Castle yard
while he was being given a meal. He was brought down and

laid on [a] stretcher in [the] ambulance. Father Sebastian and myself drove with him to Kilmainham. Stood behind firing party during the execution. Father Eugene McCarthy, who had attended Seán McDermott before we arrived, remained and anointed Connolly immediately after the shooting.

FRIDAY

Morning papers reported sensational speech by Dillon in Commons with a stinging attack on government. Mr. Asquith's reply was that he was crossing to Ireland that night to see the situation for himself.

LATER IN DAY

Visited Richmond Barracks to see prisoners—amongst them Seán T. O'Kelly, Alderman Tom Kelly, and Laurence O'Neill (Lord Mayor). Got an account from prisoners of Asquith's visit to the prison.

～

Message of Gen. Maxwell to the Archbishop,
and His Grace's reply:

Headquarters Irish Command,
6th May, 1916

Your Grace,
I shall be glad if you will convey to the clergy
of your Church my high appreciation and thanks for the
services rendered by them during the recent disturbances
in Dublin. I am aware that such services were practically
universal, but it is possible that Your Grace may desire
to bring to notice individual cases of special gallantry or
devotion. If such is the case, I shall be obliged if you will
inform me of the names of the gentlemen in question.
I am, Your Grace's obedient servant,
J.G. Maxwell,
General Officer Commanding-in-Chief the Forces in Ireland

Reply:

Archbishop's House
Dublin May 11, 1916

Dear Sir John Maxwell,
    *In reply to your letter of Monday, I beg to
thank you for your gratifying testimony to the fidelity of
our clergy in the discharge of their duties during the recent
troubles in Dublin. I have been much struck by your request
to be furnished with the names of the clergy in cases of
special gallantry or devotion that I might desire to bring
under your notice. But I quite concur in your view that
services deserving of high praise are practically universal.
Many such cases have of course come to my notice—
especially amongst the clergy of my own Pro-Cathedral
Parish in Marlborough Street, and those of the Capuchin
Community in Church Street. But I feel that it would be
invidious to treat these cases as if they were exceptional.*

    *Again, thanking you for your kind letter.
I remain your faithful servant,*

    *William J. Walsh,
Archbishop of Dublin*

MONK GIBBON—*from*:

INGLORIOUS SOLDIER

(1968)

Born in 1896 into a family
with a history of service in
the Anglican Church, Monk
Gibbon was educated at
St. Columba's College.
His student career at
Oxford was curtailed when
he volunteered for the
British army as an officer
in the First World War.
The experience made him
a committed pacifist, a
philosophy strengthened
by his witnessing of the
murder by a British officer
of another pacifist, Francis
Sheehy Skeffington, in
the course of the Rising.
He felt such conflicted
loyalties after fighting the
rebels that his family in
Taney rectory accused ↗

IT WAS NOT the moment to call Pearse a brave man
in the hearing of officialdom. Even NCOs and private
soldiers seemed infected by the same angry resentment,
the same whole-hearted condemnation of anyone who
could attack England at such a critical moment in her
history. It was just not 'playing the game'. But whose
game? Different nationalities have different games. It
would certainly not be playing Ireland's game to wait until
England had triumphed over her formidable adversary,
Germany, and then to take her on single-handed. Pearse
would have said that he was not being disloyal to England
since loyalty was the very last thing he felt he owed to her.

The rebels were a tiny minority. They were being
execrated everywhere, whereas men in khaki were being
befriended. The loyalists held a good hand but they did
not seem aware of that. Dominant races always tend to be
cruel because they sense the insecurity of their position;
just as subject races like to trade shamelessly on humanity's
inclination to sympathise with the underdog. The majority
of the insurrectionists were not in uniform. Or their
uniform might be only a belt with holster for a revolver,

equipment easily discarded. One could be soldier one minute and a civilian the next. This made the British troops suspect every man. But it is one thing to suspect a man, and another to murder him in cold blood, as had happened in North King Street.

I was helping to suppress the rebellion but I had no hatred. The few instances of bullying which I witnessed stank in my nostrils, even though they were not of a particularly startling nature. I was sick of hearing the words, 'He's a Sinn Féiner, sir,' of all and sundry. I saw prisoners being hustled along with their hands above their heads, and the aid of a prodding bayonet. And it revolted me to see a youth burst into tears, who was being questioned in the barrack square and taunted by an NCO. A green uniform had been found in his house. That did not establish treason. It could have belonged to a time, before the war, when Redmond's Volunteers wore uniforms which were green. The irony of the situation was that this young man, who was weeping, had a brother who was in the barracks and who was a soldier. ■

→ him of being a Sinn Féiner. He agreed with Shaw that Irishmen in arms were only doing what Englishmen would do, if invaded. Gibbon taught in Switzerland and England for many years; he wrote novels, stories, poems and memoirs (including one about his cousin, W.B. Yeats), and he edited for publication Michael Farrell's historical novel, *Thy Tears Might Cease*. He lived out his later years in Dublin and died there in 1987.

W.B. YEATS

'EASTER 1916'

(1916)

Yeats composed this
poem in the months
after the Rising between
May and September. It
was privately printed
and circulated by
Clement Shorter but
Yeats (perhaps fearful
of losing his British
pension) held back from
formally publishing until
it appeared in the New
Statesman of 23 October
1920. This was a key
moment, at the height of
the War of Independence
and in the course of a
seventy-four-day hunger
strike to the death by
Terence MacSwiney,
Lord Mayor of Cork. The
strategic timing has led
some critics to suggest
that the poem is 'on
Ireland's side' in the war
against England but
Yeats's divided responses
in the aftermath of
rebellion are well balanced
in the text. As a public
bard, he must name
the warrior dead and
say that the land ↗

I have met them at close of day
Coming with vivid faces
From counter or desk among grey
Eighteenth-century houses.
I have passed with a nod of the head
Or polite meaningless words,
Or have lingered awhile and said
Polite meaningless words,
And thought before I had done
Of a mocking tale or a gibe *laughing @ their caws*
To please a companion
Around the fire at the club,
Being certain that they and I
But lived where motley is worn:
All changed, changed utterly:
A terrible beauty is born.

That woman's days were spent
In ignorant good-will, *woman's place not in politics*
Her nights in argument
Until her voice grew shrill.
What voice more sweet than hers
When, young and beautiful,
She rode to harriers?
This man had kept a school *mythic*
And rode our wingèd horse;
This other his helper and friend
Was coming into his force;
He might have won fame in the end,

So sensitive his nature seemed,
So daring and sweet his thought.
This other man I had dreamed [*Gonne's husband*]
A drunken, vainglorious lout.
He had done most bitter wrong
To some who are near to my heart,
Yet I number him in the song;
He, too, has resigned his part
In the casual comedy;
He, too, has been changed in his turn,
Transformed utterly:
A terrible beauty is born.

Hearts with one purpose alone [*unification of the various groups*]
Through summer and winter seem
Enchanted to a stone [*an unchanging; fixed course*]
To trouble the living stream. [*myth*]
The horse that comes from the road,
The rider, the birds that range
From cloud to tumbling cloud,
Minute by minute they change;
A shadow of cloud on the stream
Changes minute by minute;
A horse-hoof slides on the brim,
And a horse plashes within it;
The long-legged moor-hens dive,
And hens to moor-cocks call;
Minute by minute they live:
The stone's in the midst of it all.

→ has been redeemed by their sacrifice: but the poem is a prolonged deferment of that moment. Instead, it employs a private voice to ask painful questions: about the cost in human terms of the rebels' ideals, not excluding the costs to sexuality, culture and even family happiness. It also leaves open the possibility that England may keep faith—a view which Yeats might still have held in 1916 but not by 1921, when he told the students of the Oxford Union that 'not law, but English law, had broken down in Ireland.' 'Easter 1916' appeared in the collection *Michael Robartes and the Dancer* in 1921, having been held back from the earlier *The Wild Swans at Coole* (1919).

Too long a sacrifice
Can make a stone of the heart. *no passion?*
O when may it suffice?
That is Heaven's part, our part
To murmur name upon name,
As a mother names her child
When sleep at last has come
On limbs that had run wild.
What is it but nightfall?
No, no, not night but death;
Was it needless death after all?
For England may keep faith
For all that is done and said.
We know their dream; enough
To know they dreamed and are dead;
And what if excess of love
Bewildered them till they died?
I write it out in a verse –
MacDonagh and MacBride
And Connolly and Pearse
Now and in time to be,
Wherever green is worn,
Are changed, changed utterly:
A terrible beauty is born.

(Cathleen – those who society remembers)

MAUD GONNE

LETTER TO W.B. YEATS
November 1916

17 Rue de l'Annonciation
Passy
Paris
8th Nov [1916]

'Easter 1916' is a love
lyric as well as a political
poem. Into its refrain Yeats
had tried to incorporate
Maud Gonne's response:
'tragic dignity has returned
to Ireland'—the words
'terrible' and 'beauty' being
a compound of the pity
and terror which Aristotle
proclaimed the elements
of true tragedy. The poem
showed how Ireland after
the Rising has moved
from a world of splintered
comedy (epitomised by
the half-rhymes of the
opening 'faces/houses')
to the grave decorum of
tragedy. But Maud, living
in political exile in France
and having just lost her
husband John MacBride,
was deeply irritated by
the questions preceding
the ringing refrain. Yeats
brought the poem on his
visit to her in Normandy,
as an accompaniment
to his final proposal of
marriage. He urged her
to forget the cold stone
of extreme idealism for →

My dear Willie,

No I don't like your poem, it isn't worthy of you and above all it isn't worthy of the subject. Though it reflects your present state of mind perhaps, it isn't quite sincere enough for you who have studied philosophy and know something of history, know quite well that sacrifice has never yet turned a heart to stone though it has immortalised many and through it alone mankind can rise to God. You recognise this in the line which was the original inspiration of your poem 'A terrible beauty is born' but you let your present mood mar and confuse it till even some of the verses become unintelligible to many. Even Iseult reading it didn't understand your thought till I explained your [?retribution] theory of constant change and becoming in the flux of things.

But you could never say that MacDonagh and Pearse and Connolly were sterile fixed minds; each served Ireland, which was their share of the world, the part they were in contact with, with varied faculties and vivid energy! Those three were men of genius, with large comprehensive and speculative and active brains. The others of whom we know less were probably less remarkable men, but still I think they must have been men with a stronger grasp on reality; a stronger spiritual life than most of those we meet. As for my husband, he has entered eternity by the great door of sacrifice which Christ opened and has therefore atoned for all so that praying for him I can also ask for his prayers and 'A terrible beauty is born.'

→ the joys of an ever-
changing emotional life
(hens calling to moor-
cocks, etc.). She rejected
his offer of marriage
but reinterpreted the
stone image: in her mind
the rebels' stone-like
idealism helped to create
the eddies in the living
stream all around it. By not
changing, the rebels had
in fact changed everything.

There are beautiful lines in your poem, as there are in all you write but it is not a great *whole*, a living thing which our race would treasure and repeat, such as a poet like you might have given to your nation and which would have avenged our material failure by its spiritual beauty.

You will be angry perhaps that I write so frankly what I feel, but I am always frank with my friends and though our ideals are wide apart we are still friends.

I am writing this in the confusion and weariness of a *déménagement*. Our new apartment is small but has a wonderful roof terrace from which one sees the chimneypots of all Paris and gorgeous clouds and sunsets. Money affairs are worrying and may prevent us leaving Paris for another month. I will let you know as soon as dates are settled. I would like to see the *Hawk's Well*, but fear we shall be late for that. However, you will bring it to Ireland will you not?

How nice really getting your old Castle. I hope you will succeed in that. It sounds very fascinating and it would be lovely to have a place you could put all your treasures and make really beautiful.

Always your friend,
Maud Gonne

FRANCIS LEDWIDGE

'LAMENT FOR THOMAS MACDONAGH'

(1916)

Francis Ledwidge was born to a poor family in Slane, County Meath in 1887 and he worked from an early age as a farm labourer and miner. His poems, published in the *Drogheda Independent*, won the support, literary and financial, of Lord Dunsany. Despite being a supporter of the Gaelic League and a member of the Irish Volunteers, he enlisted as a soldier in the British army in October 1914, taking part in the battle of Gallipoli. He was home on leave during the Rising and so conflicted in his response that he returned late from the leave in May and was promptly court-martialled. Later, he was restored to the rank of lance-corporal. He was killed at Ypres in 1917. His poem about his close friend combines internal rhymes of Gaelic poetry (cry\sky, blows\ snows etc.) with the alliteration of Anglo-Irish verse, along precisely those lines advocated by MacDonagh in his *Literature in Ireland*, published later in 1916.

He shall not hear the bittern cry
In the wild sky, where he is lain,
Nor voices of the sweeter birds,
Above the wailing of the rain.

Nor shall he know when loud March blows
Thro' slanting snows her fanfare shrill,
Blowing to flame the golden cup
Of many an upset daffodil.

But when the Dark Cow leaves the moor,
And pastures poor with greedy weeds,
Perhaps he'll hear her low at morn,
Lifting her horn in pleasant meads.

V.I. LENIN

LESSONS FROM THE IRISH REBELLION

(JULY 1916)

Lenin had taken the view that an Irish insurrection could be objectively progressive in effect. The growing exhaustion and cynicism of soldiers in the European war was bound, in his view, to bring imperialism to a crisis-point. Noting similar 'attempts' in French Annam and the German Cameroons, Lenin denied the contention of some fellow-Marxists that the Rising was a putsch without popular support. He sensed that, if the British were to threaten conscription (as they did in 1918), a rebellion with even wider effect would call forth a reign of official terror. He probably felt that ensuing mutinies by Irish soldiers on the western front would generate other defections across the ranks of warring nations, leading to a collapse of the imperial order. In fact a revolution broke out in Russia in 1917, and by 1918 a mass mutiny took Russia clean out of the war. V.I Lenin, born in 1870, was a leader of that revolution and of the Soviet Union until his death in 1924.

T HE MISFORTUNE OF the Irish is that they have risen prematurely, when the European revolt of the proletariat has *not yet* matured. Capitalism is not so harmoniously built that the various springs of rebellion can of themselves merge at one effort, without reverses and defeats. On the other hand, the very fact that revolts break out at different times, in different places, and are of different kinds, guarantees wide scope and depth to the general movement; only in premature, partial, scattered and therefore unsuccessful, revolutionary movements do the masses gain experience, acquire knowledge, gather strength, get to know their real leaders, the socialist proletarians, and in this way prepare for a general onslaught, in the same way as separate strikes, demonstrations, local and national outbreaks in the army, outbursts among the peasantry, etc., prepared the way for the general onslaught in 1905. ▪

JOSEPH MARY PLUNKETT

'I SEE HIS BLOOD UPON THE ROSE'

(1911)

Joseph Mary Plunkett was one of the signatories of the Proclamation of the Irish Republic. He was imprisoned in Richmond Barracks but on the night before his execution was permitted to marry his fiancée Grace Gifford. The incarnation of Jesus in worldly form is a constant theme in his work, which explores a connection between the mystical and the environmental. The association of the Rising's leaders with the imagery of 'blood sacrifice' after 1916 gave this poem and poet added fame. But there was no mention of blood sacrifice in early newspaper reports of the event: it seems more a retrospective formulation, often devised by Catholic analysts eager to identify their faith with an increasingly-admired insurrection. The romantic cult surrounding Pearse, MacDonagh, Plunkett and others recast the Rising in global propaganda as a 'poets' rebellion'. That idea was challenged by British propagandists who commissioned essays to contest its legitimacy from such leading novelists as H.G. Wells, John Galsworthy and Arnold Bennett—in prose.

I see his blood upon the rose
And in the stars the glory of his eyes,
His body gleams amid eternal snows,
His tears fall from the skies.

I see his face in every flower;
The thunder and the singing of the birds
Are but his voice—and carven by his power
Rocks are his written words.

All pathways by his feet are worn,
His strong heart stirs the ever-beating sea,
His crown of thorns is twined with every thorn,
His cross is every tree.

ROGER CASEMENT—*from*:

'SPEECH FROM THE DOCK'

(1916)

THEN CAME THE war. As Mr. Birrell has said in his evidence recently laid before the commission of inquiry into the causes of the late rebellion in Ireland, 'the war upset all our calculations.' It upset mine no more than Mr. Birrell's, and put an end to my mission of peaceful effort in America. War between Great Britain and Germany meant, as I believed, ruin for all the hopes we had founded on the enrolment of Irish Volunteers. A constitutional movement in Ireland is never very far from a breach of the constitution, as the loyalists of Ulster had been so eager to show us. The cause is not far to seek. A constitution to be maintained intact must be the achievement and pride of the people themselves; must rest on their own free will and on their own determination to sustain it, instead of being something resident in another land whose chief representative is an armed force—armed not to protect the population, but to hold it down. We had seen the working of the Irish constitution in the refusal of the army of occupation at the Curragh to obey the orders of the crown. And now that we were told the first duty of an Irishman was to enter that army, in return for a promissory note, payable after death—a scrap of paper that might or might not be redeemed. I felt over there in America that my first duty was to keep Irishmen at home in the only army that could safeguard our national existence. If small nationalities were to be the pawns in this game of embattled giants, I saw no reason why Ireland should shed her blood in any cause but her own, and if that be treason beyond the seas I am not ashamed to avow to it or to answer for it here with my life. And when we had the doctrine of unionist loyalty at last—'Mausers and Kaisers and any King you like', and I have heard that at Hamburg, not far from Limburg on the Lahn—I felt I needed no other warrant than that these words conveyed—to go forth and do likewise. The difference between us was that the unionist champions chose a path they felt would lead to the Woolsack; while I went a road I knew must lead to the dock. And the event proves we were both right. The difference between us was that my 'treason' was based on a ruthless sincerity that forced me to attempt in time and season to carry out in action what I said in word—whereas their treason lay in verbal incitements that they knew need never be made good in their bodies. And so, I am prouder to stand here today in the traitor's dock to answer this impeachment than to fill the place of my right honourable accusers. ■

→ had hounded Oscar Wilde in the witness-box in 1895 and had gone on to found the Ulster Volunteer Force in 1912— hence the bitter lucidity of Casement's references to loyalist leaders in his speech, which contended that as an Irishman he had a right to be tried only by his own people. He was hanged in August 1916.

'... I went a road I knew
must lead to the dock.'

C.S. LEWIS—*from*:

SURPRISED BY JOY
Trench War
(1955)

Born in Belfast in 1898, Clive Staples Lewis attended Oxford University but interrupted his studies to serve in the British army in 1917. He was wounded in the Somme valley in the following year. As a young poet, he had considered enlisting as a follower of W.B. Yeats and the Irish Revival: but the traumatic experience of trench warfare created in him a lifelong admiration for the decency of ordinary English people and a disinclination to excavate the inner recesses of the self—a fear to which he confesses in this passage written much later in life. Lewis achieved lasting fame as a scholar of Renaissance literature and as author of the 'Narnia' books for children. The plot of *The Lion, the Witch and the Wardrobe* has been interpreted as Lewis's much-postponed attempt to render the experience of war. He died in 1963.

CAME TO KNOW and pity the reverence the ordinary man: particularly dear Sergeant Ayres, who was (I suppose) killed by the same shell that wounded me. I was a futile officer (they gave commissions too easily then), a puppet moved about by him, and he turned this ridiculous and painful relation into something beautiful, became to me almost like a father. But for the rest of the war—the frights, the cold, the smell of H.E., the horribly smashed men still moving like half-crushed beetles, the sitting or standing corpses, the landscape of sheer earth without a blade of grass, the boots worn day and night till they seemed to grow to your feet—all this shows rarely and faintly in my memory. It is too cut off from the rest of experience and often seems to have happened to someone else. ■

GEORGE RUSSELL

'TO THE MEMORY OF SOME I KNEW WHO ARE DEAD AND WHO LOVED IRELAND'

(1917)

Their dream had left me numb and cold,
But yet my spirit rose in pride,
Refashioning in burnished gold
The images of those who died,
Or were shut in the penal cell.
Here's to you, Pearse, your dream not mine,
But yet the thought, for this you fell,
Has turned life's water into wine.

You who have died on Eastern hills
Or fields of France as undismayed,
Who lit with interlinked wills
The long heroic barricade,
You, too, in all the dreams you had,
Thought of some thing for Ireland done.
Was it not so, O shining lad,
What lured you, Alan Anderson?

I listened to high talk from you,
Thomas MacDonagh, and it seemed
The words were idle, but they grew
To nobleness by death redeemed.
Life cannot utter words more great
That life may meet by sacrifice,
High words were equalled by high fate,
You paid the price, You paid the price.

George Russell's poem was published in the *Irish Times* in December 1917. It represents an early attempt to offer an equal commemoration of the dead of World War One and of the Easter Rebellion. Russell had probably seen Yeats's 'Easter 1916'; hence his stanzas, contrasting the apparently idle talk of MacDonagh with the nobility of his ultimate sacrifice. The emotion thus summoned is made to flow like a tributary into the commemoration of another Thomas, Kettle. Kettle, born in Dublin in 1883, had served as professor of economics in University College Dublin and had been an Irish Volunteer, but he enlisted in the British army in order to defend Belgium. He gave character evidence on behalf of Eoin MacNeill at his court-martial after the Rising but died at the battle of the Somme later in 1916.

You who have fought on fields afar,
That other Ireland did you wrong
Who said you shadowed Ireland's star,
Nor gave you laurel wreath nor song.
You proved by death as true as they,
In mightier conflicts played your part,
Equal your sacrifice may weigh,
Dear Kettle, of the generous heart.

The hope lives on age after age,
Earth with its beauty might be won
For labour as a heritage,
For this has Ireland lost a son.
This hope unto a flame to fan
Men have put life by with a smile,
Here's to you, Connolly, my man
Who cast the last torch on the pile.

You too, had Ireland in your care,
Who watched o'er pits of blood and mire,
From iron roots leap up in air
Wild forests, magical, of fire;
Yet while the Nuts of Death were shed
Your memory would ever stray
To your own isle. Oh, gallant dead—
This wreath, Will Redmond, on your clay.

Here's to you, men I never met,
Yet hope to meet behind the veil,
Thronged on some starry parapet,
That looks down upon Innisfail,
And sees the confluence of dreams
That clashed together in our night,
One river, born from many streams,
Roll in one blaze of blinding light.

CANON CHARLES O'NEILL

'THE FOGGY DEW'

(1919)

As down the glen one Easter morn to a city fair
  rode I,
There armed lines of marching men in
  squadrons passed me by;
No fife did hum nor battle drum did sound its
  dread tattoo,
But the Angelus bell o'er the Liffey swell rang
  out through the foggy dew.

Right proudly high over Dublin town they hung
  out the flag of war,
'Twas better to die 'neath an Irish sky than at
  Suvla or Sud El Bar;
And from the plains of Royal Meath strong men
  came hurrying through,
While Britannia's Huns, with their long range
  guns sailed in through the foggy dew.

'Twas Britannia bade our Wild Geese go that
  small nations might be free,
But their lonely graves are by Suvla's waves or
  the shore of the Great North Sea;
Oh, had they died by Pearse's side or fought with
  Cathal Brugha,
Their names we will keep where the Fenians
  sleep 'neath the shroud of the foggy dew.

The song was a traditional lover's lament, to which new words were put by the parish priest of Kilcoo. The reference to the Angelus bell sought to intensify the Catholic sub-text of the Rising, already manifest in cards issued in subsequent months depicting Pearse in a 'pieta' pose. These lyrics are even more remarkable for their anti-recruiting focus, critical of those tens of thousands who enlisted in the British army as part of the war effort. The song is thus reflective of an already emerging orthodoxy among nationalists, who questioned the wisdom of such recruits and would ultimately reduce their profile in narrative histories of the period. The phrase 'Britannia's Huns' may →

→ be ironical, but there are
frequent references to 'the
Saxon Hun' in songs of the
period, perhaps intended
to suggest that the British
and German war-machines
were indistinguishable in
the minds of those who had
other priorities. The use by
the British of the gun-boat
Helga to pound the rebels
into submission had drawn
strong rebukes from a
range of commentators.

But the bravest fell, and the requiem bell rang
    mournfully and clear,
For those who died that Eastertide in the
    springing of the year;
And the world did gaze, in deep amaze, at those
    fearless men, but few
Who bore the fight that freedom's light might
    shine through the foggy dew.

Ah, back through the glen I rode again and my
    heart with grief was sore,
For I parted then with valiant men whom I
    never shall see more;
But to and fro in my dreams I go and I kneel
    and pray for you,
For slavery fled, O glorious dead, when you fell
    in the foggy dew.

GEORGE RUSSELL

TWO COMMENTS

(1916 AND 1937)

When the Rising happened, many cultural leaders such as W.B. Yeats felt that the Revival project had been brought to nothing. That response was rather like Henry James's reaction to the outbreak of World War One: that the slow improvement of society in the Victorian and Edwardian years had been destroyed at a stroke. It was difficult for even shrewd analysts, at the mercy of the immediate moment, to find in such events an embodiment of the preceding cultural movements. Yet the fragmentation of the human body in the trenches had already been depicted by artists, as had the destructive element in a culture which would negate itself by those very energies which defined its being. Yeats did not immediately see the link between the cult of Cuchulain, to which he, Augusta Gregory and Patrick Pearse had contributed, and the fact of dead bodies in the streets of his native city. But Russell was able to recognise that all this was what happened when images created at the writing-desk were expressed in action.

T HERE IS A danger in revolution if the revolutionary spirit is much more advanced than the intellectual and moral qualities which alone can secure the success of a revolt. These intellectual and moral qualities—the skill to organise, the wisdom to control large undertakings, are not natural gifts but the results of experience. . . .

—*The National Being.* Dublin, 1916

O'Grady said of the ancient legends of Ireland that they were less history than prophecy, and I who knew how deep was Pearse's love for the Cuchulain whom O'Grady discovered or invented, remembered after Easter Week that he had been solitary against a great host in imagination with Cuchulain, long before circumstance permitted him to stand for his nation with so few companions against so great a power. . . .

—*The Living Torch.* London, 1937

After the Revolution

IN THE SHOCKING aftermath of the Rising, a noticeable transformation took place in the modus operandi of the surviving rebels. The era of high debate, manifestos and grand revolutionary gestures inspired by Pearse and Connolly came to an abrupt end, and a more coldly pragmatic phase of combat, masterminded by Michael Collins, was about to begin. Republican prisoners interned in British jails contemplated the logistics of a new armed struggle, while the female volunteers of Cumann na mBan continued the work of agitation at home and abroad. Significantly, the strategy adopted during the subsequent War of Independence followed the guerrilla tactics deployed with success by Thomas Ashe during the Battle of Ashbourne, rather than the theatrical military gestures of Pearse and his comrades in the GPO. When Ashe died after being forcibly fed while on hunger-strike in Mountjoy Jail in 1917, the massive turnout for his funeral indicated that the public mood of hostility towards the rebels had been changed by the protracted and punitive nature of the British response. As James Stephens wrote in his account, *Insurrection in Dublin*, the effect of the executions was 'like watching blood oozing from under a door.' If the

British reaction to the Rising was disproportionate, it also killed off the allure of Home Rule in Ireland. As the English journalist Henry Nevinson realised, the Irish people had looked to British Liberal opinion for forty years in hope that a measure of political autonomy could be achieved, but after the Rising the very concept of Home Rule was regarded 'with indifference or contempt'. The Home Rule chapter was definitively closed when the Irish people responded at the ballot box, giving Sinn Féin a landslide victory in 1918.

The demand for Irish sovereignty may have been copper-fastened in that democratic moment but at the expense of Connolly's socialism, which was ordered to take a back seat while the national question was sorted out. In the new phase of Collins's militarism, it wasn't just left-wing politics that lost out: as volunteers like Colm Ó Gaora discovered, the cultural ideals on which a claim of nationality rested were often discarded in the soldierly moment. When a settlement was finally agreed, it was hailed by the pro-Treaty party as a pragmatic means to an end; however, the anti-Treaty party could see nothing in it but a betrayal of the republic to which they had sworn allegiance, and for which their comrades had died. Without question, the Civil War represents the nadir of the revolutionary phase in which unspeakable acts of violence were committed on both sides. The Free State government proved that it could be more ruthless than its former colonial master by ordering the execution of seventy-seven republican prisoners. The republicans, on the other hand, terrorised pro-Treaty politicians and their families, often burning their homes. In the end de Valera yielded to pragmatism when he ordered a cessation of hostilities on the realisation that victory for the anti-Treaty side was impossible. He may have been inspired in that moment by the actions of his fallen comrade, Erskine Childers, who shook hands with the Free State firing squad before his execution.

The establishment of the Free State on 6 December 1922 undoubtedly created a moment of great possibility for a country that had been denied any measure of self-government for well over a century. The Treaty, after all, achieved more autonomy than had been on offer with Home Rule. The excitement of a new phase of nation-building was tempered, however, with a sense that nothing would change fast, as

the new Irish Governor General took up residence in the old
Viceregal Lodge. Yet to unionists like Edward Carson the final
settlement was a disaster and a betrayal of the loyalty of the
people of Ulster. In 1925 the Boundary Commission confirmed
the partition of Ireland, leaving northern nationalists at the
mercy of unionist leaders intent on creating a Protestant
parliament for a Protestant people.

Much energy, in the early years, was invested in securing
the loyalty of the defence forces and the new Gárda Síochána
(Guardians of the Peace, the new police force), a high
proportion of whose members had seen action during the Civil
War. In this divided society, the tendency of leaders to invoke
Catholic authority and social conventions to smooth over
ideological differences was palpable. Many complained of a
censorious moral atmosphere created by the new puritanism.
The impulse towards a secular, rights-based society, which
informed the Proclamation, was threatened by the emergence
of a more narrowly defined ethnic nationalism. A number of
prominent Anglo-Irish houses had been burned down during
the Civil War and many of the Irishmen who fought for the
British army were marginalised on their return home from

the trenches. The instrumental use of the Irish language as
a tokenistic marker of cultural distinctiveness also became a
widespread phenomenon. Such a stifling cultural environment
was repugnant to a later generation of writers—both those
steeped in the Gaelic tradition, like Flann O'Brien, and those
who were not, such as Samuel Beckett. A form of suspended
animation pertained as the country hovered in its dominion
status between sovereign nation and empire affiliate. The
condition of waiting—for the full achievement of sovereignty;
the rise of socialism; the accomplishment of economic take-
off; or the reintegration of the national territory—was to
dominate the national mood as the early decades of the new
state unfolded.

COLM Ó GAORA—*from*:

MISE

(1943)

(TRANSLATED FROM IRISH BY DECLAN KIBERD)

Born in 1887, Colm Ó
Gaora grew up in Ros
Muc, where Pearse (who
came to know him) had
a summer cottage. He
had fitful employment
as a labourer but also
published prose fiction,
Connemara songs and
historical studies. Between
1907 and 1916 he was
a travelling teacher for
the Gaelic League. A
member of the IRB after
1913, he was arrested in
1916. In jail, he pioneered
a way of teaching three
fellow-prisoners at a time
during daily exercise: but,
as outlined here, he soon
realised that the study
of Irish would not be a
priority for most of the
future leaders in any state
which emerged from their
struggle. He was released
from a second period in jail
in 1920 following a hunger-
strike and led an ambush of
a police barracks in Galway
in 1921. He fought against
the Free State in the Civil
War but went to the United
States in 1925, where he
founded an Irish-language
school in New York in 1925.
He spent his later decades
back in Ireland and died
in 1954.

COUNT PLUNKETT WAS elected in a bye-election in County Roscommon while we were in Dartmoor prison. He was the first republican to defeat the Redmondites in any election until that moment. There was a prisoner with us in Lewes—Joseph Magennis, may his soul be in paradise!—and he was re-elected in the same way. As no stories against republicans could now be set before the people in these bye-elections, the reality of Easter Week and the fact that they were now prisoners stood to the candidates. Some of us prisoners began to worry that people might renege and take the wrong line, as had happened before with the Fenians and Parnell. However, as we had free speech among ourselves, the question was well and truly weighed and sifted. In the end, the debate got so sharp in the movement that prisoners alone were allowed to decide the outcome. It was put to a vote—either to adopt a new strategy or to continue straight on the road to a republic. I'm ashamed to say that there were people who had fought hard and fast for a republic just a year before and were now satisfied with something less. Dermot Lynch was one of those who was steadfast against any planned new strategy.

There was another thing which baffled me at this time. When we made Irish-language classes available in the prison, some comrades did not attempt to learn so much as a word—these were people who had risked their lives for their country! Not only that, but some of them started to study German, something which astounded me. ∎

CUMANN NA mBAN PETITION TO PRESIDENT WILSON

(1918)

*To the President and
Houses of Congress of
The United States
of America*

We, the undersigned, representing a large body of Irish women whose President was condemned to death for her share in a struggle for the freedom of our country, make an appeal to you, and we base our appeal first, on the generosity of the American administration in all things affecting women's lives and welfare and secondly, on your recognition, many times extended, of the justice of Ireland's demand for political freedom.

For many lamentable generations the women of Ireland have had to bring up their children in a country in a perpetual state of economic and political disarray consequent on its being governed in the interest of another country. Your declaration concerning a war settlement which has called into being and endowed with hope the spirit of democracy in every country, has made us feel that a new era is opening up for us. Our appeal now is to remind you of a cause which should not be overlooked when so many European nationalities are to be reconstructed in accordance with your declaration. Our country, having behind it twenty generations of repression has, we believe, a profound claim upon those who have declared their will to make the world safe for democracy. We appeal to you to recognise the political independence of Ireland in the form of an Irish Republic.

And encouraged by the knowledge that the States of Wyoming, Colorado, Utah, Idaho, Washington, California, Arizona, Kansas, Nevada, Montana, Oregon and New York

After the Rising the republican movement was seriously depleted by the execution of the leadership and the widespread imprisonment of activists. In this context, Cumann na mBan played a crucial role in sustaining the momentum for independence at home and abroad. The Irish Volunteer Dependants' Fund was set up by Áine Ceannt and Kathleen Clarke to raise funds for the families of imprisoned or dead Volunteers. Hanna Sheehy Skeffington played an important role on the international stage and lectured extensively in the United States in support of Irish independence. In January 1918, the American president announced a plan for a post-World War One peace settlement, which advocated 'a free, →

→ open-minded, and absolutely impartial adjustment of all colonial claims'. Within days, Sheehy Skeffington secured a White House meeting with President Wilson during which she presented him with this petition from Cumann na mBan.

have granted full suffrage to their women, we feel that your generous sympathy will be extended to the women of our country in our demand before the world for the recognition of an Irish Republic virtually in existence since April 1916— the only republic which from its inauguration was prepared to give women their full place in the councils of their nation.

Signed on behalf of Cumann na mBan (The Irishwomen's Council)

Countess de Markiewicz
Nannie O'Rahilly
Mary Ryan
Elizabeth Bloxam
Kathlin Clarke
Annie Kent
Louise Gavan Duffy
Niam Plunkett
Jennie Wyse Power
Mary S. Walsh

Cumann na Ban, Ard Craobh, Parnell Square N., Dublin, Ireland.

ERNIE O'MALLEY—*from*:

ON ANOTHER
MAN'S WOUND

(1936)

T HE JANSENISTIC OLDER priests, hard, austere—some
more human as they grew into age—bore on the people;
sermons, advice and the-to-be-feared calling from the
altar submerged them in a facile but unreal submission. Some
priests were hostile to dancing and gatherings; they interfered
in every aspect of life. The lack of organised social intercourse
made the young discontented, especially in the towns. The wise
domination of age, to some hard and harsh in the soul as the
cancer of foreign rule, made volunteering an adventure and a
relief. Parish priests were managers of national schools. They
had the power to appoint and remove teachers. Some, hostile
to the movement, dismissed young men and women who were
separatists. They found work in England and turned their hand
to anything they could find, or joined our export of youth to
America. We had other exports; priests to the mission fields of
the British empire; artists and writers to London, because our
nation did not support them.

My hat I seldom wore when passing through towns and
villages; when I was given it I do not remember; it was a faded
green. Sun and rain had each in turn touched it strongly. There
was a bullet hole on either side of the crown near the top. Once
in Clare, Peader, Maurteen and myself were cycling from Ennis
to Kilfenora. At a crossroad we saw police with carbines; at
the same time came a command 'Halt there!' We drew our
revolvers and fired, running for cover. The police used their
carbines. It was near sunset. We had carried our bicycles over
the ditch. When twilight came Peader brought our bicycles
across the next field whilst we replied slowly to the ragged
police firing. Then we crawled away, reached our bicycles
and cycled in the welcome friendly darkness. When I arrived

Born in County Mayo in
1897, O'Malley grew up
there and in Dublin. He
was a medical student at
the time of the Rising and
in its aftermath joined the
Volunteers and the Gaelic
League. After 1918, he
was a full-time organiser
for the Irish Republican
Army. He travelled the
countryside, as described
in the following passages,
training units and leading
attacks on barracks and
police stations. He was
captured in December
1920 but escaped
and commanded IRA
operations in Limerick,
Tipperary and Kilkenny.
He was wounded while
fighting against the Treaty
on the republican side and
later wrote an account of
the Civil War under the title
The Singing Flame (1978). In
1928 he went to the United
States to raise money for
the foundation of the *Irish
Press* and began a long →

at Maurteen's house I found the bullet hole in the hat. The most obvious sign of my light-headedness in the eyes of the old people was my not wearing a cap or hat; the men usually wore their hats—even in the house—and they always thought I would catch cold in my bare head.

I was on the outside. I felt it in many ways by diffidence, by an extra courtesy, by a silence. Some were hostile in their minds; others in speech. Often the mother would think I was leading her son astray or the father would not approve of what the boys were doing. We of the Volunteers were talked of at first: 'Musha, God help them, but they haven't a stim of sinse.' Yet there was a tradition of armed resistance, dimly felt; it would flare up when we carried out some small successful raid or made a capture. Around the fire it would be discussed; it would heighten the imagination of those who were hostile. In their minds, a simple thing became heroic and epical. Perhaps the sense of glory in the people was stirred, and the legend that had been created about myself, whom they did not know, helped them to accept me as part of it.

I felt that I should be able to fuse with my material, the people, so that I could make better use of it; yet look at them dispassionately, as if from a distance. My approach to teaching and training of the men was impersonal; they would have to learn to do without me, to depend on themselves, and avoid too much trust in what they considered leadership. This often meant a cold quality creeping in, but few could mingle with them without gaining warmth.

At the beginning it was the poor who stood by us in the country, and with them mostly I stayed. In some parts, the standard of comfort was better, as in North Tipp, or when I was in a town house, but food, irregular meals or conditions did not matter to me whilst I was busy trying to improve a command. The life of the people was hard enough, but money or comfort were not standards that interrupted their content; above all they were alive and personal. The struggle with the soil rarely ground them down.

There was always the solace of the men in the ranks; why did they turn up week after week for the same monotonous minor

→ association with an artistic circle which included painters, musicians and poets. He married Helen Hooker, a sculptor and tennis star, and returned to live in Ireland where he wrote essays and poetry. He died in 1957 and was given a state funeral.

movements? They must have felt the lack of imagination of
their officers. They were not being trained in the use of arms;
two or three men in a company would have held a rifle in their
hands, and the drill was too ragged to give them a composite
sense so that in danger they would feel each other and act
together. Anyhow they would seldom have to fight in large
bodies, but they were not being trained to any decent squad
or section sense. Yet there was a certain co-operative value in
meeting boys who thought as they did. During the European
war the English found that the platoons of a company had to
be self-contained for trench warfare. We would have to think
in terms of the quarter company, the section.

To effect any change, I would have to remain four months
in an area and insist that some of the senior officers remain
with me. My temper was ready to fly when I found that men
had shirked duties and responsibilities. I did not remember
that they had been working hard all day.

Every one of our little fights or attacks was significant; they
made panoramic pictures of the struggle in the people's eyes
and lived on in their minds. Only in the country could the
details of an individual fight expand to the generalisations of a
pitched battle. What to me was a defeat, such as the destruction
of an occupied post without the capture of its arms, would soon
be sung of as a victory. Our own critical judgements which
adjudged action and made it grow gigantic through memory
and distance, were like to folklore. To an outsider, who saw our
strivings and their glorification, this flaring imagination that
lit the stars might make him think of the burglar who shouted
at the top of his voice to hide the noise of his feet. Actually the
people saw the clash between the two mentalities, two trends in
direction, and two philosophies of life; between exploiters and
exploited. Even the living were quickly becoming folklore; I had
heard my own name in song at the few dances I had attended.

Many of us could hardly see ourselves for the legends
built up around us. The legends helped to give others an
undue sense of our ability or experience, but they hid our
real selves; when I saw myself as clearly as I could in terms of
myself, I resented the legend. ▪

THE IRISH TIMES—*from*:

'THE STRIKE AT LIMERICK'

(1919)

When James Connolly
was executed after the
Rising, Irish socialism lost
its most gifted thinker
and organiser. That the
cause of the workers
was subordinated
in the aftermath of
the insurrection was
evidenced by the decision
of the Labour Party not to
contest the 1918 election
(to avoid splitting the Sinn
Féin vote). This strategy
was encapsulated in the
slogan, 'Labour must wait'.
However, signs that the
socialist movement had
not fizzled out appeared
in Limerick where a
workers' council set up
what became known as
the Limerick Soviet, lasting
for two weeks in April
1919. In response to the
imposition of martial law
by the British army, the
workers of Limerick went
on a general strike to ↗

THE CITIZENS OF Limerick are living under an unusual regime. Their local affairs are controlled by a sort of domestic 'war government', but public order is maintained by the forces of the crown. Limerick was proclaimed a military area on account of one of the most daring of recent outrages. The local Labour leaders declared a general strike as a protest against the system of 'permits'. They have appointed a soviet which has taken charge of all food supplies, regulates prices, and controls the opening of shops and places of amusement. Strangers in the city may not buy a clean collar without 'the authority of the strike committee.' The traders and directors of industries seem to be helpless: at any rate, they have taken no steps to assert their independence. The military authorities hold themselves severely aloof from the domestic situation, and confine themselves to the strict duty of observing their special regulations and enforcing the law. Their tact and firmness seem, on at least one occasion, to have averted serious trouble. Here, as in so much that has happened in Ireland of late, comedy and tragedy walk dangerously close together. The strikers declare that their action has no connection with politics, but is merely Labour's challenge to assaults on its dignity and convenience. The Labour leaders in England refuse to accept that theory. And Mr. J. H. Thomas, MP, has warned the branches of the Railwaymen's Union in Ireland against any unauthorised support of 'what appears to be an industrial move against political action.' It is, indeed, quite clear that, while the strike may have begun as a purely local affair, it is now being used as a deliberate and very ambitious attack on the whole system of Irish government. The Central Executive of the Irish Labour movement has identified itself with the agitation, which can be dissociated no longer from the propaganda of the Irish republicans. An effort is being made to extend the strike to the rest of Ireland—in other words, to present the government with the *fait accompli* of a whole nation brought to a social and economic standstill. We are spectators today of a very bold and candid experiment in Irish syndicalism.

We think that the experiment will fail. The national executive of Labour evidently is disappointed with the result of its appeal to the workers throughout Ireland. Its project of 'promissory notes' is a sign of financial weakness. A universal strike cannot succeed without almost unlimited funds. The great English unions, which have some firsthand acquaintance with industrial Bolshevism, clearly do not intend, by financing it in Ireland, to weaken their own authority at home. Finally, the strike cannot be universal because the sturdy and highly organised Labour of north-east Ulster will have nothing to say to it. The truth is that syndicalism and Bolshevism, with their common motto, 'What is yours is mine, and what is mine is my own,' never will make any real headway in this country. In our farming classes the sense of property is as sacred and strong as in the French. Our middle classes are hard-working individualists. The bulk of Irish labour, both urban and rural, is restless today, but it is shrewd and intelligent. It will begin soon to recognise the economic limits of the concessions which our staple industries can make to its demands. The Limerick strike and the national executive's hopes are possible just now because political excitement runs high, because extremist organisations terrorise public opinion, and because the Irish people, in their insular isolation, have not learned, like the English, the lesson of recent events in Russia and Germany. We hope that they will be sobered and instructed by the story of the strike at Limerick[.] ◼

→ circumvent army control of the city. Workers' committees also took command of the food supplies and printed an alternative currency. As this editorial published in the *Irish Times* on 23 April demonstrates, establishment interests felt the threat of the initiative, and feared that the Limerick 'Bolshevism' would catch on elsewhere.

HENRY NEVINSON—*from*:

'IRELAND: THE ONE SOLUTION'

(1920)

Henry Nevinson was born
in Leicester in 1856 and
educated at Oxford. He
began a distinguished
career as a foreign
correspondent with the
Daily Chronicle in 1897
and reported on many
of the important military
conflicts of his era. During
World War One, he
witnessed events from the
western front and at the
Dardanelles. Nevinson's
journalism is distinguished
by careful reporting
of the facts and an
instinctive sympathy with
the oppressed. He took
a deep interest in Irish
affairs and met many of
the key figures of the Irish
Revival, including Roger ⊅

I HAVE FOLLOWED IRISH history very closely for thirty years, and always felt passionate sympathy with the national cause. I have been very often in the country, and have known most of the great Irish leaders and most of their friends and enemies in England. I know that, from the English point of view, the situation in Ireland is now more difficult and more dangerous than it has ever been within my memory. For the last forty years, the great mass of the Irish people have always looked with hope, if not with confidence, to a strong body of Liberal opinion and leadership in England to obtain for them that measure of independence which was called Home Rule. Today they regard with indifference or distrust every English party alike, with perhaps a touch of extra contempt for the Liberal Party, if indeed it can be said still to exist. And they regard with indifference or contempt the very name of Home Rule. For them that chapter is closed forever. It was too full of prevarication, deceit, half-heartedness, and hope deferred. The Home Rule Act was passed. It was to come into effect directly after the war, if certain conditions were fulfilled. 'We stood ready to fulfil the conditions,' they say. 'We voluntarily enrolled 170,000 Irishmen to fight for the cause of small nationalities, which you assured us, was the object of the war. Where is that Home Rule now? You have brought in a wretched substitute, framed by our greatest enemies, headed by Lord Birkenhead to represent your Law as Lord Chancellor—Lord Birkenhead who, as "Galloper Freddy" was openly acting under Carson only six years ago in stimulating Ulster to rebellion against your laws! What is the good of talking about Home Rule and your precious bill "for the better government of Ireland"? Certainly, it would not be for a worse government, but as for your bill, we will follow Swift's advice and burn it, together with everything that comes from England except her coals and her people.'

They will not burn the bill. They will take no notice of it. The lamentable history of the last ten years has entirely destroyed all belief in England's good faith and good intentions. It is a bitter thing for an English patriot like me to say, but who can wonder at the distrust? When at last, some ten years ago, the Liberals under Mr. Asquith plucked up heart to fulfil their pledges and bring in a Home Rule bill, the whole of the Unionist Party, hounded on by the Northcliffe press, incited Ulster to rebellion. In September, 1912, Carson's Covenant was signed, pledging the Ulster Protestants (rather less than half the population of the province) 'to combine in using all means which may be found necessary to defeat the present conspiracy to set up a Home Rule parliament in Ireland.' The Ulster Volunteers were openly drilled for rebellion. They paraded arms and ambulances before Carson and F.E. Smith. They imported a large cargo of rifles from England, and nothing was done against them. When the Irish or Nationalist Volunteers drilled, and imported arms at Howth, British troops were sent against them and people were shot in the Dublin streets. When the war came, the Ulster Volunteers were allowed to form a separate division with their own emblems. The Irish Volunteers who offered divisions were not admitted as separate formations. Carson and F.E. Smith were appointed Law Officers of the crown in the coalition. After the Easter Week rising of despair, the leaders were executed in driblets—not in hot blood, but one or two for breakfast at intervals. Among the victims James Connolly—

→ Casement whose work on human rights he greatly admired. Nevinson reported on the revolutionary events in Ireland for British and American publications, where he expressed outrage at the atrocities committed by the Black and Tans. This article, published in the American magazine, *The Nation*, on 29 May 1920, is critical of the British handling of the Irish problem, but hopeful that old enmities can be transcended.

one of the finest characters that Ireland has ever produced, an Ulsterman and a Protestant, too—though severely wounded was dragged out in a chair to be shot. . . .

Still there are signs of hope. The English people, always so conservative, so slow to move or change, have now as a body come up to the line of the old Home Rule. They are genuinely anxious for a settlement. They see the demand always rising with refusal and delay, and terms that once would have been welcomed with joy are now despised. The English working people must be told the absolute truth. For true settlement certain conditions are essential: a single and separate parliament for Ireland; complete financial control of all taxes and expenditures and trade; the withdrawal of the British army, and a clean sweep of Dublin Castle. Ulster might also demand the usual safeguards for religion and education and equal justice, such as Lord Midleton accepted for the southern unionists in the Convention. The main conditions are essential. My own belief is that the ultimate and triumphant settlement will come only when British statesmen have the good sense to go to Ireland with both hands open and say: 'Look here now, we are entirely honest; we want to do the right thing at last. Take the utmost you can ask. Take it as some compensation for centuries of wrong. Call yourself an Irish Dominion, or an Irish Republic, or what you like. Be free, be independent. Only be our friend, instead of being always an enemy upon our flank. Think it over for a year or two in perfect freedom, and then see if you would not prefer to join us as an ally or equal confederate. We know we are foreigners. We have different ideas, different history, and rather different temperaments. But still nearly all of you can speak our language, and those of us who go to Ireland and marry there have a long established habit of becoming more Irish than the Irish. Think it over, and give us an answer soon.'

That, I am convinced, is the natural, high-hearted, and ultimate way of escape from a tragic situation that with every year involves my country in deeper shame. ■

EDWARD CARSON

'SINN FÉIN HAS BEATEN YOU'

(1921)

I READ A STATEMENT in an essay in a paper a few weeks ago by that great statesman, so intimately connected with Ireland, Mr. Birrell. He said this, and I never knew it was true till I heard the noble Marquess speak this evening:

> It is a British characteristic, though not an amiable one, that once we are beaten we go over in a body to the successful enemy, and too often abandon and cold-shoulder and snub, both in action and writing, the suffering few who adhere to our cause in evil and difficult times.

I am one of the suffering few. I speak for a good many, I speak—I can hardly speak—for all those who, relying on British honour and British justice, have in giving their best to the service of the state seen them now deserted and cast aside without one single line of recollection or recognition in the whole of what you call peace terms in Ireland. The noble Marquess paid a generous and eloquent tribute to Michael Collins, the head of the murder gang, as Sir Hamar Greenwood described him a few months ago in the House of Commons.

For thirty years or more, the late Unionist Party has been fighting the question of modified Home Rule—as I think noble Marquess called it, 'a milk-and-watery Home Rule,' or something of that kind. All of a sudden they say that Home Rule is not good enough; you must have the real thing; the country must abandon Ireland at the very heart of the empire to independence, with an army, with a navy, with separate Customs, with ministers at foreign courts, and

Born in Dublin in 1854, Edward Carson was educated at Trinity College Dublin (where he played hurling) and later called to the bar. He won fame for the way in which he turned Oscar Wilde's prosecution of the Marquess of Queensberry for libel back on Wilde himself, whom he accused of moral depravity—the playwright was subsequently tried, imprisoned and ruined. Carson had been a Member of Parliament for Trinity in 1892 and after a stellar spell at the English bar became Solicitor General in May 1900. He opposed Home Rule and was the first person to sign the Ulster Covenant in 1912. The outbreak of war prevented the implementation of Home Rule and Carson helped to form the 36th Ulster Division in the British →

→ army from the ranks of
the UVF. The Anglo-Irish
Treaty of 1921 went much
further than previous
bills for Home Rule
and seemed to him a
betrayal, as indicated in
these excerpts from his
maiden speech to the
House of Lords. He had
never wanted Ireland to
be partitioned and feared
that Catholics would be
unfairly treated in the
Northern Irish state. He
was worried that such
injustice would threaten
the state's stability and
that the army of the new
southern state would
attack it. He declined
the offer of unionists to
become the first prime
minister of Northern
Ireland. He died in Kent
in 1935 and was given
a state funeral.

delegates to the League of Nations, where they can vote against you.

And how is it presented to the country? I do not believe, in the whole of the history of our constitution, anything approaching it has ever been attempted. It is brought out one morning cut and dried, signed, sealed, and delivered. And before making this great act of constitutional change, which is to break up the United Kingdom and, in the words of Sir Harmar Greenwood, to smash the British Empire, you are not to present this to parliament or to the country, but you are to advise His Majesty to give his consent. I say there never was a greater outrage attempted upon constitutional liberty than this coalition Government have attempted at the present time.

One thing the noble Marquess entirely forgot to tell us was how the government came to the conclusion that these Articles of Treaty were so much for the benefit of the country. The difficulty I have in commenting upon them at all is that, unless as a matter of mere pretence, when we are seeming to be very dignified and concerned, there is not a noble Lord in this House who believes for a moment that these terms were passed upon the merits. Not at all. They were passed with a revolver pointed at your head. And you know it. You know you passed them because you were beaten. You know you passed them because Sinn Féin with its army in Ireland has beaten you. Why do you not say so? Your press says so, and you may as well confess it. There may be nothing dishonourable in it.

But when we are told that the reason why they had to pass these terms of Treaty, and the reason why they could not put down crime in Ireland was because they had neither the men nor the money, nor the backing, let me say that that is an awful confession to make to the British Empire. If you tell your Empire in India, in Egypt, and all over the world that you have not got the men, the money, the pluck, the inclination, and the backing to restore law and order in a country within twenty miles of your own shore, you may as well begin to abandon the attempt to make British rule prevail throughout the Empire at all.

I hope you are proud of your Treaty. Let me say this, and it is the last word so far as this point is concerned. I think it is an innovation which this House ought very carefully to consider—namely, the entry into a treaty between different parts of one kingdom. Was such a thing ever heard of before? The next time you have a dispute in the coal fields of this country you will find suddenly coming down here, with the King's assent to it beforehand, a treaty between England and the coal-owners and coalminers of Yorkshire, Derbyshire and elsewhere.

A treaty! On the very face of the document itself it is false. It says: 'A Treaty between Great Britain and Ireland,' and before you signed it you never even asked Ulster. Nor is her signature necessary. It is only to be signed in the House of Commons of southern Ireland and by this House; and your Lordships, who only last year set up a separate entity in the six counties consisting of 1,200,000 people, disregard that as part of Ireland. But when you come to ask for contributions and taxes then you say: 'Small patch as you are' (to use Mr. Asquith's phrase) 'you must pay 44 per cent of the contribution.' I say the document has a lie on the face of it. And it is put there purposely. It is put there for this reason—that you wish to admit in the presence of those men, because you were afraid of them; that they were representative of the whole of Ireland. They are not, and please God they never will be.

In 1914, the whole Conservative Party, headed by the noble Marquess, had pledged the whole force and power of the party and, if they got into the government of this country, to maintain and keep Ulster outside the modified Home Rule Bill of 1914. What has happened since to change your attitude? When the war came on and you were in want of men, just at the point when you were turning Ulster (as she thought, at all events) out of the United Kingdom, I was asked to go over and try to raise a division. I had to go to the men who were smarting under the fact that you were trying to turn them out of the heritage of citizenship to which they were loyal and devoted, and I had to say to them: 'Never mind; that is merely an act of the government and not an act of the people; the people are all right, and, after all, our union and the United Kingdom are all wrapped up in the success of this war.' I said to them: 'Go and enlist, go and bring glory to Ulster and safety to the Empire; that is your first duty.' And they went, and they suffered, and they lost thousands and thousands of men, while your new-found friends were murdering your troops in the city of Dublin, Is it that which has turned you from your desire to help Ulster? ▪

ELIZABETH BURKE-PLUNKETT—*from*:

SEVENTY YEARS YOUNG

Into the Free State

(1937)

MICHAEL COLLINS WAS what he looked—a big simple Irishman—and remained so. One day he was at lunch at Cromwell Place, with Lord Birkenhead as another guest. Hazel had a small Peke who was pawing at Lord Birkenhead under the table. Hazel looked down and called the little dog. 'Oh, I am sorry. I thought you were making advances,' said Lord Birkenhead.

Up rose the big IRA leader, towering over him in wrath: 'D'ye mean to insult her?'
Hazel threw oil on the troubled water quickly: 'Lord Birkenhead was only joking.'

'I don't understand such jokes,' said Collins.

The Treaty was signed in December. The British troops left. The English flag was pulled down from its flag-post in Ireland after more than seven hundred years and the new Irish tricolour, with the white of peace between the orange and green, run up instead. The British troops departed and the soldiers of the new Irish army, in their dark green uniforms, took their place. And at Easter 1922, the republican Rory O'Connor held the Dublin Four Courts against the newly established Free State.

Tim Healy had been made the first Governor General. About the same time the Irish stamps were issued—not beautiful—a white map of Ireland on a red ground and a green ground. And the map appeared quite empty, which fact some cynics soon discovered, christening the stamps 'empty Ireland'. But an old countrywoman, peering at them for the new king's head, exclaimed: 'Sure that's no more like Tim Healy than I am!'

Under his rule, the Viceregal Lodge was run with simplicity and dignity. He was a man of great taste, and

The Irish Free State was officially established on 6 December 1922 under the terms of the Anglo-Irish Treaty, negotiated on the Irish side by a team that included Michael Collins. Lord Birkenhead took part on the British side. In this account, Elizabeth Burke-Plunkett, who knew many of the leading cultural and political figures of the day, portrays Collins as a cavalier military man who didn't stand on ceremony. Her description of the changeover to the Free State depicts a confusing transition in which the sense of possibility of a state yet to be made is combined with an unmistakable feeling that things are staying the same.

collected Waterford glass before others knew its value. He had a wonderful collection on his dinner table. Also he collected Spanish gold plate, which should be even more rare and wonderful now.

One day I was lunching at the Viceregal Lodge and sitting beside the Governor General. He asked me if I noticed any difference in the dining room. I looked around and discovered that the two ugly black marble chimney-pieces that I had always known there had been replaced by two lovely Bossi ones. All the Lords Lieutenant had put up with those others but Tim Healy could not bear to look at anything so ugly. ▪

'About the same time the Irish stamps were issued—not beautiful—a white map of Ireland on a red ground and a green ground. And the map appeared quite empty, which fact some cynics soon discovered, christening the stamps 'empty Ireland'.'

PIARAS BEASLAÍ —*from*:

MICHAEL COLLINS AND THE MAKING OF THE NEW IRELAND

The Shooting of Michael Collins

(1926)

Piaras Béaslaí (Percy Beazley) was born in Liverpool in 1881 to Irish immigrant parents. He spent summers in Kenmare, County Kerry where he learned Irish from native speakers. He was active in the Liverpool Gaelic League and moved to Dublin in 1906 where he became a central figure in the Keating branch of the Gaelic League. He contributed to Árd-Chúirt na hÉigse, a circle of poet-scholars, and was a founding member of the Irish-language drama company, Na hAisteoirí. He deserves recognition for adding considerably to the repertoire of Irish language theatre at a time when this new form was in its infancy. Béaslaí joined the IRB and the Irish Volunteers, and was a member of the Gaelic League executive in 1915 when Douglas Hyde resigned over the politicisation of the organisation. He fought in the Rising and was elected TD for Kerry East in 1918. A close friend of Michael Collins, he was chosen by the Collins family to write the official biography of his former friend.

THERE WERE CIRCUMSTANCES in connection with the death of Michael Collins which have never been fully cleared up. None of his companions actually saw him hit. The wound was in the back of the head, but it must have been fired from a distance, as there was no exit wound. I have referred several times to his habit of jerking his head round rapidly. Perhaps he was in this position looking to the left, when he was hit by a stray shot—for his attackers were retreating, and their fire was dying away at the time, The bolt of his rifle was drawn, from which it would appear that he was in the act of loading when he was hit. Perhaps this would also explain his head being turned to the left.

As to whether the ambushers were aware of the identity of Collins, despite assertions to the contrary by members of the anti-Treaty Party, I think there can be no reasonable doubt that they were fully aware. The fact of his presence in the district was known since morning, and the news of his death was current in the countryside for hours before it could have reached by any save Irregular channels.

The ambushers were only a small party. A large force of Irregulars had been lying in wait for several hours, but the main body of these had moved before Collins's party arrived. ■

THOMAS BODKIN—*from*:

SAORSTÁT ÉIREANN
'Modern Irish Art'
(1932)

Thomas Bodkin was born in Dublin in 1887 and graduated from University College Dublin in 1908. Although he trained as a barrister he was far more interested in the visual arts, becoming, in time, a distinguished art critic and a museum director. In 1926, he was appointed to the commission to advise the government on the design of coinage for the Irish Free State, which chose the animal and bird designs of Percy Metcalfe. The following year he was chosen to succeed Lucius O'Callaghan as the director of the National Gallery of Ireland. In this essay, he laments the underdevelopment of the visual arts in the ↗

THE ARTS OF painting and sculpture only flourish in the communities that enjoy peace and prosperity. The Free State has not yet been established for a sufficient time to redeem the promise of those Irish artists who, in the eighth century, won for their country a pre-eminence in illuminated manuscripts and precious metal work over all the other nations of Europe. The intervening dark ages of turmoil and misery effectively prevented the development of a distinctively Irish School of Fine Art.

The foundation of the Royal Hibernian Academy in 1821 gave rise to hopes which have not yet come to fulfilment, though such brilliant painters as the second Nathaniel Hone, Walter Osborne and William Orpen have more than justified its existence. . . . But we are still entitled to expect much from an institution which contains upon its roll of active membership such well-known names as Lavery, Yeats, and Hughes, and which attracts such talented younger artists as Mrs. Margaret Clarke, Estella Solomons, and Messrs. Henry, Keating, Whelan, Power, Lamb, Craig, and Sean O'Sullivan. A little more encouragement, or a little more opposition, would probably stimulate the Hibernian Academy into a period of vigorous achievement.

To [Hugh] Lane, also, Ireland owes the Dublin Municipal Gallery of Modern Art, which he founded in 1907. There is nothing negligible there, with the exception of a few of those pictures which have been acquired by gift since the death of its founder. No one who saw for the first time the decayed exterior of Clonmel House, in Harcourt Street, could dream that it hid a series of delightful canvasses by Degas, Monet, Corot, Whistler, Sargent, Brangwyn, Osborne and Hone; the finest group of Mancini portraits to be seen outside Italy, and the finest groups of pictures by Mr. Augustus John, R.A., and Mr. Wilson Steer, O.M., to be seen outside England. ∎

→ Ireland of his time, yet he celebrates the contribution of influential patrons such as Hugh Lane, and lauds the talents of a new generation of Irish painters.

GEORGE RUSSELL

'REACTION IN LITERATURE'

(1937)

WE ALL KNOW since Newton how exquisitely nature keeps the balance of its powers, but I do not know whether it has been yet accepted as a law that life maintains its balances as exquisitely around some mysterious norm. We can see this in little things. I look at the sun and that intolerable brightness is balanced by black spots which swim before the eyes until the norm is regained. I look at a red circle and when my eye wanders from that a green circle appears for a little and then vanishes. Action and reaction seem to be equal and opposite in life as in nature, and I am tempted, partly by the spirit of scientific enquiry and partly by sheer impishness, to inquire into how that law of reaction operates in literature. Twenty-five years ago Anglo-Irish literature was romantic, idealistic or mystic. But what a change in the writers who came after these!

From the most idealistic literature in Europe we have reacted so that with Joyce, O'Flaherty and O'Casey, the notabilities of the moment, we have explored the slums of our cities, the slums of the soul. Is there a law in these oscillations like that which brings centrifugal to balance centripetal? Are these writers the black spots which balance the bright stars? If a writer of powerful character appears, is it inevitable that his opposite must be born? Or if nature cannot find any single person powerful enough to form the balance must it inspire a school of smaller men and cast them into the scale? It is the spirit of scientific inquiry which prompts the question. It is, perhaps, the imp in me which makes me speculate whether James Joyce was not made inevitable by W.B. Yeats, is not in a sense the poet's creation, his child, born to him, not out of his loins, but supplied to him by nature, being called forth by a kind of necessity to balance in our national life an intense imagination of beauty, by an equally intense preoccupation with its dark and bitter opposites. It amuses me to consider this parentage. Father and son have this in common, that they are stylists even to elaboration. There was also a little poetry in the youth of James Joyce, and if nature, or the national being, had not to preserve the balance of things, if there was not a force pulling the pendulum of literature from the height of dream it had swung to in Yeats, Joyce might never have written *Ulysses*. He might have gone on writing *Chamber Music* and further innocencies of that kind.

What damp and depressing literature have not the fiery and volatile elders made inevitable! Perhaps it was as well that George Bernard Shaw was removed from Ireland before he began to write. If he had remained here, if we had to bear the full force of the reaction which that transcendental puritan virtue of his would have involved, what a literature we might have had, a literature as loose as the Restoration literature in England! And now I must dismiss the imp who has been prompting these speculations, but who refused to depart until he was allowed to make them, lest I be suspected of holding the heresy that every good deed leads to a bad deed. I think it true that every intellectual effort has a twofold effect. It tends to multiply images and shadows of itself, and also to stir into activity an opposite or balance. The moral character of that balance is not predestined, but depends on the individual who may be caught by the balancing forces. I would say that an idealist movement must create by reaction a realistic literature, but that does not imply a literature without moral character, though there are people who seem to think that the person who refers to a sin in literature is as guilty as the persons who commit the sin. The moment we read a book, either of two things takes place. We find the book is akin to us and we accept it, or if it is not ours we react from it and tend to give birth in ourselves to the opposite idea. This law of action and reaction is observable not merely in our own literature but everywhere. ■

→ comment freely on life in independent Ireland, and essays and editorials were eventually published as a collection in *The Living Torch* (1937). Here Russell argues that the idealism of the Revival was giving way to a realist antithesis, which had perhaps always been latent but was now wrongly being treated as a final, definitive insight into the Irish soul. For a man who had always balanced the visionary and the pragmatic, the cult of Joyce, O'Casey and O'Flaherty was a challenging development, worthy of analysis and critique.

ELIZABETH BURKE-PLUNKETT—*from*:

SEVENTY YEARS YOUNG
The Burning Party
(1937)

In the autumn of 1922, the anti-Treaty forces started a campaign of burning country houses. This tactic began as an organised attempt to coerce certain members of the Dáil to resign and make the Treaty unworkable. Many houses, however, were destroyed simply because they stood as highly visible reminders of Anglo-Irish dominance at a time of anarchy. Not even committed Revivalist figures such as Horace Plunkett were spared the torch of destruction. His house, Kilteragh, in Foxrock, County Dublin, was destroyed by fire in 1922. Months previous to this, he had been contemplating a move to a smaller house and the gifting of his residence to the Irish people. In this extract, Elizabeth Burke-Plunkett (Countess of Fingall) vividly describes the experience of waiting for her house, Killeen Castle in Dunsany, County Meath, to be burned.

IN THE AUTUMN of 1923, the Burners came to Lismullen, the other side of the Hill of Tara. Sir John Dillon and his wife and daughter were at dinner, when a party of young men in some sort of uniform knocked at the door. Sir John went out, and the leader said to him:

'Sir John, we are very sorry, but we have orders to burn your house.'

'But what have I done?' he asked, being one of the best landlords and kindest men in the country.

'Nothing yourself, Sir John, but there was a man killed on the road above, and this is a "reprisal".'

No use for poor Sir John to expostulate. Orders were orders, and the IRA ruthless. They said they would help him to get out his pictures and any furniture he particularly valued, but they must be quick, for they were going on to Killeen Castle—'and *that* would take a bit of doing!'

They cut some of the pictures from the frames that they could not take from the walls and carried them out with the most valuable furniture and silver. Someone remembered the gloves with the pearl-sewn gauntlets that King James had dropped at Lismullen three centuries earlier, as he fled from the Battle of the Boyne. They were flung though a window onto the lawn, where they were found in the morning. There was so little time and the usual confusion and uncertainty about what to save.

Still Sir John, good friend and neighbour that he was, managed to find a scrap of paper and a pencil and to scribble a note. Then he thrust it into the hand of a small bare-footed boy, the son of one of his men, telling him to run as fast as he could with it over the Hill of Tara to his Lordship at Killeen. The second time in the Plunkett history that a warning had been carried by such a messenger across the Hill of Tara.

That night Fingall and I were sitting in his study after dinner, I reading, he asleep as usual. The shutters were closed and the lamps lit. It was, I suppose, somewhere about ten o'clock.

Suddenly I heard a sound at the window, behind the heavy shutters. I looked up from my book and listened. It came again. Someone was knocking on the glass.

'Fingall,' I called. 'Fingall! Wake Up! There is someone at the window!'

Fingall came awake, with difficulty at first. 'What did you say?'

The tapping was repeated, with a sound of increased urgency. Fingall got up, lifted the heavy iron bar that kept the shutters in their place, and pulled them back. Outside, a small face was pressed on the pane. So clearly did I see the little face in that startled moment, that, like the click of a camera taking a photograph, my mind registered it, and I can see it now.

Fingall pulled up the window. The autumn wind blew in, and with it a scrap of paper thrust by a small hand. Then the barefoot messenger disappeared like a fairy into the night.

Fingall opened the crumpled note and held it to the light, to read the faint pencilled writing:

Dear Fingall,
They are burning my house, and they say they are going on to you. I thought I had better let you know.
John Dillon

We looked out of the window. There was nothing there. Fingall pulled it down and closed the shutters again.

He refused to believe that they would ever burn Killeen, and it would have been a big job, as they said, with some of the walks six-feet thick and stone floors in the basement and halls. However, we went upstairs and I collected what was left of the family jewellery in my jewel-case, and some other personal valuables, which I tied up in a blanket. The silver closet was built into the walls of the study, with an iron door behind the wooden one, which would have taken many tons of dynamite to blow up. Then I put on a fur coat because the night was turning chilly, and we went downstairs again, made up the fire in the study, and sat down to await our visitors. Fingall fell asleep again. ▪

'... we are very sorry, but we have orders to burn your house.'

ÉAMON DE VALERA

'LEGION OF THE REARGUARD'

(1923)

On 10 April 1923, Liam Lynch, Chief of Staff of the republican army, died of wounds received in action. As the atrocities and casualties of the Civil War mounted on both sides, the leaders on the republican side began to consider bringing hostilities to an end and called a ceasefire on 30 April. Although a decision was taken by the republican cabinet to engage no further in hostile action, it refused to order a surrender of arms. A command to cease fire and dump arms was issued on 24 May, with the following statement from Éamon de Valera.

S OLDIERS OF THE republic, legion of the rearguard, The Republic can no longer be defended successfully by your arms. Further sacrifice of life would now be vain and continuance of the struggle in arms unwise in the national interest and prejudicial to the future of our cause. Military victory must be allowed to rest for the moment with those who have destroyed the Republic. Other means must be sought to safeguard the nation's right.

Do not let sorrow overwhelm you. Your efforts and the sacrifices of your dead comrades in this forlorn hope will surely bear fruit. They have even already borne fruit. Much that you set out to accomplish is achieved. You have saved the nation's honour, preserved the sacred national tradition, and kept open the road of independence. You have demonstrated in a way there is no mistaking that we are not a nation of willing bondslaves.

Seven years of intense effort have exhausted our people. Their sacrifices and their sorrows have been many. If they have turned aside and have not given you the active support which alone could bring you victory in this last year, it is because they saw overwhelming forces against them, and they are weary and need a rest. A little time and you will them recover and rally again to the standard. They will then

quickly discover who have been selfless and who selfish—
who have spoken truth and who falsehood. When they are
ready, you will be, and your place will be again as of old
with the vanguard.

The sufferings which you must now face unarmed you
will bear in a manner worthy of men who were ready to give
their lives for their cause. The thought that you have still
to suffer for your devotion will lighten your present sorrow,
and what you endure will keep you in communion with
your dead comrades, who gave their lives, and all these lives
promised, for Ireland.

May God guard every one of you and give to our
country in all times of need sons who will love her as dearly
and devotedly as you. ▪

'Seven years of intense effort
have exhausted our people.'

GEORGE BERNARD SHAW

'SAFE HOLIDAYS IN IRELAND'

(1923)

Sir,

Several persons have complimented me on my courage in venturing into the South of Ireland for my summer holiday. These people feel safer in the friendly atmosphere of Poincaresque France, or in the land of the bottomless mark chute, where merchants chain up their typewriters with Krupp chains overnight, only to miss them, chains and all, in the morning. They are not afraid even of being dosed with castor oil in Italy by Anglophobe fascists. But they dare not set foot in Ireland. I admit that there is some excuse for them. The Irish government has just passed a Coercion Act which would make Trotsky gasp, and which makes the history of Dublin Castle under English rule seem like freedom broadening down from precedent to precedent. It contains a flogging clause, directed specially against robbery under arms, of such savagery that foreigners may well be led to believe that no man's property or person is safe.

The truth is that Cork and Kerry are much safer, in respect of both person and property, than the administrative county of London. A year ago, no owner of a bicycle in Ireland risked riding it out of call of a barrack, as it was sure to be stolen 'under arms', and even the cheapest motor cars were hidden more carefully than illicit stills. Today not only Fords, but Vauxhall 38s and Crossley 25s career over the mountain roads as carelessly as over the Surrey hills. The tourist's heart is in his mouth when he first crosses a repaired bridge on a 30cwt car, for the repairs are extremely unconvincing to the eye, but after crossing two or three in safety he thinks no more of them. Since I arrived I have wandered every night over the mountains, either alone or with a harmless companion or two, without molestation

Éamon De Valera had ordered all republican insurgents under his command to dump arms but the sense of instability persisted amid occasional gunplay, as elections were due in August of that year. De Valera, still at large, appeared at an election meeting in County Clare, but was promptly arrested by government forces. As Ireland sought to regain a modicum of normality and also to reactivate its damaged economy, Shaw did his bit in this letter to *The Times*, published on 31 July. He wrote parts of *Saint Joan*, perhaps his →

→ finest play, while
holidaying in Glengariff
and Parknasilla in the
summer of that year,
testing the scene in
which Joan is tried by the
Inquisition on two local
Kerry priests. The play's
theme is that of a nation
freeing itself from foreign
control. In keeping with the
spirit of his letter and of his
play, Shaw said 'I would
rather be burnt at the stake
by Irish Catholics than
protected by an English
garrison.'

or incivility. Naturally there is plenty of room in the hotels, and the quality of the potatoes, the butter, and the milk is such as to make one feel that one can never eat the English substitute again. In short, there is not the smallest reason why Glengarriff and Parknasilla should not be crowded this year with refugees from the turbulent sister island and the revolutionary continent, as well as by connoisseurs in extraordinarily beautiful scenery and in air which makes breathing a luxury. However, the dock strike must be reckoned with. The passengers must unload the ship, and must therefore leave Saratoga trunks behind. It is hard on the dockers to have to look on idly whilst potential employers whose rate of pay varies from twelve to thirty shillings an hour handle their own luggage and evidently enjoy it for once in a way as a holiday lark, but it need not hinder the passenger traffic from Paddington to Cork via Fishguard.

Perhaps I should explain that though the Coercion Act empowers every superintendent of police or army captain to seize any man's property, even to his clothes, leaving nothing on him but the onus of proving that he ever possessed them or had any right to possess them, this power (in force for one year only) is not exercised at the expense of the errant Englishman, and exists only because the loot from plundered houses has to be redistributed by rough-and-ready methods for which the permanent law is too slow and contentious. Ireland is at present in a reaction of quiet, with the hands of its government reinforced by extraordinarily temporary measures, and is therefore at this moment probably the safest country in the world for visitors.

Yours truly,
G. Bernard Shaw

'THE CIVIC GUARD AND THE PIONEER MOVEMENT'

(1923)

Temperance Cause

GREAT PIONEER RALLY IN DUBLIN

R EV. J. FLINN, SJ, St. Francis Xavier's, speaking yesterday at the annual meeting of the Pioneer Total Abstinence Association, Mr. J. P. O'Neill, presiding, at the Theatre Royal, which was crowded, said the organisation had grown to such an extent that there was no place in Dublin able to hold in winter-time their great jubilee demonstration.

The total number enrolled was 287, 791, of whom in Ireland there were 278,827.

One of the brightest pages in this year's story was the fine work done among the Civic Guard, amongst whom the Pioneer movement had made tremendous strides . . . No less than 645 had been enrolled in the Depot. He paid a great tribute to the help and assistance got from the Chief Commissioner, Gen. O'Duffy (applause). Without hesitation Gen. O'Duffy gave from the very start the sanction for the open wearing of the Pioneer badge in the uniform. They all wished that the army should follow on the same lines.

CALL TO THE STATE

Very Rev. Father Angeins, OSFC, who delivered the Pioneer address, said that it was heartening amid the encircling gloom to be present at such a grand and inspiring meeting. They were against drunkenness because it was a mortal sin, and being a spiritual evil it must be fought by spiritual methods.

They ought to get assistance from the state in all its various forms of activity. All schools should teach the pupils the danger of alcohol and the blessings of temperance.

They called for greater rigidness in the enforcement of the licensing laws and also for a drastic revision of these laws. They had submitted their suggestions to the government and were quite agreeable that compensation should be given to the owners of licensed premises that they held should be closed down. They called for immediate government action. ∎

Eoin O'Duffy was appointed commissioner of the new Civic Guard, which was renamed An Garda Síochána in August 1923. His objective was to form a respected, non-political, unarmed police force to replace the semi-military Royal Irish Constabulary. In an era of Civil War tensions, Free State leaders often mobilised the authority and cultural practices of Catholic Ireland to foster allegiance to the fledgling state, and to deflect ideological challenges. This is reflected in the decision to allow Gardaí to wear Pioneer pins on their uniforms, reported in the *Irish Independent* on 26 November 1923. The cultivation of a singular moral climate is unmistakable in the early years of the Free State, as those in authority attempted to rein in the radical impulses of the revolutionary years.

GEORGE BERNARD SHAW—*from*:

THE *IRISH STATESMAN*

(1928)

George Russell had joked that the Irish were lucky that a realist like Shaw had removed himself from Ireland—otherwise his sardonic thrusts might have prevented the full flowering of the Revival. In fact, Shaw wrote one full play on Revival themes, *John Bull's Other Island*, intended to mock many Revivalist values and to mark the opening of the Abbey Theatre in 1904: but Yeats claimed that its large cast meant that it was beyond the players at his disposal. (Yeats may also have objected to its undermining of some of his own most sacred beliefs). Shaw's moment came over two decades later when Russell invited him to make a comment in a context which seemed more likely to confirm his analysis. Shaw, who was born in Dublin in 1856 and died in England in 1950, needed no second invitation to inform his many readers in Ireland that the Revival was well and truly over.

IRELAND IS NOW in a position of special and extreme peril. Until the other day, we enjoyed a factitious prestige as a thorn in the side of England, or shall I say, from the military point of view, the Achilles heel of England?. . . When we were given a free hand to make good we found ourselves out with a shock that has taken all the moral pluck out of us as completely as shell shock. We can recover our nerve only by forcing ourselves to face new ideas, proving all things and standing by that which is good . . .

The moral is obvious. In the nineteenth century, all the world was concerned about Ireland. In the twentieth, nobody outside Ireland cares two-pence what happens to her. If she holds her own in the front of European culture, so much the better for her and Europe. But if, having broken England's grip of her, she slips back into the Atlantic as a little grass patch in which a few million moral cowards cannot call their souls their own . . . then the world will let 'these Irish' go their own way into insignificance without the smallest concern. ■

AFTERWORD

BY

PRESIDENT MICHAEL D. HIGGINS

Collected here in this Handbook is a selection from the
writings of an extraordinary group of people who shared
a belief that the future was for the making. They lived in
conditions of immense change. Standing to the back of
them was a rural Ireland where, as an eminent historian
put it, rather than fields giving way to families, families now
gave way to fields, and the ethos of property established
itself in the mind of a previously impoverished tenantry.

A great silence may have hung over a land that had
emptied its rural areas of agricultural labourers as a result
of famine and its subsequent emigration. Holding the
land would be an informing principle that for many would
be more important than political freedom itself. In time
the change in values would include all of the institutional
structure of what would become the new State, and a
commitment to respectability would serve as a seal on sense
and sensibility, as it suggested itself or as it might have been
recalled or imagined.

By the end of the nineteenth century, however, from
their different perspectives there emerged an exciting
motley of competing modernisms that sought to break
the silence induced by the devastating events of famine
and emigration. I cannot but sense a contradiction in
their distance from the most immediate forms of the
suffering, and yet their intellectual engagement with it.
There is a sense of suggesting a vision of the future and
yet a great debate as to whether a reinvention of the past,
an invocation of the past, a call to action as to the future
should serve as contact.

What these readings will have shown was that there was
a connection between intellectual work, not simply sourced

in Irish experience, but drawing on the philosophical and literary work of Europe and indeed the world. Readers will equally have appreciated the connection between artistic work and activism that is both sought and delivered in the readings. All of this was delivered not only in the formal communication system of the time—the newspapers—but in journals, letters and on the stage.

My hope is that in reading these pieces readers will be encouraged to go on to engage with the writers involved in more depth. What the editors have done is to have saved for us the evidence of some of the most sensitive, idealistic, often combative people of an extraordinary set of decades that ended a century of devastation and began a new century that presented both a promise and a set of conflicts whose consequences would endure into our own times.

There is some merit too in the opportunity that has been provided for engaging with some of the writers at different phases of their lives, and in differing circumstances of the context to which they were responding. It suggests how the search for consistency may be a flaw rather than an achievement in the efforts of those who have sought to reach back and select a particular emphasis of one period in the life of any one of the writers. The contradictions and the conflicts come to life in these extracts. Neither is there a style that we can say is singly emblematic of the period. Sometimes the writing is of a restrained and formal kind as would meet the expectations of an argument within an empire. At other times it is not just polemical or denunciatory but inflammatory.

If we are to draw best benefits from the moral and intellectual tasks of commemoration, it is surely appropriate that we recall what we might regard as 'the scattering of the revival', as important perhaps as 'the gathering' which we recently celebrated. These writings may have been recovered in their individual senses by academic work, but it is when one encounters the full range of the discourse of the three formative decades of our modern times that one can sense the passion of the period, the moral intent of creating something new out of the darkness.

The writings stand there now. They have informed our present and they will draw forth I am sure a new set of responses from those who may want to break away from the darkness of contemporary experiences. We cannot but admire the courage that is revealed in the writings. There is too, however, the agony of the time. This may be revealed in the division between Anna Parnell and her brother Charles, or it may be revealed in the lonely challenges of those who sought to locate within nationalism the important themes of women's rights, of new forms of economic life, or indeed the fullness of equality as the necessary ingredient of citizenship.

What the writings share is a period of time and a context of possibility, recovery, or disintegration depending on how you constructed your experience and your hopes. Some of the writers could be so hopeful as to go on to suggest a practical agenda for what they presumed would be an emerging and unavoidable freedom. Others contested the connections that must now be broken or retained. What is striking is the public discourse, its unrestrained figure and its willingness to engage in disputation, drawing energy as the introduction suggests from one's opponents as much as one's allies.

Engaging with these predecessors of ours through their own words can, I believe, be invigorating for those in our contemporary experience who seek an informed public discourse in the public space. It will remind us that there never was any simple moment of modernism in our formative decades. Rather what there was was a continuous set of attempts in words and actions at construing something new. Nor does it matter whether it be regarded as idealistic, utopian or simply necessary. What matters is that it be taken as the honest expression of its authors, writing out of their experience as they had found it.

This collection of readings too will, I am sure, help bridge the gap between academic work and a public that will benefit from accessing the writings of some of the most sensitive, courageous and brave people, whose literary and political intentions were far beyond any limiting individualism. The public availability of the readings is an invitation to build a bridge between the academy and the public. It would simply be unfair to the life and the work of those whom these extracts recall to be confined to the occasional and partial resurrection, or invocation, for academic or political purposes. The French philosopher Paul Ricoeur once wrote 'to be forgotten is to die twice'. Re-engaging, taking up the invitation from the passages in this *Handbook*, will be not only a source of information, of recovery of writers unfairly neglected, it will be an opportunity of experiencing the humanity of the end of an era and the beginning of a new one. It will be an invitation to mark our own times drawing on an engaged scholarship and a respect for the artistic, for the dissenting intelligence, and for ideas, that will give us the energy to shape our contemporary existence with its own version of humanity shared and celebrated.

Michael D. Higgins
The President of Ireland

SELECT BIBLIOGRAPHY

Birrell, Augustine. *Things Past Redress*. London, 1937.

Brennan, Helen. *The Story of Irish Dance*. Dingle, 1993.

Brooke, Stopford A. *The Need and Use of Getting Irish Literature into the English Tongue*. London, 1893.

Casement, Roger. *Heart of Darkness: The 1911 Documents*. Ed. A. Mitchell, Dublin, 2003.

—. *The Amazon Journal*, Ed. A. Mitchell. Dublin, 1997.

Colum, Mary. *Life and the Dream*. London, 1947.

Colum, Padraic. *The Road Round Ireland*, New York, 1927.

Connolly, James. *Selected Writings*. Ed. P. Berresford Ellis, London, 1973.

—. *The Lost Writings*. Ed. A. Ó Cathasaigh. London, 1997.

Coffey, Diarmuid. *Douglas Hyde*. Dublin, 1938.

Corkery, Daniel. *The Hidden Ireland*. Dublin, 1924.

Eglinton, John. Ed. *Literary Ideals in Ireland*. Dublin, 1899.

—. *Irish Literary Portraits*. London, 1935.

Fay, Frank J. *Towards a National Theatre*. Ed. R. Hogan. Dublin, 1970.

Field Day Anthology of Irish Writing. Ed. Seamus Deane. Derry, 1991.

Gibbon, Monk. *Inglorious Soldier*. London, 1968.

Gonne MacBride, Maud. *A Servant of the Queen: Her Own Story*. Ed. R. McHugh. Dublin, 1950.

Gregory, Augusta. *Selected Writings*. Ed. Lucy McDiarmid and Maureen Waters. London 1995.

—. *Cuchulain of Muirthemne*, Gerrards Cross, 1970.

—. *Poets and Dreamers*, Gerrards Cross, 1974.

—. *Seventy Years*, Gerrards Cross, 1974.

—. *Our Irish Theatre*, Gerrards Cross, 1972.

—. Ed. *Ideals in Ireland*, London, 1901.

Griffith, Arthur. *The Resurrection of Hungary*. Dublin, 2003.

Hyde, Douglas. *Love Songs of Connacht*. Dublin, 1969.

—. *Language, Lore and Lyrics*. Ed. B. Ó Conaire. Dublin, 1986.

Irish Feminisms 1810-1930. Five volumes. Ed. Mary S. Pierse. London, 2010.

Jeffares, A.N. and A. S. Knowland. *A Commentary on the Collected Plays of W. B. Yeats*. London, 1975.

Joyce, James. *Dubliners*. London, 1991.

—. *A Portrait of the Artist as a Young Man*. London, 1991.

—. *Poems and Critical Writings*. London, 1995.

MacBride White, Anna and A.N. Jeffares Eds. *The Gonne-Yeats Letters 1893-1938*. London, 1994.

MacDonagh, Thomas. *Literature in Ireland*. Dublin, 1916.

MacNeill, Eoin. *Phases of Irish History*. Dublin, 1919.

Meyer, Kuno. *Ancient Irish Poetry*. London, 1915.

Moran, D.P. *The Philosophy of Irish Ireland*. Dublin, 1905.

Moore, George. *Hail and Farewell*. Gerrards Cross, 1976.

Ní Fhaircheallaigh, Úna. *Smaointe Ar Árainn/Thoughts on Aran*. Ed. Ríona Nic Congáil. Galway, 2010.

Nic Congáil, Ríona. *Úna Ní Fhaircheallaigh agus an Fhís Útóipeach Ghaelach*. Dublin, 2010.

Nic Shiubhlaigh, Máire. *The Splendid Years*. Dublin, 1955.

Ó Buachalla, Seamus. *The Letters of P. H. Pearse*. Dublin, 1980.

O'Casey, Sean. *Drums Under the Windows*. London, 1972.

Ó Gaora, Colm. *Mise*. Dublin, 1943.

O'Grady, Standish. *Toryism and the Tory Democracy*. London, 1886.

—. *Selected Essays*. Ed. E. A. Boyd, Dublin 1918.

Ó Laoghaire, Peadar. *Mo Sgéal Féin*. Dublin, 1915.

O'Malley, Ernie. *On Another Man's Wound*. Kerry, 1990.

O'Riordan, Michael. *Catholicity and Progress in Ireland*. Dublin, 1905.

Pearse, Patrick. *Political Writings and Speeches*. Dublin, 1924.

Plunkett, Horace. *Ireland in the New Century*. Dublin, 1982.

Pyle, Fergus and Owen Dudley Edwards Eds. *1916 The Easter Rising*. London, 1968.

Rooney, William. *Prose Writings*. Dublin 1909.

Russell, George. *The National Being*. Dublin, 1982.

—. *The Living Torch*. London, 1937.

—. *Letters from AE*. Ed. Alan Denson. London, 1961.

Ryan, Desmond, Ed. *The 1916 Poets*. Westport, 1963.

Sayers, Peig. *Peig (Scéalta ón mBlascaod*. Kenneth Jackson do scríobh ó bhéal Pheig Sayers). Dublin, 1968.

Shaw, George Bernard. *Shaw: Autobiography 1898-1950 Playwright Years*. Ed. S Weintraub. London, 1970.

—. *The Matter with Ireland*. Ed. David Greene and Dan H. Lawrence. London, 1962.

Sigerson, George. *Bards of the Gael and Gall*. Dublin, 1897.

Stephens, James. *The Insurrection in Dublin*. Gerrards Cross, 1992.

Synge, J. M. *Collected Works: Prose*. Ed. Alan Price. Oxford, 1966.

Yeats, W.B. *Uncollected Prose 1*. Ed. John P Frayne. London, 1970.

—. *Autobiographies*. London, 1955.

—. *Essays and Introductions*. London, 1961.

—. *Explorations*. London, 1962.

—. *Collected Poems*. London, 1952.

Where recent editions are available we have cited and used these—otherwise we have cited and used the original publication.

USEFUL WEB RESOURCES

www.abbeytheatre.ie/archives/

www.breac.nd.edu/

www.bureauofmilitaryhistory.ie

www.nli.ie

www.historyhub.ie/

www.rte.ie/centuryireland/

www.ucd.ie/scholarcast

9 780268 101312